BEN HOFFLER grew up in the Midlands, UK. He studied geography at Hertford College, Oxford, before working as a shipwreck hunter for Odyssey Marine Exploration. He moved to Egypt in 2008 and soon discovered the Sinai, walking the peninsula as widely as possible. Ben lives in Alexandria now and spends a few months in the Sinai every year. He is a fellow of the Royal Geographical Society.

Sinai: The Trekking Guide
First edition: Aug 2013

Publisher
Trailblazer Publications
The Old Manse, Tower Rd, Hindhead, Surrey, GU26 6SU, UK
🖳 www.trailblazer-guides.com

British Library Cataloguing in Publication Data
A catalogue record for this book is available from the British Library

ISBN 978-1-905864-41-6

© Ben Hoffler 2013
Text, maps and photographs (unless otherwise credited)

The right of Ben Hoffler to be identified as the author of this work has been
asserted by him in accordance with the Copyright, Designs and Patents Act 1988

Editor: Jim Manthorpe
Layout: Anna Jacomb-Hood
Additional editing: Nicky Slade
Proofreading: Anna Jacomb-Hood
Cartography: Nick Hill
Index: Anna Jacomb-Hood

Warning: mountain walking and desert travel can be dangerous
Please read the notes on the Egyptian Revolution (p4), when to go (pp19-20) and how to
stay healthy and safe on the trek (pp86-94). Every effort has been made by the author and
publisher to ensure that the information contained herein is as accurate and up to date as
possible. However, they are unable to accept responsibility for any inconvenience, loss or
injury sustained by anyone as a result of the advice and information given in this guide.

A request

The author and publisher have tried to ensure that this guide is as accurate and
up to date as possible. Nevertheless, things change. If you notice any changes or
omissions that should be included in the next edition of this book, please contact
the author (🖳 benhoffler@hotmail.com) or publisher (address above or
🖳 info@trailblazer-guides.com). A free copy of the next edition
will be sent to persons making a significant contribution.

Updated information will be available on 🖳 **www.trailblazer-guides.com**

Front cover: Camel trekking between Jebel Barqa and the Haduda Dune
Back cover: View from the summit of Jebel el Deir (Photos © Ben Hoffler)

Printed by Sahara (🖳 www.saharaprinting.com), Nasr City, Cairo, Egypt

Sinai
THE TREKKING GUIDE

BEN HOFFLER

TRAILBLAZER PUBLICATIONS

Dedication

In memory of my grandmother, Kathleen Hoffler

Acknowledgements

This book was made possible with the kind help of many people. My biggest thanks go to Faraj 'The Fox' Mahmoud (Jebeleya), who told me more about the Sinai than anyone. A similarly big thanks to Faraj Soliman of the Muzeina and Nasr of the Gararsha (who died before this book was published). Other special guides include Rajab Saadi (Jebeleya), Salah (Gararsha), Ismaieel (Gararsha) and Ibrahim Abu Yasser (Hamada).

For filling in important gaps: Hatem Hussein, Naser Ashour, Mohammed Khalil, Metowah Musaad, Andrew Power, Neill Ghosh, Matthew Teller and Ahmed 'The Invincible' Ghaffer. Others: Patric Holm, Mohammed Eissa, Robert van Pietermann, Karim Thebault, Clare Thacker, Kathy Evans, Rory Deane, Dr Adel Taher, Tim Simond (author of *Dive in Style*), Olivia Norfolk and Katy Thompson.

Thanks also to Saqi Books, for allowing us to reproduce the poem on p71, from Clinton Bailey's *Bedouin Poetry from Sinai and the Negev*.

A collective note of thanks to the Trailblazer team, always patient and helpful: Jim Manthorpe for editing; Anna Jacomb-Hood for layout, proofreading and the index; Nicky Slade for eleventh-hour editing and updates; Nick Hill for his marathon with the maps; and publisher Bryn Thomas, for enduring the near-Biblical saga of doing a book in the Egyptian revolution. Finally, to my family for their support, especially my Grandma and Mum.

لم يكن هذا الكتاب ليرى النور لولا المساعدة الكريمة من العديد من الأشخاص .الشكر الكبير لكل من فرج (الثعلب) محمود (جبالية) الذان علماني عن سيناء أكثر من أي شخص أخر .الشكر كل الشكر أيضا لفرج سليمان من مزينة ونصر من قرارشة –الذي مات قبل أن يرى هذا الكتاب – فالاثنان فرج ونصر أجابا على كم لا ينتهي من الأسئلة وساعداني على خوض واستكشاف أبعد الأماكن.أتوجه بالشكر أيضا الى أخرين من بينهم رجب سعدي (جبالية) ،صلاح (قرارشة) ،إسماعيل (قرارشة) وابراهيم أبو ياسر من (حماضة) ،كذلك أشكر الشيخ أحمد محمد أبو رشيد (جبالية)، حميد محمد وحميد فرحان (جبالية) ،حاتم حسين ،محمد عيسى ،محمد خليل وأحمد غفار

وأخيرا أتوجه بالشكر للغرباء الذين قابلتهم في رحلتي ،لقد نسيت الأسماء لكنني أتذكر المساعدة ...ألف شكر

❏ NOTES ON THE TEXT

The Egyptian Revolution Egypt saw massive change in the revolution and has remained a country in transition since. Things are changing fast and travellers will therefore have to be extra vigilant in asking round for the latest information. Check the Trailblazer website (see p2) for updates.

The Bedouin In Arabic the plural for Bedouin is *Bedu*; the singular, *Bedawi*. *Bedouin* is an English derivative and, in keeping with common parlance, it's used here to refer to both a collective group of Bedouin or a single Bedouin person.

Mountains and deserts Distinction is made between the 'mountains' and 'desert'. Correctly, all of the Sinai is a desert, including its mountainous parts. Likewise, those areas called the 'desert' have mountains. All the same, the contrast is striking enough to make this distinction clear and it's one that follows the way local people talk.

The desert Three trekking areas are covered in this book. One is around St Katherine, another around Wadi Feiran. The third is a large territory stretching between Nuweiba and an oasis called Ein Hudera. This area doesn't have an all-embracing name; for ease of reference, and in keeping with the convention above, it's referred to simply as 'the desert'.

CONTENTS

INTRODUCTION

The Sinai is the jagged tooth of wilderness between Africa and Asia; a frontier of rugged mountains and wild, windswept deserts whose epic Biblical legends have echoed through the ages. Humans walked out of Africa through here and civilisations from the Pharaohs to the Nabataeans and Ottomans have followed since, making journeys that shaped the history of the Middle East; even the history of the world.

There's nowhere on earth like the Sinai: it grew at a great continental crossroads under a unique set of influences, developing as a land unto itself. It's an extraordinary place to walk but its troubled politics have long kept it off the mainstream map. That's beginning to change now and trekking is getting ever easier. But there's still some way to go — which is perhaps why it's so exciting.

This isn't a destination of neat trails, signposted paths and easy conveniences. It's a vast *terra incognita* of wild wadis, unclimbed peaks and hidden ruins; a brooding Bedouin wilderness whose severity strips away the excess in landscapes and people. The opportunities for exploration and discovery are still rich but, above all, there's adventure. Great, epic adventure to remember for a lifetime.

The Sinai can be trekked at any time of year. There are daily flights from Europe and you can get by on very little. There are coral reefs, shipwrecks and beaches, and Egypt's pyramids and temples are a short hop over the Gulf. Tourism has been hit hard by the revolution but it'll recover in time; Egypt always does. If anything, now is the best time to visit. It's cheaper and even quieter on the trails and the fabled Arab hospitality is extra warm.

About this book
This book is about South Sinai. The north is yet to be developed for any real sort of trekking or adventure travel.

There's practical information on planning every aspect of your trip. There are full reviews of the gateway towns (including town plans) and trekking bases, plus detailed route descriptions, 74 large-scale maps and hundreds of GPS points. In addition there's background on history, culture and the environment, along with tips on riding camels, speaking Arabic, and more.

This is the most comprehensive trekking guide to the Sinai yet published and is an all-in-one travel guide for the peninsula; it's the only book you will need.

1

PLANNING YOUR TREK

With a group or on your own?

No man can live this life and emerge unchanged. He will carry, however faint, the imprint of the desert, the brand which marks the nomad; and he will have within him the yearning to return, weak or insistent according to his nature. For this cruel land can cast a spell which no temperate clime can match.
Wilfred Thesiger *Arabian Sands*

BEDOUIN TRIBES AND TREKKING

The Bedouin are a tribal people and the Sinai has many different tribes. Each tribe has its own territory and most rule that trekkers need guides within it. It's also usually specified that the guide must be one of their own tribesmen. In the High Mountain Region of the Jebeleya tribe, you need a Jebeleya guide. In Wadi Feiran, guides have to be from the local Gararsha tribe and so forth. Everything is outlined in the relevant trekking chapters. This guide requirement goes back centuries; before trekkers, traders, pilgrims and explorers had to take them too. Guiding is one of the few ways the Bedouin have been able to make a living out of their land; it's not a modern-day money-making scheme rolled out purely for tourism.

TREKKING WITH A GUIDE

Don't have any concerns about a guide limiting your independence on trek. The Bedouin are a fiercely independent people and a good guide will understand exactly what it is to want freedom in a wild place. Going with a guide means you don't have to think about the humdrum practicalities that'd constrain you anyway. Guides do much more than just keep you on the right track too. They tell you about wildlife and history, explain place names, local legends and Bedouin culture. The whole trek is enriched.

The Bedouin make trekking in the Sinai what it really is; without them, you'd miss something essential. Guides can become companions who live as long in the memory as the scenery does.

Finding a guide yourself

Guides are found easily at trailheads: ask around and you'll be pointed the right way. They influence treks more than anything so always **choose carefully**. Chat with any guide, getting a feel for his character and likely abilities. How well do you communicate? Does

> **❏ So what happens if I go alone?**
> Not every tribesman will care. Sooner or later though, one will. Mountain tribes are stricter than those in the desert (especially the Gararsha). As well as creating trouble with the tribe, it can be a problem with the police. This book fully recommends you take a guide. As much as respecting local laws and supporting a legitimate Bedouin economy, it's about safety. The Sinai is tough and the Bedouin know how to get through it better than anyone. What's more, they'll smooth the way with opium farmers, smugglers and any other rough-and-ready characters along the way.

he seem reliable, knowledgeable and enthusiastic? As much as anything, will you get on? A lot of the time, success simply rests on an interpersonal dynamic. Remember, there's no obligation to use the first guide you meet: if you don't like one guide, find another. And if you get a bad feeling, heed it. Some so-called guides should be avoided at all costs.

Two more considerations are the route and schedule. Different **routes** may go between the same basic trekking highlights and they won't necessarily be of equal merit. Trek names are specific to this book so they won't tell guides all they need to know; detail the route by reading out key locations on the treks (they're in bold section headers throughout the trek descriptions). As for **schedules**, these vary: you, your guide, the camels, the season and other things all have an effect. Some guides push for longer than you need; others rush to finish. The times in this book are just suggestions. It's best to aim for couple of days' flexibility either side, seeing how you go and adjusting accordingly from there.

Organising yourself is cheapest – but you have to haggle hard. In the desert the cheapest **rates** are about LE150/£15/US$25 per day, but LE200/£20/$35 is more standard (even for good hagglers). In St Katherine and Wadi Feiran, the minimum is about LE200/£20/US$35. Negotiate for an all-inclusive price that factors in guides, camels and food, plus extras such as jeeps (when needed). When a trek ends a few days from where it starts, you usually have to pay the guide for the return trip. As a rule of thumb, give one day's extra pay for every three you've been on trail (eg if you've trekked six days, pay for an extra two). It's common to pay half the money up front (your guide will buy food, camel fodder and a mountain of cigarettes), but never give the whole lot. Things can often be ready in a couple of hours if you're alone. For groups of three or more, or for more complicated, remote treks, it might be the next day.

When do I need a camel?

Camels carry water, food and bags. They're essential in the desert, where water is scarce (you'd struggle to get between wells carrying all your stuff). The mountains have more water, meaning treks can usually be done unsupported, at least over a couple of days. Camels become essential again on longer routes, when you need more supplies. Only one trek in this book has a village where you can re-stock on the way. Most of the time you have to carry everything needed from start to finish. Camels can also be good to ride (see box p81), especially on long, winding wadi treks. If you want a camel to ride *as well* as the

❏ **Female guides**
Every guide in the Sinai is male. Local women hardly feature in trekking at all. It's not because they don't know the area; to the contrary, some know it better than the men. Bedouin culture is just very conservative in this respect. Female guides could do a superb job, and especially for female trekkers; but most men remain opposed. Things do change though. Until recently, only a few Bedouin girls went to school. Today, many more go, at least in the bigger towns. If nothing else, ask questions about it to fix it as a point for local discussion and debate.

one for baggage it'll cost about LE100-200 per day (per camel). Take one per trekker; they walk about one-and-a-half times the pace of people – faster on sand – and if everyone rides the expedition can move at the same speed.

Guides and cameleers

These are usually distinct in the mountains. You go one way with a guide – often a more difficult way – as the camel takes another one, meeting you at a rendez-vouz in the evening. In the desert you stay with camels pretty much the whole way. Guides and cameleers are essentially one and the same thing here (this is one reason it's often cheaper to trek in the desert).

Independent women

Harassment is common in Egypt and although it's rare for women to have prob-lems from Bedouin guides it's not unknown. Single women should at least be extra selective in choosing a guide. Trekking with a friend can be the most com-fortable option of all. See also pp56-7.

GROUP TOURS

Trekking tours are taking off in the Sinai and it's easy to find an all-inclusive package with a trek, flights, transfers and accommodation. Most packages focus on the best-known trails in the High Mountain Region or the desert, sometimes throwing in excursions to Cairo or Upper Egypt. There are benefits: there's no hassle with organisation, expeditions are more comfortable and medical know-how is usually better. You get the social benefit of meeting like-minded others too. The downsides are the rigid schedules, limited independence and lack of genuine, spontaneous contact with the local culture. Whether you'd like one just depends on your travel philosophy. Typical prices range from £800 to £1200 for a 10-day package and sometimes more.

TREKKING AGENCIES

Many of the trekking agencies in the Sinai are run by Bedouin. Use them to organise anything from a guide to a jeep or an entire trek. They're especially useful for long, complicated, or remote routes.

When organising with a Sinai-based company from home, don't forget to haggle. Emails carry little of their culture; it's easy to forget prices quoted will be deliberately high in the expectation you'll negotiate. Drive the price down over several messages; there'll almost always be leeway (see p48).

Trekking agencies based elsewhere in the world offer places in bigger, Western trekking groups. They work through local agencies like those listed for the Sinai but that's not to say they're exactly the same. These add value in bringing the big groups together in the first place and their know-how makes trips extra comfortable.

In the Sinai

● **Desert Fox Safari** (🖳 www.sinaidesertfox.com, ☎ 069-347 0344, mob ☎ 0109-473 2417, Desert Fox Camp, St Katherine) An unparalleled knowledge of the peninsula and one of the best. Along with treks it can organise Bedouin herbalists, trackers and pretty much anyone else you'd want.

● **Sheikh Mousa** (🖳 www.sheikhmousa.com, ☎ 069-347 0457, mob ☎ 0100-641 3575, Bedouin Camp and Guesthouse, El Milga, St Katherine) Another top option, able to organise programmes in most trekking regions.

● **Sheikh Sina** (🖳 www.sheikhsina.com, ☎ 069-347 0880, El Milga, St Katherine) An EU-funded, Bedouin-run agency with an interesting range of treks, including a good coast-to-coast programme.

● **Wilderness Ventures Egypt** (🖳 www.wilderness-ventures-egypt.com, mob ☎ 0128-282 7182, El Rasees, St Katherine) Good expat-run agency with a night telescope and camel-riding school.

● **Bedouin Safari Dahab** (🖳 www.bedouin-safari-dahab.com, ☎ 069-364 0317, Mashraba, Dahab) Good, family-run Bedouin business. Can tailor-make camel safaris in the desert, mountains and Serabit el Khadem area.

● **Crazy Camel Safaris** (🖳 www.crazy-camel.de, mob ☎ 0100-557 5161, Masbat, Dahab) Also offers camel safaris, especially near Ein Hudera.

● **Hike Dahab** (🖳 www.hikedahab.com, mob ☎ 0122-457 7586, Dahab) Good expat agency, runs short hikes around Ras Abu Galum and a deeper desert trek.

● **Sinai Safari** (🖳 www.sinai-safari.com, Dahab) Excellent Bedouin-Egyptian agency with a strong cultural and eco-focus. Offers a trek from St Katherine to the desert and a few itineraries around Ein Hudera.

● **Sinai Bedouin Safari** (🖳 www.sinaibedouinsafari.com, mob ☎ 0100-284-7015, Masbat, Dahab) Bedouin agency offering camel treks around Ein Hudera.

● **Bedouin History Desert Safari** (🖳 www.bedouinhistorydesertsafari.com, mob ☎ 0122-268-1938) Excellent Bedouin agency covering more off-beat locations in the desert. Also offers a trek from St Katherine to Sharm el Sheikh.

● **School of the Desert** (🖳 www.schoolofthedesert.com, mob ☎ 0128-321-8280) Excellent Egyptian-Bedouin agency with a strong cultural emphasis. Can tailor itineraries across most parts of South Sinai.

In the UK

● **360 Expeditions** (🖳 www.360-expeditions.com, ☎ 020-7183 4360, London) Experienced firm with a good coast-to-coast desert trek.

● **Bedouin Trails** (🖳 bedouintrails.com) Excellent new firm, investing all profits back into the Bedouin community.

PLANNING YOUR TREK

● **Wind, Sand & Stars** (🖳 www.windsandstars.co.uk, ☎ 0122-532 0839, Bath) Over 20 years' experience in the Sinai. Offers a good range of programmes, sometimes accompanied by experts in local history or culture.

● **Sam McConnell Expeditions** (🖳 www.sam-mcconnell-expeditions.com, mob ☎ 07826-292632) A specialist desert-trekking agency working in Africa and the Middle East. Offers a good camel trek from Serabit el Khadem to St Katherine, with the option to continue towards the Ein Hudera region.

In continental Europe

● **Austria BergSpechte** (🖳 www.bergspechte.at, ☎ 07-3277 9311, Linz). Offers a High Mountain Region circuit and a few desert treks.

● **Belgium Anders Reizen** (🖳 www.andersreizen.be, ☎ 013-334 040, Diest) Offers both mountain and desert treks.

● **France Allibert Trekking** (🖳 www.allibert-trekking.com, ☎ 04-7645 5050, Paris) Offers mountain and desert treks. Another is **Visages** (🖳 www.visages-trekking.com, ☎ 04-9245 1805), with a desert trek.

● **Germany Hauser Exkursionen** (🖳 www.hauser-exkursionen.de, ☎ 089-235 0060, Munchen) Offers High Mountain Region treks and a camel option in the desert. Also see **Moja Travel** (🖳 www.moja-travel.net/, ☎ 0781-932 2970).

● **The Netherlands Angie Barth** (🖳 www.feel-the-desert.com) is a Dutch expat who can fix programmes in the desert.

In Israel

Israelis trekked the Sinai widely in the occupation. Many Israelis know the region well and their agencies have good local links to the Bedouin. Most firms have scaled back since the revolution, re-focusing in Jordan and Israel. The information here is thus especially liable to change.

● **SK Tours in Nature** (🖳 www.sktours.net, ☎ 02-672 6095, Jerusalem) Developed in the Sinai and has over 30 years' experience.

● **Desert Eco Tours** (🖳 www.desertecotours.com, Eilat) Offers a good range of treks in the mountains and desert.

● **Benayuh Blum** (🖳 www.benayahblum.co.il, ☎ 08-637 7022) Experienced guide offering treks in the High Mountain Region.

● **Yoel Oren** (🖳 www.yoeloren.com) Another knowledgeable guide; offers a four-day programme in the High Mountain Region.

In North America and Australasia

● **Footloose Travel Guides** (🖳 www.footloosetravelguides.com, USA ☎ 720-220-6998, Colorado, USA) Offers a good coast to St Katherine trek. Experienced Texan expat accompanies trips.

● **World Expeditions Canada** (🖳 www.worldexpeditions.com/ca/, CAN ☎ 613-241-2700, Ottawa) Offers same trek as World Expeditions UK.

● **World Expeditions Australia/New Zealand** (🖳 www.worldexpeditions.com /au/ and 🖳 www.worldexpeditions.com/nz/) Trekking agencies are limited in Australasia; this is about the only one.

Getting to the Sinai

BY AIR

Direct flights go to the Sinai from across Europe, with journey times about five hours. The main international airport is Sharm el Sheikh (SSH). There's a smaller one at Taba (TCP). Finding flights is easiest with an instant comparison engine such as 🖳 www.skyscanner.net or 🖳 www.kayak.com.

From the UK

The UK has more scheduled flights to the Sinai than anywhere. **Easyjet** (🖳 www.easyjet.com, ☎ 0843-104 5000) runs daily flights from Gatwick, Luton and Manchester. Both **Thomson** (🖳 www.thomsonfly.com, ☎ 0871-231 4787) and **Thomas Cook Airlines** (🖳 www.flythomascook.com, ☎ 0871-895 0055) fly from airports across the UK. Also consider **Monarch** (🖳 www.monarch.co .uk, ☎ 0871-940 5040) and **Avro** (🖳 www.avro.co.uk, ☎ 0871-423 8550).

There are no direct flights from the Republic of Ireland but there's a Thomson flight from Belfast. Flights can be as little as £180 return (Nov to Feb is cheapest, especially if you book ahead) but £250-500 is more typical.

From German-speaking Europe

The German-speaking countries of Western Europe are also well connected.
● **Germany** Air Berlin (🖳 www.airberlin.com, ☎ 0303-434 3434) flies from German airports every day. **TUIfly** (🖳 www.tuifly.com, ☎ 0900-1000 2000) and **Condor** (🖳 www.condor.com, ☎ 01805-767 757) are other options.

● **Austria** Air Berlin (🖳 www.airberlin.com, ☎ 0820-737 800), **TUIfly** (🖳 www .tuifly.com, ☎ 0900-190 150); **Lauda Air** (🖳 www.laudaair.com, ☎ 0820-320 321).

● **Switzerland** Both **SWISS** (🖳 www.swiss.com, ☎ 0848-700 700) and **Easyjet** (🖳 www.easyjet.com, ☎ 0848-282 828) fly from Geneva. Fares vary but an average return to Sharm el Sheikh would be about €250-600.

From other parts of Europe

From the **Netherlands**, there's Transavia (🖳 www.transavia.com, ☎ 0900-0737). From **Russia**, Aeroflot (🖳 www.aeroflot.com).

Most other countries have charter options and you can always fly to Cairo with **Egypt Air** (🖳 www.egyptair.com) or your national airline.

From the United States and Canada

There are no direct flights to the Sinai: everything goes to Cairo, usually via Europe. **Egypt Air** (🖳 www.egyptair.com, USA ☎ 1-212 581 5600) offers flights from across the USA, including the New York JFK to Cairo service which is the only direct, scheduled one between North America and Egypt. Several other airlines fly indirectly from both the US and Canada, including

British Airways (🖥 www.ba.com, USA/CAN ☎ 1-800 247 9297) and **Lufthansa** (🖥 www.lufthansa.com, USA ☎1-800 645 3880, CAN ☎ 1-800 563 5954). Fares are typically US$750-1500 from the eastern seaboard but up to double from west-coast cities such as LA or Vancouver.

From Australia and New Zealand
Flights go to Cairo, usually via the Gulf states; some can be epic slogs over 30 hours. **Emirates** (🖥 www.emirates.com, AUS ☎ 1-30 030 3777, NZ ☎ 050-836 4728) is the airline with the most frequent services from both countries.

Fares are usually about AUS$1800-2600 from Australia and NZ$2200-3200 from New Zealand.

From within Egypt
Egypt Air (🖥 www.egyptair.com, ☎ 1717) has a near monopoly on internal flights. There are seven flights a day from Cairo to Sharm el Sheikh and it's just a short hop at 50 minutes. Flights also go from Luxor and most other places, usually with a change in Cairo. Wherever you go from, a one-way ticket is about LE400-1000. Booking on the Egypt Air website is easy; just take your booking reference to the airport. As we were going to press in 2013 the St Katherine airport – closed for many years – was handling flights again. **Smart Aviation** (🖥 www.smartaviation.com.eg) now offer direct flights from Cairo to St Katherine from LE350, making travel to the trekking areas much easier.

OVERLAND

The Sinai connects the world's biggest continents and the overland route is easy. Take your passport with you when travelling from the Egyptian side; they're checked at the Suez Canal and at checkpoints throughout the Sinai. Travelling the other way involves crossing an international border. The main one is with Israel at Eilat–Taba (beware of the Taba visa, noted on p17). The other is a Hamas-controlled crossing with the Gaza Strip at Rafah. This has been opening up lately, but mostly to Egyptians, Palestinians and other Arab nationals; it's still difficult for Westerners. Check the latest with your embassy.

By public bus
From Cairo Buses are regular, cheap and the best way of getting to the Sinai. Stock up on food and take a sweater for night journeys. It's best to book ahead, especially with night buses to Sharm el Sheikh, Dahab or Nuweiba, or on a big religious holiday, like one of the two Eids (see p44).

East Delta Travel Company (☎ 02-2405 3482, 🖥 www.bus.com.eg) is the main firm covering the Sinai, with the following services from Cairo: Sharm, 5/day, including night buses at 11pm and 1am (LE90, 9-10hrs); Dahab, 4/day including a night bus at 11.45pm (LE60-80, 9-10hrs); Taba and Nuweiba, 3/day, 6am, 9.30am and 11.30pm (LE70-90, 6-8hrs); St Katherine, 1/day 11am (LE55, 6-8hrs).

In late 2012, the bus to Taba and Nuweiba (which goes across central Sinai) was closed to foreigners; ask for service updates or use a bus via Sharm.

❏ **Bus stations in Cairo**

Bus stations can be obscure in Cairo. When taking a taxi, give the name of the bus station and bus company. Use these pointers when walking:

● **Go Bus/El Gouna** From Abdel Minim Riyadh, a busy intersection north of the Egyptian Museum (Midan Tahrir). Look for the Ramses Hilton, a brown skyscraper with blue letters on top. The bus office is just a stone's throw from the bottom.

● **East Delta and Superjet** From Turgoman Garage (aka Cairo Gateway Plaza). From the bus office above, walk north-east up Sharia Gala (below a flyover). The 26th July St crossroads is 10 minutes up (always busy). Cross and continue to the shiny black Al Ahram news building. Turn left after this – just before a church – and walk ahead.

● **High Jet** From Ahmed Helmi, outside Ramses Railway Station. Take the metro to Al Shohadaa (it means The Martyrs and used to be called Mubarak). Enter the railway station, and go through to the other side. There's a minibus depot with a church outside here. High Jet's office is on the main road on the very far side.

To travel between Taba and Ras Shaitan (east coast) use any East Delta bus between these towns and tell the driver where to stop – it's best to give the name of a camp or hotel (see pp118-19 and p228).

Other companies serve the Sharm route too. The best is **Go Bus/El Gouna** (☎ 19567), with tickets costing LE45-135. It runs 'elite' buses at 1pm and 10pm. They have spacious, reclining seats and an on-board meal, and they're the most painless way of travelling (LE135). Others are **High Jet** (☎ 16108; 5/day, LE55-70, 8-9hrs) and **Superjet** (3/day, LE85, 8-9hrs).

From elsewhere in Egypt East Delta runs buses to **Sharm** and the Sinai's west-coast towns from **Suez**, **Ismaila** and **Port Said**. There's another bus from **Luxor** to **Sharm** and **Dahab** but it's a 16hr trip that involves driving a country-sized hairpin bend around the Gulf of Suez and it's better to fly (see opposite).

From Israel There are regular **Egged** buses (🖥 www.egged.co.il) to Eilat from Jerusalem, Tel Aviv, Beersheba and other destinations. They get busy – especially during holidays such as Sukkot and Passover when many Israelis flock to the Sinai – so reserve a ticket online.

By minibus
Minibuses go to Sharm from outside the New El Marg metro, but they're irregular, crowded and a headache best avoided.

By rail
The closest you can get is Suez, from where there are connecting East Delta buses. Trains go from Cairo's Ramses Railway Station but they're old, rickety and slow, with no romantic charm to make up for them.

❏ **Eilat–Taba border crossing**

This is open 24/7 but is slower on both sides on Fridays. NIS103 (US$27) departure tax on the Israeli side and LE75 road tax is payable to leave the Taba area for the Sinai.

By sea

It's always great approaching the Sinai by sea. **AB Maritime Company** (☎ 03-201-3236, 🖳 www.abmaritime.com.jo) runs a ferry from Aqaba to Nuweiba. As of 2013 there was one daily (7pm, US$60/JD42 one-way, three-hour crossing). It doesn't go on Saturdays and departure times are always liable to change. Arrive two hours before departure, with JD5-8 for the exit tax.

   A note on the AB ferry: It's busy, chaotic and a bit of a mission, especially during the *Hajj* (it's worst in Eid el Adha, when everyone flocks back to North Africa, see p44 for dates). Delays are routine and there are safety issues too. The ferry caught fire in 2011; 1200 passengers were evacuated and one died jumping overboard. The ferry sank a few days later.

Other options Meenagate (☎ 03-201 3137, 🖳 www.meenagate.com) operates a catamaran between Aqaba and Taba. It leaves Aqaba's Royal Yacht Club daily between 7pm and 8pm, taking 30-45 minutes. All tickets are returns (US$100) that must be used within seven days. If you don't return you (apparently) risk a US$500 fine from authorities.

   Book by emailing 🖳 info@meenagate.com at least 24 hours before travel, attaching a photo of your passport ID page.

   Sindbad (☎ 03-205-0077, 🖳 www.sindbadjo.com) used to run a service between Aqaba and Taba. Called the **Sindbad XPRESS**, it stopped after the Egyptian revolution, but operators said it was scheduled to return sometime in 2013. It's a good, fast option but, like the service above, only offered compulsory return tickets. Contact **Al Jawad Tours** (☎ 03-201-4337, 🖳 www.jawad.com.jo) for the latest information. With both Taba ferries, you get the restricted 14-day Sinai visa at the marina (see p17).

   Hurghada and Sharm were at one time connected but the boat stopped years ago. It might still return so ask around for the latest. It's a great short-cut for getting between Upper Egypt (Luxor, Aswan etc) and the Sinai.

Visas and entry

STANDARD TOURIST VISAS

Europeans and most other nationalities need visas (although many Arab nationals enter visa free). They're cheap and hassle-free to get at Egyptian airports on arrival. Your passport should have at least six months until expiry and visas are a flat-rate US$15 (or equivalent in Egyptian currency, about LE90). It's the same procedure at every airport: get them at the foreign-exchange bank windows near the passport control points.

   For those arriving from Aqaba, visas are available at Nuweiba port. Visas are issued at Taba Marina too, but they'll be the restricted visas outlined next.

❏ **Israeli border stamps and Taba stamps**
Many Arab countries will prohibit entry if they suspect you've visited Israel. Anything can give it away: an El Al airline sticker on your hand bags, a Hebrew receipt in your passport and so on. Most of the time it's just a passport stamp and it can be one from either the Israeli border *or the border of the country you left to get to Israel (or entered from Israel, if going the other way)*.

Israeli border guards might be persuaded to stamp a bit of paper instead of your passport (though not always). The Egyptian guards at Taba sometimes do this; others, they don't. The chances of getting the stamp seem to be about 80-20. To guarantee avoiding it, use the Nuweiba ferry to/from Jordan.

There's a trick for concealing stamps. Egypt visas are usually given as stickers, which you can put anywhere in your passport. Travellers have stuck them over unwanted stamps to get through borders but — with electronic passports catching on — it's getting ever-more difficult and is always a risk now.

RESTRICTED VISAS AT TABA

All Taba entry points issue special 'Sinai-only visas' (except the airport). These are valid for 14 days and prohibit all movement off the Sinai's east coast and the town area of St Katherine. Wadi Feiran, the desert, El Tur, North Sinai, and mainland Egypt stay off-limits. These visas are useless for trekking and are a pain to get rid of once you've got them. Sometimes, officials at Sharm airport upgrade them but it depends. Usually, you have to leave Egypt, pick up a proper visa from an Egyptian embassy, then enter again.

If you arrive unaware there's a last-ditch option, but only at the land border (ie not the marina). Touts in the arrivals hall will write a 'letter of introduction' for upwards of US$40/LE240. Give this and the standard US$15 visa fee to the border guards, who'll issue the proper visa. It feels like a racket (and *it is*); but it's an official one and the visas are the real deal.

Look out! Restricted visas can be given at Nuweiba and Sharm, usually when it's not clear what you want. Get the full visa before passport control (as described above). As a quick rule of thumb, remember restricted visas are *free*; as long as you've paid the US$15, everything's fine.

Getting Egyptian visas in Israel and Jordan
Egyptian missions in Israel and Jordan do the full visa. Those mentioned here open Sunday to Thursday 9-11am; take your passport, a passport photo and the visa fee of US$15 (or local equivalent). Visas are usually ready by 1pm.

In **Israel** the Egyptian Embassy (☎ 03-546 4151) is in Tel Aviv at 54 Rehov Basel. The consulate is in Eilat at 68 Afrouni St, Bna Betkha.

In **Jordan** the Egyptian Embassy (☎ 06-560 5175; 14 Riyadh Al Mefleh St, between 4th and 5th Circles, Jebel Amman) is in Amman. The consulate (☎ 03-201 6171; 9th of Sha'aban St, between 3rd and 6th Residential Districts) is in Aqaba (it's quite a way from the town centre so use a taxi).

RENEWING A VISA

Tourist visas are valid for a month but you usually get two weeks' lee way. There's sometimes a fine after this — about LE150 — but it depends on the official (generally, it's easier to get out of Cairo than Sharm on an outdated visa; Cairo officials are overworked and few want the extra paperwork). It's not so much the getting out as the getting around that's difficult in the Sinai. An outdated visa prompts questions at checkpoints. To renew, go to the government office in El Tur (daily, 8am-3pm excl Friday). One-year extensions are LE91, with six months LE61 and shorter periods less. It takes about 45 minutes and you need a copy of your passport ID page and one of your visa (ask in a local bank or post office if you don't have one). For office directions see p120.

CUSTOMS AND ENTRY

You can enter Egypt with one litre of spirits and 200 cigarettes. Another three litres and 600 cigarettes can be bought at duty-free shops in Sharm or Nuweiba within 48 hours of arrival (foreign cigarettes such as Camel go down a treat with Bedouin guides). LE5000 is the cash limit, entering or leaving.

Budgeting

Budgets have to be flexible because of all the haggling. Don't underestimate the difference it makes: it can cut costs by over half. The sooner you get to grips with it the cheaper your trip will be. Prices in this book are realistic ones, achievable with limited haggling experience; you might get them for less. In most towns you can get by on as little as LE50-80/£5-8/US$8-13 a day. In 2013 the following rates were about right for trekking: you may be told they're out of date but this will probably all be part of the haggle. Of course, they'll increase over time but incrementally, like most things.

Trekking costs

It's cheapest to deal directly with the Bedouin. Daily rates vary but in the desert it's usually LE150-450 for a guide and camel. In Wadi Feiran a guide costs LE200 and it's roughly the same for a camel. In the St Katherine region, guide costs are about LE180-250 and LE80-120 for a camel (though the Mount Sinai trek is cheaper). Food isn't always included in these prices; if not, add LE20-30 a day based on one person and a guide (LE10-15 for each additional person). Jeeps to trailheads, taxi pick-ups and *baksheesh* might add to these costs.

Accommodation

Budget accommodation is everywhere. Basic rooms cost about LE20-50. For a room with a/c and a bathroom expect to pay LE60-120. Upmarket hotels on the coast can be as expensive as anywhere in the world. Since most rooms are doubles if you are travelling on your own you will get a discount on the room rate.

Transport
Public transport is always cheap. Sharm to Dahab by bus is LE20 and from the Sinai to Cairo as low as LE45. Taxis aren't too bad over long distances: 200km from Sharm to St Katherine is about LE350. The cost is proportionately greater over short distances in towns (LE15-20 for as little as 3km).

Eating
Eating like the locals, going to street stalls and cheap *shisha* cafés, you can get by on LE20-30 every day. Eating at more upmarket restaurants like those on the Dahab promenade it's about LE35-65 for a main meal, which is still good.

Other expenses
Budgets are broken by little things: bottles of water, cups of tea, mobile phone credit, postage stamps, internet use, chocolate, ice creams etc. LE20-30 each day should be enough to cover these.

When to go

The big changes in altitude across the Sinai give each trekking region its own climate. The High Mountain Region is twice the height of the desert and sometimes up to 10°C cooler. It's also significantly higher than Wadi Feiran and Serabit el Khadem. Whenever you visit, one region will have suitable conditions. Early spring or late autumn gives you the best of everywhere.

SEASONS IN THE SINAI

Mid-March to May
This is springtime and the busiest trekking season. It's probably the prettiest time too: ephemeral flowers bloom, orchard trees come into season and wildlife becomes more active. Water levels are usually high and seasonal creeks form in some mountain wadis. Temperatures are manageable everywhere but things warm up significantly in the desert from the end of April.

June to mid-September
Temperatures are absolutely searing in the desert. It's hard enough swinging in a hammock, let alone trekking. Some guides don't even work their camels. This is the time for the mountains but even here, on the open trail, the heat shouldn't be underestimated. You have to carry more water and do treks more slowly. Ramadan (see pp43-4) will also fall in this period until 2018.

Mid-September to November
Temperatures cool steadily and by late October it's manageable in the desert again. The High Mountain Region is a good spot, with Bedouin gardens going through pretty autumnal displays. Heavy rain fell in 2012 but most autumns in the last decade have been dry and water levels low. If it's a dry autumn, plan your water needs carefully (especially in Wadi Feiran).

December to Mid-March

This is prime time for desert trekking: temperatures are pleasant and the land-scape can be enjoyed properly. It's bitterly cold in the mountains; often sub-zero high up (sometimes with snow). Rain is more likely and creeks often form in the wadis again. The whole place has a desolate feel which might be an attraction in itself. January and February are big camel-racing months (see p45).

Route options

There's an extraordinary diversity of scenery in the Sinai: high mountains, sandstone plateaus, sweeping deserts and immense seaboard plains. The treks in this book give a representative selection of the best. Classic trekking highlights are the focus but the spectacular wild and untrodden parts haven't been forgotten. There's plenty of variety: some routes are classic mountain walks, others wadi-based treks, and one or two mostly scrambles. Along with the scenery, many treks have an historical attraction: some are notable for their Nabataean and ancient Egyptian history, others for their early Christian heritage. Treks can be done as shorter routes or linked into bigger circuits and there's a range in difficulty. There's plenty to choose from and you should find something suited to your interests and capabilities. See map opposite back cover.

Note: Trek names are specific to this book and may also be known by other titles.

HIGH MOUNTAIN REGION

This is an area of rugged granite peaks, sometimes dubbed 'The Roof of Egypt'. Home to Mount Sinai and the Monastery of St Katherine, the area is steeped in history and fable and is the peninsula's most popular trekking region.

Mount Sinai/Jebel Musa (1-2 days)

Mount Sinai – or Jebel Musa as the Bedouin know it – is a holy peak for millions of people. This is where it's said God gave Moses the Ten Commandments. There are two tourist routes to the top: the Camel Path and Steps of Repentance (both often combined in a circuit). This trek takes you up another way, long favoured by local monks, pilgrims and the Bedouin. You can wander around the mountain's forgotten chapels and climb the pretty peak of Jebel Safsafa ('Mountain of the Willow') before finishing on Mount Sinai itself.

Jebel el Deir (1-2 days)

Jebel el Deir stands opposite Mount Sinai; a mass of bulging cliffs and rounded pinnacles. It's seldom climbed and has virtually no trails; it's more a scramble than a trek and this route will appeal to the adventurous. The mountain has a hidden complex of Byzantine ruins, along with a beautiful high basin where you can gaze down on the Monastery of St Katherine.

Galt el Azraq (3-4 days)

This shows the High Mountain Region at its finest – it's the best trek in the area. It begins by winding through rugged wadis to the blue pool of Galt el Azraq (where you can swim). You move into the wilder, western parts of the mountains from here, climbing the frontier summit of Jebel Bab el Dunya ('Door to the World'). This looks over the Red Sea to Egypt and the jagged summits of Africa rise in sharp outline on a good day. You traverse a line of high cliffs after this – some dropping off nearly a vertical kilometre – before finishing in some pretty wadis lined with green Bedouin orchards.

Northern Peaks Circuit (2-3 days)

The northern massif is the most untrodden part of the High Mountain Region. Its three major summits are ascended in the first half of this trek: Jebel Suna, Jebel el Ojar and Jebel Banat. The second half is more a wadi walk; you pass the high waterfall of Sed el Nugra before cutting out of the High Mountain Region to the lowlands. You re-enter on a beautiful old pilgrim trail to the Monastery of St Katherine, through Naqb el Hawa ('Pass of the Winds').

Jebel Katherina and Jebel Abbas Basha (2-3 days)

Jebel Katherina is Egypt's highest summit; an obvious, time-honoured trekking target. Jebel Abbas Basha, the second highest peak in the local area, is crowned with an Ottoman palace. This isn't a remote trek but both peaks are climbed by adventurous, off-the-beaten trail routes harbouring Byzantine ruins. You can do it in two days or spend the second night on Jebel Katherina, making it three. Africa and Asia are both visible from the top and you'll see the sunset, sunrise and shimmering lights of faraway towns at night.

Jebel Umm Shomer (3 days)

Egypt's second highest summit, Jebel Umm Shomer, is a mass of sharp teeth and foreboding pinnacles. It remained unclimbed until 1862, defying several intrepid explorers. The way is well-trodden today, but it's strenuous with plenty of scrambling. The second half is all downhill; you follow an ancient mountain road that once linked Mount Sinai with the port of Raithu.

There's a spectacular gorge in the last stretch; one of the peninsula's great natural wonders. You finish on the immense Plain of Qa, from where you can move on to the city of El Tur and beyond.

❏ **Connecting routes in the mountains**

Many routes overlap and you can combine them as you want (see colour map opposite inside back cover). An entire circuit of the area can be walked in 10-14 days, linking the trails in this order: Northern Peaks Circuit, Galt el Azraq, Jebel Katherina and Jebel Abbas Basha, Mount Sinai and Jebel el Deir. To extend it further, it's possible to walk from Jebel el Deir or Mount Sinai to Jebel Umm Shomer in a day.

You can also walk from St Katherine to Wadi Feiran in one or two days; for a brief route description, see p180. It's a two- to three-day walk to the desert and the route is a bit more complicated.

WADI FEIRAN

Wadi Feiran is a gigantic wadi surrounded by summits up to 2000m; not as high as those in St Katherine, but perhaps more beautiful. Feiran has a feel of the Sinai's 'Wild West' about it; it's untrodden and the Bedouin carry traditional *shibriya* (daggers) in places. There are no hotels or restaurants and English is almost non-existent; but it all adds to the adventure.

Jebel Serbal Circuit (3-4 days)

Jebel Serbal is a mass of rugged pinnacles, gigantic cliffs and deep, shadowy ravines: a dream of a mountain. Early travellers called it the 'Crown of Sinai', for all its pointed peaks. The Nabataeans climbed here 2000 years ago and early Christians thought it was the real Mount Sinai of The Bible. Israelis trekked here in the occupation, but only a handful of trekkers visit today. The classic trek is a short two- to three-day circuit; but this book makes the mountain the focal point of a bigger, circular route – which is exactly what it deserves. You climb the peak in the first half, moving around the back of it in remote, bouldery wadis (with pools and waterfalls in winter) on the second.

The scenery is tremendous, as is the history. Ancient graffiti is found all along and you can sleep in old Christian hermit cells and tread crumbling Byzantine stairways. It's a superb trek but a serious undertaking; you'll have to be experienced and in good shape. Gradients are steeper and altitude gains bigger than elsewhere and there's also plenty of scrambling.

Jebel Salla (½ day)

This is a half-day trek to a high, sugarloaf-type peak. It's capped with one of the most spectacular set of ruins in the Sinai: Byzantine churches, cells and 'walkways of faith' straddle precipices around the top. It makes a good 'warm up' trek but you can also tag it onto the end of Jebel Serbal.

Wadi Feiran to Serabit el Khadem (3 days)

This route connects Wadi Feiran with Serabit el Khadem and has exceptional historical interest. You'll see mines worked under the Pharaohs 4000 years ago and the best-preserved Egyptian temple outside Africa.

There's also Wadi Mukattab ('The Written Valley') with its hundreds of Nabataean inscriptions. The trek starts through low, unremarkable ranges but the scenery soon improves as you follow a sheer ravine through one of the wildest and least trodden mountain massifs on the entire peninsula. The beautiful, stark plateau lands of the north come afterwards.

There are difficulties organising this route: it's little-trodden and only a few guides know the way. On top of this you go through a patchwork of Bedouin territories, sometimes needing a new guide in each. If you just want to see Serabit el Khadem you can do the last stage of the trek. Details on getting to Serabit can be found in the 'Abu Zenima' section on p221.

THE DESERT

This stretches over the east of the Sinai. It has rugged mountains along its coasts, but is best known for its colourful canyons, rugged sandstone peaks, and wide horizons. Treks are usually done in wadi bottoms – meaning the walking is easier – and camels stay with you the whole way (the lack of water dictates their necessity). Trekking here feels different, touching on a more traditional side of Bedouin life. See also box below.

Ras Shaitan to Ein Hudera (3-4 days)

This takes you from the coast to the heart of the desert. The first part cuts through the coastal ranges, passing the dramatic Wishwashi Canyon. The more famous Coloured Canyon follows. The second half is a long wadi walk that passes the little oasis of Ein Furtaga. You finish at the bigger oasis of Ein Hudera ('The Green Spring'); one of the Sinai's most fabled retreats.

Desert Traverse (5-6 days)

This covers the best of the desert around the Ein Hudera oasis. You visit its three most famous canyons: the Arada Canyon (or 'Double Canyon'), Closed Canyon and White Canyon. The popular sandstone peaks of Jebel Gunna, Jebel Berqa and Jebel Mileihis are climbed between these, each offering beautiful views as far as the Hejaz. Scrambling is involved in the canyons and, to get to the top of Jebel Berqa, there's a short rock climb, for which a 15m rope is recommended (all scrambling is optional so don't let it put you off). Most of the trek is done on flat, sandy terrain so it's excellent for camel riding.

The Haduda Dune (2 days)

This takes in the best of the desert south of Ein Hudera, starting at the prehistoric Nawamis tombs. From here you climb the rugged peaks of Jebel Mutamir and Jebel Barqa, finishing on the Haduda Dune – the highest in South Sinai. It's a good trek if you're limited for time but want to see something of the desert, or if you want to make a longer route of either trek above.

HOW LONG DO YOU NEED?

Obviously it depends what you want to do, but two to three weeks is enough to see something worthwhile in each trekking region. Remember to factor in time off the trail. A day or two to settle in and perhaps a few more for heat acclimatisation. Time spent travelling, organising a trek, recovering from a trek, snorkelling etc all limit days thereafter.

❏ **Connecting routes in the desert**
There is potential for combining routes here (see map opposite back inside cover). The Haduda Dune trek can be tagged on to the end of the Ras Shaitan–Ein Hudera trek. Likewise it gives an alternative end to the Desert Traverse. You could also finish the Ras Shaitan trek with the last two days of the Desert Traverse, continuing towards Jebel Mileihis.

PLANNING YOUR TREK

What to take

Whatever you take, keep it light. Heavy bags limit freedom and you'll always wish you'd brought less. Above all, bring any specialist trekking gear you need as you can't get it in the Sinai (or elsewhere in Egypt).

WHAT TO PACK EVERYTHING IN

A **backpack** is best. It might be on a camel when trekking but you'll still have to lug it about off-trail. Get one with a specially stiffened back, a hip-belt and enough dangly straps to adjust things. 65-75 litres is ample and if you don't fill it you can always bring more back.

A **day sack** is what you'll walk with most of the time so make sure it fits comfortably. Get one with a bigger capacity of 40-45 litres; you'll often have to carry up to three bottles of water, food, cooking equipment, a jacket, a first-aid kit and other essentials. It'll also be useful on short overnight trips where you need a few additional overnight supplies.

A **bumbag** is good for valuables and anything you need quickly: passport, wallet, camera and so on. **Stuff sacks** or plastic bags help divide kit in a bigger bag.

FOOTWEAR

Travellers have long bemoaned the damage the Sinai does to footwear and it still rings true today. Everything I've used, including a top of the range pair of leather boots, has been shredded within six weeks of heavy trekking.

Trails are rough, the rock is hard, sharp and abrasive, and hot surfaces make soles all the more vulnerable to nicks and tears. Go for something balancing comfort and durability and don't bring anything near the end of its life. If you'll be staying for an extended period bring two pairs.

Boots and trekking shoes

Leather boots give the best protection but can feel hot and heavy. You might spend the whole trek just wanting to tear them off. **Fabric boots** are lighter, cooler and a better option. **Trekking shoes** are really just a pair of low-cut fabric boots and they're the most comfortable of all. They don't give your ankle so much support but the extra flexibility is good for scrambling and they're a good compromise for mountains and desert.

Trekking sandals

These leave your feet open to falling rocks, scorpions and sunburn but they're cool, lightweight and don't fill with sand. Don't use them in the mountains;

they're best in the sandy deserts and for wearing around camp. Take moisturiser as heels can develop painful cracks.

Other items

Walking socks with anti-blister lining are good (blisters are always more common in hot environments). Whatever you use, wash socks free of sand, grit and hard edges to keep your feet in good nick. **Camp shoes** or **sandals** are a relief after a hard day and well worth taking. Shops in Dahab sell flip flops, fake Crocs, wet-suit shoes etc that do the job. **Spare laces** are useful too as they can snap after a few weeks in the abrasive air.

CLOTHES

Look at what the Bedouin wear. Their *jelebeyas* cover skin down to wrists and ankles, and they're baggy enough for air to circulate freely. The head is protected with a traditional head cloth or *shemagh* (see box p26). Whilst you don't have to dress like the Bedouin it helps to understand the principles that underpin their clothes, using them to inform your own.

Base layer

This covers things like T-shirts. Cottons soak sweat up and leave it soggy on your skin. Specialist modern synthetics make it evaporate more quickly. Materials such as Argentium by Berghaus and Duofold are good options. **Long-sleeved T-shirts** protect arms, and the collar on a **trekking shirt** can be turned up to cover your neck. A good, tight-hugging thermal is good in cold months.

Mid-layer

Carry a **woolly jumper** all year as evenings can be cold. You'll need a **thick fleece** and sometimes even more layers when it's really cold.

Outer shell

Rain comes every year so be prepared. Carry a **stuff sack waterproof** or **poncho** between September and June, wherever you're trekking. For cold-month mountain trekking bring a jacket that's windproof, waterproof and breathable.

Underwear

Take loose-fitting cotton garments. There's rarely enough water to wash underwear on trail so pack enough to allow for a regular change.

Leg wear

Respect local culture and **avoid shorts**. Some trekkers know the sensitivities full well and go in them anyway. Lightweight trekking trousers are good and khaki ones with plenty of pockets are best. Check they don't restrict leg movement as it's a nuisance when scrambling.

Headwear

Wide-brimmed sunhats give good protection. A **baseball cap** with a neck curtain is another option. **Woolly hats** are good in winter but the Arab *shemagh* beats all these options whenever you're trekking (see box p26).

PLANNING YOUR TREK

❏ **The Shemagh: made for the desert**
The *shemagh* or *shaal* (or *keffiyeh*) is the traditional Arab head dress. They're not just for show though; they've been integral to Bedouin life through the ages. They give excellent protection from the sun, cold and sandstorms. They're good as pillows, towels and head nets and you can use them to strain bigger sediments out of water and to soak it up from wells. Camel loads can be tightened with them and there are all sorts of first-aid improvisations: sling bandages, normal bandages, emergency joint supports and tourniquets. The ones in tourist areas are often smaller and thicker. Go for the biggest one you can find in a thinner fabric. It should be nearly 1.5 sq metres when you unfold it fully. The best cost about LE45-65.

Other items
Gloves and **sweat bands** are handy at the right time of year. **Swimwear** is good for taking a dip in pools. Men can go in shorts but women should at least wear a big T-shirt over a bikini or a swimming costume (local women swim fully clothed). **Towels** are needed more off-trail than on it. Specialist trekking towels are lightweight and usually coated with an anti-bacterial agent.

TOILETRIES

Unless you're picky, most things are available in the Sinai: soap, shampoo, razors etc. Limited water means limited washing so take smaller amounts of everything or share.

Essentials are a **bar of soap**, some **toothpaste** and a **toothbrush**. A **razor** and **shampoo** are good if you're going somewhere with plenty of water. **Baby wipes** or **antibacterial gel** are good for sterilising hands in dry places (antibacterial gel is hard to find so bring it from home).

Toilet roll is vital and zip-seal bags help store soiled paper when you can't burn it. Keep toilet paper handy off-trail too; few toilets have it.

HEALTH SUPPLIES

Medical help can be a long time coming and basic when it arrives. Carry a decent first-aid kit and know how to use everything in it. It'll be deadweight otherwise. It's worth doing a first-aid course or reading up before your trek. *Pocket First Aid and Wilderness Medicine* by Jim Duff and Peter Gormly is an excellent choice and will fit easily in the top of a rucksack.

Basic first-aid supplies
Bring **plasters/Band Aids** in various sizes and **Steri-strips** to close bigger gashes. A good stock of blister plasters such as **Compeed** or **moleskin/Second Skin** is essential. **Crêpe bandages** have many uses. **Dressings** are useful for bigger wounds and **non-adhesive dressings** are suitable for burns. **Micropore tape** helps strap them on. Also useful are: **antiseptic cream**; **safety pins**; **tweezers**; **tick-removal forceps** and **small scissors**.

Medication supplies

The first thing to pack are **rehydration salts**: potential lifesavers when you're hit by dehydration. An anti-diarrhoeal like **Imodium** is equally vital. **Ibuprofen** is good for fever and pain and its anti-inflammatory properties help limit swelling from sprains. A few **paracetamol** tablets are useful too. **Antihistamine** relieves irritation from bites but **repellent with a DEET ingredient** stops you getting them at all. **Piriteze** is an anti-allergy medication some swear by. Remember **inhalers** and **personal medication**. Broad spectrum **antibiotics**, such as Augmentin, are easy to get in Egypt (see box p51).

Water purifying tablets

Iodine or **chlorine tablets** are best. Be generous as you can get through a lot of water (up to eight litres a day at the extreme). Keep two separate stores in case you lose one. For more see pp88-9.

Sun protection

There's no place to hide. Good **sunscreen** and **lip salve** are essential (lips become dry and chapped fast). **UV-rated sunglasses** protect your eyes (if you don't have any smear a line of ash under your eyes to limit glare and knot your shemagh so it protrudes at the front for shade).

WATER BOTTLES

Ordinary plastic bottles can spring leaks if dropped. A good rule of thumb is to bring two specialist **trekking bottles** from home – most are made from tough plastic or aluminium; you can top up from here with ordinary ones. **Bladder bottles** by manufacturers such as CamelBak and Platypus fit nicely in the top of a rucksack and have a drinking tube. Water stays on-tap all day, encouraging you to drink and keeping dehydration at bay. See box below.

CAMPING GEAR

Sleeping bag

Get a three-season bag with a sub-zero rating for colder times. A two-season bag is enough in hotter months. Down-filled bags are better than synthetic ones: they're lighter and pack down smaller. Good synthetic ones are still available and cost about half as much. **Sleeping bag liners** come in cotton, silk and fleece and they're worth it too. They make sleeping bags warmer and can be sleeping bags in their own right. They're also good for when you have to sleep in dirty blankets. The Bedouin usually sleep in the **thick fleece blankets** used to pad camel loads. Ask for a couple to be included if your bag won't be warm enough.

❏ **Bedouin water skins**

The Bedouin once used animal skins to store water (and other things like ghee and butter). Small skins that hung on a saddle were called a *semzemeeyah* and bigger ones a *girbeh*. They were comfortable for camels to carry but both gave water a horrid, bitter taste and strong winds could deplete them by half.

Sleeping mats

These make both rocky ground and sand more comfortable. **Thermarest-style mats** give maximum luxury for minimum weight but frequently puncture (the desert is full of thorns). Bring a **repair kit** or improvise with a blister plaster. **Roll-up foam mats** have no puncture risk but they're bulkier.

Tents and other options

Tents aren't commonly used in the Sinai; you usually sleep under the stars. Even so, they're still useful; they give warmth, security from rain, and a barrier against mosquitoes. The private space is good too. Don't invest in anything too high-performance. A reasonable quality two-season model is fine.

Bivvy bags are waterproof (and, ideally, breathable) sacks for sleeping bags and they're as good as a tent. A **basha** is a waterproof sheet to rig up from walls, boulders or trees, and it's another decent option.

Cooking equipment

Gas cylinders are taken for bigger trekking groups; guides make fires for smaller ones. Wood is becoming scarce now (see p80) so a **camping stove** is better. The only snag is you can't fly with gas canisters or get them in the Sinai. They're available in Cairo but even then just a few models in the Campingaz range (try Alpha Market on Al Malek al Afdel St in Zamalek).

The best alternative is an MSR-type multi-fuel stove. These can be used to burn diesel, kerosene and other fuels that are readily and cheaply available in Egypt. See 🖳 cascadedesigns.com.

A **pot or pan** can be useful, along with a **mug, plate/bowl, cutlery** and a **can opener** — but don't bother with much else. Most food is canned; cook it by opening the can and just standing it by the fire. For tea, your guide will have a boiler and shot glasses (they never leave home without the latter). Pots, pans etc will be thrown in when you have a camel anyway.

OTHER IMPORTANT KIT

Carry **matches** and **cigarette lighters**. Take at least two lighters for every few days on the trail; sand wears ignition cogs down fast. **Candles** are useful and a good, windproof lantern is made by putting one in half a plastic bottle.

A **torch/flashlight** is vital, with a **headtorch** that keeps your hands free best. LED bulbs have the best efficiency. For **batteries**, get a long-life brand like Energizer Lithium so you don't have to carry as many. **String** has many uses, including getting water up from wells. **Whistles** summon help but **reflectors** are often better: flashed in the sun they're seen from search helicopters. You can improvise with a cosmetic mirror, CD or even a shiny knife blade.

Knives are important and the Swiss Army type is best (can openers and tweezers are the most useful tools). **Trekking poles** help the knees but can sink in sand. **Binoculars** are excellent for wildlife, views and stargazing.

Some bits and bobs

Other things to consider: a **mobile phone**; an **alarm clock**; an **adaptor**; a **passport photocopy**; an **insurance policy**; a **return boarding pass**; a pair of earplugs; **nail clippers**; a **sink or bath plug**, an **i-Pod (or MP3 player)**; a **shortwave radio**; **pocket travel games**; a **journal, pencils** and **pens**.

CAMERA EQUIPMENT

Take care with cameras in the desert; windblown sand enters to corrupt the inner workings fast (even when it's not windy). The mountains aren't so bad but there's still enough dust to cause problems over periods of a few months. One option is a so-called **rugged camera**. These are shockproof, freeze proof, waterproof and as such, impervious to sand. Alternatively, wrap your camera in **clingfilm** or a **cellophane bag** (bring spares as they jade quickly). Bring enough **memory cards** (the Sinai is a photographer's paradise). To upload photos in the Sinai itself take a **flash card reader/USB stick** (you can do it in most internet cafés). For film, 100ASA or 200ASA is best. If you have a good camera, a **UV-filter** protects from sunlight. **Tripods** are useful, especially in twilight times (always the most picturesque). As a final word, keep your camera somewhere you can get it fast. Desert wildlife is there and gone in a flash.

RECOMMENDED READING

Guidebooks

Mainland Egypt is covered well by all the major guidebooks: Rough Guides, Footprint Guide and Lonely Planet. If you'll be staying a while by far the best practical guide is the *Cairo Guide* (AUC Press). There aren't many books on the Sinai itself. One of note is Alberto Siliotti's *The Guide to the Exploration of the Sinai* (AUC Press). This outlines the main sights – including overlooked ones in the North – and some good 4x4 routes. Another is *Discover Sinai* by Zoltan Matrahazi and others. This outlines lesser-known parts of the peninsula, showing trekking highlights and giving useful route pointers in each: download at 🖥 www.discover sinai.com. Also by Zoltan Matrahazi is the short book *Trekking in South Sinai*, outlining eight of the peninsula's most popular treks.

Phrasebooks

Egyptian Arabic phrasebooks are published by Lonely Planet and Rough Guides. They're small enough to fit in a pocket but still big enough to keep you going. Egyptian Arabic has differences to the various Bedouin dialects of the Sinai but it's still widely understood.

Wildlife

For a good bird-watching guide get *Common Birds of Egypt* (AUC Press) by Bertel Brunn and Sherif Baha. *Birds of the Middle East* (Helm Field Guides) by Richard Porter and Simon Aspinall is also excellent. About the most comprehensive animal guide is Richard Hoath's *A Field Guide to the Mammals of Egypt* (AUC Press). The *Discover Sinai* guide noted before has an illustrated wildlife section by Professors Francis Gilbert and Samy Zalat (see above). Also worth a look is the recently released *Wildlife in South Sinai*, a beautifully illustrated and extremely informative guide by Dina Aly and Rafik Khalil.

Diving guides

The Red Sea is one of the world's most written-about diving destinations. Amongst the stand-out books are the *Sinai Diving Guide* (Geodia) and Lonely Planet's *Diving and Snorkelling: Red Sea*. Ned Middleton's *Shipwrecks from the Red Sea* (Ashgrove Publishing) is the most authoritative book on wrecks. For underwater wildlife get the *Coral Reef Guide; Red Sea* (Collins) by Ewald Lieske and Robert Myers. *Reef Fishes and Corals of The Red Sea* (New Holland Publishers) by Peter Harrison and Alex Misiewicz is also worth a look.

Travelogues and expedition reports

Travellers have been visiting the Sinai for well over a thousand years and some wrote highly readable accounts of their journeys. Edward H Palmer's *The Desert of The Exodus* (Harper and Brothers) is of special note. He was the translator on the British Ordnance Survey and stayed on to explore after the expedition had finished (he was killed in the Sinai in 1882). Few have matched his understanding of the region and his skill in describing it. *Travels in Syria and the Holy Land* (Cambridge University Press) by John Lewis Burckhardt gives a good read too. Credited with discovering Petra, Burckhardt travelled through in the early 19th century, keeping interesting notes. *Traveling in Sinai* (AUC Press) is a compilation of diary excerpts with passages from both books above, edited by Deborah Manley and Sahar Abdel-Hakim.

The best expedition report is Sir Charles W Wilson's *Ordnance Survey of the Peninsula of Sinai*. Wildlife, culture, history, place names, routes and everything else of note is documented; it's the exploration document *par excellence*. It also gives the first photos of the Sinai Bedouin (always in demand by Sheikhs). Unfortunately, you won't be able to take it as it's in five huge volumes but you can see it in the British Library Map Room (🖥 www.bl.uk, Maps1787.d). Anybody interested in its preliminary expedition notes can see them at the UK National Archives (🖥 www.nationalarchives.gov.uk, OS 3/32).

The Bedouin

A good introduction to the Bedouin is Wilfred Thesiger's *Arabian Sands* (Penguin). It's an account of his travels across the Empty Quarter of Arabia – 'Rub al Khali' – but his observations of the Bedouin still ring true in the Sinai. Joseph Hobbs's *Bedouin Life in the Egyptian Wilderness* (University of Texas Press) is a short, readable outline of Bedouin culture in Egypt's Eastern Desert. For something specific to the Sinai look out for anything by Clinton Bailey: the region's most distinguished anthropologist. *A Culture of Desert Survival* (Yale University Press) compiles over a thousand local proverbs, distilling centuries of hard-won wisdom into short, simple sentences. *Bedouin Poetry from Sinai and the Negev* (Saqi Books) is also worth a look. Arabic poems aren't so beautiful in English; but they still give valuable insights into the culture.

Other books

Mount Sinai (University of Texas Press) by Joseph Hobbs is a good book on just about everything to do with the High Mountain Region: its geography, history, people and culture.

❏ **Useful websites**
The best website for independent travel in Egypt is ⌨ www.alternativeegypt.com. In the Sinai, ⌨ www.discoversinai.net. For tips on desert travel and for finding a trekking partner join this excellent forum ⌨ www.saharasafaris.org.
   For getting the latest information from fellow travellers try the Lonely Planet Thorn Tree Forum, ⌨ www.lonelyplanet.com.

For a smaller, more popular title, try Janet Soskice's *Sisters of Sinai* (Chatti and Windus); the true story of two Scottish sisters who travelled in the region in the 19th century and stumbled upon a long-lost gospel.

Not the average holiday material – granted – but a Bible can bring out the Sinai's Exodus legends all the more; its 'waste howling wilderness' and 'fiery serpents and scorpions'. Just a lightweight pocket one will do and everything worth reading is in Exodus, Numbers and Deuteronomy.

MAPS, SATELLITE IMAGES AND GPS

Trekking maps
Finding maps is difficult and almost everything's at least 30 years out of date. They don't show new roads or settlements and water sources, once full, might now be dry. Nonetheless, they're still worth taking.

   Quite apart from helping with orientation, a map enhances your appreciation of an area. You'll know place names, ruins, camel routes, and spot heights and your surroundings will suddenly mean a lot more.

● **British Survey of Egypt, Southern Sinai, 1:100,000** Published in the 1930s these are the highest-scale English-language maps available. They don't have contours and accuracy is lacking in places, including the High Mountain Region. Even so you can get by in big, easy wadi country in the desert.

   Copies are available from the Royal Geographical Society at 1 Kensington Gore, London (☎ 020-7591 3000, ⌨ www.rgs.org). They come in 12 sheets. The High Mountain Region treks are on sheets 8, 9, 10 and 11 with those in Wadi Feiran on sheets 5 and 8. The desert treks are on sheets 4, 7 and 9. Each sheet is about £10; order with reference is MR EGYPT D 35.

● **Survey of Israel, 1:100,000** The Survey of Israel made excellent maps in the 1970s. The best was a 1:100,000 map, with accurate co-ordinates, contours and an overlay of English names. Unfortunately it's no longer sold. You can see it in the Royal Geographical Society but important sheets are missing and it can't be copied (MR EGYPT D 43). A 1:250,000 Israeli map is the next best option and it'll give a broad idea of what's where. A derivative version called *Sinai Map of Attractions* can be purchased in the Sinai today.

● **Soviet military maps, 1:200,000** These are similar to the Israeli maps but everything is in Cyrillic. You can get them online and they're so detailed you can zoom in to a scale of about 1:50,000.

   Once you've identified the areas to cover, you can print copies. They're available at the slightly dubious-looking website: ⌨ maps.vlasenko.net. Find the

❑ **Place names of the peninsula**

The Sinai might look like a big emptiness; but everywhere has a name. Actually, it's richer in place names than many of the world's most heavily settled regions. Most names were given by Bedouin tribes that arrived from the 14th century. Many nod to water: eg Wadi el Ein (Wadi of the Spring), Wadi el Galta (Wadi of the Waterpool) or Wadi Shellal (Wadi of the Waterfall). Water quality was often referenced too: eg Bir Melha (The Salty Well), Moiyet Ramliya (The Sandy Water) and Ein Marra (The Bitter Spring). Others underlined resources: eg Wadi Zatar (Wadi of Oregano), Farsh Loz (Basin of the Almonds) or Farsh Arnab (Basin of the Rabbit).

Physical features or dangers were noted too eg Jebel Ahmar (The Red Mountain), Wadi Ramla (Valley of the Sand), or Wadi Abu Seila (Valley of the Floods). Some had real and long-standing historical associations eg Serabit el Khadem (Heights of the Slave), Bir Nasrani (The Christian's Well), or Jebel Abbas Basha (Mountain of the Pasha).

Others played on Biblical legend: eg Jebel Musa (The Mountain of Moses), Badiyat el Tih (The Wilderness of the Wanderings) and El Raha (The Plain of Rest). The oldest names are pre-Islamic: some say Jebel Serbal is derived from the god *Baal*; others that Sinai itself comes from the moon god *Sin*.

small English title at the bottom left corner of the homepage reading 'Soviet Military Topographic Maps'. Click on the '1:200,000' link below it and a page will come up showing a world map with a red grid over it. Click on the relevant Sinai squares and go from there. Alternatively, Stanfords (🖥 www.stanfords.co.uk) in London can source colour reprints for £20 per map or copies on a CD for £26 per map.

● **Other maps** A High Mountain Region map with English names is available online. It's good for orientation, but not intricate route finding. Get it at the maps link on this website: 🖥 www.st-katherine.net.

Satellite imagery

Widely available online, this is an interesting development in navigation. Satellite images don't mark names, trails or water sources but they give a better, more naturalistic feel for a landscape. Knowing what you're looking at can be tricky if you're not familiar with the area, but if you can figure that out using the maps mentioned above and those in this book, these can be very useful if printed, especially in sandy desert terrain.

Trekking with GPS

GPS isn't essential, especially with guides being compulsory. Nevertheless, it gives security. And as much as anything it's good for the add-ons: many GPS handsets have a compass, altimeter, pedometer, sunrise clock and so on. Remember though, never let GPS take your eye off what's around you.

Watch the landscape carefully and keep a constant note of where you are. GPS devices get lost and broken, batteries die, satellite signals can be scrambled and so on.

Health preparations

INOCULATIONS

Yellow Fever vaccination certificates are compulsory when arriving from an infected region (South America and tropical Africa). There are no other official requirements but get all the basic inoculations anyway. Start making enquiries about six weeks before you go.

Travel clinics are often better informed than GP surgeries and some do injections on the spot. The International Society of Travel Medicine (ISTM; 💻 www.istm.org) has a directory of travel clinics in over 80 other countries. In the UK, Nomad Travel (☎ 020-7833 4144, Russell Sq; ☎ 020-7823 5823, Victoria) has clinics in London. Trailfinders (☎ 020-7938 3999) also has a branch in London. Find others in UK towns at 💻 www.traveldoctor.co.uk/clinics.htm.

Others to consider having
● **Hepatitis A** This is spread by poor hygiene, like not washing hands after the toilet. Get the standard Hep A injection two weeks before you go. An alternative is the Hepatyrix jab, which gives dual immunity with Typhoid.
● **Typhoid** Also spread by poor hygiene. One jab, or a course of tablets, is needed two weeks before you go. Keep the Hepatyrix injection in mind. Typhoid vaccines are just 75% effective so focus on prevention.
● **Tetanus** Most Westerners are immunised and just need boosters every 10 years. It's now given as a three-way vaccine with diphtheria and polio.
● **Diphtheria and polio** Egypt was declared 'polio-free' by the World Health Organization in 2006, but it might not be completely gone. Diphtheria is still found in places. Make sure you're up to date with boosters.
● **Rabies** This is given as a course of three injections over a month. It is a 'pre-exposure' vaccine that gives extra time to get to a hospital for prophylaxis: it doesn't give full immunity. For more on rabies see p90.

For further information on travel health check out 💻 www.netdoctor.co.uk and 💻 www.nathnac.org.

Additional preparations
It's sensible to keep a note of **vital medical information** on your person for others to find. List major conditions and any medication you're taking, along with your blood group (ie A, B, AB, O). Take a print out of your insurance policy and keep everything somewhere obvious for others to find.

Bring enough **personal medication** and a **prescription** in case you need to re-stock. It should note the drug brand and its active ingredient.

Visit your GP for any prescription medication like antibiotics.

Trekkers using **contact lenses** should bring a moisture-rich type and eye-drops. Lenses dry out quickly and eyes get sore.

INSURANCE

Insurance is vital and you need a policy for everything you'll be doing. Look out for the trekking small print: some policies only cover you up to altitudes of 2000m, but the mountains of the Sinai rise over 2600m. Scrambling, camel riding and 4x4 travel are other essentials and remember a good watersports package if you'll be diving. Get a policy with air-rescue cover and don't skimp on medical allowances. Always shop around as policies and prices differ widely. The following are worth considering: How much is deductible if you need to make a claim? How long do you have to make a claim? What evidence do you need to provide (hospital bills, crime reports etc)?

The **British Mountaineering Council** (🖥 www.thebmc.co.uk, ☎ 0161-445 6111) offers good trekking insurance for UK residents but there's a joining fee (about £25). **Essential Travel** (🖥 www.essentialtravel.co.uk, ☎ 0845-803 5434) do a trekking policy suited to the Sinai as well.

GETTING FIT FOR YOUR TREK

Trekking will be more enjoyable if you're fit on arrival. You don't need to be at a tip-top athletic standard; just a comfortable sort of wellbeing where your body is used to activity is fine. Don't be deterred if you can't hit this level. Treks can be done more slowly, with camels carrying heavy bags. In the desert you can ride a camel pretty much the whole way on many treks. **Aerobic exercise** makes the body better at using the oxygen it takes in, keeping you more comfortable and less breathless. Walking, jogging and cycling all help so build some into your daily routine before you go.

❏ Help in the desert – an oral legend as told by Sheikh Ahmed Mohammed Abu Rashid of the Jebeleya tribe

A poor Bedouin once lived in the Sinai with a beautiful horse. Everywhere he went the horse drew admiration and its legend soon spread across all Arabia. One day a rich man came to offer great wealth for the horse — gold and camels — but the Bedouin refused. Burned by the rejection, the rich man called a warning: 'no man refuses such generosity', he said; 'so know this: one I day I will take your horse'.

Some years later the Bedouin was riding when he saw a man lying bloodied on the ground. Finding him alive he hauled him up on the saddle and rode in haste. But it was all a trick: the man threw the Bedouin down, tearing off his bearded disguise and crying in triumph 'I told you I'd take your horse!'. The Bedouin knew his horse was lost and sighed. 'So take my horse', he said; 'but do one thing – never tell people how you took him'. Puzzled, the rich man agreed but asked why: 'because if they knew', said the Bedouin, 'then nobody would ever help anybody in the desert again'.

EGYPT

2

Egypt is often defined by the glories of its past: its pyramids, temples and legendary Pharaohs. In the Middle East it's firmly a place of the present. It's an Arab leader in the arts, media and politics and its culture has been influential across the region for decades.

The first part of this chapter sketches out some background on Egypt, setting the Sinai in its wider national context. The second has practical information relevant to both regions. A trip to the mainland is always worth it; Egypt has an incredible history and geography and its people are some of the warmest in the world. Getting there is easy from the Sinai and if you use flights and night buses you can get a lot out of a few days in Upper Egypt, Cairo or Alexandria.

Facts about the country

GEOGRAPHY

Egypt covers one million square kilometres, making it about twice the size of Spain. From space, it's a gigantic desert plateau, interrupted only by the dark, meandering line of the Nile. The Nile is the longest river in the world (6695km) and it divides Egypt's two great deserts. The Western Desert stretches towards Libya; a vast emptiness of sweeping sand seas. The Eastern Desert goes the other way, running to the Gulf of Suez. The Red Sea Mountains (or Red Sea Hills) run down the east coast, rising over 2000m in places. Their towering, jagged peaks are visible from the high places of the Sinai. Another massif is Jebel Uweinat, in the south-west corner of Egypt (also extending into Libya and Sudan).

Geographically, the Sinai is probably Egypt's most interesting – and certainly its most distinctive – region. It's the land bridge between the world's biggest continents and on the shores of a newly forming sea; it has some of the oldest, most varied rocks in the world, and more endemic species than anywhere in the country.

HISTORICAL OUTLINE

The first Pharaoh
The lush banks of the Nile were settled from the earliest times but ancient Egypt, as we know it today, really began about 3100BC. This

was when King Narmer (or King Menes) united Upper (South) and Lower (North) Egypt into a single kingdom. He was the first in a glorious line of Pharaohs that would rule for thousands of years, giving humanity some of its finest cultural treasures.

The Old Kingdom
Lasting from about 2700-2200BC, this was Egypt's first great golden age. Government was strong and organised and significant leaps were made in art, agriculture and engineering. Pyramid building was perfected around 2560BC, when the Great Pyramid of Giza was finished (using about 2½ million blocks of stone). The Pharaohs also reached the Sinai at this time, establishing turquoise and copper mines to furnish their fast-rising kingdoms.

The Middle Kingdom
The Old Kingdom was ravaged by power struggles, and Upper and Lower Egypt broke apart. Pharaoh Mentuhotep II re-unified them in 2050BC, driving Egypt into the so-called Middle Kingdom. The capital was moved to Thebes – now called Luxor – and there was a renaissance in architecture and the arts. Mining boomed in the Sinai, but everything went into decline when the Hyksos (an Asiatic people) invaded, bringing Egypt under its first foreign occupation.

The New Kingdom
Lasting from about 1550-1100BC, this was perhaps Egypt's greatest age of all. Pharaoh Ahmose expelled the Hyksos and the kingdom flourished as never before. The monumental temples of Luxor and Upper Egypt were built; celebrated Pharaohs such as Ramses II, Queen Hatshepsut and the nine-year old boy king Tutankhamun reigned, and Egypt expanded to conquer foreign lands. It's believed The Exodus (see pp75-6) happened at this time too, with the Israelites following Moses out of Egypt to Sinai (c1450-1200BC).

End of the Pharaohs
The New Kingdom dwindled under weak rulers and the Persian King Cambyses II conquered Egypt in 525BC (at the Battle of Pelusium, North Sinai). Egypt won its independence, but the Persians returned in 343BC, with Egypt's last native Pharaoh – Nectanebo II – fleeing to Ethiopia. Alexander and his Greek/Macedonian legions invaded in 332BC, expelling the Persians just a decade after they'd arrived. Alexander crowned himself the new Pharaoh and built the city of Alexandria to mark the achievement.

Ptolemies and Romans
When Alexander died in 323BC Egypt came under the rule of Ptolemy, one of his surviving generals. It thus entered the so-called Ptolemaic period. Male rulers had the title Ptolemy; female ones were sometimes called Cleopatra. The most famous Cleopatra of all was the fabled beauty queen Cleopatra VII, who seduced some of Rome's most powerful men to Egypt's national advantage. Octavian defeated her and her Roman lover, Mark Antony (both committed suicide in Alexandria). Egypt became a realm of the Roman Empire in 30BC.

EGYPT

Arab and Islamic Egypt

Egypt came under Byzantine rule as Rome dwindled in the Eastern Mediterranean. It was governed as a Christian state until the mid 7th century, when it fell in the Islamic Conquest. Islam became the official state religion and, a few centuries later, Arabic the first language. Various Islamic governments ruled after this – some of them from outside Egypt – including the Fatimids, Ayyubids and Mameluks (a slave people who became emperors). The Ottomans invaded to bring Egypt under Turkish rule from 1517.

Modern Egypt

Napoleon invaded in 1798, but was pushed out in three years. Modern Egypt saw two more occupations. The British arrived at the end of the 19th century, displacing the Ottomans. The Israelis occupied the Sinai from 1967 to 1982, capturing the peninsula in the Six Day War of 1967. Egypt saw action in most major wars of the 20th century – both World Wars, the 1948 Arab-Israeli War, the 1956 Suez Crisis, the 1967 Six Day War, and the 1973 October War. It also became the first Arab country to make peace with Israel in the late 1970s.

POLITICS

Egypt is a key player on the international stage; an ally of the US, Europe and (more reluctantly) Israel, and a leader of the Arab League. Its domestic politics haven't been so progressive. Air force commander Hosni Mubarak took office in 1981, ruling for almost three decades with his so-called National Democratic Party (NDP). Egypt was a dictatorship; opposition was suppressed and elections rigged. Millions languished in poverty as plutocrats guzzled vast sums of the national wealth. Unemployment was rife; corruption, abduction and torture virtually routine, and the prospect of meaningful change bleak (Mubarak's son, Gamal, was being groomed for the next presidency).

The 2011 revolution was borne of desperation; Egyptians felt they had nothing left to lose. It was a true peoples' uprising at the beginning; men and women of all faiths and backgrounds united. Inevitably, when Mubarak fell, groups split down their own lines of interest. The biggest winners were the Islamists. Their parties had survived underground even under Mubarak and they could drive millions to the polls when elections came round. The Muslim Brotherhood's Freedom and Justice Party won a parliamentary majority; the harder line Al Nour Party (following a politicised sort of Islam called 'Salafism') came in behind. Liberal parties had a smaller presence behind these.

The Egyptian Revolution

The Egyptian uprising drew inspiration from the revolution that toppled President Ben Ali in Tunisia (January 2011). Protests began on 25 January 2011, as Egyptians took to the streets to demand the departure of President Mubarak. Momentum gathered quickly and just three days later, on 28 January, Egypt exploded in the so-called *Friday of Rage*. Thousands of protestors gathered in major cities after midday prayers, fighting the police in running street battles. It was civil unrest on a massive scale and by evening, the Egyptian government

---

❏ **Khaled Said: face of an uprising**

Khaled Said was a 28-year-old Egyptian man killed by plainclothes police in 2010. Wanted (supposedly) for theft offences he was dragged out of an internet café and battered to death in a public doorway. Police brutality was common in Egypt – abduction, torture and killings were all known too well – but with this being so open and with national dissatisfaction at an all time high, it sparked outrage. Images of Khaled's broken face – with the slogan *We are all Khaled Said* – were circulated widely and became a powerful rallying symbol as the revolution gathered pace. Hailed as a martyr, his death was of comparable significance to that of Mohammed Bouazizi, the street vendor who set himself on fire to spark the revolution in Tunisia.

---

was on its knees. One of the biggest and most untouchable police forces in the Middle East had collapsed and the headquarters of Mubarak's NDP stood blazing on the banks of the Nile.

In a last-ditch bid for survival, Mubarak mobilised the military and flooded the streets with tanks. The heavily armed presence restored stability but it soon became clear he couldn't rely on the army's full support. Soldiers took a non-confrontational approach and the protestors welcomed them with kisses and Egyptian flags, feting them as friends of the revolution.

It was a day of epic national catharsis, forcing more change in a single afternoon than Egypt had known in half a century (arguably longer). But still, Mubarak clung doggedly on. He made conciliatory speeches and rolled out reforms to tame the revolution; but the protestors demanded nothing less than his outright resignation. They began to occupy Cairo's symbolic heart – Midan Tahrir (Liberation Square) – vowing to stay until he'd gone.

With the army refusing to use violence, Mubarak rallied the battered remnants of his security services to break the occupation. Days of bloody fighting followed but the protestors put up defiant resistance to hold the square.

The occupation soon pushed Egypt into economic meltdown and internal pressure from Generals finally brought change. Mubarak stepped down on 11 February, having held out for 18 days. About 850 lives were lost in the uprising; both protestors and police. The Supreme Council of the Armed Forces (SCAF) took control afterwards, promising to oversee the transition from a military to a democratically elected civilian government.

Mubarak flew to a villa in Sharm, vowing never to leave Egypt – but hopes of a Red Sea retirement were soon dashed. His old police officers came knocking; arresting and charging him with ordering the use of lethal force against protestors (though not with any of the human rights abuses he stood accused of in the 30 years before). Egypt came to a standstill as the once-indomitable figurehead was wheeled into a Cairo courtroom, lying prostrate on a hospital bed. He looked an old man, every one of his 83 years, but few felt sympathy.

Symbolically, the trial seemed a step forward; but Egyptians soon came to question it, dismissing it as a smokescreen behind which SCAF was consolidating its own grip on power. Egypt was as corrupt as ever, they said – it just had a new cast of villains at the helm. One regime had been replaced by another; or rather, the same regime had re-asserted itself, minus Mubarak.

Midan Tahrir saw more deadly battles; things only settled in November, as parliamentary elections got underway. Egypt's new parliament was formed in January 2012. The presidential race was held in June, with the Muslim Brotherhood's Mohammed Morsi winning a close run-off against Ahmed Shafik. Morsi's win sealed a clean sweep of the presidency and parliament for the Islamists but a second popular uprising – led by the Tamarud (*Rebel*) movement – saw them ousted a year later. Egypt remains a country very much in the making.

PEOPLE

Egypt has a population of around 84 million and is the Arab world's most populous nation. Demographers predict it will overtake Ethiopia to become the second biggest country in Africa at some point in 2013 (Nigeria is currently the biggest). Its population was just 10 million in 1900, so the increase has been nearly tenfold in a century. Egypt calls itself the 'Arab Republic of Egypt' but its Arab roots are widely questioned and by none more than Egyptians themselves. Some research suggests only a minority of Egyptians might actually be Arab: not entirely surprising given the country's diverse settler history. Within Egypt, a few groups are notably distinct in ethnicity, or at least identity, to the majority. There are the Bedouin, the Berbers of the Western Desert (around the Siwa oasis), the Nubians of Upper Egypt and the Greeks of Alexandria.

RELIGION

The official religion is Islam and about 90% (76 million) are Muslim. The majority follow Sunni Islam but there are still plenty of Shias (estimates vary widely from a few hundred to over 50,000). Shia Islam is a 1000-year leftover of Fatimid rule and there are still theological and political sensitivities about it. Some hardline Sunnis don't see Shias as Muslims at all. The other 10% are Christian, mostly of the Coptic Orthodox faith. The Coptic church is one of the oldest in the world and it's highly independent with its own Pope. Alongside the Copts are a few Greek Orthodox and Catholic groups, mostly in Alexandria. There used to be a Jewish population but the Sinai wars saw most leave: about 100 Egyptian Jews are thought to live in Egypt today.

ECONOMY

Egypt's economy has a GDP of about US$257 billion/year, putting it in the world's top 50. Tourism is important, especially in South Sinai, where it employs around 50% of the workforce. Oil, natural gas and mineral wealth are also significant, along with agriculture, manufacturing and the Suez Canal. Egypt receives about US$1.5 billion in foreign aid from Washington every year (though the US has dubbed this 'under review' at strategic junctures since the revolution). In fact, for the better part of the last three decades, Egypt has been the world's second-largest recipient of US foreign aid, behind Israel.

Practical information for the visitor

Crossovers exist between Egypt and the Sinai but there are differences too: it's inevitable given that the Sinai has only been properly integrated into Egypt since the 1980s. Much information in this section has a relevance to both regions but, where necessary, it is targeted specifically at the Sinai, beginning with the first section on transport below.

GETTING AROUND

Public bus
The East Delta Travel Company runs buses along the east and west coasts but there's a major gap with coverage inland to St Katherine. A bus used to run between St Katherine and Nuweiba but it stopped in 2007. Buses are perfectly comfortable but note two things: toilets stay locked and some have monster truck horns and blaring TVs that get irritating (ear plugs or an iPod are useful). They can also get chilly on night journeys, so take a sweater.

Public minibus
Minibuses run mostly on the west side of the Sinai and they're used commonly by locals. A useful service goes between St Katherine and El Tur, stopping in Wadi Feiran. A traveller-focused minibus called Bedouin Bus started in late 2011, linking St Katherine with Dahab and Nuweiba, and going every other day. Minibuses (though not the Bedouin Bus) are hot, cramped and noisy, with loose schedules and obscure departure points; but they're always cheap and fast.

Private taxi
Taxis are never difficult to find in the Sinai; drivers find you. They're colour-coded cars in major towns but in Bedouin areas they're usually white minibuses. You can use them for short hops or long-distance travel between towns and they're quick, convenient and comfortable. Prices rise with each person in the taxi, but the overall cost comes down when split at the end.

Collect the telephone numbers of good taxi drivers. They're some of the most useful people to know and using the same one gets better rates (without the hassle of haggling). Bedouin drivers are usually best; they know the wadis, trailheads and pick-up points better than their Egyptian counterparts.

❏ **A note on the roads**
Road accidents kill about 16,000 people every year in Egypt, injuring 35,000 more. Get used to the roads when it's quiet and expect the unexpected. People might sit a metre behind you at 90kph or dazzle you with their headlights at the very moment you pass at night. If someone else is driving and you feel unsafe, don't feel silly about telling them. Take responsibility for your own safety.

Don't try to get a taxi from where you arrive in Egypt: drivers exploit your shortcomings in local knowledge and the likelihood you'll want to end a tiring journey and move on. They can charge three times the price. Arrange one in advance through a camp or hotel (they can always arrange pick ups easily) or use a driver noted in this book.

Shared taxis
People can often be found going the same way, especially along the east coast or from Dahab (less so Nuweiba) to St Katherine. Sometimes camps can put you in touch with other hopefuls so ask around.

Service taxis
These run between set places and leave when full. If you're the first one in you might have to wait an age but it's sometimes possible to pay the remaining seat fares to go sooner. These go mostly down the east coast from Taba, and frequently between Sharm, El Tur and the mainland (Cairo and Nile Delta towns).

Private hire
Cars are most useful for short excursions around Sharm. Outside Egypt, Jerusalem, Petra and Wadi Rum make great trips but some firms prohibit international travel. Go with a well-known firm or one attached to a big hotel. Cars and insurance are better and it's easier if something goes wrong. Get the best insurance available and check the excess (it can vary by up to US$1000 between companies). Also read the contract small print; you might be charged extra for every kilometre over an allotted number. You usually have to be over 23 and in possession of your full national driving licence (but even big firms often bend their own rules with a bit of persuasion). **Scooters** and **motorbikes** are available but make sure you get a decent helmet.

Hitching
Hitching can be useful when treks finish on a remote highway (which all will in the desert). Flag vehicles down like a bus and see if the driver wants payment; many will (especially around tourist areas). Also keep enough water for a long wait in the open sun. Women should only hitch in the company of a man.

LANGUAGE

Arabic
The Middle East is an Arabic-speaking region, but there's a great variety in its everyday, colloquial dialects. Egypt has its own dialect — Egyptian Arabic or *Ammeya* (or *Masri*) — and owing to the decades long influence of Egyptian TV, cinema and music, it's also the most widely understood.

Even within Egypt people speak Arabic in their own way and this is especially true for the Bedouin. Bedouin Arabic has close parallels with the dialects of the Arabian peninsula (betraying their cultural roots). Even if you don't speak Arabic you'll hear an obvious difference in the Egyptian and Bedouin tongues. Egyptians speak with a hard 'G'; the Bedouin, with a soft 'J'. The word mountain — which you'll use daily on trek — is thus said 'Gebel' and

---

❏ **The Arabic 'el'**
The word 'el' approximates to Arabic's definite article, a bit like the word 'the' in English. When spoken (at least with many letters) its pronunciation mirrors the first sound of the following word. Thus, Sharm el Sheikh is actually said as Sharm esh Sheikh; Jebel el Deir is Jebel ed Deir; Mawlid el Nabi is Mawlid en Nabi and so on. This is sometimes transliterated in written English, though it depends. This book standardises the use of 'el' throughout.

'Jebel' respectively. Being able to speak a little Arabic will be to your advantage, even if you just learn the standard Islamic greetings. It doesn't matter how tongue-tied or clumsy you sound, people will respect the effort.

Other languages
English is common in tourist areas such as Sharm, Dahab and St Katherine. Hardly anybody speaks it in remote places like Wadi Feiran. Hebrew is a linguistic leftover of the Israeli occupation, spoken by some older Bedouin (and a few enterprising younger ones). Greek is the language of the monasteries.

OPENING HOURS

The **Egyptian weekend** is on Friday and Saturday. Friday is an Islamic holy day and anywhere that's open usually shuts around midday for public prayers (except Christian businesses). Prayers usually last about an hour.

Major public services follow the standard Friday-Saturday weekend, including **banks**, which mostly open Sunday to Thursday, 8am-2pm. **Post offices** are an exception as they only close on Fridays (Sat-Thur, 8am-2pm).

Small private shops and **pharmacies** often observe a slightly different weekend, closing on Friday and Sunday but staying open on Saturday. All private shops open until late (usually until at least 1am).

HOLIDAYS AND FESTIVALS

Secular festivals
These mark important political anniversaries in Egyptian life and fall on the same day every year. The dates listed are public holidays on which banks, government offices and public services usually close.

● **1 January** New Year's Day.
● **25 January** National Police Day Ironically, this marked the start of the protests that saw the police collapse across Egypt in 2011. It might be re-named to commemorate the revolution in the coming years.
● **25 April** Sinai Liberation Day Marks Israel's withdrawal in 1982.
● **1 May** Labour Day Celebrates the world's workers.
● **23 July** Revolution Day Commemorates the overthrow of King Farouk by a group of young officers in 1952.

● **6 October** Armed Forces Day Celebrates Egypt's famous 1973 advance through Israeli lines into occupied Sinai.

● **24 October** Suez Day Marks the brave civil resistance of Suez residents in the 1973 Sinai war against Israel.

● **23 December** Victory Day Marks the end of the Suez crisis in 1956.

Islamic festivals

These are the most widely celebrated festivals. Dates vary with the Islamic lunar calendar and religious authorities finalise them nearer the time. It's still possible to predict them to within a couple of days though. All are public holidays and the closure of businesses is widespread.

Islamic New Year or **Ras el Sana** heralds in the first month of Muharram. As with the Gregorian New Year, there's no real religious meaning.

Mawlid el Nabi marks the Prophet Mohammed's birthday and comes in the third month (Rabi el Awwal). It's celebrated with religious services and feasts.

Islamic New Year	Prospective dates
2014	25 October
2015	14 October
2016	2 October
2017	21 September
2018	11 September

Mawlid el Nabi	Prospective dates
2014	13 January
2015	2 January
2016	12 December
2017	1 December
2018	20 November

Ramadan

Ramadan is the ninth month of the Islamic calendar and the holiest period of the whole year. Muslims believe it's when God revealed the first verses of The Koran to the Prophet Mohammed and there's a fast every day, with people shunning food, drink, cigarettes and all other temptations. The fast starts at sunrise and it's broken at sunset with much merriment and feasting (*iftar*). The first few days are always the most important. Families and friends get together and poor people are fed on big public tables, in the streets.

Ramadan can be a nice time to visit: it's less crowded and the streets are decorated with streamers and pretty lanterns or *fawanees*. Hospitality is even more noticeable and strangers commonly invite you to share food. Nonetheless, there are practical difficulties. Most cafés are shut during the day, banks and other services close early, and most of Egypt goes nocturnal. Public transport runs reduced services and travelling becomes more difficult.

Most guides observe the fast when trekking. The pace is slower, rest stops are longer and the distances you cover are less. Your guide will make tea and food but eating it alone doesn't feel right. You could consider skipping your daytime meals, but it's essential to keep drinking. Most guides shrug off the fast but that's just Bedouin bravado; they feel it, like anyone else. Remember, your

Ramadan	Prospective dates
2014	28 June–27 July
2015	18 June–17 July
2016	6 June–5 July
2017	27 May–25 June
2018	16 May–14 June

EGYPT

guide will be operating under heavy physical stresses in the hottest time of the year and his dehydration risk is high. Anything that happens to him will affect you so be extra vigilant with safety. It's always best to trek in greater numbers and with non-fasters in case something happens to your guide.

The two Eids

The first Eid festival is **Eid el Fitr** or **Eid el Sughair** (little Eid) and it falls at the end of Ramadan. It involves three days of unrestricted feasting.

The other one is **Eid el Adha** or **Eid el Kebir** (big Eid) and it falls about two months later. It commemorates Abraham's readiness to sacrifice his son for God and also marks the end of the *Hajj* pilgrimage. In a symbolic nod to Abraham Muslim families traditionally slaughter a goat, sheep or other livestock animal. It lasts about three or four days and finding a guide for trekking is virtually impossible on the first day. It becomes easier on each following day, but you might have to a pay a bit more.

Eid el Adha	Prospective dates
2014	4 October
2015	23 September
2016	11 September
2017	1 September
2018	20 August

Easter Sunday	Date
2014	20 April
2015	12 April
2016	1 May
2017	16 April
2018	8 April

Christian festivals

The Sinai has big Coptic Orthodox communities and a handful of Eastern Orthodox monks in the monasteries. The most important festival for both is **Easter**, celebrated over a long weekend from Good Friday to Easter Monday. Easter Monday is a national holiday in Egypt and it's used to mark a 'coming of spring' festival called **Sham el Nessim**, that dates back to ancient times.

The other big festival is **Christmas**, which falls annually on 7 January in the Orthodox calendar. There's also the **Feast of St Katherine**, usually in late November or early December. It's celebrated with special gusto at the Monastery of St Katherine. Christian businesses will be closed on major festivals.

Bedouin *ziyarahs* ('*zoowarahs*')

These venerate Bedouin holy men or saints. Each tribe has its own saint and some have several. They were typically buried in small whitewashed tombs, usually on major desert thoroughfares where they'd remain in view. Tribesmen were buried around the tomb to stay close to the saint in the afterlife and each is thus surrounded by a small cemetery. Up until recently these tombs were the focal points of annual ziyarahs. Each tribe gathered around them and there was singing, dancing and feasting over a day or more.

As well as having a religious function, ziyarahs were important social events that united the tribe in a single place and affirmed their collective identity. Ziyarahs have all but died out today but small ones occur every now and then. Look out for them at the back end of summer. Visitors are welcome but it always feels most comfortable to go with a Bedouin escort.

Camel races

Nothing generates excitement for the Bedouin like camel races. They occur both within and between tribes. Sometimes Bedouin tribes come from North Sinai or the Eastern Desert. Whatever the opposition, the race is always fiercely contested. Jockeys are typically boys, sometimes taken out of school for up to a year to focus solely on riding. There are two types of track. One is circular and measures endurance. The other is straight and the camels are sprinted from start to finish (more exciting). Races occur throughout the cooler months, usually from early autumn, but the calendar is busiest in January and February. Favoured spots include flat desert wadis such as Wadi Zeleqa and Wadi Migerah. Everything is arranged at short notice by Bedouin Sheikhs; ask around with tribesmen and you'll usually find one. These are some of the most authentic Bedouin events you can see and visitors are welcome.

TIME

Egyptian Daylight Saving Time was scrapped on popular grounds after the revolution. The clocks are now set at GMT+2 all year.

❏ EMBASSIES AND CONSULATES

Embassies are in Cairo but some keep individual consuls in Sharm. It's worth registering online as the embassy will have you on the radar in the event of an emergency. All embassies are available 24/7 for emergencies.

- **Australia** 11th floor, World Trade Centre, 1191, Corniche el Nil, Boulak, Cairo, ☎ 02-2770 6600, 🖳 www.egypt.embassy.gov.au
- **Austria** 5 Wissa Wassef St, 5th floor, Corner el Nil St, Riyadh-Tower, Giza, 11111 Cairo, ☎ 02-3570 2975, 🖳 www.bmeia.gv.at
- **Belgium** 20 Kamel El Shenawy St, Garden City, 11511, Cairo, ☎ 02-2794 7494, 🖳 www.diplomatie.be/cairo
- **Canada** 26 Kamel el Shenawy St, Garden City, 1667, Cairo, ☎ 02-2791 8700, 🖳 www.canadainternational.gc.ca/egypt-egypte/index.aspx
- **France** 29 Charles de Gaulle Ave, 1777, Giza, Cairo, ☎ 02-3567 3200, ☎ 0122-210 4133 (emergency mobile), 🖳 www.ambafrance-eg.org
- **Germany** 2 Berlin St, Zamalek, Cairo, ☎ 02-2728 2000, 🖳 www.kairo.diplo.de
- **Italy** 15 Abdel Rahman Fahmy St, Garden City, Cairo, ☎ 02-2794 3194, 🖳 www.ambilcairo.esteri.it/
- **Netherlands** 18 Hassan Sabry St, 11211, Zamalek, Cairo, ☎ 02-2739 5500, 🖳 www.hollandembassy.org.eg
- **New Zealand** Level 8, North Tower, Nile City Towers, 2005c Corniche el Nil, Ramlet Beaulac, Cairo, ☎ 02-2461-6000, 🖳 www.nzembassy.com/egypt
- **South Africa** Building No 11, Intersection Rd 200 & 203, Digla, Maadi, Cairo, ☎ 02-2535 3000, 🖳 www.saembassyinegypt.com
- **Switzerland** 10 Abdel Khalek Sarwat St, 11511, Cairo, ☎ 02-2575 8284, 🖳 www.eda.admin.ch/cairo
- **United Kingdom** 7 Ahmed Ragheb St, Garden City, Cairo, ☎ 02-2791 6000, mob ☎ 0100-169 5074 (Consul, Sharm el Sheikh), 🖳 www.ukinegypt.fco.gov.uk
- **United States** 5 Tawfik Diab St, Garden City, Cairo, ☎ 02-2797 3300, 🖳 cairo.usembassy.gov/.

EGYPT

ELECTRICITY

Electricity is **220 volts AC, 50Hz**. Bring continental European plugs with two rounded pins. The same ones can be used in most of Egypt's neighbouring countries, including Jordan and Israel.

Power cuts are common in mountain areas like St Katherine. Many remote desert settlements have generators but they're only used in the evening and the output is always weak and unreliable.

MONEY

Egyptian currency (the 'ginay')

The **Egyptian Pound (LE)** is the basic unit of currency and it's divided into 100 piastres (pt). Almost everything comes in notes and you get these denominations: LE200, LE100, LE50, LE20, LE10, LE5, LE1, 50pt and 25pt. There are coins for smaller amounts, including LE1, 50 pt and 25pt. Actually, there are even smaller ones but they're rarely seen and barely worth carrying anyway.

Euros and US dollars are accepted widely in Sharm and other tourist towns. Bedouin in remote areas might accept them for bigger payments but it's best not to use them. Exchange rates are poor and they mark you out as a *khawaja* or foreigner. People see you as straight out of the West with money to burn and bargaining suddenly gets tougher.

Managing money

ATMs are best for managing money on the move. They're common in east-coast tourist towns but there's just one inland at St Katherine. Always stock up with a generous supply of hard cash when going to the interior.

Credit and debit cards are accepted in places such as big hotels, airline offices and car hire firms, but they'll be useless elsewhere. **Travellers' cheques** are a thing of the past and most banks won't accept them now. Those that do give poor rates and charge a commission and you'll also be restricted to banking hours when you want money.

For **currency exchange** wait until you get to Egypt. Airports and borders have 24/7 exchange tills and rates will be better. All banks change money and some ATMs have an exchange facility now too (try the Banque Misr ones).

Note to visitors from Scotland and Northern Ireland National bank notes aren't usually accepted in Egypt so change them before you arrive.

Small change

Egypt has a **chronic lack of change** meaning small notes are much more

❑ Exchange rates	
The exchange rates of the Egyptian pound have been variable with the recession and political unrest. Rough ones are below, rounded into the nearest whole figures. Check the latest at ⌨ www.xe.com/ucc.	
AUS$1	LE 6
CAN$1	LE 6
€1	LE 8
Israeli Shekel 1	LE 2
Jordanian Dinar 1	LE 9
Swiss Franc 1	LE 7
UK£1	LE 10
US$1	LE 6

EGYPT

❏ Arabic numerals

The numbers we use in the West are often called 'Arabic numerals' but they're not seen much in the Middle East. They actually originated in ancient India and became known as Arabic only as they last reached Europe from North Africa.

The digits used in the region today are called Eastern Arabic Numerals and they probably came from ancient India too, but some say they're from Iraq. Whatever the history you need to recognise them so you know what to pay.

There are a couple of tricky ones: the number six looks exactly like our seven, and the five a little bit like our zero. They're read left to right, like numbers in English, and a comma is used instead of a decimal place. Buying a cheap local watch keeps them on hand when you need them. See also p278.

1	١	2	٢	3	٣	4	٤	5	٥
6	٦	7	٧	8	٨	9	٩	10	١٠

0	·	345	٣٤٥	6.50	٦,٥٠	1980	١٩٨٠

useful than big ones. It's hard to use big notes for anything, simply because people rarely have enough change to give back. Taking a short taxi ride worth LE5, for example, an LE10 note will be more valuable than an LE100. Break up big notes, offering them before small ones and pocketing the proceeds. Don't give change away easily and, if you get stuck, change big notes at the bank.

Other pointers

Check change for tears; damaged notes are common and everyone wants to offload them (unsuspecting arrivals are easy targets). If you get them banks will issue replacements if the unique ID code is still visible. Also look out for people giving you the LE1 coin instead of the similar-looking, but more valuable euro. It's a common trick in Sharm.

Money precautions

The hassle involved in losing your wallet makes precautions sensible. Keep an emergency reserve of cash and put bank cards in different places. Extras can be picked up as pre-paid disposable debit cards before you leave home: check out the options at 🖳 www.cashpassport.com.

When you have no recourse to funds you'll have to get an emergency supply wired over. There are Western Union branches in Sharm or Dahab that do instant cash transfers over the counter.

Baksheesh

Baksheesh is a tip, sweetener, or incentive for getting something done. It's common in Egypt and the Middle East and is generally expected, asked for and given. There's no obligation but if you have the means (and it will be assumed you do), it's the local way.

❏ Baksheesh in kind

Many trekkers give guides equipment in lieu of baksheesh. This is to be encouraged as it helps guides do their jobs: equipment is hard to get in Egypt. The three most sought-after items are knives, boots and, especially amongst the Gararsha, binoculars.

EGYPT

❏ **The last word**
Halas (*khalas*) is one of Arabic's most important words. The exact meaning varies with context but it translates roughly as '*done, understood; nothing more to say*'. You might say it on making an agreement or to show you've had enough of something – like being hassled – and people generally respect it.

Make it about 10-15% of the original price: this is a fair and standard cut. For porters and others who give a one-off service, tip LE2-3 (more in expensive hotels); for toilet attendants who hand out tissues 25-50pt per visit. Leave a tip on the table for waiters even if service is included; frequently the latter just goes straight into the manager's pocket.

Haggling

Haggling is widespread in the Arab world and nowhere more so than Egypt. There's a special onus to haggle as a foreigner as you're often charged over the odds (at least in big tourist towns). Few bother haggling for simple things like groceries, but most other things – taxis, hotels and treks – are all open game.

Haggling doesn't come naturally to all; it can feel awkward questioning prices and people but forget any inhibitions. Jump in and get a feel for it: the more you do it, the more you'll understand it. You'll see how vendors work and you'll be able to perfect your own style. Prices soon drop and you might even come to enjoy the liberation it gives you in setting value rather than being dictated to by a price tag. Every haggle is different but the following tips will get you started.

● **Have a price in mind** Before anything, know your price. Think in hard-headed economic terms about what something's really worth to you and whether that's about right in the local economy. This gives you a target to aim for and streamlines your thinking during the exchange.

● **Let the vendor name the price** Naming your price shows too much of your hand at the start. Name half the price you're willing to pay. This gives the proverbial 'room for negotiation' and you can work up from there. Vendors work the other way, often quoting at least double.

● **Haggling tactics** Following the exchange of prices expect mock outrage, disappointment, flattery, sweet talk, life stories, sob stories, cups of tea and more. These are haggling tactics; stay clear-headed and remember your price.

● **Reply tactics** Use any of your own of the above and build a rapport that works to your advantage. Make it clear that if this deal doesn't work out you'll be disappointed but that it doesn't matter in the grand scheme of things.

● **Seal the deal** Dig your heels in as you approach your price. If you can't get it, walking away sometimes prompts the vendor to close. Having cash and a hand outstretched to shake might do it too. If not, walk away and think things over with a bit of space; you can always go back later.

WEIGHTS AND MEASURES

Egypt uses the metric system for weights and measures: kilometres (1km = 0.62 miles, 50km = 31 miles, 100km = 62 miles), kilograms (1kg = 2.2lbs, 5kg = 11lbs, 10kg = 22lbs) and litres (1 litre = 0.22/0.26 imperial/US gallons, 5 litres = 1.1/1.3 imperial/US gallons, 10 litres = 2.19/2.64 imperial/US gallons).

Don't expect exactitude in remote areas: traditional scales are used to weigh vegetables and petrol dispensers have tick-tock counters.

POST AND TELECOMMUNICATIONS

Postal service

The Egyptian postal service does a pretty good job. Postcards take about 5-10 days to Europe and 10-14 days to North America (and elsewhere). Posting from the mailboxes of bigger hotels fast tracks them to the front of the English-language sorting line and usually takes a couple of days off delivery times. In late 2012 stamps were LE2.50 each and you needed two per postcard.

Egyptian post offices handle bigger parcels but they're not particularly cheap. It's about LE120 to send 1kg to Europe, LE260 for 5kg and LE630 for 10kg. For anything urgent **DHL** or **FedEx** are better but more expensive still (DHL is cheapest). Both have offices in Sharm and guarantee delivery within three working days. When packages are going to international destinations you have to provide an itemised contents list and show your passport.

Post restante is available and most post offices hang on to things for about a month. Write your name on, underlining your surname. Mark it clearly as 'poste restante' in big, easy-to-read English, give a mobile phone number for the recipient, and address it: GENERAL POST OFFICE, TOWN NAME (eg ST KATHERINE), GOVERNORATE NAME (eg SOUTH SINAI), FIVE DIGIT POSTAL CODE (see below), ARAB REPUBLIC OF EGYPT.

The main **postal codes** are: Sharm el Sheikh 46619; Dahab 46617; Taba 46621; El Tur (Tur Sina) 46511; St Katherine 46616; and Nuweiba 46618.

Parcels get rifled by officials and hit with taxes. Taxes vary but they're always on the steeper side for hi-tech things such as memory cards, USB sticks, camera batteries and so on (some report the taxes to be more than the item itself but for a few CDs and memory sticks expect to pay about LE50).

Internet

Internet cafés are widespread in tourist towns and the wi-fi scene is growing too. Coverage is limited elsewhere and the only place it's available inland is St Katherine. Expect to pay about LE5-15/hr in tourist towns like Dahab and Sharm and LE2-5/hr elsewhere.

If you're staying a long time the mobile phone operators mentioned on p50 do USB modems that plug into a laptop (Vodafone ones are the fastest and best).

Internet calling means you can chat with home for the basic cost of getting online. Every internet café in the Sinai has webcams and headsets; just set up a Skype account: 🖳 www.skype.com.

Mobile phones

Mobiles are best for staying in touch in the Sinai and virtually everyone has one (a staggering 80% of the population, according to a recent survey). Having one yourself makes independent travel much easier. Get into the habit of exchanging numbers with useful people: guides, taxi drivers etc.

> ❏ **Emergency numbers**
> Emergency lines are open 24/7 and operators speak English or will find someone who can. Call the following numbers from a mobile:
> | | |
> |---|---|
> | **Ambulance** | 123 |
> | **Fire** | 180 |
> | **Police** | 122 |

Don't bother with an international roaming service: buy an Egyptian SIM card on arrival. They're available from three companies (Vodafone, Mobinil or Etisalat) and mobile phone shops are everywhere. They should cost LE10-20 but expect to be quoted LE30-70. You're supposed to show your passport when registering (although many vendors don't care).

The real thing to consider is the difference in coverage. Vodafone has the edge in the High Mountain Region but Mobinil is the only one with a signal in Wadi Feiran (and in parts of the desert like Ein Hudera). Mobinil is thus the best overall option but be sure to choose a number beginning 0122 or 0128. Occasionally 0127 works but other Mobinil numbers won't.

Credit is very cheap and you can buy it in scratch cards of various denominations. Otherwise, re-charge electronically from a mobile phone store.

Telecom offices

Every town has a so-called *telephone centrale*. These were once thriving hubs of communication for everyday Egyptians but the massive surge in mobile phone ownership has left them near deserted today. The government still funds their upkeep and if nothing else their booths give a nice, quiet place for making calls. You can dial internationally for about LE5/min, which is cheaper than calling on a mobile. It's also possible to send faxes.

Street phones

These are going the same way as telecom offices and falling out of business. They work on pre-paid cards but it's hard to buy them now.

Telephone numbers

Egyptian landlines have seven or eight digits. If you're dialling one from another part of Egypt, add the relevant area code (given in the box opposite).

In this book telephone numbers are given as you'd dial them in the country you're in. So, those in Egypt are as you'd dial them in Egypt and in Jordan as you'd do there and so on. They're not preceded by international codes.

> ❏ **Area codes and calling from a mobile**
> The most useful telephone area codes are:
>
> | City/region | Area code |
> |---|---|
> | Alexandria | 03 |
> | Aswan | 097 |
> | Cairo | 02 |
> | Luxor | 095 |
> | North Sinai | 068 |
> | South Sinai | 069 |
>
> **Egyptian mobiles** are easy to call from outside Egypt. From your own mobile, dial +2 in front of the *whole Egyptian number*. From a landline, dial 002 before.

E G Y P T

MEDIA

Egypt is one of the Middle East's media leaders with lots of **English-language publications** to keep you going. *Al Ahram Weekly* is the biggest and best read, out every Thursday. For daily headlines, try *Daily News Egypt* or *The Egyptian Gazette*. An interesting current affairs magazine is *Egypt Today* (monthly).

It's easiest to follow things online in the Sinai. The titles above have their own **news websites**; others to look out for are *The Egypt Monocle* (🖥 www.egypt monocle.com), *Mada Masr* (🖥 www.madamasr.com) and *Egypt Independent* (🖥 www.egyptindependent.com).

The BBC World Service can be picked up on shortwave pocket **radios** in many remote areas, but you'll have to twiddle with the tuning.

Satellite TV is big; even remote Bedouin villages now have it. *BBC World* and *Al Jazeera English* are the main English-language news channels.

TOILETS

Public toilets aren't common and few have toilet paper. Get into a habit of carrying a pack of pocket tissues with you.

HEALTH CARE

Every town in the Sinai has a small hospital and, generally, they're not too bad. Equipment is sterile and they nearly always stock drips, antiserum and rabies prophylaxis. What's more, doctors speak basic English and do simple, GP-type consultations. Payment isn't always asked for but give something if you can. Medical salaries are low in Egypt: for a newly qualified doctor, often under LE1000/month. Sharm has some of the best hospitals in Egypt; of comparable quality to those in Western Europe. Pharmacies are easy to find too. Actually, it can be cheaper to wait until Egypt to buy supplies – see box.

WHERE TO STAY

Most of the **gateway towns** provide accommodation ranging from camps and budget hotels up to five-star international resorts providing all the comforts you might want.

❏ Medicines in Egypt

Medicines are cheap but always get a doctor's advice before taking them. Pharmacists often hand out antibiotics for common complaints, which can do more harm than good.

Remember, doses can vary too; one pill in an Egyptian brand doesn't necessarily equal one from home. The Egyptian names of Western medicines are below:

Aspirin	Aspocid
	Rivo
Ibuprofen	Brufen
Rehydration salts	Hydrosafe
Mosquito repellents	Off Spray
Antihistamine	Zyrtec
	Claritine
Antibacterial creams	Fucidin
Anti-diarrhoeals	Kapect (avoid Streptoquin, an antibiotic that is often prescribed but that's banned in some parts of Europe).

EGYPT

❏ **Mountain orchards of the Sinai**

Bedouin orchards are found all over the High Mountain Region. Tapping deep reserves of groundwater, they grow fruits such as apricots, figs and pomegranates, along with nuts, vegetables and herbs. Orchard gardening actually stretches back over a thousand years here: it started out of a survival necessity in early Christian times and became progressively more sophisticated.

Orchards are found in many mountain wadis – even small, remote ones – but most stand ruined and forgotten. Only about 20 remain productive today. Decades of drought, the import of cheap Nile valley produce and changing livelihoods have all contributed to the demise. Nevertheless it isn't too late; these gardens offer superb sleeping spots for trekkers and if you actively seek them out and pay a fee, you'll encourage the gardeners to diversify their business and preserve a dying piece of history.

On the trail

Under the stars is the classic Bedouin way: they call it 'the million star hotel'. There's usually a low risk of rain and the night skies are big, clear and beautiful. Caves, overhangs and hollows under boulders give natural shelter.

Stone **huts**, ruined houses and Bedouin storerooms are sometimes found. **Hermit cells** (see box p170) from early Christian times can be used too, but leave them exactly as you find them; these are precious pieces of the Sinai's past.

There are a couple of EU-funded **eco-lodges** near St Katherine. They're built with local materials and have composting toilets, solar-heated showers and candlelight at night. They're staffed by local Bedouin and are generally good initiatives to support. It's possible to stay in one called Al Karm Ecolodge (p137) on the Northern Peaks Circuit; the other is noted on p130.

About 400 **Bedouin orchards** are found in Jebeleya land and it's often possible to stay in them (see box above). They're tranquil havens of green and some are becoming integrated into the trekking scene. Most have a shelter where you can sleep, along with a well or water pool. A few have washing facilities and composting toilets. Reckon on paying about LE10-25 per night. When the owner isn't in his garden it's sometimes possible to enter with your guide and pay the owner on your return to town.

Note: The abbreviations '**a/c**' and '**att**' are used throughout this book. Att means 'attached bathroom' (ie en suite) and a/c, 'air conditioning'.

FOOD

Egypt is the Arab leader in many things, but not so much in food – many of the dishes on restaurant menus came from nearby countries. Nevertheless, things are given a distinctive Egyptian twist, and there are still authentic Egyptian dishes to try, all at reasonable prices. Look out for the following:

● **Fuul** A brown paste of mashed fava beans, popular for breakfast.
● **Taameya** Egyptian falafel, made from fava beans, not chickpeas, and eaten at breakfast. It comes in deep-fried balls or discs, usually in flat bread.

● **Shakshouka** Fried or scrambled eggs in a sauce of tomatoes, peppers, onions and spices. Eaten across the Middle East, at breakfast or dinner.

● **Kushari** Egypt's national dish: a filling mix of lentils, pasta and chickpeas, covered in a tomato sauce and topped with fried onions.

● **Molokhia** A slimy green broth of jute leaves, sometimes containing meat or fish. Some say the psychotic Fatimid Caliph Al Hakim was so appalled he banned it in the 11th century, but it persisted stubbornly nonetheless.

● **Stuffed pigeon** Stuffed with peppers and rice; another Egyptian classic.

● **Shawerma** Usually beef or chicken, cooked on fat rotating spits. Shavings are cut for sandwiches and other dishes (sometimes kushari).

● **Kofta** Minced beef, lamb or goat meat, skewered and cooked over charcoal. Kebab is similar but it's chunks of clean-sliced meat.

● **Umm Ali** A pastry pudding topped with cream, cinnamon and nuts.

● **Muhalabiya** A creamy blancmange type desert with rosewater.

● **Oriental pastries** There are lots of honey-drizzled pastries such as kunefa, basboosa and baklawa. Sometimes they're stuffed with cream and pistachio fillings. One of the two Eids is the best time to try them.

Traditional **Bedouin food** doesn't lend itself to modern kitchen preparation. It's a wilderness cuisine cooked with natural materials: bread is made in hot sand and ash, chicken is cooked underground with rocks, eggplants are roasted whole on the fire and so on. 'Bedouin dishes' are seen on menus, but they're not the real deal – you have to wait for the trail to try it. For trekking food see below.

Western food features on tourist menus in east coast towns. International fast-food outlets are found in Sharm.

There are Western-style **supermarkets** in Sharm and Dahab. In St Katherine minimarkets stock basics and there are fruit shops and a bakery. In remote areas a pick-up truck drives by every few days with groceries.

On the trail

Bedouin guides get everything sorted with food. They'll buy it before you go and make meals to share on the trail. Guides often buy more than you need when you have a camel. Carrying more is safer and you'll also have to be hospitable and share food if you meet people on the trail (see p85).

Eating on the trek: a typical day You will burn about 4000 calories a day when trekking, or double the normal. Make sure you get enough energy and

---

❏ **Vegetarianism**
Vegetarianism is often seen as a Western eccentricity but it's still not too hard to get by. Everyday staples like fuul, taameya and kushari are meat-free and restaurants in big tourist areas have vegetarian options. It can be a bit awkward if someone cooks meat in a remote area, wanting to give you the finest hospitality they can afford. Make things clear at the outset, before anything's killed. Either show them the Arabic text (left: 'I don't eat meat, I'm a vegetarian') or say أنا ما باكلش لحمة أنا نباتي 'ana ma-bakoolsh la-mah, ana nabairtee'.

❏ **Bedouin staples: bread and tea**

Bread, the basis of the Bedouin diet, is served with almost every meal. There are two types, with *libba* the most common. Dough is rolled into a thick circle, then cooked in the embers of a fire for 15 minutes. *Farashee* is a thin flat bread like a tortilla. Dough balls are thrown hand to hand to stretch them thin, then cooked on a metal plate heated over the fire (about 30 seconds).

Equally important is **tea**. It's the one thing the Bedouin can't do without. They drink it the whole day; on meeting, making a deal and in every other conceivable situation where there's an excuse (and even when there isn't). It's black, clean and extremely sweet with sugar often measured in by the handful. The real attraction is the cultural side: the fire, the desert etc. Once you've had it a few times you'll probably look forward to it as much as your guide does.

cover all the main food types; carbs (slow energy), sugars (instant energy), fats and proteins.

The Bedouin diet covers these well: for **breakfast**, expect bread, jam, white cheese, *halawa* and biscuits; for **lunch**, white cheese, tuna salad and perhaps something like hot *fuul*.

For an **evening meal** you will probably get something hot based on rice or potatoes, often with canned meat. Fresh meat might be available on a shorter trek or in the first days of a longer one, but it spoils quickly.

EGYPT

❏ **Buying food: what to pay**

Food prices have been rising across Egypt. In the Sinai, the cost of tomatoes, sugar and oil have been especially variable. Nevertheless, prices will remain broadly similar and those below give a rough idea of what to pay. See also p19.

Bottle of water (1.5 litres)	LE3	Can of plain fuul (400g)	LE3-7
Can of Coke/7 Up etc	LE3	Soft white cheese (250g)	LE3-5
Carton of fruit juice (1 litre)	LE7-8	Packet of 8 cheese triangles	LE2-4
Packet TANG (30g)	LE1-2	Pot of jam (340g)	LE5
Rice (1 kilo)	LE5	Pot of honey (340g)	LE8-9
Lentils (1 kilo)	LE5	Tomatoes (1 kilo)	LE3-5
Pasta (500g)	LE4-5	Cucumbers (1 kilo)	LE4
Bakery bread (5 pieces)	LE1	Aubergines (1 kilo)	LE4-5
Sugar (1 kilo)	LE5	Potatoes (1 kilo)	LE3
Packet of tea (250g)	LE7-8	Onions (1 kilo)	LE3
Carton milk (1 litre)	LE7-8	Oranges (1 kilo)	LE3-4
Milk powder (125g)	LE6-7	Dried dates (1 kilo)	LE10
Bottle of cooking oil (750ml)	LE8	Dried apricots (250g)	LE15
		Twix Bar/Snickers etc	LE3-4
Bottle of olive oil (250ml)	LE12	Large packet of biscuits (150g)	LE4-6
Can of tuna (200g)	LE5-8		
Tin of corned beef (340g)	LE12-15	Bag of cashew nuts (250g)	LE15
Frozen chicken (average size)	LE20-25	Bag of raisins (250g)	LE6

Expect to be plied with **sweets**, especially by the Jebeleya tribe around St Katherine. Wafers, halawa and hard-boiled sweets keep best in the heat. Dates, prunes, dried apricots, figs and nuts are natural options.

Note If you're not sure your guide will get the food you want, go with him to buy it. Western snacks are available at supermarkets in Sharm and Dahab so if you want these, always stock up before you go inland.

Getting food on the trail Bedouin gardens grow produce in the High Mountain Region. You can't rely on these for food but you can sometimes get fresh fruit to snack on. Only one trek in this book (Wadi Feiran to Serabit el Khadem) has a village where you can buy food on the way.

Carrying the food Food takes a battering on the back of a camel so pack to avoid damage. Keep things such as rice, flour and sugar in their own plastic bags and take spares for when these split. Fasten jam-jar lids (which can unscrew themselves) and keep vegetables on top of heavy food packs.

DRINK

Alcohol

Islamic attitudes to alcohol are conservative but Coptic Christians keep liquor stores going on the east coast. Stella and Sakkara are perfectly passable **beers**; Sphinx is a new one that slips down well too. Egypt has a small but thriving **wine** industry; Chateau des Reves is the critics' choice'.

Look out for **fake liquors**: the labels might look real but a close inspection shows them up as moonshine and contraband. Johnny Walker is *Johnny Waler*, Bercadi, *Bercardoi*, and so forth.

Soft drinks

Tea (*shay*) is taken strong and black. Nobody ever drinks it with milk. **Hibiscus** (*karkaday*) is delicious hot or cold; other infusions like **mint** (*nana*), **aniseed** (*yansoon)* and **cinnamon** (*irfa*) are available too. Look out for **sahleb** in winter, a milky drink topped with coconut shavings.

Thick, grainy **Turkish coffee** (*ahwa*) is another local favourite and you can have it any amount of sweetness: try it medium (*mazbut*) to begin with and go from there. For **instant coffee** order *Nescafe*: it's called Nescafe whatever the brand.

Ramadan is known for its **evening feast drinks**. *Amar el deen* is a popular apricot concoction and *tamr hindi*, a slightly sour tamarind option. There's also the white, coconut-flavoured *sobia*. Others include *carob*, made with pods of the carob tree, and *erksoos*, from liquorice roots (definitely an acquired taste). Some of these stay available all year, being served alongside standard juices (*asir asab* (crushed sugar cane), orange, mango etc). The best place to try them is Sharm's Old Market.

International soft drink brands are widely available. TANG is a **fruit powder drink**, which is good for improving the taste of bad desert water and anything with purifying tablets in it. It comes in apple, orange and other flavours and it's worth stocking up with a few sachets for the trail.

Many Egyptians drink **tap water** but it's heavily chlorinated and tastes awful. Avoid glasses of water served in shisha cafés as it's all from the tap. Bottled water is ubiquitous and cheap (LE2-3 per 1.5-litre bottle).

WHAT TO BUY

The wandering Bedouin culture of the Sinai didn't give rise to the great souks of Cairo, Damascus and other Middle East trading centres. As you'd expect though, lots of tourist shops have moved in to fill the void. Fez hats, papyrus scrolls, backgammon boards and other such merchandise is all widely available. Remember though, this has more to do with mainland Egypt than the Sinai. Something reflecting Bedouin culture is more authentic.

Bedouin handicrafts made by local women are amongst the most authentic souvenirs you can buy. They're made with the same handiwork skills that supplied Bedouin tribes with their material needs (tents, saddles, water skins etc). Rugs, bags and clothes are just a few of the many items available today. Each tribe has its own, distinctive style of decoration. The women of the Jebeleya tribe are famous for their use of colourful little beads, for example. The Bedouin women from El Arish in the North are known for cross-stitching.

Herbs and produce give something of the Sinai itself and can be highly evocative. Oregano (*zatar*), sage (*mardagush*) and rosemary (*zanzabil*) are available, along with other things such as dates and mountain honey. Make sure these have been grown in orchards rather than harvested from the mountainsides (some will have been). A sustainable and fair-trade producer in the St Katherine area is the Medicinal Plants Association (see box p82).

The Christian culture is arguably the oldest on the peninsula. **Monastery mementos** such as crucifixes, icons and CDs of the monks singing plainsong are available. The Monastery of St Katherine also does a nice set of lithographs by the Scottish artist David Roberts.

CRIME AND THE POLICE

Crime has increased since the revolution but Egypt is still much safer than the West. Violent street crime isn't really an issue. Petty pilfering happens but it's rare. The **police** are helpful and they'll give a crime report for insurers if needed. If something happens in a Bedouin area it's best to tell the local tribe. Tribes police themselves more effectively than outside authorities.

SEXUAL HARASSMENT

Sexual harassment is common, especially for Western women. It's complicated and there are many reasons; the biggest is just the idea that Westerners are sexually loose. They're seen as an easy, no-strings option next to local women and as such become the focus of all male attention. It's hard to stop it entirely but a few things help limit it. Start with dress and wear baggier clothes, covering legs, shoulders and arms. Sunglasses help avoid persistent male stares and a wedding ring will make it look as if you're attached (though it still won't deter all males). Minibuses usually have a row of seats reserved for women (at the front). As much as anything, it's about the way you interact: follow local women and look to strike a manner that's polite but very reserved. There's no physical contact between the local sexes and even talking alone together is frowned upon in conservative areas. The way you interact with Egyptians of the opposite sex shouldn't be like it is at home: norms and expectations are fundamentally different and innocuous gestures can be completely misunderstood. Harass Map is a great new support network for victims of harassment in Egypt. See 🖳 harassmap.org/en/ for more information.

● **Don't let it get on top of you** Harassers never give their actions a second thought. Hard as it is on the receiving end, don't let it reverberate to ruin a day.
● **Report harassment** If it happens in a Bedouin area tell someone who has a bit of standing like a camp owner. The tribe is honour-driven and offenders will be dealt with when they can be identified.
● **Help others when you can** When you see a woman being harassed, lend a bit of moral support. Many report the feeling of being alone is the worst part.

HOMOSEXUALITY

Homosexuality isn't illegal in itself, but gay men can be arrested for offences against religion and public decency laws. The whole practice is looked on unfavourably and it's worth keeping it quiet. Don't be fooled by the sight of Egyptian men holding hands. This is done all over the Arab world.

TERRORISM AND SECURITY

The rise and fall in terror
The Sinai has seen its fair share of conflict in recent decades, but it remained mostly free of the terrorist violence that rocked Egypt in the 1980s. Things changed in 2004 when bombs killed 34 people in Taba and other places on the east coast. Another set of bombs hit Sharm in 2005, killing 88, then Dahab the following year, with 23 more fatalities. The police began a big crackdown after the Dahab bombs, raiding villages and arresting thousands of Bedouin all over

---

❏ **Tourist kidnappings in South Sinai**
Early 2012 saw several tourist kidnappings. They weren't the horror kidnaps seen elsewhere in the Middle East, but they grabbed global headlines nonetheless. Families in two local tribes were responsible and tourists were used as leverage in negotiating kinsmen out of jail. Every kidnap was over within three days and most much sooner, within hours. The kidnappers followed strict hospitality codes (after they'd done the kidnapping, of course), treating the tourists well; the most they had to fight off were lashings of tea and lectures on Bedouin rights. Pressure from Bedouin tribes had brought them to a near standstill in mid 2013. If, for whatever reason, they start again, don't worry unduly. Kidnaps in South Sinai have their own style.

❏ **A note to Israelis**

Israelis trekked in the Sinai through the 1990s, but tourism nosedived with the bombs of 2004 and has never recovered. Over the years there have been ongoing stories about terrorists hiding in the Sinai mountains, lying in wait for Israelis. Bedouin Sheikhs reject these outright — on moral and logistical grounds — and point out the interior, trekking parts of South Sinai have never known a terrorist attack. That certainly tallies with my experience: out in the mountains of South Sinai, you're probably safer than in much of Israel itself. I've been mistaken for an Israeli several times and during the revolution — when I was taking notes for this book — some Bedouin even thought I was an Israeli spy. It didn't make a difference and the welcome was as warm and hospitable as it would've been for anyone.

Check travel advice but just balance it with reasonable insights from elsewhere. The Israeli trekking agencies on p12 have good links to the Bedouin and are worth contacting. North Sinai, by contrast, should be avoided.

Trekking regulations for Israelis   Officially, Israeli trekkers need an armed escort. You and a guide might slip on to the trail unseen as a pair; but not in a bigger group. The Bedouin insist it has more to do with Egyptian–Israeli relations than danger on the ground and they're lobbying for change. The chances are it'll remain in place for a while. Check the Trailblazer website for updates 🖥 www.trailblazer-guides.com.

the peninsula (resent still lingers about the raids today). Nevertheless, the blitz approach worked and the terrorist cell was found and destroyed. Millions of tourists have visited without issue since then. South Sinai remained calm as hundreds were killed across Egypt in the revolution.

The Sinai: since the revolution

The Sinai isn't the unified peninsula it might appear. The Tih Plateau is a natural north-south divide and each region has its own alliance of Bedouin tribes. North Sinai is one of Egypt's poorest governorates and has been unstable for a long time. The region's gas pipeline to Israel was bombed repeatedly through 2011. Things came to a bloody head in August 2012, with the 'Ramadan Massacre', when 16 Egyptian soldiers were gunned down at sunset. Inter-tribal violence and smuggling – including people smuggling – have also afflicted the area.

The south is completely different. 2012 saw minor Bedouin protests against long-standing political grievances, as well as the kidnaps noted on the previous page. But the area has mostly been safe and calm. Always remember though: Egypt can change quickly post-revolution. Check government travel advice and news. Just read between the lines with a bit of common sense. Places are rarely as dangerous as governments or anyone else make them sound; especially South Sinai. Think smart, make good local contacts and you should be fine.

THE SINAI

3

Geography

The Sinai is 61,000 sq km or roughly the size of Ireland. The Pharaohs established a presence here some 4000 years ago and it has been ruled as part of Egypt ever since. Nevertheless, it has always been something of a detached province; one far removed from the life and politics of the Nile Valley. Throughout history, Cairo governments have consistently overlooked the Sinai and it grew up very much as a land unto itself, with its own people, culture and traditions. Egypt and the Sinai, the Egyptians and Bedouin, often seem out of sync. This chapter aims to bring out the unique side of the peninsula, putting things you'll see in their local context.

Geographical regions
To generalise, South Sinai is mostly rugged mountain country; North Sinai is flat, barren desert. Trekking takes place entirely in the south and a quick breakdown of its physical geography looks like this:

● **Southern mountain massif** Most of the south is covered with a rugged swathe of granite mountains. They reach up to 2642m at Jebel Katherina.
● **High Mountain Region** This is a cluster of high peaks around St Katherine. High mountains are found elsewhere too (most notably around Wadi Feiran and the Jebel Umm Shomer region).
● **Jebel Tih (Badiyat el Tih)** Pronounced Jebel 'Tee' this is a high, flat-topped escarpment that stretches across the Sinai. It's about a third of the way up and is a natural divide between north and south. You'll see it stretching across the distance from high summits and it's the much-fabled Biblical 'Wilderness of the Wanderings'.
● **The Tih divide** A break zone between Jebel Tih and the southern mountain massif. Sandstone areas such as Ein Hudera and Serabit el Khadem are found here.
● **Wadi Feiran** The biggest wadi in the west of the Sinai. It's home to a gigantic palm grove, with over 10,000 trees.
● **The Plain of Qa** An immense seaboard plain stretching from the edge of the mountains to the Gulf of Suez. It's a long, barren walk.
● **The Aqaba foreshore** This is a smaller plain around Sharm. Further up the coast there's no plain at all; the toes of the mountains dip into the very edge of the sea.

GEOLOGY

The Sinai is the most geologically varied part of Egypt and, as such, has an extraordinary diversity of scenery. Contrasts can be sudden and dramatic. The area has been dubbed a 'geologist's wonderland' before and, with patchy vegetation putting every small detail in the rock on show, it's about right.

Mountain building

Most of the Sinai's mountains formed 600-800 million years ago. Some might even be up to a billion years old and, thus, amongst the oldest in the world (the Earth itself only formed 4.6 billion years ago). The rock is mostly red granite and some say its colouring gives the neighbouring Red Sea its name.

The mountains are known for their gigantic hemisphere-summits and bulging convex cliffs; these are the result of geological features called *plutons*; balloon-like masses of rock that rose from deep within the earth. They pushed up and cooled underground until erosion exposed them on the surface. Granite is often shot through with lines of different (often darker) rock: these are called 'dikes' and were created more recently (less than 30 million years ago). Molten rock ran into passages and hollows in the plutons, cooling within.

Sandstone deserts

There are lots of sandstone areas in the Sinai. They formed some 580-320 million years ago when the peninsula was under a shallow sea. Sediments settled on the sea bed, with millions of years of pressure compressing them into solid rock. What you see today is the dessicated remnant of an ancient sea bed; seashells, fossils and even water ripples can be found in places.

The Sinai: becoming a peninsula

Most mountain building was completed long before the Sinai became a peninsula. For most of its history it was an integral piece of the African Plate; a big slab of the earth's crust upon which most of modern Africa sits today. Things changed about 60 million years ago when molten rock rose from below, splitting the plate down lines of weakness.

❏ **A Sinai sandstorm – by Arthur Penrhyn Stanley, *Sinai and Palestine: In Connection with their History*, 1875**
'Soon Red Sea and all were lost in a sandstorm, which lasted the whole day. Imagine all distant objects entirely lost to view – the sheets of sand fleeting along the surface of the desert like streams of water; the whole air filled, though invisibly, with a tempest of sand driving in your face like sleet. Imagine the caravan toiling against this – the Bedouin – each with his shawl thrown completely over his head, half of the riders sitting backwards, the camels meantime, thus virtually left without guidance, though, from time to time, throwing their long necks sideways to avoid the blast, yet moving straight onward with a painful sense of duty truly edifying to behold. Through this tempest, this roaring and driving tempest, that sometimes made me think that this must be the real meaning of a "*howling* wilderness", we rode on the whole day.'

Ongoing pressure saw these splits grow into bigger rifts; these continued to grow into valleys hundreds of kilometres wide. One was the so-called Red Sea Rift Valley, which split Africa from Asia (with waters running between to form the Red Sea). The rift extended north and about 22 million years ago carved out the Gulf of Aqaba, giving the Sinai an east coast. It actually went further north still; creating the Dead Sea Depression and Lebanon's Beqaa Valley. About the same time as this other rifting occurred to give the Sinai a west coast and leave it as a triangular peninsula. Rifting in the Gulf of Suez was more superficial, as seen in its depth: the Gulf of Suez is mostly less than 50m deep; the Gulf of Aqaba is up to 1850m.

The environment

CLIMATE

Rainfall in a desert

However you measure it, the Sinai is a desert. The UNESCO Aridity Index identifies four classes of aridity; every part of the peninsula is in its two most extreme bands. Precipitation is lowest on the Plain of Qa; just 13mm a year. Half the peninsula gets 25-50mm a year; only the High Mountain Region and north coast approach 100mm a year. To put this in context, the average annual precipitation in Scotland is about 1500mm a year. This general aridity results in clear blue skies: in Sharm 80% of days are cloudless, in St Katherine 70%.

Temperatures

Temperatures vary greatly with altitude. Summers are always hot on the coasts, with daytime averages just under 40°C and 45°C at the extreme. Winters are mild with temperatures hovering around 20°C. The mountain areas usually average about 30-32°C in summer (daytime). Temperatures can go sub-zero in winter. Extremes of minus 14°C have been recorded on Jebel Katherina, but strong, dry winds can make it feel much colder.

The *khamsin*

This is a hot wind that blows over North Africa and Arabia, usually between April and May. It comes from the south-west, whipping up big clouds of sand that turn the skies a foreboding yellow (as if a Biblical plague has set in). Visibility becomes limited and airborne particulates make it difficult to breathe. *Khamsin* means 'fifty', after the number of days during which it's said the wind might blow. Fortunately, it's only felt for a few days during that time.

FAUNA

This guide gives only the most cursory overview of wildlife in the Sinai: for more extensive supplements see p29. The species below are the ones deemed most notable or interesting in the region. When known, Arabic names are *italicised* by

> ❏ **Camels: a very quick overview**
> Camels in the Middle East have one hump and are called Dromedaries (or Arabian Camels). Their two-humped cousins – Bactrian Camels – are native to the deserts of Mongolia and Central Asia. Camels are extremely well-adapted to the desert: water is stored in their bloodcells and they can go 10-14 days without drinking. The hump is a fatty reserve broken into on long desert journeys without grazing. In addition their big snowshoe feet stop them sinking in sand and their knee pads prevent burns when they crouch. Their long legs keep their bodies high and cool, whilst thick, matted coats keep them warm. They have bushy eyelashes, nostrils and ears to filter out airborne dust, and tough, thick tongues for grazing on thorny vegetation. If you wanted to buy your own camel you'd pay LE5000-8000 in the Sinai, but the finest thoroughbreds cost much more.

English ones; in the absence of either, Latin names are given. Desert wildlife is cautious and always difficult to spot; if there's something you really want to see, camps in St Katherine can fix you up with excellent Bedouin trackers.

Birds
The mountains are rich with bird life; in the desert, they're most common around water. Found widely in both regions is the **white-crowned black wheatear** (*bagar*), a small white-headed bird that often flutters up close. The **Sinai rosefinch** (*jazama*) is a handsome finch with a light pink breast. Similarly pretty is the **Palestine sunbird**: males have green, iridescent plumage in the mating season. The **Tristram's grackle** (*shahrour*) has shiny black plumage and faded orange strips below its wings. It whistles loudly and often grooms camels for ticks. The **chukar partridge** (*shanir*) has a fat, rounded body but it's a nippy sprinter over short distances. The **Verraux's eagle** is the largest bird of prey. It's thought to live in the St Katherine area and feeds on mice, hyrax and, some say, goat kids. Millions of birds, such as the **white stork**, pass through the Sinai on migrations every autumn and spring (see box below).

Butterflies and dragonflies
There are about 40 species of butterfly (*faraashat*) in the mountains. The **Sinai baton blue** is the world's smallest; about the size of a small thumbnail.

> ❏ **The continental migrations**
> Millions of birds fly through the Sinai when migrating between Eurasia and Africa. It's important for soaring species, being the only land bridge between the continents. Buzzards, falcons, jays, eagles and others take part, but white storks are the most impressive. Their wingspan can be nearly two metres and up to 80% of the global population joins the journey. They can fly in flocks of several thousand, soaring past mountain tops like gigantic white clouds. Listen for the distant squawking as they're often so high you'd completely miss them otherwise.
> The outward migration in autumn is more impressive than the spring return, with October and November the best months. Ras Mohammed (p105) and Nabq (p107) are well-known sighting grounds on the coast, but the High Mountain Region is best for seeing them in flight.

Documented in 1974, it's endemic to the mountains of Mount Sinai, Jebel Safsafa and Jebel Ahmar. The **Sinai hairstreak** is another endemic species, known for a white band across its wings. Dragonflies and damselflies come in intense reds and blues and are perhaps the most beautiful of all. The **red-veined darter** is common in the springtime.

Reptiles

Lizards are seen more than anything. The **Sinai agama** (*blayus*) is a common mountain lizard. They vary in colour; but most of them show flashes of brilliant turquoise. The **starred agama** (*hardhun*) is bigger, darker, and seen just as much. The **desert monitor** (*rawwal*) lives at lower elevations and can be a metre long. Another big one is the **ornate dabb lizard** *(dabb)*; it has multi-coloured skin and is endemic to the Sinai and Hejaz. There are also **skinks** and several types of snake, including **vipers** and the **desert cobra**. Lesser-known snakes are the endemic **Sinai banded snake** and **Jan's desert racer**. The animal hazards section has more on snakes (see pp92-3).

Mammals

The lack of water and vegetation puts strong limits on mammal life. Deserts like the Sinai have fewer species and population sizes are always restricted.

Mice are the most common species and can be seen at the top of Jebel Katherina, usually nibbling crumbs left by trekkers. Prettiest of all is the **Asian garden dormouse** (*irsa*); it has dark eye blotches and looks as if it's wearing a bandit's mask. About the size of a rabbit, the **rock hyrax** (*wabar*) is a furry creature with hooves. It's something of a biological curiosity, being a distant relative of the elephant. The hyrax's song lasts several minutes and has its own syntax; actually, hyrax are one of the world's most brilliant animal communicators, comparable to primates and whales. **Hares** (*arnab*) are found widely and they're favourite prey for the region's two types of **fox** (*lehseen, abu reesha*).

Of the bigger mammals, the **Nubian ibex** (*bedan*) is an agile mountain goat, sometimes seen around St Katherine and Wadi Feiran. Males have big, recurved horns, much prized by Bedouin trophy hunters. The **Dorcas gazelle** (*ghazal*) lives in flatter wadis and is a graceful sprinter; unfortunately, over-hunting has put it on the brink of local extinction today.

Wolves (*deeb*) have been documented recently, but only in breeding pairs or small packs. The **striped hyena** (*dab*) is common at lower altitudes but is nocturnal so it's rarely seen and nothing to worry about (they're most common around fresh camel carcasses). **Arabian leopards** (*nimr*) once roamed the mountains but they're probably extinct now. The Bedouin say the last was one killed in Ras Abu Galum in 1996 (the last before that was in 1955). The closest population today is in the Negev desert of Israel.

❑ **Legend of the leopard**
Many Bedouin believe the leopard was once a man. He performed his prayer ablutions using milk instead of water and God turned him into a leopard for his hubris.

FLORA

The Sinai might be a desert but there are still at least 800 plant species (constituting about half of Egypt's total flora). By comparison, the Sahara has around 200 species. There's some overlap between mountain and desert vegetation, but the prevailing theme is one of difference. Mountain vegetation is more diverse and many species originated faraway, in the high places of Turkey, Iran and Afghanistan. They blew in about 30,000 years ago when the peninsula was cooler; the mountains were the only place they could survive as things warmed up again. They're the relic of a bygone age; a refuge community detached from their parent stands by thousands of kilometres.

Fragrant shrubs of the mountains

The High Mountain Region is rich with scented shrubs. They catch on the breeze, making trekking pleasant; but the scent is mainly there to deter grazing herbivores. **Judean wormwood** (*beartheran*) is one of the most common, with crumbly, beaded leaves and a menthol scent; the Bedouin put a teaspoon in water to treat diarrhoea. **Tanacetum sinaicum** (*murr*) is a near-endemic with small, comb-like leaves. It's boiled into an infusion to treat skin rashes. **Pulicaria desertorum** (*rabil*) has small, yellow flowers and a strong scent. It's added to tea to relieve rheumatism. **Horsemint** (*habak*) is a telltale sign of water. **Oregano** (*zatar*) and **desert lavender** (*zayta*) are plentiful. **Sinai thyme** (*zataran*) and **sage** (*bardagoosh*) are both rare and endangered.

Other plants of note

Spiny zilla (*zilla*) is a ubiquitous thorn bush. It's used to feed camels and the Bedouin heat its thorns to make prison-style tattoos. **Bladder dock** (*homaath*) is a small plant with pink leaves. The leaves have a refreshing lemon taste and the Bedouin eat them as snacks on the trail. **Common asphodel** (*aaslan*) has long, grass-like leaves and is also edible (if heavy on the chlorophyll). **Capers** (*lissuf*) grow as bushes and usually hang off cliffs.

Jointed anabis (*ajram*) is a succulent shrub with bulbous stems; crushed to make soap. **Cleome droserifolia** (*samwa*) has small, sticky leaves and a menthol scent; it's often used as an antiseptic. **Henbane** (*sakraan*) is a bush with purple-white flowers. It's poisonous and its Bedouin name literally means 'intoxicated'. There's also the **colocynth/desert melon** (*handl*), a satsuma-sized fruit growing on the ground. Just a single seed is enough to give a terrible stomach upset.

Poppies (*ofyoon*) have dispersed from plantations and grow wild in some areas, coming into a beautiful bloom in spring; see box on p65.

Trees

Several trees are especially common. The **date palm** (*nakhl*) will be familiar to all. The **acacia** (*seyal*), the classic desert tree, has thorny branches. It's important for grazing and gives the Bedouin many useful materials. **White broom** (*retem*) is more like a bush than a tree and has clusters of stringy leaves. Its branches are sometimes used as camel sticks. The **tamarisk** (*tarfa*) is slightly taller and grows as a series of slender branches. Some believe its exudates were the manna of The Exodus. Also look out for the **ziziphus** tree (*nabak*), seen in

Judean wormwood (*beartheran*)
Artemisia judaica

Bladder dock (*homaath*)
Rumex vesicarius

Sinai tansy (*murr*)
Tanacetum sinaicum

Henbane (*sakraan*)
Hyoscyamus boveanus

Capers (*lissuf*)
Capparis

Acacia (*seyal*)
Acacia tortilis raddiana

Spiny zilla (*zilla*)
Zilla spinosa

Rabil (*rabil*)
Pulicaria desertorum

Sage (*bardagoosh*)
Salvia multicaulis

White broom (*retem*)
Retama raetam

Colocynth/Desert melon (*handl*)
Citrullus colocynthis

Samwa (*samwa*)
Cleome droserifolia

Ziziphus (*nabak*)
Ziziphus spinosa

Common asphodel (*aaslan*)
Asphodelus aestivus

Sinai baton blue
© Katy Thompson

White-crowned black wheatear
(*bagar*) © Andrew Power

Nubian ibex (*bedan*, seen
St Katherine/Wadi Feiran)

Mountain lizards are commonly seen. The **starred agama** (*hardhun*, left) is bigger than the **Sinai agama** (*blayus*, right © Andrew Power) but both have very long tails.

Colour photos (following pages)

● **C4 Top**: The Monastery of St Katherine; built about 1500 years ago on the site of the Burning Bush, this is one of Christianity's oldest and most sacred sites. **Bottom left**: On the Northern Peaks Circuit, Jebel el Ojar (**top**) is one of the lesser-climbed peaks in the High Mountain Region. Farsh Suna (**bottom**) on a freezing morning. **Bottom right**: Sed el Nugra, on the Galt el Azraq trek, is a gigantic waterfall below the north face of Jebel Banat.

● **C5 Top**: High on the rocks of Masba Abu Garun, on the Galt el Azraq trek. **Bottom left**: Scrambling in Wadi Sagr. **Right top**: Deir Rahab (Monastery of the Poor Doctors) in Wadi Talla. **Right bottom**: Jebel Katherina's summit chapel; built where it's said a band of angels laid St Katherine to rest after she was martyred in Alexandria.

● **C6 (Clockwise from bottom left) 1**: Mount Sinai, crowned with a summit chapel. **2**: Glowing amber in the heart of the High Mountain Region: sunrise on the rugged peaks of Jebel Safsafa. **3**: Jebel Safsafa – Mountain of the Willow – at dusk. **4**: The Steps of Repentance, Mount Sinai; on a rare flat stretch. **5**: Crucifixes perch on precipitous ledges around the Monastery of St Katherine.

● **C7 Top**: High on Jebel el Deir; Mount Sinai is the high peak on the far left. **Bottom left**: The Monastery of St Katherine has been damaged by many flash floods through the ages: dams like this have been built to limit damage. **Bottom right**: Trekking in Wadi Isleh.

● **C8 The Desert – Top**: The Haduda Dune is the highest in South Sinai. **Middle**: Farsh Fureh: trekking past a hidden oasis. **Bottom left**: Drooping rocks on Jebel Mutamir. **Bottom right**: Nawamis tombs are found throughout the wadis of South Sinai. They're about 6000 years old and their doors usually face west, towards the setting sun.

● **C9 Wadi Feiran – Top**: Edge of the Serabit el Khadem plateau, looking over Wadi el Khaseef. **Middle left**: Seil Aleyat, a Bedouin village in Wadi Feiran. **Bottom left**: Wadi Iqne, with green acacia trees; on the way to Serabit el Khadem. **Bottom right**: Egyptian stelae (funerary monuments) at the Temple of Hathor, Serabit el Khadem.

● **C10 Wadi Feiran – Top**: Deir Banat (Convent of Feiran), built on the site of Sinai's first episcopal city and home to a small community of nuns today. **Middle left**: Jebel Salla is a sugarloaf-like peak of exfoliated granite. **Middle right**: High, sweeping cliffs on Jebel Serbal. **Bottom left**: Ibex hunting has a long history in Sinai, as this ancient Nabataean graffiti shows. **Bottom right**: High on Jebel Serbal; the peak in the top left is Jebel Banat, where it's said two Bedouin sisters tied their hair together and jumped to their deaths.

C5

C6

C7

C9

❏ **Poppies and opium production**

The Sinai became a centre of opium production in the 1990s, as authorities stamped out the farms in Lebanon's Beqaa Valley. The poppy (*ofyoon*) is cultivated widely today, along with plenty of marijuana (*hasheesh*). With the Bedouin facing routine discrimination in the job market it's often the only way they can make a living. Expect to go past poppy plots in remote mountain areas, especially in poorer districts. Farmers might look fearsome, with their unkempt beards and old hunting rifles, but don't worry; they'll be friendly and hospitable in the best Bedouin traditions.

Even so, their job carries a stiff sentence and they don't like having their photos taken: don't ask for photos or take them, either of the farmers or the plots. The treks in this book have been steered away from the biggest centres of production that are easily accessed from roads (mostly in the desert).

---

lower mountain elevations. It has a small, cherry-sized fruit (edible) and is from the family of trees whose branches were used to make Christ's crown of thorns.

A brief history

EARLY PEOPLES

The dawn of history

The Sinai has featured in the earliest ages of our collective history, being the land bridge by which humans first left Africa (probably about 100,000 years ago). Arrows, axes and other artefacts show it was inhabited in the Stone Age, but the population first boomed in the world's great metal ages. Large numbers wandered in at this time, attracted by rich surface deposits.

By 3500BC mining communities were scattered all over the peninsula. They'd exhaust the supply at one site before moving on to the next, covering large distances between the generations. They kept livestock and cultivated cereals; some anthropologists regard them as pioneers of the nomadic pastoralism that has remained so central to life here since. Their eerie last relics are seen in tombs called *nawamis* (see p246).

(Opposite) Life on the trek

(Clockwise from top left): **1.** The Arabs know the camel as the 'Safeenit el Sahra' or 'Ship of the Desert'. Its face is covered in thick, bristly whiskers to protect it from windblown sand. **2.** Camels can carry heavy loads and walk long distances but they don't usually sleep more than a few hours a day. **3.** Bedouin cooking is minimalist and makes use of readily available desert materials; wood, hot sand, ash and rocks. **4.** Natural spring (*ein*). Springs often occur at the bottom of cliffs. When water evaporates in hotter months, dig down until you reach it. **5.** A favourite Bedouin instrument, the *simsimiyya* has six strings, a wooden frame and sometimes a tin-can body. **6.** The *oud* is an 11-stringed lute-like instrument popular in the Middle East. **7.** Hermit cells are great spots to sleep; some date back to the Roman persecution when Christians took refuge in the wilderness. **8.** Making thin *farashee* bread.

Pharaohs and the Sinai

The Sinai's mineral deposits didn't go unnoticed by the Pharaohs, whose Bronze Age Kingdoms were rising fast in the Nile Valley. Pharaohs of the Old Kingdom sent exploratory mining expeditions to the Sinai from about 2700BC; by the Middle Kingdom in 2000BC, big mining colonies were operating. The first mining peoples worked these as slaves; their expertise and labour much valued. The ruins of one such colony are seen at Serabit el Khadem, complete with mine shafts, hieroglyphs and miners' graffiti. These remote colonies are as close as the Pharaohs ever got to settling the Sinai. It was seen as a hard desert frontier; good for resources but utterly unsuited to habitation. It was on the lush banks of the Nile that ancient Egypt really flourished.

The Nabataeans

The first major civilisation to settle was that of the Nabataeans (most famous for Petra in Jordan). They moved in around 200BC as their trading networks expanded into Egypt from the Dead Sea. They lived mostly in North Sinai, occupying major oases on trading routes. They cultivated crops, grazed live-stock and were known to be great hunters. They were a highly literate people and left thousands of inscriptions (graffiti!) across the peninsula; mostly names and simple statements. Actually, their alphabet remained in use by the native people of the Sinai for centuries after they'd left. The Nabataean alphabet was a local variant of the Syriac alphabet and has major significance in the Middle East, being the script that gave direct rise to Arabic in the 4th (or 5th) century.

ROOTS OF CHRISTIANITY

Rome and the Christians

Rome conquered Egypt in 30BC and the Nabataean influence dwindled over the next century in the Sinai. Christians were the next to arrive, attracted by the peninsula's rich Exodus legend. Christian settlement increased heavily in the 2nd and 3rd centuries, as the Roman Empire began its persecutions.

Thousands fled to the Sinai to escape the bloodshed, scattering across the rugged mountain wilderness. Most settlers knew nothing of their environment and life was extremely hard. They endured constant physical deprivation and some were killed or sold into slavery by marauding desert bands.

Nevertheless they persisted, putting down the roots of a Christian culture that survives to this day. In keeping with its own traditions, Christianity in the Sinai grew out of oppression elsewhere. The peninsula was a sanctuary for the world's first Christians as it had been for their prophets and kings before.

The days of Byzantium

The Emperor Constantine converted to Christianity in 313AD and the persecutions soon stopped. Egypt became a Byzantine, Christian land and the Sinai's ascetic communities grew still further. By the 5th century a large episcopal city stood in Wadi Feiran (Pharan), complete with its own archbishop.

The prosperity wasn't all good news though. It made Christians an easy target for plunder and attack; by the 6th century, things had become so precarious

THE SINAI

that they appealed to the Emperor Justinian for help. He responded by ordering the construction of three fortress monasteries. There'd be one in St Katherine and others at Raithu (modern-day El Tur) and Clysma (Suez).

The Emperor probably acted with political as much as altruistic motives; as well as protecting the Christians, the monasteries would give him a much-needed military presence on the far-flung borderlands of Byzantium. Whatever the real motives though, these monasteries gave Christianity its strongest-ever foothold in the region and allowed it to blossom as never before.

The Monastery of St Katherine

The Monastery of St Katherine didn't start out as such: it was the Monastery of the Holy Virgin (or Monastery of the Transfiguration) to begin with. It was built on the site of a much-earlier chapel, said to incorporate the original Burning Bush. Hundreds of Egyptian Christians provided the labour, quarrying out gigantic blocks of granite and stacking them into walls up to 3m thick and 20m tall. A battalion of East European soldiers was dispatched to give extra security and by 565AD the whole complex was fully functional.

ARRIVAL OF ISLAM

As Christianity flourished in the Sinai, Islam was on the rise over the Red Sea. The Prophet Mohammed had revealed the Koran to the desert tribes of Arabia and Islam was established by 630AD. Mohammed died in 632AD but this only increased the zeal with which his surviving companions spread the faith. Lightning military conquests brought most of the Arabian Peninsula and Levant under Muslim control, but Egypt remained unconquered: the great jewel of the Byzantine Empire and a rich prizeland of ancient civilisation.

The Conquest of Egypt started under General Amr Ibn al Aas in 639AD. His forces were vastly outnumbered but determined and battle-hardened. Within just three years they'd fought off the mighty Byzantine army to win Egypt and make Islam the official religion. Many converted to Islam in the Sinai but Christian monasteries were given special exemption.

The Christian cause was aided greatly by a charter of rights bearing the hand stamp of the Prophet Mohammed himself. This set down their right to religious freedom and protection by authorities if Egypt ever became an Islamic land. The monks claim Mohammed had given it to a delegation they sent to Medina in his twilight years. There's no doubt this document existed but its veracity remains open to question. The chances are it was a clever forgery: a self-authored charter of rights written in desperate times to guarantee Christianity's survival in a suddenly hostile new environment.

THE BEDOUIN

Egypt was ruled by various Islamic governments after the Conquest, including the Fatimids, Ayyubids and Mameluks. Almost without exception, Egypt meant the Nile Valley; the Sinai was largely a forgotten desert frontier. It was in this vacuum of centralised authority that Bedouin tribes began to enter. Most

THE SINAI

wandered in from the Hejaz; others came from Yemen. Each had their own reasons: some came to escape wars and drought, but others to find new lands for growing populations. Bedouin oral lore records 73 tribes arriving through the centuries, but most moved on soon after. It was only by the 14th century that the tribal patchwork was beginning to look as it does today.

The Bedouin have long been the real masters of the Sinai. Whenever governments wanted to get anything done, they had to work through the Bedouin (not entirely unlike it is today). The same was true for the Christians: monks kept tabs on tribal politics, drawing alliances to serve their survival.

THE OTTOMANS AND THE BRITISH

The Ottoman occupation

Sultan Selim swept through the Middle East in 1517, bringing Egypt and the Sinai under an Ottoman (Turkish) occupation that would last nearly 400 years. The Ottomans overlooked the Sinai, much like their predecessors; at least at the beginning. Things changed in the 19th century, as Egypt became a more ambitious, independent-minded state under the rule of Mohammed Ali, a renegade Ottoman Viceroy. Modernisation programmes were rolled out to integrate the Sinai more closely with the mainland. From 1849 Abbas Pasha I built roads, military outposts and even a mountain-top palace in the region.

Said Pasha continued the development drive in 1854, giving the go ahead for the Suez Canal (Port Said is named after him). The canal was finished in 1869, giving the first direct sea route between Europe and the East. If one point was a critical juncture in the Sinai's past, this was it. The canal fixed it in the designs of the world's superpowers, transforming it from a forgotten desert frontier into perhaps the most strategic piece of land in the world.

The British occupation

The Suez Canal was of supreme importance to Great Britain. The preservation of British India – the jewel of the Empire – rested critically on its control. By the 1870s the Ottomans had become so wracked with debt — partly because of their previous modernisation programmes — that they had to sell their stake in the canal. Britain snapped it up to become a major shareholder.

About a decade later (1882), the British army entered Egypt following a nationalist uprising against ongoing foreign interference. It claimed it was there to keep the peace and restore stability; really though, Britain was beginning to tighten its grip on Egypt and the canal. The British were the latest in a long line of foreign occupiers but – unlike those before (and because of the canal) – the Sinai was key from the start. Military surveys were made, which gave them a head start when WWI broke out. The Ottomans invaded from the east, attempting to take the canal; but British forces soon pushed them back out.

A British-backed Arab (more specifically, Bedouin) uprising soon forced the Ottomans out of the Middle East altogether, ending their 400-year occupation (see box opposite). The Ottoman struggle left the British overstretched in mainland Egypt and a home-grown revolution soon got into full swing. By 1922 civil unrest had forced Britain to grant Egypt independence. But it came with

---

❑ **Lawrence of Arabia**
Thomas Edward Lawrence studied history at Oxford University, writing his thesis on Crusader castles. He worked on a survey in the Negev before moving to Cairo when WWI broke out. Operating in army intelligence, he was despatched to help spur an Arab uprising against the Ottomans. Lawrence helped unite the Arab tribes with each other and the British, turning them into a formidable guerilla force that brought the mighty Ottoman empire to its knees. In October 1918, the Arabs marched on Damascus to end the 400-year occupation. But victory was short-lived. When encouraging the rebellion the British had —many believed — promised the Arabs an independent state if the Ottomans were defeated. Now they just divided Ottoman lands between themselves and the French. The Arabs never got a state; just new foreign occupiers. T E Lawrence has legendary status in the West; for some, he's 'Lawrence of Arabia' and a champion of Arab rights. He's comparatively little known in the Middle East and opinion remains divided. Some see him as a well-meaning ally; others as a double agent who encouraged the Arabs to rebel, knowing they'd ultimately be betrayed. It's a difficult issue: read Lawrence's book *Seven Pillars of Wisdom*, and see what you think.

---

strings. The British would leave Egypt, but they'd remain in the Suez Canal zone with an ongoing political influence.

THE SINAI: MODERN TIMES

The Suez Crisis
The Middle East saw great turmoil as Israel was created in 1948. Its statehood was secured with a war Israelis know as 'The War of Independence' and which most Arabs just call 'El Nakba' ('The Catastrophe'). Egyptian forces were involved and there were skirmishes on the Sinai's borderlands. Not long after this Egypt saw its own revolution, with a group of army officers overthrowing the unpopular government of King Farouk. Egypt was declared a republic and by 1956 the charismatic General Nasser was the new Egyptian President.

Nasser was a fierce nationalist who believed Egypt was for the Egyptians; similarly, he was a loyal Arab, aggrieved at the loss of Palestinian lands to Israel. One of his first acts was to order the British out of the Suez Canal Zone, closing it entirely to Israeli shipping. This prompted the so-called Suez Crisis in which British, Israeli and French troops invaded the Sinai and Port Said to claim the canal. The invasion was unpopular around the world and diplomatic pressure soon forced them out. The Suez Canal became Egypt's and the country was now truly independent for the first time in several millennia.

The Sinai and Israel
The Suez Crisis set a bloody tone that echoed through the next decades. The first war came in 1967, as Nasser's Egypt joined a coalition of Arab states seeking to force Israel into national surrender. The Israelis got last-minute intelligence of the plans and launched their own pre-emptive air strikes. They flew into Egypt – staying low enough to remain off the radar – and bombed hundreds of grounded fighter jets; Egypt lost several hundred jets in a day.

THE SINAI

With the skies clear, Israeli forces swept out to capture the whole of the Sinai. They also took Gaza, East Jerusalem, the West Bank and the Golan Heights (most of which remain under Israeli control or influence today). It was a humiliating defeat for the Arabs. The alliance was defeated in just six days; hence the immortal name – the 'Six Day War'.

The loss of the Sinai rankled deeply and the new leader, President Sadat, resolved to get it back. Following months of secret planning, and on the Jewish holy day of Yom Kippur (1973), Egyptian commandos assaulted Israeli lines. They crossed the Suez Canal in dinghies, blasting sand ramparts away with water cannon to send the Israelis into a full retreat. Egypt surged forward and looked set to re-take the peninsula, but the Israelis soon re-grouped. They focused their offensive on a single part of the Egyptian lines, punching through to encircle the Egyptian army. Most of the Sinai stayed under Israeli control – although the UN administered a ribbon of land along the Suez Canal.

The Sinai functioned much like other parts of Israel in the occupation; new settlements, roads and resorts were built and existing ones re-named. Sharm was Ophira, Dahab, Di-Zahav and Nuweiba, Neviot. A hearts and minds battle was waged with the Bedouin too: they had jobs, healthcare and freedom of movement. The Sinai seemed destined to become part of Israel.

The Israeli departure

The 1973 war was a reality check for Egypt. Conflict had proved a bloody and largely unsuccessful strategy in the Sinai. To achieve anything President Sadat knew he'd have to work by other means and began to focus on diplomacy. By the end of the 1970s Egypt and Israel were negotiating for peace at Camp David. Sadat made the Sinai a central bargaining chip: if Israel gave it back, Egypt would recognise its right to statehood and all aggression would end. Israel was reluctant to leave but saw sense in nullifying the Arab military leader and in setting a precedent for peace that others might follow.

The deal was signed and Sadat held up as a hero for getting the Sinai back. Even so, the admiration wasn't universal: some felt he'd made peace with the arch enemy, betraying the Arab cause and abandoning the Palestinians to their fate. Sadat was gunned down at a military parade in Cairo in 1981; he never saw the last Israeli tanks pull out in 1982.

(For a historical and political background to Egypt see pp37-9).

People of the peninsula

THE BEDOUIN

The Bedouin – '*El Bedu*' – are a people of nomadic origin found all over the Middle East and North Africa. Estimates put their numbers at about four million. Saudi Arabia, Libya, Israel, Iraq, Syria and Jordan all have big Bedouin communities. There are about 200,000 in the Sinai; mostly in the north. The

Bedouin are typically portrayed as wanderers; as a people moving constantly in search of water, but this isn't entirely accurate.

Tribes typically migrated once a year between established winter and summer pastures, mostly in their own territory.

In the Sinai, tribes rarely travelled more than 40km; resources were close together and they didn't have to go further. The Bedouin in the mountains made a vertical migration – switching between high gardens in hotter months and lower pastures in winter. Many tribes kept fishing camps along the coast. The Bedouin of the Sinai are perhaps best described as semi-nomadic.

Whatever the extent of their wanderings, make no mistake – the Bedouin were a people of the desert; their closeness to the land meant they were reluctant to renounce footloose freedom for the trappings of settled, domestic life.

The desert has forged the most essential parts of their identity and it marks every part of their culture. Their diet evolved around available desert foods: dates, skinks and ibex, for example. Livelihoods came from local produce such as acacia charcoal or Gum Arabic. Bedouin Islam became highly unorthodox in isolation, developing superstitions much-frowned on in classical Islam.

The desert made the Bedouin entirely oral too; written records were only a burden for a people on the move. Their culture became exceptionally rich in stories and poems. Much of the great Arab folk literature is of Bedouin origin and, even today, the Bedouin are famous storytellers. Virtues of courage, loyalty, cunning, ingenuity, vengeance and hospitality were all sharply pronounced as well: good or bad, they were essential for physical and social survival in self-regulating wilderness communities.

❏ **A poem of disappointed expectations**

This poem records a guest's experience of a cold welcome: as with all Bedouin poetry, it would be circulated widely, shaming the offenders and reminding others of an important lesson.

> 'We came to Beersheba; may a drought strike the town
>   And a star-wrought quake bring her tall buildings down!
> Their guest tents are tiny and give no repose;
>   Their guest tents seem burdened with worry and woes.
> Bin Sudes and his friends found no work to do
>   And Bin Khalaf wished coffee that no one would brew.
> If your luck is outstanding, you might get one cup
>   But you'd better not blink or ever look up;
> Even their barley-bread – half bran and dry –
>   For the same loaf the children and ninety dogs vie.
> We came to Beersheba; may a drought strike the town
>   And a star-wrought quake bring her tall buildings down!'

(Anonymous, 1970s, translated by Clinton Bailey in *Bedouin Poetry from Sinai and the Negev*, Saqi Books)

The Bedouin tribes of the Sinai ('The Towarah')

The Bedouin are a tribal people. Each tribe has its own history, culture, and a firm sense of its own identity. There are hundreds of tribes in the Middle East and the Sinai has about 23 (numbers vary depending on whether tribal sub divisions are counted as tribes in their own right). Bedouin tribes are always subsumed in bigger, regional alliances; the one in South Sinai is called the 'Towarah' ('People of the Mountain') and it comprises seven or eight tribes.

A few tribes in the south aren't in the alliance. These arrived after the alliance was made, or live on its borderlands and ally themselves with other groups to the north. A few things are sketched out about each Towarah tribe below, but bear in mind Bedouin oral law is flexible: things are told, re-told, half-forgotten and mis-remembered by many tribesmen. Such is the richness of the spoken word. What's here might well be contested: as the old saying goes – 'ask two Bedouin, get three different answers'.

● **Muzeina** The Muzeina are the biggest tribe in South Sinai, with a huge territory encompassing Sharm, Dahab and half of Nuweiba. They came from the Hejaz, probably in the 1500s, and still have branches around Medina today.

● **Aulad Said** This tribe holds the mountains south of St Katherine. Their holy man is Nabi Saleh, who was an early prophet of Islam, mentioned in the Koran. They're one of the region's poorest tribes today.

● **Jebeleya** This small tribe (see p124) lives in the High Mountain Region, mostly in the town of St Katherine; the name literally means 'The Mountain People'. They're an anthropological oddity for the Bedouin, claiming roots that are European and Egyptian Christian, not Arab and Muslim.

● **Gararsha** The Gararsha hold Wadi Feiran and it's said they came as refugees from the Hejaz. They have close historical ties with the Sowalha.

● **Hamada** This small tribe is said to be the oldest in the Sinai. It's suggested they might even have bloodlines from the earliest miner groups. They occupy a few valleys around Wadi Sahu, near Serabit el Khadem.

❏ **The bloodiest Bedouin battle**

The Alegat and Sowalha were once big and powerful tribes. Both lived in the west of the Sinai and had frequent disputes over territory. War erupted in the 1500s and the explorer John Lewis Burckhardt explains it thus: the Muzeina migrated to the Sinai from Arabia and appealed to the Sowalha for pasturage. The Sowalha agreed, but only on the condition they'd get an annual gift of sheep.

This was a grave insult to the Muzeina: the sort of demand that'd put on a rabble of outcasts. Seeing an opportunity for political advantage, the Alegat stepped in and offered the Muzeina some of their land. Both tribes soon clubbed together and launched a conquest against the Sowalha. The Gararsha joined the Sowalha and a tribal war raged for over 40 years, being fought between generations. It culminated in a battle in Wadi Barak, won by the Alegat and Muzeina.

There was such wide bloodshed the Bedouin said the wind blew remains of the dead for many years after. The Alegat and Muzeina remain 'brother' tribes today, often occupying the same lands and helping each other resolve blood disputes.

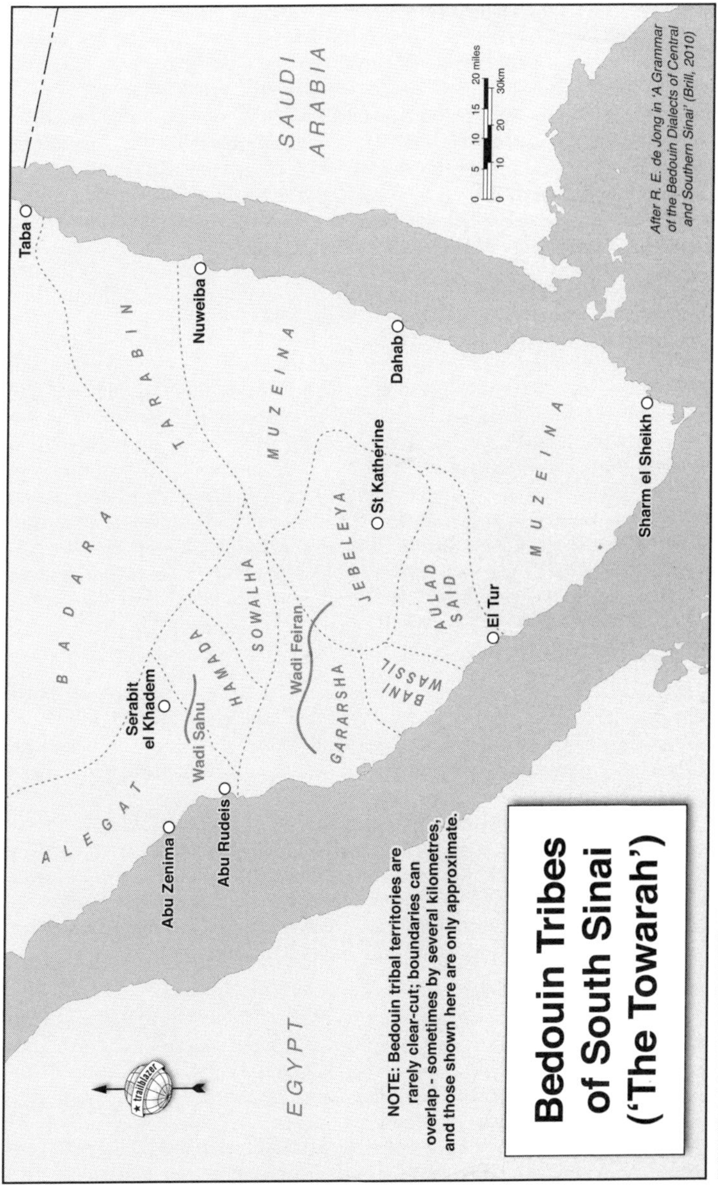

Bedouin Tribes
of South Sinai
('The Towarah')
NOTE: Bedouin tribal territories are rarely clear-cut; boundaries can overlap - sometimes by several kilometres, and those shown here are only approximate.
EGYPT
SAUDI ARABIA
trailblazer
Taba
Nuweiba
Dahab
Sharm el Sheikh
St Katherine
El Tur
Abu Rudeis
Abu Zenima
Serabit el Khadem
Wadi Sahu
Wadi Feiran
BADARA
TARABIN
MUZEINA
MUZEINA
ALEGAT
HAMADA
SOWALHA
GARARSHA
JEBELEYA
AULAD SAID
BANI WASSIL
0 5 10 15 20 miles
0 10 20 30km
After R. E. de Jong in 'A Grammar of the Bedouin Dialects of Central and Southern Sinai' (Brill, 2010)

● **Alegat** The Alegat used to be a big, powerful tribe and travellers reported a branch of them as far away as Nubia in the 19th century. They occupy a territory around Serabit el Khadem and have close ties to the Muzeina.

● **Sowalha** The Sowalha were once said to be the first Bedouin tribe in the Sinai. This probably wasn't correct but they were the most powerful for a long time. Their influence declined after they lost a war against the Alegat and Muzeina (see box p72). They live on the west side of the Sinai today.

● **Bani Wassil** The Bani Wassil are such a small tribe they're often not counted in the Towarah. Their territory is on the Plain of Qa and they were noted in the Sinai as early as the 13th century.

The Bedouin: settling down

The Bedouin are now giving up their nomadic lives and settling down across the Middle East. It's partly down to political pressure: like the Gypsies of Europe, they're seen as a law unto themselves; governments prefer them as good, settled citizens, easy to control. Even so, a lot of the settlement is voluntary. Tap water, TV, shops and health care have all proved hard to resist after centuries in the wilderness. Some say settlement marks the end of Bedouin culture but at least for the moment, this isn't quite so.

The Bedouin might be settled, but they don't live like settled people. Old Bedouin tents are seen tied onto homes, and many families own camels. Most Bedouin still speak in their own tribal dialect and dress in traditional *jelebeyas* and *shemaghs*, welcoming you in a house like they'd do in a tent. The Bedouin are changing, but their culture is still Bedouin.

THE EGYPTIANS

This title might seem unnecessary: the Sinai is in Egypt and everyone should therefore be called Egyptian. The Bedouin don't see it like this: few call themselves Egyptian and some make it explicitly clear they're not. Whereas the Bedouin are a wandering people from the deserts of Arabia, the Egyptians are a settled agricultural people of the Nile Valley.

There are tensions between both at times: some Bedouin see the Egyptians as the latest in a long line of outside occupiers. The Egyptians see the Sinai as an integral part of their homeland, with the Pharaohs having established a presence over 4000 years ago. Nevertheless, there are overlaps between both groups and their cultures are becoming closer. The relationship will likely change further as the Sinai finds its place in post-revolution Egypt.

Settlement in the Sinai

In the 1960s South Sinai had a population of about 4500, mostly Bedouin. From the 1980s Mubarak encouraged Egyptian settlement, seeking to strengthen the national claim should it ever be in question again. Jobs, tax breaks and subsidised housing were created and thousands of migrants arrived from overcrowded Nile Delta towns like Tanta and Zagazig.

By 1996, South Sinai's population was thought to number about 55,000; in 2003, up to 100,000. Some estimates suggest it will be near 300,000 in 2017.

Whatever the precise number, one thing is indisputable: in many parts of the Sinai the Bedouin are now a minority.

THE CHRISTIANS

Christianity is the oldest surviving religion in the Sinai, but the Christian population has been in steady decline for the better part of the last thousand years. Hundreds lived here in Byzantine times, but numbers dropped amidst anti-Christian sentiment in the Crusades. The Black Death arrived on trade routes in the Middle Ages, decimating the population still further.

For the last few centuries, the Monastery of St Katherine has had fewer than 100 monks. About 20 remain today. The Convent of Feiran has four nuns, and there are a few monks at the Monastery of St George in El Tur. There's concern the population could soon disappear entirely and there has even been periodic talk of admitting Coptic monks (whose theology differs in some key respects).

Life in the monasteries

Christianity developed a unique character in its wilderness isolation. The Holy Monastery of Sinai is part of the Eastern Orthodox Church but it's an autocephalous (ie highly independent) order with its own archbishop. Its Byzantine heritage is reflected in a strong Greek culture in the monasteries. Monks must be of Greek descent, they have to speak Greek and they're given Greek names. Sometimes Greek flags are flown from the chapels.

Life is the same as it has been for centuries: the day begins with a service at 4am, followed by a period of reflection. Work comes next, with each monk having his own trade, from cooking, to archiving and gardening. The afternoon involves prayers, followed by a communal meal and bed.

The Sinai and religious legends

THE EXODUS

Legends of The Exodus resonate around the Sinai. The story goes like this: the Israelites (or Hebrews) were a slave people living under the Pharaohs in Egypt. Moses was an Israelite who fled to the Sinai as a fugitive, after killing a cruel Egyptian slave driver. He lived the simple life of a mountain shepherd, grazing his flocks until God spoke to him one day from a Burning Bush. He commanded him to go back to Egypt and set the Israelites free; leading them out of slavery to the Promised Land (Canaan). God helped by bringing down the Ten Plagues, striking down the last – the killing of every first-born Egyptian son – as the Israelites stole away one night. They moved out over the desert, following a pillar of cloud by day and a column of fire by night, soon reaching the shores of the Red Sea. God drew its waters apart to give them safe passage across to the Sinai, lashing them back on the Pharaoh.

They continued through the wilderness – stricken with thirst, exhaustion and doubt – to reach Mount Sinai. Moses climbed it alone, staying on top for 40 nights. Fire and clouds swirled around in the sky as the peak trembled and God delivered the Ten Commandments (on the Tablets of Law). The Israelites set out again but disaster soon struck. Advance scouts reported giants lying in wait in the Promised Land and they refused to go any further.

Enraged by their lack of faith, God condemned them to wander in the Sinai for another 40 years; hence, 'The Wilderness of the Wanderings'. It was only after the unfaithful generation had passed away that Moses led them to the Promised Land – the 'Land of Milk and Honey' – dying a happy old man (well over 100 years old) as it came into sight.

Mapping the Exodus

Biblical geographers have long tried to map the route of the Exodus, comparing scripture with the landscape. The most widely accepted theory suggests the crossing of the Red Sea took place near Suez; early travellers said you could see the Pharaoh's chariot tracks running down to the sea. They moved down the coast before turning into Wadi Feiran and following it up to Mount Sinai. The modern Mount Sinai has long been the most popular choice of peak. Only a few ever believed it was another one, with most favouring Jebel Serbal.

Modern revisionist theories suggest the Israelites dodged South Sinai altogether. The Red Sea is interpreted as 'The Sea of Reeds': not a sea at all, but part of the Bitter Lakes of the Suez Canal depression. Mount Sinai is one of the peninsula's lesser northern summits like Jebel Hellal or Jebel Maghara. Some iconoclasts scrap the Sinai altogether, claiming most of The Exodus actually happened in the Hejaz mountains of Saudi Arabia.

The Exodus: fact or fiction

The Exodus debate has shifted today; the question isn't so much where it happened but whether it ever happened at all. Historians point out that ancient Egyptian sources make virtually no mention of any people called the Israelites (or Hebrews) nor any mass departure from Egypt. No economic records show a significant downturn in the economy, which would certainly be expected with the overnight loss of the workforce and their dependents: 600,000 men are said to have left, as well as women, children and a 'mixed multitude' of others (probably putting the total nearer two million).

Archaeologists report similar findings: no material evidence suggests such a large group ever passed through the region. Language critics add their voice and say a textual analysis of the Exodus books shows a varied authorship across several centuries. It is partly on this basis that some claim The Exodus was in fact a politically motivated origin myth; one written as it needed to be, to consolidate a peoples' identity when it happened to be socially useful. Whatever the hard history of The Exodus there is no doubting the power of the story: its fable of a people rising up against slavery has struck a universal chord with every culture through the ages.

ST KATHERINE OF ALEXANDRIA

St Katherine is the Sinai's most important saint, giving her name to a monastery, a mountain and a town. According to Christian tradition, she was born into a pagan family in 3rd century Alexandria, converting to Christianity in her teens. She became an eminent scholar and soon denounced the anti-Christian persecutions of the Emperor Maximinus. Taken aback – but bewitched by the beautiful, outspoken young woman – Maximinus requested her presence. She travelled to debate Christianity with his 50 finest court scholars, persuading many to convert on the spot (all of whom were promptly killed).

Enraged at his humiliation, the Emperor threw her in a dungeon. When his wife announced she was converting too he gave Katherine a stark choice: renounce Christianity and marry him, or die – she chose to die. She was to be mangled by a contraption of rotating wheels and knives (hence the term 'Katherine Wheel'); but in a miraculous, last-minute twist, it suddenly cluttered to pieces. This still wasn't enough to save her: she was just beheaded instead. It's said angels carried her body to the Sinai's highest peak — (now called) Jebel Katherina — and laid her to rest on the summit.

The monks of the Sinai provide a footnote. They say the whereabouts of Katherine's remains were revealed by God in the 9th century, then retrieved for safekeeping. The monastery re-named itself the Monastery of St Katherine to mark the find, prompting a resurgence of interest in her life across Europe (not to mention a flood of sorely needed donations). Schools, universities and chapels were named after her, and she became a popular women's icon. It's said Joan of Arc even held regular counsel with her ghost. Her popularity waned through the Reformation but she remained important in the Orthodox and Catholic faiths. She's the patron saint of scholars (for all her early self-education), oppressed women, and people who use wheels in their work: wheelwrights, clockmakers, mechanics, mill men, spinsters and so on.

ISLAM AND THE SINAI

Muslims hold the Sinai important like Jews and Christians, with The Koran recounting the story of The Exodus. It doesn't go into the same detail as the Biblical sources but it mentions major events: the Burning Bush, The Crossing of the Red Sea and the Forty Year Wanderings, for example.

It also identifies Mount Sinai as the peak on which Moses received The Law, as well as one of the four sacred symbols on which God created mankind ('*By the Fig, And the Olive, And the Mount of Sinai; And this City of Security – We have indeed created man, In the best of moulds*': Sura 95: 1-4).

4

MINIMUM IMPACT TREKKING & TRAIL SAFETY

The Sinai remained unsettled for most of its history: a land of rugged mountains and wild, windswept deserts. A few Bedouin tribes wandered. Everyone else – and there weren't many – passed through on major desert roads such as the pilgrim trail to the Monastery of St Katherine, or the *Darb el Hajj* to Mecca. That's all changed today; the Sinai has seen more development than any other part of Egypt and millions of tourists visit its resorts every year.

Tourism *can* be a force for positive change but all too often, it's not. It's important to travel in the right way, with an understanding of local issues and an awareness of our own impact. Otherwise we'll play a part in killing the things that should be there to love.

ENVIRONMENTAL IMPACT

The Sinai has been made suddenly accessible by jeep travel. Hundreds visit the desert every day, or walk the trails up Mount Sinai, and the strain is starting to show. As much as the numbers, it's about attitudes; all too often, visitors don't show the environment the care it needs. They don't live with it, connect with it, or see any reason to preserve it once they've gone. The chances are you'll be in the environmentally conscious bracket, but extra care is still needed. The desert is very sensitive and once disturbed it can take decades to recover.

Litter management

The Sinai is beautiful and litter wrecks its virgin landscapes. Orange peel can take over six months to decompose, plastic bags more than 10 years, aluminium cans 85 years and glass bottles thousands of years.

● **Minimise group size** Bigger groups create more litter and it's harder to manage the waste.

● **Strip packaging** Remove excess packaging before you hit the trail.

● **Burnable flammables** Burn food, cardboard, paper and anything else that's combustible. Use it as fire-starting material through the day.

● **Carry out waste** Keep a pocket purse for ring pulls, cigarette butts and other little bits of waste you build up. Crush bigger refuse and keep it in a bag. When you find bins in Bedouin gardens don't use them. It just shifts the dilemma of what to do with it to the owner. Carry everything back to town and get rid of it there. It'll end

❏ **Littering for the next person**
The Bedouin are resourceful with waste and it's sometimes left to help out the next person. Old tin cans are used for boiling water, sawn-off oil drum lids are there for making bread, and half-full bottles dot waterless trails for thirsty wayfarers. Don't add to this supply; just let the Bedouin manage it in their own way.

up in a desert landfill but it's still better in a designated one than it is blowing about elsewhere.

● **Pick up any litter left by others** This sets an excellent example.

Respect local wildlife

Desert wildlife has narrow margins for survival and is extremely sensitive to disturbance. There's an extra onus to respect it.

● **Don't pick wild herbs or flowers** Insects live in them, herbivores graze on them and some are critically endangered now. Just leave picking them to the Bedouin. Plants that look dead are often just dormant until the rains.

● **Don't feed the wildlife** Crumbs, fruit peel and vegetable waste have become part of the wildlife diet on heavily touristed trails. However, this weans wildlife off natural foods and out of foraging habits so it's not necessarily good for them.

● **Don't linger around wildlife** Get one good look and a photo, then leave. Even at a distance your presence is stressful for the animal, especially if it has young.

● **Discourage ibex hunting** Some guides carry guns in the hope of seeing an ibex, especially in Wadi Feiran. Ibex (see p63) have been hunted for thousands of years here but the introduction of modern firearms has seen their numbers drop sharply. There are only a few hundred left now and you shouldn't have any part in their ongoing demise. Where the guide has a gun lay it down very straight that he has a choice: he can either go with the gun, or with you.

● **Camp carefully** Camp over 100m from open water. Animals drink from these sources and most will go without rather than risk approaching a human camp. Don't camp near burrows as it'll disturb nocturnal patterns.

Conserve water

Every drop is precious. The Sinai has been in one of its worst droughts for decades recently. Vegetation is dying, creeks have disappeared and wells, once full, are now empty. Water use has increased with population growth, mass tourism and opium farming too. Water conservation thus has an added importance. Aim to preserve both its quantity *and* quality:

● **Keep drinking sources pristine** Impeccable hygiene is a basic duty as everyone uses these. Never wash hands, brush teeth in them etc.

● **No chemical pollution in other sources** Be careful with other sources too; they support water-loving fauna and animals drink from them. Avoid chemical soaps and bio-detergents; even ones purporting to be eco-friendly.

● **Never waste water** Try to think about why you really need water. Wash clothes after a trek, clean pans with bread etc. The Bedouin don't wash on trek and you could do this too; you'll certainly appreciate the first shower when it comes.

Good fire practice

Fires are communal hearths that bring people together and they're integral to Bedouin culture. They're common on trek but with more people visiting now, wood is getting ever-more scarce. Mountainsides are looking bare in places and many acacia trees have had their branches lopped off. It's a pressing environmental issue and it's only going to get worse. Help by doing the following:

● **Use gas where possible** Bigger trekking groups should use gas cylinders. Camping stoves should be taken by smaller groups where possible (you can't get them locally so consider the options on p28).

● **Use wood sustainably** Dead shrubbery is scattered about on trek. Sometimes, the Bedouin dig down, cutting dead roots off a live shrub. Trees aren't used in the mountains, but they're important for fuel in the desert. The Bedouin take single branches, but only from trees with enough greenery to withstand the loss. When they're very dry, you can sometimes use camel droppings to make a fire that's sufficient for tea.

● **Buying firewood** Wood is sometimes sold but it's local and there's no guarantee it's been sourced sustainably. The upside is it's taken from lesser-trodden areas that have more chance to recover. A big armful costs about LE40-50.

● **Other tips** Use established fireplaces when you can. Where you have small fires, cover the remains with sand. Don't blacken any rocks or cliffs.

Going to the toilet

A few Bedouin gardens have composting toilets but most of the time you just have to find your own place to go. Get clear of any water sources to begin with.

On the advice of the National Parks of Egypt you should be at least 100m away from the nearest water source. Choose your spot carefully, avoiding any water channels where rain would wash the excrement down into bigger wadis. Use the heel of your boot to dig a small trench (making it at least 30cm deep in sand) and cover it back up when you're finished. Toilet paper should be burned or put in a zip-seal bag and carried out. Otherwise, animals can dig it up or it can be exposed by winds and scattered about the landscape.

Other ways to help

● **Walk out of season** Peak season puts maximum strain on water, wood and other resources. Coming at a different time spreads the impact.

● **Never leave graffiti** Never make markings on rocks, especially at graffiti sites of ancient origin. Many people have added their names or doodles. It

---

❏ **Out of toilet paper on the trail?**

The Bedouin have long made do using nothing but stones. Some stones are better than others: size, shape and surface texture affect fitness for purpose. Nonetheless, when you get the right one, it can be as good as toilet paper. Doing this is to be encouraged. No toilet paper means no litter and faeces dry fast on the stone, dispersing across the landscape with a fertilising effect. This might all sound a bit improbable, but it's true.

defaces an extremely rich historical record in the same way that scribbling over a precious ancient manuscript would.

● **Don't take rocks** Semi-precious stones are harvested for the tourist market. Jebel Gunna is a sandstone plateau, once rich with seashells and fossils but comparatively bare now. Quartz is chiselled out of mountains around St Katherine, leaving unsightly scars on the rocks.

● **Use camels not 4x4s** To get to an advanced trailhead, consider a camel (see box below).

❏ Camel skills: a quick guide

Camels are amazing creatures – the fabled 'ships of the desert' – and the bedrock upon which Bedouin culture has been built. Few animals are so well adapted to their environment; sometimes, camels seem like an animated extension of the desert itself. They have a superb memory of routes, water and food sources, and they're astute watchers of life and people. The Bedouin have a great affection for their camels, regarding them as companions. All that said, they can be hard work. Camels are loyal to their owners and are usually stubborn with strangers. Aim for firm, clear leadership from the start; give commands only when you have to, and don't pet a camel like a domestic animal. Superficial affection just irritates them.

● **How to sit** Don't sit on a camel like a horse. From the horse position, raise one leg and rest it on the bit of hump in front. This gives a lever against the rocking motion and you can use it to spring up suddenly. A *shemagh* (see box p26) is good for stuffing between your back and the rear saddle horn.

● **Getting up** The camel gets up in a series of forceful jerks. This is when the unsuspecting passenger falls so hold tight (see box p121).

● **Moving** To start moving or quicken the pace, click with your salivary glands or growl out the long sound *hareee!* Keep up with other camels: when one falls away, others get agitated and the whole expedition slows. When you can't get a camel moving, hit its haunch with a stick (doing it harder than you might expect). Sometimes just raising it into the camel's side vision is enough.

● **Steering** Camels don't need much steering. When you have to give it direction just a gentle tug of the bridle is usually enough.

● **Stopping** Tug on the bridle and make the long sound *ageeeef!* Where the camel refuses to stop you might have to pull the bridle back until its head is nearly touching yours. This is highly uncomfortable and it won't be able to continue. To make the camel kneel, blow air out of the sides of your mouth, a bit like a scowling cat. Hold on tight when it kneels down, just like when getting up.

● **Leading** Lead camels over rugged terrain and give them breathers when going uphill. Never go too close to others on a pass as this can hurry them and lead to disastrous falls. Legs are often broken like this and camels may have to be killed where they fall. There's no chance of moving something as heavy and killing it is kinder than letting it die a long death in the open sun.

● **Feeding** This is the basis of the owner-camel bond. Outsiders can undermine it and it's easy to give the camel something that's bad for it. Out on trek, it's fine to let it graze naturally; camels get moisture from herbage and your guide will hobble its forelegs so it can wander and graze more during meal times.

● **Loading** Get the saddle tight. You'll have a nasty fall if it slips but, more importantly, a loose saddle burns painful sores into the camel's back. If it refuses to move and you're a long way from water, it's a problem. Saddles are tightened with straps under the belly – accompanied by yelps and groans – and loads are balanced evenly either side.

● **Encourage sensible driving** If you take a jeep tour, tell your driver to stick to the tracks. Many rove around to entertain passengers, flattening burrows, tearing up plants and crushing the hard sand that protects seedlings below. It also leaves unsightly tracks across the landscape. Follow the same advice if you use a quad bike or dune buggy or better still – avoid them altogether.

ECONOMIC IMPACT

South Sinai was transformed into Egypt's 'Red Sea Riviera' in the 1990s. Mubarak trumpeted it as a success story, but the Bedouin didn't see it like this; they claim vast chunks of ancestral land were sold off to foreign hotel chains. What's more, they had no place in the beach-based economy built up on it after-wards. Nature-based tourism, like trekking, to which Bedouin lifestyles would have been so perfectly suited, was left chronically under-developed. Some sug-gest authorities deliberately impeded it to limit Bedouin influence. Unemployment is as high as 80% in some tribes and many turn to drug cultiva-tion and smuggling to make ends meet. The Sinai's development thus has a dark underbelly; as much as helping, it has deepened divides, split communities and criminalised hundreds of young men. Hopefully things will change in the new Egypt; but it'll take time. Use your money to make a difference, getting it to the people and communities who really need it.

Spread the wealth

The east coast gets more tourism than anywhere and by heading into the Bedouin interior you'll be making a difference already. Even here though, there are great inequalities; some tribes are notably poorer than others. The Bedouin in places like Wadi Feiran or the Jebel Umm Shomer region have had almost no income from tourism. These are some of the most spectacular areas in which to trek and by visiting you'll inject money where it's needed and help create a legitimate Bedouin economy. You can spread the wealth over time by trekking off-season, when many guides and cameleers find themselves out of work.

❏ **Local NGOs (non governmental organisations)**
These are good places to use up leftover holiday money, making a donation or buy-ing gifts. Here are just a few good ones to consider.
● **Medicinal Plants Association** This monitors local plant species. It also grows endangered ones in greenhouses and works with local farmers to promote eco-friendly horticulture in the mountains (🖳 www.mpcpegypt.com).
● **Makhad Trust** This aims to protect traditional Bedouin livelihoods. It has built dams to keep mountain gardens productive and a community centre to teach tradi-tional skills (it's at the Nawamis trailhead and offers accommodation). It's also devel-oping the Sinai's first proper Bedouin museum (🖳 www.makhad.org).
● **Community Foundation for South Sinai** This is a broad-focus organisation; it has deepened wells, trained local people with modern job skills and bought instru-ments to help keep traditional music alive (🖳 www.southsinaifoundation.org).

Support local women

Bedouin men have suffered in the Sinai but women are the most economically excluded group of all. One of the only ways they can earn disposable income is by selling their handicrafts. You can also give women work by asking them to repair any damaged trekking gear; they do a superb job and it's well worth it. A few widows live on their own and offer accommodation in gardens on trekking routes too. Where there's a chance to stay somewhere like this it's listed.

Support locally owned businesses

Use small, locally owned businesses over bigger, international ones. Local shops, hotels and shisha cafés give an area its character and they face tough competition. To survive, they have to be used.

Buy local garden produce

Fruit, vegetables and other local garden produce is often available if you ask. Buying this puts money in the pockets of people who use the land to live. These are the ones most tied to the place; they have its best interests at heart and they're the best guardians for it. Not only this, but it cuts down on pollution caused by bringing food in from outside: the so-called 'food miles'.

Encourage local skills and trades

Traditional skills and trades are becoming irrelevant to modern life and thus forgotten. As much as being worthy of preservation in their own right, they give a unique economic niche for locals. The best way to keep them going as such is to put down an economic incentive. As well as trekking, consider organising a Bedouin herbalist and learning about plants, using a wildlife tracker etc.

CULTURAL IMPACT

Mainland Egyptians outnumber the Bedouin in many parts of modern Sinai. Westerners have a big permanent presence too. Bedouin culture has become suddenly exposed to outside influences and it's changing. Some are worried it's changing so fast traditional knowledge could be lost within a generation. Take every opportunity to remind younger Bedouin why their culture is deserving of preservation.

Avoid flaunting wealth

Don't flash things about that local people couldn't afford, nor boast about wealth. Apart from being crass it just reinforces the assumption that Westerners are rich and the West is better, deepening divisions.

Discourage begging

Local children can pester you all day for 'caramela', 'shikolata' or 'one dollar'. Giving in just breeds a culture of dependency. Moreover it reinforces the view that Westerners are good for getting things from. Sadly, these attitudes persist in later life; do your bit to nip them in the bud.

Photograph with sensitivity

It is a basic courtesy to ask before you shoot. Don't photograph a woman unless both she and her husband agree. Sometimes people expect baksheesh and all like to see their picture on a camera. Do a good turn by taking a picture of a family and sending it back to the nearest post office. It'll become a treasured family possession and perhaps the only one they have to remember things.

Aim to understand

Local culture has different norms to Western culture. There are contrasting attitudes on everything from homosexuality to women's rights and how an animal should be slaughtered. Take care not to come across like you're trying to enlighten people on the best way with these ie the Western way. Ask questions, listen, and try to understand why the local culture adds up as it does, even if the resulting principles are a sharp moral contrast from home. Wherever we are; Egypt or the West, nobody likes a lecture.

Speak a little Arabic

People like to hear outsiders speak their language. No matter how clumsy you sound, they respect the effort. Learn at least the standard Islamic greeting 'Peace be Upon You' and a few everyday words. Obviously, the more you can communicate, the richer your contact will be. See pp276-7 for some useful words and phrases.

Dress appropriately

Dress codes are conservative and you should try and fit in. It might not seem a big deal but dress affects how you're seen and sends out signals about how much you respect local norms. People might not say anything if you're not dressed how you should be, but it doesn't mean they like it. Being dressed inappropriately will make you feel more awkward than anyone a lot of the time.

　　Men should avoid shorts. Trousers are best and three-quarter length trousers between the knees and ankles are fine too. Cover your shoulders and don't wear vests. **Women** should wear trousers at all times. Shoulders and upper arms should always be covered and sleeves to the wrists are best. Loose clothing is best and you must wear a headscarf if you enter a Sheikh's tomb or mosque.

Everyday etiquette

Like everywhere, the Sinai has its own customs. Misunderstandings are tolerated from outsiders but it's good to hit the ground running when you arrive.

● **How to greet people** When someone new arrives in a tent stand up and shake their hand. Men and women can acknowledge each other with a simple hello.

● **Take shoes off in a home** Shoes are considered unclean and a lot of symbolism goes with them in Arab culture (a popular insult is 'jazma!' – shoe! To offend someone seriously, 'sitteen jazma' – 'sixty shoes!').

● **Don't show your soles** This is considered rude and it's easy to forget. Try kneeling or go cross-legged like the Bedouin.

● **Take gifts** If invited to a special occasion take a small gift. The gesture is most important: a box of dates, or a pocket Koran, is fine.

Etiquette with food

Food has a great cultural importance in the Arab world and nowhere more so than in Bedouin society, where it's central to hospitality.

● **Always share**   The Bedouin will share what they have with you and it's imperative to do the same. It's not unusual for people to come out of nowhere at dusk, arriving at the precise moment your food is being served. Give them their fill, without question and with the best will, even if you go to bed on an empty stomach. It might be infuriating after a long day, but hospitality like this is almost sacred. Acts of warmth mean a lot in places as hard as the desert; it's through them that people have survived here, both physically and spiritually.

● **Accept hospitality**   This is just as important as giving it. Acknowledge the generosity, even if you take just a small, token amount. Be the best guest you can; accepting your host's generosity freely and showing your gratitude.

● **Three cups of tea**   The Bedouin rarely drink more than three cups of tea in a single sitting. More is considered greedy.

● **When finished, leave a little**   If you eat everything off the plate the host will see it as a sure sign you want more. You can protest all you want, but it'll just be seen as an obligatory show of politeness. Leave a few morsels on the plate when finished and say '*hamdelelah*' (thank God).

● **Eat only your portion**   A big circular plate or *sineeya* is used for communal eating. Its contents are divided into imaginary equal-sized wedges and you should only eat from yours. Dipping freely into others would quite rightly raise eyebrows. If you've finished and others are still hungry you can help by nudging some food from your wedge into theirs.

● **Don't use your left hand**   This is the hand locals use to clean themselves after the toilet (and it'll be assumed you do the same). Avoid using your left hand when eating and accept cups of tea with your right hand.

● **Avoid alcohol**   Some trekkers take alcohol for the campfire but many Muslims consider it *haram* (forbidden by God). Guides might not remark on it but the reality is most don't like it and it creates barriers between you.

Relations between the sexes

These are constrained from teen years onwards. Men and women sit in separate quarters on most social occasions. Foreigners should follow local norms and behave with restraint to locals of the opposite sex. With men, a nod of acknowledgement and a few words to the local women should be the extent of things.

The West: tell it like it is

The 'West is best' mentality is becoming more prevalent. When you encounter it, acknowledge the good parts of the West: higher standards of living and health care, good education, democracy and so on. Just balance it out with a realistic picture of the bad sides: higher rates of violent crime, homelessness, family breakdown and mental illness.

Encourage local pride and keep local knowledge alive

Taking an interest in local culture breeds pride. Tell people when you see something you like as it underlines its importance and reminds them to value it.

Modern life renders traditional Bedouin knowledge of plants, starlore, place names and local legends largely superfluous. This took centuries to build up and, as an oral people, the Bedouin never put it down in writing. When it's gone, it'll be gone for good and it'll be a loss for all of humanity. It reflects a wilderness culture that'll never be replicated in the same way again. Asking questions about it helps keep it in circulation.

Don't play doctor
Westerners can be seen as travelling doctors and medical supplies come under heavy strain. Giving out a few plasters and the odd aspirin probably won't do too much harm but people should see real doctors if they feel unwell.

See the funny side
Travelling in the Sinai can be stressful: the heat, the haggling, the delays. Take a step back and see the funny side; it'll always be there.

Health and safety on the trail

HEAT ACCLIMATISATION

Heat acclimatisation is the process by which the body gets used to working in a hot climate. A big raft of changes set in: the core body and skin temperatures drop; blood flows nearer the surface of the skin to dissipate heat, and sweating begins sooner and is more profuse. Fluid chemistry is also altered to reduce vital salt loss. Changes become noticeable after a couple of days but it takes about two weeks for the physiological process to complete. To trigger the level of acclimatisation needed for trekking you actually have to get out and exert yourself in the heat. Lazing around will only result in partial adaptation.

Don't do too much too soon: take it slowly and ease into the climate over a few days. Step things up with a short, easy trek or do a long one more slowly.

DEHYDRATION

Dehydration happens when you lose more water than you take in. It's the most common cause of hospitalisation for trekkers in the Sinai. Most water is lost by sweating but four litres a day can be lost just by breathing too. Early warning signs are thirst and a headache. You'll also pass darker urine, less regularly. If it worsens either heat exhaustion or heat stroke might come on.

Heat exhaustion
This involves nausea, muscle cramps and an absolutely crippling fatigue. Even raising a water bottle feels like lifting a dumbbell. The surprising thing is how quickly it can set in: someone can go from walking to being completely disabled in less than 30 minutes. Lie victims in the shade and put their feet up on a rucksack. Drape a wet shemagh over their forehead and give them water with

rehydration salts in it, encouraging short sips. Snacks help when they hit the upward curve and, if everything goes well, the victim can feel better within an hour.

Treating heat exhaustion can be tough: the victim can be too lethargic and the temperatures too great to make the gains necessary to stop a more serious downward slide. Vigilance and prevention are key.

Heat stroke

The body gets so intensely dehydrated with heat stroke that it can't cool itself. Organs such as the brain overheat and it's classed as a medical emergency. It's the next stage of dehydration along from heat exhaustion, but this won't neces-sarily happen as a preliminary stage. Heat stroke can come on in itself. Victims look flushed, red and dry, all because their bodies don't have enough water to sweat out. Dizziness, confusion and fits soon start. Breathing becomes rapid and shallow, before a coma sets in, followed by death.

Give victims water with rehydration salts in it and get them into the shade, removing hot clothes and boots. The idea is to become a substitute for their body's defunct cooling system: cover them in a wet shemagh and sprinkle them with water whilst fanning them down.

Preventing dehydration

Dehydration is preventable; you just have to drink more water than you lose. It's best not to think about it purely in terms of drinking enough though. Aim for a trekking style that limits water loss in every way.

● **Have a drinking regime** People get it wrong by just drinking when they're thirsty. Drink in a regular regime, having a good gulp every 15-30 minutes at hotter times. Remember, it's better to drink too much than too little.

● **Trek in cooler periods** In hotter months trek in cooler periods of the day. Find a shaded rock and break in the afternoon.

● **Move slowly and steadily** Going at a steady pace helps you maintain a reg-ular drinking pattern: bursts of high activity disrupt the rhythm. Look at the camels: they perfect the desert walking rhythm to an art.

● **Avoid dehydrating drinks/foods** Coffee and alcohol are natural dehydrators. Tea has a milder dehydrating effect but Bedouin tea also has useful sugars and your guide will insist you drink it anyway. Just drink a bit more water to offset the effects. Meat, dry and salty foods dehydrate you too.

● **Look out for your companions** Look out for other people as much as your-self. During Ramadan be extra vigilant over your guide (see pp43-4).

Drinking water on the trail

The amount of water you need varies with the season; most people get through two to five litres every day. Always keep half a litre for emergencies and get into the habit of topping up at every source you pass: there are no guarantees on the next ones. For more on water see pp88-9.

In the mountains The High Mountain Region is the wettest part of South Sinai and water sources are dotted helpfully around on trails. You can usually go between each carrying two to three litres or less, just filling up on the way. Water levels are usually highest in winter and spring and lowest in early autumn, just before the rains.

● **Wells** These are the main drinking source, usually found in big wadis and Bedouin gardens. Wells can run dry in summer and even when full, they won't all have ropes; carry a good length of string in case you need to use one. If it has no bucket lower a shemagh down to soak the water up.

● **Cliff drips** Small pools have been built on cliffs to catch perennial drips.

● **Big pools** There are two types of natural pool. A *galt* is fed by a permanent subsurface spring. A *kharaza* is a hollow that fills with rain and it evaporates gradually over the year. Neither is used for drinking water.

● **Other sources** Water collects in pools, hollows and cracks after rain, often remaining there for several weeks. Creeks sometimes form in wetter months, especially in big wadis draining on to the west coast. The most notable ones in this book are Wadi Sigillia (on the Jebel Serbal trek) and Wadi Isleh (on the Jebel Umm Shomer trek). There are plenty in the High Mountain Region too.

In the desert There's much less water here and camels have to carry what you need. Water is stored in jerry cans and they're usually topped up whenever there's a source. Desert water isn't as good as water in the mountains; it's often tepid with a slightly stale or salty taste. The water you set out with will probably be from a desert well so purify it like everything else.

● **Wells** These are found at oases but they're rare elsewhere.

● **Springs** These occur where underground water reaches the surface and they're most common at the bottom of cliffs. Water can stay on the surface a few weeks after rain and sometimes longer.

● **Seep wells** Water is sometimes reached by digging down. The best spots are known springs, like those mentioned above. The water seeps into the hole as you get lower; you can scoop it up or sponge it into a shemagh.

● **Pools** Rock pools form after rain and, in the shade, they can lie for a couple of months. They're a source for local animals and the quality deteriorates quickly: use them for watering camels or emergencies.

Should I purify the water? The Bedouin gulp it straight down from drinking sources and they'll expect you to follow (some even look mildly offended if you don't). Many trekkers do and most suffer no ill-effects; but it's still best to purify. Even drinking water can be contaminated: some sources can be birdbaths or breeding pools for water-loving fauna. Consider the following methods:

● **Boiling** It's usually enough to bring water to the boil but let it stand boiling for about 30 seconds if it's very polluted. Boiling is no use when you want cool water for bottles during the day but it's perfect for tea, soups and stews. You can also let it cool overnight for the next day.

● **Chemical purification** Iodine gives the widest protection. It comes in tablets or solution. Chlorine is slightly less effective against amoebic cysts but it's a good second best. Both make water taste terrible so try adding neutralising tablets or TANG to improve the flavour (see p55).

● **UV purification** UV purifying pens are a new technology. You dip them in the water and wait about a minute. They don't actually kill microbes: they just sterilise them so they can't reproduce, rendering them harmless. Prices start from about £60/US$100. Check out Steripen 🖳 www.steripen.com.

● **Water filters** You can buy extremely fine filters that sift everything out of water to a microscopic level. Even so, the filter isn't fine enough to remove viruses so get one that treats the water chemically too. Filters are small, light-weight and convenient, with prices from about £70/US$110.

DIARRHOEA

Diarrhoea is common on arrival and it's usually nothing much to worry about. Most bouts are minor and clear up in a few days. Occasionally you'll ingest something much nastier, causing diarrhoea of nightmare proportions that will stop a trekking holiday at the start.

Extra care is needed with diarrhoea in a desert: the huge fluid loss it occasions can make heat disorders impossible to prevent. Never attempt a trek until any diarrhoea has fully gone and if you get it badly on the trail, think about getting off.

How to prevent diarrhoea There is no reason why serious diarrhoea shouldn't be prevented. Follow these steps to enjoy a trouble-free trip:

● **Drink bottled water** and purify all water on trail.
● With **fruit and vegetables** 'cook it, peel it or forget it'.
● Flies crawl over everything. **Use a shemagh to cover food**.
● If you have to consume something obviously unsafe, **limit the quantity**.
● Food is eaten communally so **get everyone to wash their hands**. You could pass a bottle of anti-bacterial hand gel round.

How to treat diarrhoea Rest and drink copious amounts of water with rehydration salts in it. When you're on trail take an anti-diarrheal like Imodium. This won't cure it but it blocks the bowels, limits fluid loss and can be a lifesaver.

If things are really bad get off the trail entirely: in an emergency a camel can be trotted to help within a day from pretty much anywhere in South Sinai.

OTHER POTENTIAL HEALTH PROBLEMS

Sunburn
Sunburn is a risk all year, especially in the mountains where UV rays are more intense. Burns can be excruciating. Cover your skin or use a high-factor sun cream, re-applying it several times a day. Remember all those easy-to-forget places: your ears, below your chin, the V-neck in a shirt and so on. Also bring a good lip salve and some UV-filtering sunglasses.

Prickly heat
This is a painful rash caused by blocked sweat glands. It's common with heavy sweating; avoid it by giving your skin a good, regular scrub.

Blisters

Blisters are an everlasting bane and even more so in hot environments. Give your feet a regular air and inspect them at lunchtime. Use special plasters like Compeed if you find blisters developing, catching them early.

Athlete's foot and fungal infections

Like blisters, these are common. Just air your feet and clean them with an anti-bacterial soap such as Dettol (available in the Sinai). Wash between your toes and dry them properly when finished. Food powders and creams help.

Joint problems

Old problems can flare up. Walk in elasticated supports and consider trekking poles. Deep Heat might help evening pain. Take an anti-inflammatory such as aspirin if a joint swells. Swelling causes damage in itself.

Rabies

Rabies is a nasty viral disease, rife in the Sinai. Foreigners have to be treated every year. It gets transmitted in the saliva of an infected animal, usually in a bite or a scratch. Fever-like symptoms can come on quickly and they get progressively worse, soon reaching a 'point of no return' where death is inevitable. There are hundreds of strays around, especially in the open-air restaurants in Dahab and St Katherine. Avoid handling them: most carriers show no outward signs. If wounded, get to a hospital ASAP. Most stock post-exposure prophylaxis and you'll get a routine shot. You still need to get to a hospital if you've had your rabies jab: this just buys you a bit more time (see p33).

Hypothermia

There's a misconception that the Sinai doesn't get cold, which is where the danger lies: people don't come prepared. Winter temperatures can drop below minus 10°C on Jebel Katherina and people have died. Hypothermia happens when the body gets extremely cold: early signs are shivering, stumbles, slurred words, and odd behaviour. Warm the victim with blankets, a hot drink and some energy food and get them to a lower altitude. This is rarely too difficult, even in the highest parts of the Sinai. Where things are beyond that put the victim in a sleeping bag with someone else: get both to strip as skin-on-skin is warmest.

ALTITUDE PROBLEMS

Most **trekking** is below 2500m, the line at which altitude sickness typically occurs. Two treks in this book reach summits over 2500m but ascents are brief

---

❏ **Why is it so cold in the desert?**
Travellers have long complained about the bitter cold of the world's deserts. There's no doubt they can be chilly, but are they really *that cold*? The heat-acclimatisation process may be the reason. This comes on to a degree even in winter and the changes that work to keep you cool in the day chill you to the bone at night. It takes two weeks' continuous exposure in a cold climate for heat acclimatisation to wear off.

and problems virtually unheard of. The time altitude becomes really important is after **diving**. Going up too high too soon can trigger **decompression sickness (DMS)**. People often attempt the Mount Sinai trek after a dive (and several have died). There's a debate on how long to wait before you leave sea level, with figures between 12, 18 and 24 hours: the safest rule of thumb is to wait 24 hours. Call the Hyperbaric Medical Center in Sharm (☎ 069-366 0922) if concerned.

Importantly, it's not just going to the mountains that can trigger DMS. People often develop problems when travelling on coastal roads, unaware of how high they go. The following are death traps:

● **Sharm–Dahab highway** This goes over the Sharira Pass, around 630m. It's the most common DMS trigger site in the Sinai.

● **Dahab–Nuweiba highway** This is higher than the Sharm–Dahab road.

● **St Katherine highway** This crosses South Sinai, through Wadi Feiran, St Katherine and the deserts near Ein Hudera, rising over 1500m.

● **Nuweiba–Suez highway** This crosses the 500m Mitla Pass.

● **Avoid all treks after a dive** All treks in this book take place at altitude, or gain it quickly enough to trigger DMS.

Altitude problems in the Sinai

The only time you exceed the 'altitude sickness' line of 2500m is on Jebel Umm Shomer (2586m) and Jebel Katherina (2642m). You only remain high on Jebel Umm Shomer for a brief period. It's the same with Jebel Katherina, unless you sleep on the summit. Even then, altitude problems are almost unknown. Drink and eat well and if you feel nausea or dizziness that isn't clearly down to something else, go down. There's a good path and you lose altitude quickly.

HAZARDS

Natural hazards

Sand storms and dust storms These are most likely in khamsin season (see p61). Even so, the Sinai doesn't have enough sand to make them hazards like they are in parts of the Sahara. Trekking is just unpleasant: sand stings your face, gets in your eyes and it makes it hard to breathe (often triggering the gag reflex). Find a good windblock or pull a shemagh over your head, looking through the fabric. Dust storms are the equivalent in the mountains, and they can be just as nasty. The most relevant forecast information on winds is for Dahab; see 🖥 www.windfinder.com/forecast/dahab.

Flash floods Flash floods, or *seils*, can occur after heavy, localised storms. They're most common in the mountains where steep solid rock creates rapid run off, but they can happen anywhere. A storm in the mountains can send a flood tearing down through dry, distant deserts. It's unlikely you'll see one, but the risks involved make a few precautions sensible. Avoid camping out in narrow gorges you couldn't climb out of quickly and stay vigilant in unstable weather.

Snow and ice This is common in the mountains in winter and both can lie in north-facing gullies for weeks. The level of snow/ice is too thin to get any benefit from crampons so take extra care placing your feet.

❏ **Witness to a desert flood in Wadi Feiran, F W Holland (abridged). Ordnance Survey of the Peninsula of Sinai, 1869**
'The rain fell in torrents and the roar of the thunder echoing from peak to peak and the howling of the wind were quite deafening. It soon grew dark but flashes of lightning were so incessant that we could see everything around us. In less than a quarter of an hour every ravine and gully in the mountains was pouring down a foaming stream and we kept an anxious look out for the flood we saw must ensue. Presently I heard a distant roaring behind us, which drew nearer and nearer, and in a few minutes a tremendous torrent burst down a little wadi just below our tent, carrying with it a mass of debris into Wadi Feiran. The bed of Wadi Feiran was still dry but a white line of foam soon appeared in the watercourse and grew in size. Suddenly a huge wave came rolling down, and then another, and another. With a desperate effort I seized my tent and dragged it to a wall, escaping to high ground. As we were sitting congratulating ourselves, another rush of water came down. The lightning soon ceased and the moon began to shine brightly. The Arabs succeeded in lighting a fire and we sat around it drying our clothes. Looking back it seemed impossible to believe that scarcely more than an hour's rain could turn a dry desert wadi upwards of 300 yards broad into a foaming torrent from eight to ten feet deep. Yet there it was, roaring and tearing down, and carrying with it tangled masses of tamarisks and hundreds of beautiful palm trees. The roar of the torrents was tremendous; the boulders ground along beneath the water with the noise of a hundred mills at work. Nearly thirty people perished but only two bodies were found: the rest were swept away'.

Animal hazards
Scorpions *(akrab)* These are more common than snakes but still rare. Two types have stings powerful enough to kill (especially in children, sick and old people). The **fat-tailed Arabian scorpion** is black. The other, the so-called **deathstalker** (and the most feared in the Middle East), is yellow. Take care picking up rocks and shake kit down when it's been on the floor (scorpions can scuttle in). Don't put sleeping bags down until you're ready to sleep and keep tents zipped up. Wear shoes at all times, especially at night.

Snakes *(thabaan)* There are six types of poisonous snake but only two are especially aggressive. The **desert cobra** is a shiny black snake with a 'hood', found mostly in sandy desert areas. It doesn't spit venom like some cobras but the Bedouin say it can jump from several metres. The most dangerous mountain snake is the **Burton's carpet viper**. It's about a metre long with black spots and often saws its scales as a warning. Take care reaching to high hand holds and

❏ **A desert cure**
The Bedouin have a remedy for almost every ailment, including scorpion stings. The Jebeleya tribe even have their own method of immunisation. A scorpion is killed, roasted and crushed. A previously immunised Bedouin then spits into the mixture, which is stirred and readied for an infant's consumption. It's sometimes smeared on the nipple of a mother. Otherwise, it's put on a lucky coin. Beneficiaries claim to have been stung ten times by scorpions with no ill-effects.

make noise going through shrubbery, taking heavy footsteps to send out vibrations. Look out for tracks in sandy areas; they're long, wiggle lines, easy to spot.

Dealing with a sting or bite Obviously, if you can, get to a hospital ASAP; most stock antiserum. Tell doctors everything about the incident so they can identify the creature and how to treat you. Otherwise, the following advice might help:
● **Get somewhere safe** Move the victim somewhere safe, shaded and cool.
● **Clean the wound site** Don't try the 'cut and suck' technique to extract venom: it's of debatable use. Just wipe the wound clean.
● **Reassure the victim** A fast heart pumps venom quicker. Simply, the symptoms will be nasty but the survival odds are in the victim's favour.
● **Restricting bandage** The Bedouin suggest a tourniquet but these are easy to misapply and you can kill a limb. It's safer to use a crêpe bandage, wrapping it round and above the wound site and going down over it. This restricts the spread of the venom but won't cut off the blood supply.
● **Treat symptoms as they appear** A wide raft of symptoms appear with stings and bites: fever, vomiting, delirium, a loss of bowel control, respiratory difficulties and so on. Treat each as it occurs and remain vigilant for heat disorders on top; the fluid loss makes them an extra complication.

Irritating bugs and bites Mosquitoes are rife on the coasts all year. They're bad in St Katherine and Wadi Feiran in springtime too. They descend round you in a deafening drone and bites can keep you up all night. Sleep somewhere windy, with a shemagh over you, or otherwise use a good repellent. **Camel ticks** like humans as much as camels. Cover your skin and check exposed areas regularly. **Bedbugs** infest dirty mattresses and blankets so always check cleanliness. **Common flies** are everywhere and some even bite. A shemagh is good for covering your face when dozing. **Antihistamine** is good for insect bites: it relieves the itchiness that makes you to scratch them into an even worse condition.

Other creepy-crawlies Look out for the **camel spider**: a huge hairy creature with a leg span up to 12cm. They're not poisonous, despite what some Bedouin say, but they have powerful jaws and the bite is bloody and nasty.

Man-made hazards
Unmarked wells These are dotted about in the High Mountain Region, occasionally near trails. They can be man traps and plummeting down one would be an ignominious end. Take care round the tops of wells too as they can collapse.

Landmines Egypt has more landmines than any country in the world. There are 23 million in the Western Desert (all leftovers of WWII), and five million more in the Sinai (from the Egypt–Israel wars). Clearance isn't complete and won't be any time soon. Egypt and Israel don't reveal the whereabouts of their mines; no doubt both feel they might need them again. Known danger spots are the Israel border, the Suez Canal zone, and the Mitla Pass (central Sinai). The desert of South Sinai was mined in places but the mountains remained pretty much mine-free. Don't worry about trekking; trails are well-trodden and some even have jeep tracks along them. The danger comes in beating way off into

❏ **Inshallah, Inshallah!**
The Koran tells Muslims: *And do not say of anything 'I shall do this tomorrow' unless you add: 'Inshallah'* (Sura 18: 23-24). Inshallah means 'God Willing' and you hear it everyday in the Sinai and Egypt. Everything happens because God wills it: our lives and deaths are written and the feeling we are free agents is just an illusion. Danger isn't to be shrunk from; fate is to be accepted and life lived. This sort of thinking creates a wonderful philosophical easiness of which the West has no real equivalent but it can also give rise to an alarming risk-taking culture. Guides are usually responsible with safety but a few take big risks. Take a firm stance early on and make it clear when you're not comfortable with something.

unknown regions. There are definitely mines in wadis near Dahab and perhaps Sharm. You can also get into trouble with inexperienced jeep drivers (one group got stranded in a mine field in North Sinai a few years ago). If in doubt ask the Bedouin; more often than not they actually saw the mines being laid.

BASIC SAFETY PRECAUTIONS

The difficulty involved in rescue demands a few basic precautions. Think about safety before you go and whilst you're on trail.

● **Always use a Bedouin guide** It's an age old law but some trekkers still flout it. The Bedouin know the Sinai better than anyone: how to get through it and how to survive it. Most trekkers who get into trouble are alone.

● **Tell others where you're going** At least one other person should know your itinerary: where you're going and on what schedule.

● **Don't over-rely on your guide** Accidents happen to guides too. One of mine was disabled by food poisoning in the desert. Try and understand the landscape independently of your guide, remembering anything important like water sources, signs of settlement etc.

● **Take a mobile phone** These usually work from the highest ground and you can get a signal on most mountain peaks. Get the number of a Bedouin or Bedouin camp and call them if in trouble. Help will come sooner than it would from the emergency services (see box below), and these would usually just go through the Bedouin anyway (see box p50).

● **In the event of an accident** As difficult as it is, stay calm and rational. This is the basis for good decisions and these are ultimately what get you out of trouble. Remember to keep drinking too: it's easy to forget when anxious.

❏ **Trail rescue: don't bank on it**
There's no official rescue service yet. The Bedouin always help when they can but rescues are improvised and first-aid basic. You'll usually be stretchered out in a blanket, then humped on a donkey or camel. An air rescue costs anything up to US$4000/hr and involves a mountain of bureaucracy. Embassies might help but with things being drawn out you'll probably miss the window of opportunity. The Multi National Force of Observers (MFO) have been known to act as the cavalry, swooping in with their helicopters, but there are no guarantees.

GATEWAY TOWNS

Sharm el Sheikh

Sharm el Sheikh is the biggest town in South Sinai; an ever-expanding mass of resorts, casinos and gleaming shopping malls. Tourists are more common than the Bedouin here and the whole place feels a long way from the rugged mountain wilderness on the doorstep.

Some people hate Sharm; others enjoy a few days here. It has plenty of plus points, including the best range of diving in the Sinai and some great restaurants and bars. As much as anything though, think about your budget. You can rough it on LE150/day but you'll need significantly more to get the most out of it; reckon on European prices. If that's too much, head north to Dahab.

WHAT TO SEE AND DO

The **Heavenly Cathedral** ('Kineesa el Samayeen'; see map p99) is Sharm's biggest and newest Coptic church. Its construction was funded by three Christian businessmen and it was voted one of the world's ten most beautiful churches when finished in 2010.

The inside is covered with Biblical scenes such as The Creation and The Exodus. St John's vision of The Apocalypse stares ominously down from the ceiling. It was done by two Egyptian artists and their 17 assistants in a remarkable two years. The cathedral is in the Hay el Noor district, not far from the twin minarets of El Mustafa mosque.

With hotels so territorial about their coast, **public beaches** are the only way to see the sea on a budget. There's one in Sharm el Maya (see map p100) and another in Na'ama Bay (see map p101); both beaches open daily 8am-sunset, LE10 entry. Neither has a coral reef.

For details about **diving and snorkelling** in the area see box pp96-7. Equipment for all kinds of **water sports** (kayaks, catamarans, jet skis etc) can be rented in Na'ama Bay. Shark's Bay doesn't have the same range but everything's cheaper.

Quad biking might be fun but the erosion, noise and exhaust fumes damage desert wadis. Consider **Sinai Moto Cross** (see map p99) dirt track on Sharia Salem instead.

Mountain biking is more eco-friendly altogether and is offered by Blackjack Bike (mob ☎ 0122-370 3116, 🖥 www.blackjackbike.com).

PRACTICAL INFORMATION
Orientation
Sharm is a continuous strip of coastal development, but it has two main hubs.

The first hub is **Sharm el Maya** (see map p100; 'Old Sharm' or simply 'Sharm el Sheikh'), at the southern end of the town. It's home to the Old Market: an important local service centre.

The other is **Na'ama Bay** (see map p101), about 7km north up the coast. This is an upmarket district with big hotels, shopping malls and an all-night party scene. Sharm el Maya and Na'ama are connected by Sharia Salem (the Peace Road). There

are a few other areas to note: **Hadaba** (see map p99) is a hotel district on a clifftop plateau above Sharm el Maya; **Shark's Bay** is a sandy cove with a few hotels north of Na'ama Bay; up at the very northern end of the city is **Nabq**.

Arrival
By air Sharm's airport (**SSH**) is about 10km north of Na'ama Bay and 17km north of Sharm el Maya. Travel agents might vie for attention when you enter (they sell visas at a commission). Walk past and look for the foreign exchange bank windows to get your visa (see p16). They're within sight of

---

❑ DIVING AND SNORKELLING AROUND SHARM EL SHEIKH

Diving sites
Diving sites have suffered with the thousands of irresponsible visitors, but they're still rightly regarded as some of the best in the world. There are excellent options, including reefs and shipwrecks. A few suggestions follow but the level of previous experience needed for each differs. Chat to diving companies.

● **Sharm coastline** You can dive the snorkelling spots in the next section, so have a read of those too. Otherwise, look out for the Amphoras reef near Hadaba, where a few amphoras lie scattered on the reef; remnants of an old wreck. Pinky's Wall is a colourful reef nearby.

● **Tiran Island** A few kilometres off Sharm's coast, this offers excellent reef and wreck diving. Thomas Reef has an impressive canyon, whilst the nearby Gordon Reef is capped with the rusty old wreck of the *Loullia* (1981). Jackson Reef is home to the *Lara* (1982) wreck. Most of the ship lies deep below.

● **Ras Mohammed** This is the Red Sea's most famous dive destination. The Shark Observatory has an impressive vertical reef, whilst Jackfish Alley is known for its underwater caves. Shark and Yolanda give an unmissable diving excursion. You do them together, entering at Shark and letting the current carry you down to Yolanda. Here, cargo and other bits of the *Jolanda* (1980) wreck lie scattered across the reef (the ship is 200m below).

● **Thistlegorm** The *Dunraven* (1876), *Kingston* (1881) and *Million Hope* (1996) all offer excellent wreck-diving but the real gem is the *Thistlegorm* (1941). This was a British merchant ship sunk in a WWII bombing raid. It was carrying two locomotives along with a cargo of military trucks, motorbikes, Bren carriers, aircraft parts and so on. Most dive clubs in Sharm offer the trip.

Snorkelling sites
Sharm isn't snorkeller-friendly like Dahab: every bit of the coast is owned by big hotels and some charge LE200 for access. Some reefs come into season at different times; diving firms give the best tips on which to see.

● **Shark's Bay** A colourful reef, cut up by little channels that you can dive down and swim through. Sharks aren't very common, but there are several types of ray, as well

the passport control points, near a couple of ATMs.

Sharm's airport was once one of the toughest places to haggle a taxi in Egypt. Things changed in 2012, when authorities put up a sign showing these tariffs: Na'ama Bay, LE70; Shark's Bay, LE60; Hadaba/Sharm el Maya, LE100; Dahab, LE250; St Katherine, LE500. These are sometimes cheaper if you flag taxis down on the road outside the airport.

Bus and coach East Delta buses arrive at a station (see map p99) on Sharm's outer ring road, about 2km off Sharia Salem

(don't confuse it with the old station near Sharia Salem itself, which closed in 2010). Almost next door is another station where Go Bus/El Gouna, High Jet and Superjet buses come from Cairo.

A taxi is the easiest way to move on from either; it's about LE25-30 to Na'ama or Sharm el Maya.

Ferry port Sharm–Hurghada boats stopped years ago but they might return in 2014. Arriving at the port (see map p99), you can walk to the Old Market in 15 minutes or get a taxi for LE5-15; to Na'ama costs LE25-30.

---

as eels, squid, octopuses and lion fish. Umbi Shark's Bay Hotel charges a reasonable LE25 for daily access.

● **Ras Umm Sid** This is a big, vertical wall near the Ras Umm Sid headland. It's one of Sharm's most colourful and is also the easiest to access. The Renaissance Golden View Beach Resort charges LE70.

● **Na'ama Bay** A reef fringes the headland on the northern side of Na'ama Bay. Rent snorkels from Oonas Dive Club (€8/LE70) and you can use the Sonesta beach next door; this is the best place to start swimming from.

● **Middle/Far Gardens** These have impressive coral pinnacles. They're found a few kilometres round the headland from Na'ama Bay; too far to reach by swimming. They're accessed from the Hyatt Regency for LE200.

● **The Tower** An impressive, three-sided wall or 'tower' drops to the seabed here. It's half-way between Sharm el Maya and Na'ama Bay, down Tower St. The nearby Sharm Club Village charges about LE170.

Dive companies

Dive companies are found widely; check websites as they often have special deals. The following are some of the stand-outs: **Shark's Bay Umbi Diving Village** (☎ 069-360 0942, 💻 www.sharksbay.com); **Oonas Dive Club** (☎ 069-360 0581, 💻 www.oonasdiveclub.com); **Camel Dive Club** (☎ 069-360 0700, 💻 www.cameldive.com); **Sunshine Divers** (mob ☎ 0122-783 1388, 💻 www.sunshine-divers.de).

Diving safely in the Sinai

Most dive clubs maintain good safety standards, but a few operate below the level they should. Use well-known ones, or those run from big hotels.

The important thing isn't that they're PADI-accredited but that they're members of the CDWS (Chamber of Diving and Watersports). This is an Egyptian regulating body that maintains European-level safety standards, making regular checks on equipment, instructor qualifications and so on.

CDWS insignia should be seen around the dive club. If in any doubt as to a club's legitimacy, the CDWS website lists all its members as well as blacklisted illegal operators: 💻 www.cdws.travel/.

Local transport
Public minibuses These are dark blue
and run 24 hours, going up and down the
coast between Sharm el Maya and Nabq.
They're especially frequent along Sharia
Salem, between Sharm and Na'ama. Flag
them down and pass the money over the
heads in front. The fares are next to nothing. From Sharm el Maya you should pay
the following: Na'ama, LE1; Shark's Bay,
LE2-3; Nabq, LE5.

Official taxis These are blue and white.
Drivers rarely use meters so negotiate the
fare before leaving and aim for the follow-
ing rates from Sharm el Maya: Na'ama,
LE20-25; Shark's Bay, LE50-60; airport,
LE60-70; Nabq resorts, LE80-90. To go
from Na'ama to the airport or Shark's Bay,
LE40-60.

Car rental Cars are good for visiting Ras
Mohammed or the Nabq Protectorate. AVIS
(map p101; mob ☎ 0122-789 4063, 💻 www
.avisegypt.com) have an office on Sharia
Salem in Na'ama with various vehicles for
rent, including off-roaders. A normal car
starts from about US$40/LE240 per day.

Services
Airline offices Egypt Air (☎ 1717, 💻
www.egyptair.com; daily 9am-9pm) has an
office in Sharm el Maya.

Telecommunications The main **post
office** (see map p100; daily 8am-2pm, limited hours on Fridays) is in Hadaba. It's
always very busy so arrive before it opens.
   Fed Ex (map p101; ☎ 02-2268 7888, 💻
www.fedex.com/eg/; Sat-Thur, 9am-6pm)
has an office on Sharia Salem near Na'ama.
DHL (map p101; mob ☎ 0106-661 8017, 💻
www.dhlegypt.com; Sat-Thur, 10am-2pm &
4-8pm) is across the road and cheaper.
   The Old Market has the cheapest
internet cafés including. Speednet (see map p100;
daily, 24hrs, LE10/hr) is near the west gate,
down a small alleyway with an orange sign
over it. In Na'ama, there's Hi Max Internet
(see map p101; daily, 24 hours, LE20/hr),
above DHL. Wi-fi is becoming more widespread in hotels, restaurants and bars.

The **telephone centrale** (see map
p100; daily, 8am-10pm) is in Hadaba, near
the banks. Calls to Europe and North
America are about LE5/min.

Police The police station (see map p100)
is at the top of the road from Sharm el
Maya to Hadaba.

Banks and finances Most Arab **banks**
are on Sharia Benouk in Hadaba, including
Banque Misr and the National Bank of
Egypt (both Sun-Thur, 8.30am-2pm). All
offer exchange and have ATMs outside.
   Western banks are common in Na'ama
and there's an HSBC (Sun-Thur 8.30am-
5pm, Sat 10am-7pm) on Sharia Salem.
Barclays and BNP Paribas are next door
(both Sun-Thur, 8.30am-5pm).
   Exchange shops in the Old Market
usually give the best rates on foreign currency. Thomas Cook has branches in
Sharm el Maya and Na'ama. An increasing
number of **ATMs**, including several
Banque Misr and CIB ones, now do for-
eign-currency exchange too.
   Western Union (see map p101; ☎ 069-
360 2222; Sun-Thur, 9am-5pm) is next to
Tropicana Rosetta Hotel in Na'ama. Wire
transfers can be made.

Hospitals and health Sharm has some
of the best **hospitals** in Egypt. The pyramid-
shaped Sharm International Hospital (see
map p99; ☎ 069-366 0895), on Sharia
Salem, is the main public hospital.
   Also on Sharia Salem is South Sinai
Hospital (see map p99; ☎ 069-366 6020, 💻
www.southsinaihospital.com); a newer, private alternative. GP-style consultations are
available at smaller clinics.
   Hyperbaric Medical Center Sharm (see
map p99; ☎ 069-366 0922, emergency mob
☎ 0122-212 4292) is run by Dr Adel Taher,
a world authority on diving medicine. It has
two **hyperbaric chambers** including the
newest one in Egypt, opened in 2011.
   There's a third chamber at Sharm
International Hospital. The centre is also
Sharm's best GP-type clinic, dealing with
all sorts of everyday complaints.
(cont'd on p102)

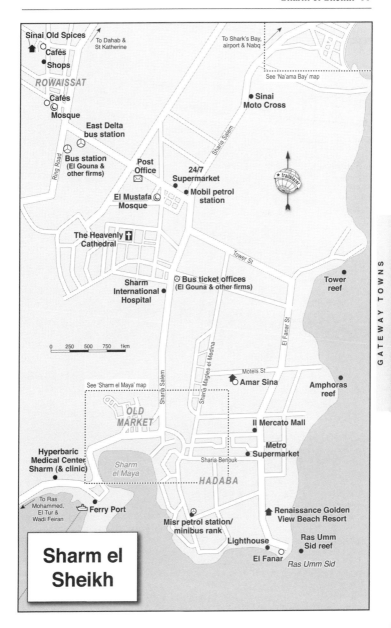

Sinai Old Spices
To Dahab & St Katherine
To Shark's Bay, airport & Nabq
See 'Na'ama Bay' map
Cafés
Shops
ROWAISSAT
Cafés
Mosque
Sinai Moto Cross
East Delta bus station
Ring Road
Bus station (El Gouna & other firms)
Post Office
24/7 Supermarket
Sharia Salem
El Mustafa Mosque
Mobil petrol station
The Heavenly Cathedral
Tower St
Bus ticket offices (El Gouna & other firms)
Tower reef
Sharm International Hospital
El Fanar St
0   250   500   750   1km
See 'Sharm el Maya' map
Sharia Salem
Sharia Maqles el Medina
Motels St
Amar Sina
Amphoras reef
OLD MARKET
Il Mercato Mall
Metro Supermarket
Sharm el Maya
Sharia Benouk
HADABA
Hyperbaric Medical Center Sharm (& clinic)
To Ras Mohammed, El Tur & Wadi Feiran
Ferry Port
Misr petrol station/ minibus rank
Renaissance Golden View Beach Resort
Ras Umm Sid reef
Lighthouse
El Fanar
Ras Umm Sid

GATEWAY TOWNS

Sharm el Sheikh

GATEWAY TOWNS

Sharm el Maya

HADABA

To Ras
Umm Sid

South Sinai
Protectorates
Office

Sharia Benouk

Main
Post
Office

Sharia Magles el Medina

Banque
Misr

National
Bank
of Egypt

Mosque

Aida Hotel

Telephone
Centrale

South Sinai
Governorate
Office

Police
Station

To Ras Umm Sid

Sharm International
Youth Hostel

● South Sinai
Hospital

Mosque

● Metro Supermarket

● Pharmacy

Post Office &
Telephone
Centrale

● High Jet
bus ticket
office &
stop

Shaira Salem

To Naama Bay,
Shark's Bay
& airport

Minibus
rank

Public
Beach

Egypt Air
Office

Kushari
el Sheikh

● El Sheikh

Sandy
Hotel

OLD
MARKET

El Masrien

Thomas
Cook Exchange

Tiran Center

Cobbler

Duty Free
Shop

Fares

Speednet

Safsafa

Minibus &
taxi rank

CIB Bank

Iberotel
Palace

Sharm el Maya

★ military

To Port,
Hyperbaric Medical Center
& Ras Mohammed

0   100   200   300m

Na'ama Bay

To Sharm Hyatt Regency, Shark's Bay, airport & Nabq

Sonesta Beach Resort & Casino

Thomas Cook

Shaia Salem

Sonesta Beach

Oonas Hotel & Dive Club

Na'ama Reefs

Na'ama Bay

Western Union

Pedestrian Esplanade

Hilton beach

Public beach

Hilton Fayrouz Resort

Tam Tam

Kanabesh Hotel

Pomodoro

CIB Bank

Hussein Salem St.

Bahrain St.

HSBC

King of

Fairuz

Radio Shack

Duty Free Shop

Camel Dive Club & Hotel

Na'ama Center

Sultan Qabos St.

Abou el Sid

Golden Pyramid Mall

Carrefour Supermarket

Yahya Delivery

Avis Car Hire

Shaia Salem

DHL/ Hi Max Internet

Marina Dental Clinic

FedEx

HSBC

To Sharm el Maya

0   100   200   300m

(cont'd from p98) **Pharmacies** are all over town and assistants usually speak decent English.

The **Marina Dental Clinic** (see map p101; ☎ 069-360 4809; Sat-Thur, 1-3pm & 7-10pm) of Dr Ashraf Mahmoudey is near the Fed Ex office in Na'ama.

Laundries, stitchers & cobblers The Old Market (see map p100) has **laundries**; most do items for LE1-3. In the same area are **stitchers and cobblers** who work with foot-pedal sewing machines. They can repair damaged trekking equipment (clothes, boots, rucksacks etc) and it's quick, cheap and absolutely worth it.

News stands and bookshops News stands at big international hotels sell newspapers, magazines and books. The Sinai's best **bookshops** are in Dahab.

Shopping
Visit a **duty-free shop** within 48 hours of arrival if you want to stock up on cigarettes and alcohol; see p18. There is one in Na'ama (map p101) and another in the Old Market (map p100). Take your passport and air/ferry ticket.

Radio Shack shops sell cameras, gadgets and **electrical items** and might help with minor repairs; they're the only places for it in the Sinai. There are shops in Il Mercato mall in Hadaba (map p101) and Sharia Salem in Na'ama (map p100).

Where to stay
Most hotels are high end, international brand types. Rates vary with the season and the following are just ballpark indicators. Check websites before you arrive as some hotels have special deals if you book ahead.

Budget accommodation Expect to pay about LE60-200 a night. To stay in Sharm on a rock-bottom budget go for the Sharm el Maya/Hadaba area. Everything is cheap there: food, transport and the internet.
● **Sharm el Maya and Hadaba (see maps pp99-100)** *Sandy Hotel* (☎ 069-366 1177) is outside the east gate to the Old Market. It's a popular place with Egyptians and has

friendly staff and a pool. Rooms have a dated 1970s' feel but with a/c and att, they're good value with singles from LE150 and doubles LE200.

The cheapest place in town is *Sharm el Sheikh International Youth Hostel* (☎ 069-366 0317, 🖳 www.hihostels.com), on the Hadaba clifftop. A berth in a two-person dorm with a/c costs LE60. Rooms are same-sex unless you're a married couple. There's no English sign: it's on Sharia Magles el Medina opposite Fares restaurant/Il Mercato St and it has a basketball court outside (for taxis, it's 'Bayt Shabab' in Arabic).
● **Shark's Bay** This is a quiet cove 7km north of Na'ama. It has a nice beach, a pretty reef and a notable Bedouin presence. Budget travellers are made to feel noticeably more welcome. *Shark's Bay Umbi Diving Village* (☎ 069-360 0942, 🖳 www .sharksbay.com) is the longest-running hotel here and something of a rarity for Sharm in that it's Bedouin owned. It offers huts with fans; singles/doubles are €17 (LE145)/€20 (LE170). Nicer cabins with a/c and att are singles/doubles €24/30.

Shark's Bay Oasis (☎ 069-360 0450, 🖳 www.sharkbayoasis.com) is next door; it rents attractive clifftop apartments with spacious living areas and kitchens. They're a bargain with singles for LE250 and doubles LE300. Friends could get a four-person apartment for LE500. *Sunshine Divers* (mob ☎ 0122-783 1388, 🖳 www.sunshine-divers.de) has a few rooms, with singles for LE160 and doubles LE250.
● **Rowaissat (see map p99)** This is a Bedouin suburb near the bus station. The only option is *Sinai Old Spices B&B* (mob ☎ 0128-336 0477, 🖳 www.sinaioldspices .com) but it warrants a special mention. It's run by a friendly Italian couple who go out of their way for you. Each room has its own decorative theme and a bathroom, mini kitchen, a/c and TV. There are just four rooms, with singles for LE150 and doubles LE240. It's good value but it's LE30 each way for a taxi into town, which adds to the costs. The owners will pick you up from wherever you arrive as it's hidden in obscure back streets and is hard to find.

Mid-priced hotels These would be classed as expensive elsewhere in the Sinai but Sharm's stratospheric level of opulence keeps them in the mid-price bracket here. All have a/c and bathrooms and prices range from LE250-600.

● **Sharm el Maya and Hadaba (see maps pp99-100)** The best option in **Sharm el Maya** is *Iberotel Palace* (☎ 069-366 1111, 💻 www .iberotel.com). The beach doesn't have coral but you get free access to other Iberotels, which have their own reefs. Singles start at €47 (LE400) with doubles from €62 (LE530).

Aida Hotel (☎ 069-366 0720, 💻 www .aidahotelsharm.com/index.htm) is on the clifftop in **Hadaba** and the real pull is the incredible city view; it extends over the Old Market to the twin minarets of the El Mustafa mosque and the rugged mountains beyond. Singles start from LE220 and doubles LE480. *Amar Sina* (☎ 069-366 2224) is nearby on the so-called Motels St. Rooms are decorated in an Arabian style with domes, arches and mosaics, and it's a nice boutique option. It's also reasonable value, with singles for LE250-320 and doubles LE350-420.

Sharm Renaissance Golden View Beach Resort (☎ 069-366 4694, 💻 www .marriott.co.uk) is on El Fanar St in Hadaba. It's one of the nicest, with the Ras Umm Sid reef on its doorstep (see box p97). Singles go from US$68 (LE405) and doubles US$80 (LE475).

● **Shark's Bay** To upgrade from the budget hotels go for a higher-priced room at *Shark's Bay Umbi Diving Village* (see box p97). Most come with an impressive clifftop view, with singles from €35 (LE300) and doubles €45 (LE380). There are more expensive hotels but they're not on the main bay, which is the real attraction of staying here in the first place.

● **Na'ama Bay (see map p101)** *Camel Dive Club & Hotel* (☎ 069-360 0700, 💻 www.cameldive.com) is a friendly, laid-back place. The only downside is that it's next to the Ministry of Sound's Pacha Club, with its thumping, night-long raves. Expect to pay about €70 (LE590) for a single and €90 (LE760) for a double.

Oonas Dive Club Hotel (☎ 069-360 0581, 💻 www.oonasdiveclub.com) has a similar vibe but is in a quieter location at the northern end of Na'ama Bay. It's a good-value option, with singles from €45 (LE380) and doubles €60 (LE510). Rooms have balconies looking out on the bay and a group of friends can get a four-person suite for €152 (LE1290).

Kanabesh Village (☎ 069-360 0184), on the promenade, is an Egyptian-owned hotel with a more down-to-earth vibe than its neighbours. The rooms aren't so luxurious but they're perfectly habitable and good value with singles from LE360 (US$60) and doubles LE420 (US$70).

Hilton Fayrouz Resort (☎ 069-360 0136, 💻 www.hilton.com) is next door and a notch higher, with an excellent beach for water sports. Singles go from US$100 (LE560); doubles, US$120 (LE720).

Expensive hotels These are a long way from the dusty cobblers' streets of the Old Market. Expect to be treated like a king, and put a king-sized budget aside to pay for it: prices start from around US$120 (LE720).

● **Shark's Bay** *Four Seasons* (☎ 069-362 1200, 💻 www.fourseasons.com) is just north of Shark's Bay. This is the best hotel in town with singles from US$260 (LE1550) and doubles from US$290 (LE1725). Just for the record, the Royal Suite is the most expensive place you can stay in the Sinai. It covers 500 sq metres, has two king-size beds, three marble bathrooms, a powder room, several walk-in wardrobes, a private beach, a garden, pool and whirlpool.

● **Na'ama Bay (see map p101)** *Sonesta Beach Resort and Casino* (☎ 069-360-0725, 💻 www.sonesta.com), near Oonas Dive Club & Hotel, is the top five-star option in the main bay. Rooms have an appealing Islamic design and singles go from US$120 (LE720) and doubles US$150 (LE900).

Sharm Hyatt Regency (☎ 069-360 1234, 💻 www.hyatt.com) is a short way up the road from Na'ama, offering a similar level of luxury to the Four Seasons. Singles

GATEWAY TOWNS

start from US$125 (LE745); doubles, US$160 (LE955).

Where to eat
Budget food The **Old Market** (see map p100) has the best budget eating. *El Sheikh* café is the top pick, offering an excellent range of sandwiches for LE2-3 (try the *shakshouka*). Walk up from the east gate; it's just before the fruit stalls. *Kushari el Sheikh* is further up and sells good, filling bowls of *kushari*.

Budget eating is harder in **Na'ama Bay** (see map p101); *Yahya Delivery*, near the Golden Pyramid Mall on Sharia Salem, is the only real place for it, with *fuul*, *taameya* and other sandwiches from LE2.

Seafood Sharm rivals Alexandria as Egypt's number one seafood city. Everything is caught and cooked on the same day. What's left is boiled into soups for the next one.

The **Old Market** (see map p100) has the best options and most restaurants are clustered around the west gate. Locals put *Fares* down as the top pick. For something small, quiet and a bit more personal try *Safsafa*.

Middle Eastern Na'ama Bay (see map p101) has the best options. *Abou El Sid*, on Sultan Qabous St, above Hard Rock Café, does Egyptian dishes such as stuffed pigeon and kushari. *Fairuz*, nearby in the Na'ama Center, is a popular Lebanese place. *Tam Tam*, on the promenade, is also good for Lebanese dishes. *El Masrien*, in the Old Market, specialises in traditional meat grills.

Other options *El Fanar* (see map p99), near Ras Umm Sid lighthouse, offers **Italian-style** cuisine. It's a higher-end option with big Red Sea views, especially beautiful at sunset. In Na'ama Bay, *Pomodoro* (see map p101) offers good Italian and international cuisine.

McDonalds, KFC and other **fast-food** places are dotted around in Na'ama Bay and in Il Mercato mall in Hadaba (near the youth hostel).

Self catering **Metro** (see map p99 and p100) and **Carrefour** see map p101) have supermarket chains. They sell things from home such as hobnob biscuits, porridge oats and Earl Grey tea. Buy any special food you want before going inland (see pp53-5).

Evening entertainment
Sharm has bars, casinos and raves till sunrise. If you're coming straight from the desert you might just prefer a relaxed beer somewhere like the Camel Bar, above the hotel of the same name. There are *shisha* cafés in the Old Market.

Moving on
Sharm is well connected to most places except St Katherine. To get to St Katherine go to Dahab and find onward transport there (see p115). For Wadi Feiran, go to El Tur and get a minibus or taxi (see p121).

By bus East Delta runs the following services: Dahab, 9am, 3pm, 5pm and 8.30pm (LE20, 1-1½hrs); Nuweiba, 9am and 5pm (LE25, 2½-4hrs); Taba, 9am (LE25, 3½-5hrs); El Tur, buses every 30 minutes between 7am and 3.30pm (LE11, 1¼-1¾hrs); Cairo, nine buses between 7.30am and 1am (LE80, 8-9hrs); Luxor, 6pm (LE110, 14-16hrs). All buses go from East Delta bus station (map p99).

Other buses go to Cairo from a station (also map p99) near the East Delta one. **Go Bus/El Gouna** (☎ hotline 19567) has 13 buses daily (LE45-135). Look out for the 'elite' night bus at 2am, with big seats and complimentary food (LE135). **High Jet** (☎ hotline 16108) has seven buses a day between 9.30am and 2am (LE55).

Superjet has five through the day and night at similar rates. Buy tickets at the main bus station or in outlets opposite Sharm International Hospital, near an NPCO garage.

By service taxi Service taxis go to El Tur, Cairo and Delta towns such as Tanta from outside the East Delta station. They're cramped and uncomfortable so buses are best.

By private taxi Private taxis can be used to go anywhere at these rates: Dahab, LE150-220; Nuweiba, LE350-400; Taba, LE400-450; El Tur, LE150-200; St Katherine, LE350-400. Taxi drivers are used to getting inflated fares so dig your heels in and haggle hard.

To go to the trekking towns you can find Bedouin drivers in St Katherine on p131 and in Nuweiba on p228.

EXCURSIONS FROM SHARM EL SHEIKH

Side trip to Ras Mohammed National Park [map p106]

Ras Mohammed ('The Head of Mohammed') is the southernmost tip of the Sinai. It's a small headland that divides the two Gulfs and is fringed all the way round with beautiful coral reefs. They brim with every one of the Red Sea's 1000 species of fish and it was this exceptional marine diversity that saw it declared Egypt's first-ever National Park in the 1980s. It remains the only one in the Sinai today. Out of the water it's a scene of barren, windswept desolation and only foxes, gazelles and a few other hardy desert creatures eke out an existence. You can visit on a dive boat where you snorkel reefs a few hundred metres out to sea. Alternatively, go by land and snorkel the reefs nearer the shore. You could camp here too.

Getting there The park is about 15km outside Sharm on the road to El Tur. Taxis will drive you there and around the various sites for LE300-400 per half day. A better option would be to rent your own transport. It's US$5 per vehicle and US$5 per person for entry. The park opens from sunrise to sunset, but rangers aren't always up at the crack of dawn so go at about 7am.

Camping You need a photocopy of your passport ID page. The US$5 entry fee covers the first night of camping and it's US$5 for each following night. There's a designated site on *Khashaba Beach*, behind the Visitor Centre. A Bedouin man rents tents for LE100/night and LE150/night with food but you can wander to a quieter spot. Take a lot of water, and gas to cook with as there's no wood.

Snorkelling sites Signposted dirt tracks connect the main sites and you could wander between them in a long afternoon. See the map on p106 and consider the following:

● **Main Beach** This has a nice reef but it can get busy with tour groups.
● **Observatory Beach** This is a small, little-visited cove just round the headland from the Main Beach, directly under the Shark Observatory. It's a good spot for bigger species such as turtles and wrasses.

GATEWAY TOWNS

❏ **Protectorates and national parks**
There are four special Protected Areas or '**Protectorates**' in South Sinai. The biggest is the St Katherine Protectorate, covering 4350 sq km of the southern mountains. The others are on the east coast and include Nabq, Ras Abu Galum and Taba.

Alongside these is the **National Park** at Ras Mohammed. A National Park differs from a Protectorate in that it has a higher level of protection; permanent human settlement is forbidden and visiting hours are limited.

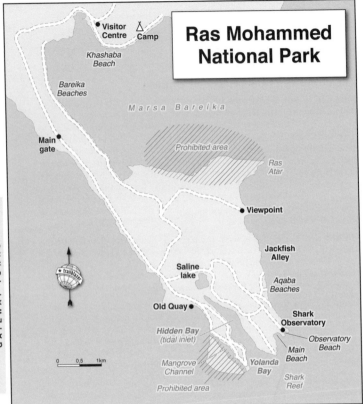

Ras Mohammed National Park

- **Yolanda Bay** This is the southernmost beach in Ras Mohammed, with another impressive reef. The Yolanda dive site lies further out but don't try and swim as the currents are strong enough to sweep you away.
- **Old Quay** On the east side of Ras Mohammed, this is one of the few sites in the Gulf of Suez. It's probably the best too, with steep, colourful coral cliffs, all bursting with big schools of fish.

Things to see on land Nothing compares to what's under the water but a few sights enliven the barren walks. There's a stand of **mangroves** (see box opposite) near the tip of the headland.

Hidden Bay is a tidal inlet where migrating birds flock (see box p62). Look out for an evaporated **saline lake**, where you can get a bit of salt for a camp meal. Also of note is a **high lookout point** to Sharm and the **Shark Observatory**, another high lookout with a free binocular station.

> ### ❏ Mangroves
> Mangroves grow in tidal zones where most plants would die. They tolerate salinity by extracting salt from the sea water and excreting it through special glands on their leaves. If the leaves become too full of salt they drop off. The roots are special 'air roots' or 'pneumatophores' that stick up above the water most of the day for oxygen. They grow as a thick mat, dense enough to trap sediment and cushion the mangroves from breaking waves. Mangroves provide a home for crabs, molluscs, birds and insects. Sometimes hyenas swim in the swamps, looking for prey.

Side trip to the Nabq Protected Area   [map p108]

Nabq stretches up the coast from Sharm, covering 600 sq km. The northern stretches have beautiful, rugged foothills, but the rest is mostly just a monotonous seaboard plain. Coral reefs and mangrove swamps fringe the shallow shores, and a few Bedouin villages dot the beaches.

Most visitors skip Nabq for Ras Mohammed and, whilst it's true Ras has better coral, Nabq has an excellent shipwreck you can snorkel from the shore. It also has a superb campsite so, at least if you're going overnight, go to Nabq.

Getting there The main entrance is from the Sharm–Dahab coastal road but you can drive straight in through the Nabq resort area too (at the very northern end of Sharm). Take the main road through here and follow a dirt track off from a little roundabout near the end. The Tropicana Sea Beach and Albatross Moderna hotels are seen shortly before. It's US$5 per vehicle and US$5 per person and the park opens 8.30am to sunset.

Dirt tracks are deep in places and normal cars only just got through in 2012. An off-road vehicle would be safer.

Camping Camping is covered by the US$5 entry fee for the first night and it's the same for each following night. Take a photocopy of your passport ID page (rules are enforced). The designated *campsite* is opposite the *Maria Schroder* shipwreck.

Fires are allowed and you can sometimes buy fresh-caught fish at the Bedouin village of **Ghargana**, further south on the coast.

What to see and do There is no need to wander over long distances. Most sights are around the *Maria Schroder* wreck.

● **Mangroves** Nabq has 5km of mangroves (see box above) and they're the most northerly ones anywhere in the Indian and Pacific Ocean basins. The one near the *Maria Schroder* is called the Ruweissia mangrove.

● **Shipwreck** The *Maria Schroder* hit the reef in 1956 and has been crumbling here slowly since. It's easy to wade out and swim around but do it on a calm day without swell. Never swim under overhanging bits of metal: half the ship has already collapsed and these are the next to go.

● **Coral reefs** Nabq has up to 200 species of coral and 350 species of fish in its reefs. It's possible to snorkel but sediments often wash out of the mangroves to limit visibility. The best reef is Nakhlet El Tal.

● **Visitor Centre** This is near the *Maria Schroder*. It's open daily (8.30am to sunset) and has a display on the environment. Even so, with its broken windows and doors it's in need of a makeover from the authorities.

To Dahab

Ras Tantour

El Monquatta mangroves

Maria Schroder wreck

Ruweissia mangrove lagoon

Visitors' Centre, campsite & toilets

0 1 2 3km

Main gate

Wadi Khereiza / Wadi Kidd

Arak plant dunes (restricted access)

Abu Zabad mangroves

Coastal Highway

GHARGANA

□ **Nakhlet el Tal**
□
□

Ghargana mangroves

Wadi Umm Adawi

Nabq Oasis

Nabq Protectorate

Coastal gate

To Sharm

GATEWAY TOWNS

Dahab

Dahab is a small town 85km north of Sharm el Sheikh. It's set on a coast of rugged mountains and sandy shores and it looks out to the beautiful Hejaz ranges of Arabia. Travellers discovered it a few decades ago and it has since grown into one of Egypt's most vibrant independent travel hubs. There's a good social mix here: a big expat community, plenty of Western students from Cairo and a continuous stream of young Egyptians.

The Bedouin are more visible than in Sharm and the whole place has a laid-back and down-to-earth feel. You can get by on a low budget and all the snorkelling in town is free. Added attractions are excellent diving and the Protectorate of Ras Abu Galum (see pp115-16). Dahab is a major gateway to the desert and mountains and simply a good place to relax.

WHAT TO DO

The Sinai has epic potential for **rock climbing**. There are longer routes in the mountains but the most popular spots are near Dahab, in Wadi Gnai. Grades range from easy to extreme and a few firms offer trips. Desert Divers (☎ 069-364 0500, 🖥 www.desert-divers.com) have climbs from €55 (LE460) and Above Sea Level (mob ☎ 0109-921 7029, 🖥 www.abovesealevel.co.uk) offer them for €45 (LE380). The Expedition Consultancy (🖥 www.expeditioncon sultancy.com, UK ☎ 020-3291 2312) is a UK outfit that has been developing climbing in the Sinai for years and it's a good source of further information.

Dahab is one of the world's top **windsurfing** spots, with 80% of the days windy between autumn and spring. The hub is the Laguna area. Up in Masbat Fantasea (☎ 069-364 1373) rent inflatable **sea kayaks** with transparent bottoms; great for paddling along the bay looking at the reef below.

For details about **diving and snorkelling** in the area see box p110.

PRACTICAL INFORMATION

Orientation

Dahab is a strip of coastal development divided into three areas. The southernmost area is **Mashraba** (see map p113) and its main thoroughfare is Mashraba St. Further up, this gives way to Masbat, which bends around the town's main bay. **Assalah** (see map p112) is further north and beyond it Dahab ends and an open coastline starts. You can walk between the three areas on a promenade.

Quite disconnected from here is a modern town area known as **Dahab City** (see map p112). It's the administrative centre and close by is an area called **The Laguna** (see map p112), a sheltered lagoon behind a big coastal spit where most high-end hotels are based.

Arrival

East Delta buses arrive in Dahab City; a taxi to town is LE10-20.

Local transport

Dahab is pedestrian-friendly but the various modes of transport available are still useful.

Bicycles Use these around town or for reaching outlying snorkelling sites. You can rent them along Mashraba St, with prices varying from LE25 to LE40 per day (plus a deposit).

Taxis Official taxis are white and orange but plain cars operate too. None of these has a meter so agree the fare before you go. A short ride around town is about LE10.

Private transport Scooters are available on Mashraba St for about LE150 per day; they're good for getting to snorkelling sites (always get a helmet). Cars are little use unless you want to go further afield. The Hilton has a rental place.

Services
Dahab's big expat population means it is well stocked with essentials. Get special food and enough hard cash before you go inland.

Banks and finances ATMs are dotted around town. For **foreign exchange**, the National Bank of Egypt (Sun-Thur, 8am-2pm) is at the southern end of Mashraba St. The CIB bank (Sun-Thur, 9am-5pm) is close and it has a 24-hour foreign exchange ATM. Banque Misr in the Hilton is useful too. It's the only bank open daily, working 9am-9pm and catering to non-guests.

Hospitals and health Dahab Central Hospital is in Dahab City; it's the main

GATEWAY TOWNS

❏ DIVING AND SNORKELLING FROM DAHAB

Dahab has excellent dive sites and all can be snorkelled. Snorkelling is easy as the coast is public property, unlike in Sharm or Nuweiba. Masks, snorkels and fins can be rented locally at reasonable rates.

● **The Blue Hole** This is a world-famous dive site where a huge sinkhole plunges 100m down in the seabed. The edges are fringed with beautiful coral and swimming over it feels like flying. It's about 12km north of Dahab (map p116) and dive clubs run buses out here in the morning (all tearing along a hair-raising dirt track). Taxis are about LE40-60; LE70-100 if the driver waits an hour to take you back. It's best to arrive just after sunrise; you'll have the whole place to yourself at this time, and it's a special place to be.

● **The Canyon** This is a big chasm in the sea bed. It has a famous coral hollowing called 'The Fish Bowl' at the end, but this was closed in 2011 to stop further damage from divers. It's on the road to the Blue Hole, where the tarmac section ends and the dirt track begins. A taxi costs about LE30-40 one way.

● **Eel Garden** A writhing mat of eels is sometimes seen on the sea bed here. It's off the Assalah promenade (see map p112), a few minutes north of the Coral Coast Hotel. Take care as currents can develop in high winds.

● **The Lighthouse Reef** A popular reef (see map p113) in the main bay. It gets crowded with beginners and women report harassment being especially bad.

● **The Islands** At the very southern end of the Mashraba promenade (see map p112), this is the richest reef in town, being comparatively little-visited.

● **Three Pools and Southern Oasis** About 10km south of Dahab and a favourite with locals. There are three coral pools and you can swim from one to the next. A taxi costs LE40-60 one way.

Dive companies

These are found widely and amongst the best are: **Sea Dancer** (☎ 069-364 0887, 🖳 www.seadancerdivecenter.com); **Poseidon Divers** (☎ 069-364 0091, 🖳 www.posei dondivers.com); **Fantasea** (☎ 069-364 1373, 🖳 www.fantaseadiving.com); **Penguin Divers** (☎ 069-364 0117, 🖳 www.penguindivers.com); and **Sunsplash Divers** (☎ 069-364 0932, 🖳 www.sunsplash-divers.com).

Dubious firms operate in places; see p97.

public **hospital**. A smaller private option is Dahab Specialized Hospital (☎ 069-364 2714). Smaller clinics do GP consultations or simple operations, the best being Sadek Polyclinic (mob ☎ 0122-348 6209) on Mashraba St. It has one of the few female doctors in the Sinai, plus its own **dental practice**, and it's open daily, 10am-11pm.

Pharmacies are found all over town, some are open 24 hours.

Hyperbaric Medical Center (mob ☎ 0100-143 3325, or ☎ 069-366 0922) is just past Swiss Inn Resort and it has the best **hyperbaric chamber** and doctors. Dahab Specialized Hospital has a chamber that's used only if the previous place is full.

Telecommunications Dahab **Post Office** (Sat-Thur, 8am-2pm) is in Dahab City and does **poste restante**. It gets busy so arrive ten minutes before it opens.

The **telephone centrale** (Sat-Thur, 8am-4pm) is next door and does cheap international calls; LE5 per minute to Europe and North America.

Internet cafés and wi-fi Internet cafés are widespread and most open late morning until about 2am, charging LE5-8/hr. DSL Online is a 24hr option at the northern end of Mashraba St.

Budget camps, hotels, and many restaurants have **wi-fi**.

Photography The Snapper Photo Lab, near the bridge in Masbat, does passport photos.

Police The police station is on the south side of the Masbat bay.

Supermarkets Ghazala supermarket is open 24 hours and stocks Western products. It's near the police station in Masbat Bay.

Bookshops Dahab is the only place in the Sinai with decent bookshops. There's a good second-hand one called Safari 1, opposite New Sphinx Resort in Mashraba (though at the time of research the owners were considering moving to new premises). It stocks hundreds of titles in every

genre (all leftover holiday material). Haggle the prices down as they're all marked new.

Barbers You can try a traditional cut-throat razor shave at the Why Not? barber (LE20) near the New Sphinx Resort. A traditional Egyptian *fatla* shave can be done too, where a string is vibrated over your eyebrows, ears and nose.

Laundry Go to Mashraba St; it's LE2-3 per item on a next-day basis.

Where to stay

Budget Dahab began as a budget destination and it still has good options today (though since the revolution some places have become a bit shabby round the edges). Beds go for as little as LE15-120.

Mashraba has the biggest range of budget facilities and is the best overall place to stay. Only rooms with higher prices should be expected to have a/c and att.

● **Mashraba** (see map p113) *Ghazala Hotel* (mob ☎ 0100-117 5869, 💻 www.ghazaladahab.com) is at the southern end of Mashraba. The rooms have nice Arab dome ceilings, with a/c and att. Singles start at LE90 with doubles LE120.

Jowhara (mob ☎ 0109-206 9005, 💻 www.jowhara.com), further up Mashraba St, is a Bedouin-run place with rooms from LE50. Not far from here is *Penguin* (☎ 069-364 1047, 💻 www.penguindahab.com), one of the most popular budget options. It's clean and comfortable but the staff can border on the puerile. Singles start at LE60 and doubles LE80, with prices rising through other options. Dorm beds are LE25.

Bishbishi Garden Village (☎ 069-364 0727, 💻 www.bishbishi.com) is just a short way from here. It's a backpacker hive with huts from LE40 and LE60. The accommodation isn't the cleanest but the breakfasts are good.

Bedouin Lodge (☎ 069-364 1125, 💻 www.bedouin-lodge-dahab.com) is nearby with singles from LE85 and doubles LE110; not the best value for local rates. *Auski* (mob ☎ 0100-888 7102) is next door and has clean huts from LE40. *Sindbad*

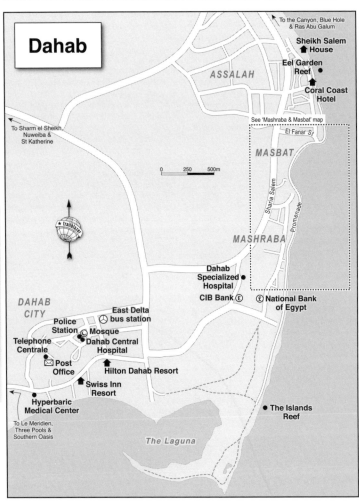

Dahab

To the Canyon, Blue Hole & Ras Abu Galum

Sheikh Salem House

Eel Garden Reef

Coral Coast Hotel

ASSALAH

To Sharm el Sheikh, Nuweiba & St Katherine

See 'Mashraba & Masbat' map

El Fanar St

MASBAT

0   250   500m

Sharia Salem

Promenade

MASHRABA

Dahab Specialized Hospital

CIB Bank £

£ National Bank of Egypt

DAHAB CITY

East Delta bus station

Police Station

Mosque

Telephone Centrale

Dahab Central Hospital

Post Office

Hilton Dahab Resort

Swiss Inn Resort

Hyperbaric Medical Center

To Le Meridien, Three Pools & Southern Oasis

The Islands Reef

The Laguna

Camp is a basic, Bedouin place but friendly and cheap with singles from LE35.

● **Masbat** (see map opposite) Everything is off the promenade around the bay. At the southern end, near Ghazala supermarket, is *Crazy Camel Camp* (mob ☎ 0100-557 5161); a basic Bedouin camp with singles from LE50 and doubles LE60.

Over the bridge is *Alaska Camp and Hotel* (☎ 069-364 1004, 🖳 www.dahab escape.com). The rooms are clean and comfortable but they don't have a/c which makes LE80 for singles and LE150 for doubles slightly overpriced.

Seven Heaven Hotel (☎ 069-364 0080, 🖳 www.7heavenhotel.com) is the

To Canyon, Blue Hole
& Ras Abu Galum

El Fanar St

Sindbad
Camp

Alf Leila

MASBAT

Red Sea
Relax Resort

The
Lighthouse

Dahab Coach
House

Lighthouse
Reef

Carm Inn

Sharia Salem

Seven
Heaven

El Fanar

*Masbat
Bay*

Snapper
Photo Lab

Blue House

Alaska Camp
& Hotel

0   50   100 150m

Bridge

Bookshop

Crazy Camel
Camp

The Kitchen

Ghazala
Supermarket

Police
Station

Abo el Reesh Café
(good for taxis)

DSL Online
(24hrs)

Nabataean
Port

Mosque

Pharmacy
(24hrs)

Mashraba St

King
Chicken

Nesima

Nesima Bar

Bookshop

Taxi Rank

El Masreen

Auski Camp/
Bedouin Lodge

Yum Yum

Safari 1

New Sphinx Resort

Bishbishi
Garden Village

Acacia Hotel

Sahara

MASHRABA

Penguin

Penguin
Restaurant

Jowhara

Lakhbatita

Sadek Polyclinic/
dentist

Mashraba St

Ghazala
Hotel

**Mashraba
& Masbat**

★ trailblazer

cheapest place in town, with dorm beds for LE15. A range of other rooms go up to LE120. The owners are friendly Upper Egyptians but the huge backpacker vibe won't appeal to everyone.

Well-worth a look is the travellers' dormitory at *Red Sea Relax Resort* (☎ 069-364 1309, 🖳 www.red-sea-relax.com). Everything is well-chilled by a/c and you can use the resort facilities: pool, gym and so on. Beds are just LE40.

● **Assalah** (see map p112) Assalah is quieter, with a more detached feel. *Sheikh Salem House* (mob ☎ 0122-730 4871, 🖳 www.sheikhsalemhouse.com) is on the northern edge of the city; a place to get away. It's owned by the family of a local Muzeina Sheikh and offers a range of rooms with singles from LE80 and doubles LE90.

Mid range These are mostly local-run places with prices ranging from LE150 to LE450. All rooms have a/c and att.

● **Mashraba** (see map p113) *Acacia* (☎ 069-364 0401, 🖳 www.acaciadahab.com) is a good, newly renovated hotel in the middle of Mashraba. It has nice singles from LE250 and doubles from LE350.

New Sphinx Resort is nearby and you walk in between the outstretched paws of a sphinx. It has nice simple singles from LE150 and doubles from LE180; it offers the best value.

Nesima (☎ 069-364 0320, 🖳 www.nesima-resort.com) has the nicest rooms; all dimly lit with ceiling domes and attractive decor. It's a bit of a price hike with singles for LE430 and doubles LE565.

● **Masbat** (see map p113) *Dahab Coach House* (mob ☎ 0100-981 1321, 🖳 www.dahabcoachhouse.dk) is the best-kept secret here. It's a small, tranquil place, run by a Danish couple, with singles for LE335 and doubles LE350. From the promenade, turn into an alleyway signposted to the 'Sabry Palace', near the Sea Dancer dive centre.

Alf Leila (mob ☎ 0100-612 8484, 🖳 www.alfleilahotel.com) is set away from the sea entirely. It's a boutique-style option and each room has a name and its own decorative theme. The room called Cinnamon is a stand-out so ask to see if it's available.

Prices start from about LE300 for a single and LE350 for a double.

● **Assalah** (see map p112) Further up the promenade is *Coral Coast Hotel* (☎ 069-364 1195, 🖳 www.fantaseadiving.com), a big hotel which at least aims at eco-friendliness. The bathrooms have water-saving devices and it sources vegetables from local Bedouin gardens. Singles are LE270 with doubles LE320.

Expensive These are mostly international-brand hotels and they're found in their own colony around the Laguna. The rooms have a/c, att and all the other things you'd expect for these prices.

● **The Laguna** (see map p112) The most luxurious option is *Swiss Inn Resort Dahab* (☎ 069-364 0471, 🖳 www.swissinn.net), with singles from US$160 (LE952) and doubles US$200 (LE1190).

Better value is *Le Meridien* (☎ 069-364 0426, 🖳 www.lemeridiendahab.com) with its nice beach and reef. Singles are US$100 (LE595) and doubles US$110 (LE655).

Hilton Dahab Resort (☎ 069-364 0310, 🖳 www.hilton.com) is the oldest and cheapest with rooms from US$80 (LE475).

Where to eat
One of Dahab's big pulls is the food. There's excellent eating at every budget level and it's a good place for a last supper before the desert.

Budget food The best budget cafés are on Mashraba St. *Yum Yum* does good sandwiches for around LE2-3 (always good at breakfast). *El Masreen* is close by, offering a similarly superb selection of sandwiches at even better prices (all stuffed to the brim). *King Chicken*, further along, does generously sized meals of chicken, rice and soup from LE17.

More expensive options Dahab's promenade (see map p113) is an uninterrupted line of restaurants and main courses cost LE30-50. Most menus stick to the same formula but one stand-out is *Lakhbatita*, with excellent Mediterranean and Middle Eastern fare. It's on the promenade by the Penguin Hotel and, rather confusingly, its sign reads 'Ramez and Paola'.

Penguin and *Sahara* are nearby, offering food in big cushion lounge settings.

Up in Masbut, *The Kitchen* serves Asian food on a roof terrace with big bay views, good at sunset.

Blue House, outside Seven Heaven Camp, is a Thai restaurant with its own Thai chef; an expat favourite. Not far away is *El Fanar*, an atmospheric place with excellent seafood.

Carm Inn, further up the promenade, serves a varied international cuisine, and is another good choice.

Evening entertainment
Masbat is the main nightlife spot with bars, live music nights and the odd disco. The Mashraba promenade is quieter and *Nesima bar* is a nice, quiet place to get a drink. Mashraba St has a few *shisha cafés*.

Organising a trek in Dahab
It's possible to organise desert treks in Dahab. Guides and fixers are found easily and several agencies are listed on p11. Even so, prices are higher and Nuweiba is an overall better spot.

Moving on
Dahab is a transport hub but there's no bus to St Katherine. The only scheduled option is the twice-weekly Bedouin bus.

By public bus East Delta has these services: Sharm, 11 buses, 8am-10.30pm (LE20, 1-1½hrs); Nuweiba, 10.30am, 6.30pm (LE15, 1-1½hrs); Taba, 10.30am (LE15, 2½-3½hrs) El Tur, 8am, 10am, 10pm (LE20, or use a Cairo bus); Cairo, 9am, 12.30pm, 3pm and 10pm (LE90, 9-10 hrs); Luxor, 4pm (LE120, 16-18hrs).

By private taxi The taxi rank is at the northern end of Mashraba St. Another good place for taxis is Abo el Reesh café on Sharia Salem. Haggle for these rates: Sharm, LE150-220; Tur Sina, LE200-250; Nuweiba, LE150-200; Taba, LE250-300; St Katherine, LE200-220.

By minibus Bedouin Bus (💻 www.bedouinbus.com) runs minibuses to St Katherine at 5pm on Tuesdays and Fridays, leaving from outside Jowhara Hotel. You can use it to get to desert trailheads including Ein Hudera, the Nawamis village and Wadi Arada (see p230). When it isn't running, there are other options.

Budget camps organise minibuses to Mount Sinai every night. Try Seven Heaven; they're laid-back and don't care if you're not a guest. Most buses leave around 11pm (going for the sunrise climb) and tickets are about LE70 (make it clear you're going one-way and don't want to climb Mount Sinai). Services are reduced on Thursdays and Saturdays (with the Monastery of St Katherine closed on the following Fridays and Sundays).

GATEWAY TOWNS

Excursion to Ras Abu Galum Protected Area   [map p116]
Ras Abu Galum is the most beautiful of the Sinai's coastal protectorates (see box p105). The mountains dip into the edge of the sea here: the Bedouin say it's where they both kiss. It's a place of wild rugged peaks and lonely lagoons and it's especially rich with wildlife (some say the Sinai's last leopard was shot here in 1996). A few days wandering around here is never wasted.

Getting there Get a taxi to the Blue Hole for LE40-60. A camel track starts behind the restaurants, running over the low pass of Naqb Shahin. After this, it descends to continue straight up the coast.

It takes about 1-1½ hours to walk to the Protectorate, marked by an abandoned ranger's office and the Bedouin village of Dahayla. Alternatively, get a 4x4, turning off the main Dahab to Nuweiba highway. A track leads down

Wadi Rasasah, about 20km south of Nuweiba.

Things to do Ras Abu Galum has untapped potential. Ask questions and you'll find interesting places to explore. The following are a few suggestions:

● **The Blue Lagoon** A sheltered lagoon a few kilometres north of Dahayla.

A *camp* offers empty huts with mattresses for LE25 (water and food are available). It's idyllic but the mosquitoes are horrendous so bring repellent.

● **Snorkel Dahayla reef** There's a reef at Dahayla and a few deeper diving sites elsewhere.

Ras Mamlah is popular but access to its underwater cave system was barred a while back, after some divers got lost and died.

● **Wadi el Uqdah** A rugged wadi with a dramatic narrow section and a spring. It opens near Dahayla and is a good place to explore and camp. There are other nice wadis too; Bedouin guides might be found in Dahayla.

● **Trek to Nuweiba** Hire a camel at Dahayla and follow the coastal track up to Nuweiba. The trek can be done in two days. It's more interesting than the bus and you should pay about LE150-200 per day.

Taba

Taba is one of the Sinai's most important international gateways. It has a land border with Israel and an airport that handles flights from Europe. It's also

❏ **People of the wilderness**
The wilderness marks every part of Bedouin culture; even the name. Bedouin is *Bedu* in Arabic, a derivative of *badiya*, the wild lands outside the cities (*mudun*).

served by a catamaran from Aqaba in Jordan. Before coming to Taba read the section about restricted visas on p17. If you're bound the other way, be equally aware of the difficulties a Taba or Israel stamp will cause you elsewhere in the Middle East (see box p17).

There's little to recommend Taba in itself; it's a small, unremarkable border outpost, almost completely devoid of cafés, culture and anything else that'd incline most travellers to stay.

PRACTICAL INFORMATION
Arrival
By air Taba International Airport (TCP) is about 30km out of town and is the only entry point at which full tourist visas are available. Actually, Eilat airport is closer to Taba than Taba airport itself and some airlines use this too.

By boat In 2012 **Meenagate** (🖳 www .meenagate.com) re-routed their Aqaba–Nuweiba catamaran (which had started in 2011). It now runs between Aqaba and Taba and arrives at Taba Heights Marina, about 20km south of town.

The **Sindbad XPRESS** used to sail from Aqaba to Taba too, docking at the same place. For a bit more info on these services see p16 and p118.

By bus East Delta bus station is a walkable few hundred metres from the border.

Services
The Hilton and Taba Sands have branches of Banque Misr (daily 9am-9pm) and **ATMs**.

There's a **post office** and **telephone centrale** on the main road (both open Sat-Thur, 8am-2pm), along with a **hospital** and **pharmacy** (both 24hrs).

The **Egypt Air** office (☎ 1717, Sat-Thur, 9am-3pm) here could be useful if you need to change/book flights.

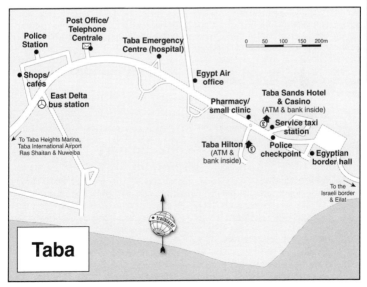

GATEWAY TOWNS

Where to stay

There are better places south of Taba but if you want to stay here there's **Taba Hilton** (☎ 069-353 0140, 💻 www.hilton.com). This was bombed in the 2004 terrorist attacks but —in a statement of defiance from management — it's been 're-built even better than before'. Another option, just over the road, is **Taba Sands Hotel and Casino** (☎ 069-353 0446). There are other hotels towards the bus station.

Moving on

East Delta buses are the best so try and co-ordinate your arrival with a departure time (don't believe taxi drivers who say the bus isn't running, at least not without checking yourself).

Nuweiba is the first major town, 65km south. Ras Shaitan, 15km before, is a trail-head for the trek to Ein Hudera (see p229). The places between Taba and Ras Shaitan are outlined below.

By bus East Delta runs the following buses: to Nuweiba, 3pm, and *sometimes* another about 1.30pm (LE11, 1-1½hrs); Dahab and Sharm, 3pm (LE25/30, 2½-3½ hrs and 3½-5hrs) and Cairo, 10.30am and 4.30pm (LE60-80, 7-8hrs).

In late 2012 the bus to Cairo, which crosses central Sinai, was closed to foreigners. Ask for service updates and if it's still off limits, go via Sharm. East Delta buses stop anywhere between Taba and Nuweiba; just tell the driver where you want.

By service taxi Minibus service taxis leave from outside the border when full. Most go to Nuweiba (LE10-15); a few continue to Dahab (LE20-30).

By private taxi There's a welcoming committee of taxi drivers when you enter Egypt.

Haggling is hard but aim for the following: Ras Shaitan, LE80-100; Nuweiba, LE100-150; Dahab, LE250-300; Sharm, LE400-450; St Katherine, LE350-400. It's simpler to book a taxi ahead. Drivers in Nuweiba are the closest (see p228).

By ferry **Meenagate** (mob ☎ 0112-059 5506, 💻 www.meenagate.com) operates a daily catamaran to Aqaba. It departs the Taba Heights Marina (20km south of town) between 7am and 8am. The crossing takes 30-45 mins and you can only buy returns (US$100). These have to be used within seven days, otherwise (it's said) you risk a US$500 fine from authorities.

Book by emailing 💻 info@ meenagate at least 24 hours before travel, attaching a photo of your passport ID page.

The **Sindbad XPRESS** boat used to sail to Aqaba from Taba Heights Resort Marina too. It stopped after the revolution but was intending to return when tourism picked up in 2013. Check ahead using an agency such as Pro Tours Travel (☎ 069-358 0076, 💻 www.protourstravel.com).

Between Taba and Ras Shaitan

This coast of rugged mountains and golden shores once thrived with Israeli tourism. The bombs of 2004 saw business fall away and many camps now stand abandoned; the surviving ones only just scrape through. Everything is basic but it offers something different from east coast tourist towns.

Where to stay Beach camps appear about 35km south of Taba. They're cheap, idyllic and welcoming, but ask around to see which have survived.

One sure to be open is **Basata** (☎ 069-350 0480, 💻 www.basata.com), the first eco-lodge in Egypt. It runs an environmental management scheme that hits nearly 100% sustainability. Organic waste is fed to animals or used as fertiliser; with everything else shipped out for recycling; there's an on-site desalination plant, and a small farm and allotment. Camping costs €14 (LE120) and a hut €18 (LE150). Rates are cheaper if you're an expat in Egypt. There are recent reports of Israeli guests being refused lodging.

Getting around Everything has to be flagged down on this stretch of coast; East Delta buses, minibuses and private vehicles. Alternatively, call a taxi from Nuweiba (p228) or organise one through a camp.

Things to see and do **Jezirat Faraun (Pharaoh's Island)** is a small island with a Crusader castle, about 7km south of Taba. Originally a Byzantine fortress, it was enlarged by Crusaders in 1116 and used as an advance outpost for the conquest of the Holy Lands. The Islamic forces of General Saladin captured it in 1182 but it was deemed of little use and abandoned soon after. The battlements have been extensively restored but original features like the furnace, water cistern and communal baths remain.

A motorboat runs out to it from Helnan Hotel for LE25 and entry is LE20. It looks close enough to swim but don't be tempted as the currents are strong. Dive firms offer trips to snorkel reefs around the island.

Castle Zaman (mob ☎ 0128-214 0591) looks like a Crusader castle but was built a few years ago. It's actually a restaurant that does slow-cooked food; call at least five hours ahead of any visit. The food's good but there's an LE100 minimum charge for every guest and the door policy feels exclusive.

El Tur (Tur Sina)

El Tur is on the west coast, about 100km up from Sharm. It was the famous port of Raithu in Byzantine times. Today it's the capital of South Sinai and a major hub of transport, services and administration. It's useful for two main things: renewing visas and finding onward buses.

Few like Tur enough to stay but you can easily kill a few hours here: there's the macabre attraction of a perfectly preserved monk's corpse or the hot, therapeutic springs of Hammam Musa, always good for soothing aching limbs.

WHAT TO SEE AND DO

The **Monastery of St George** is a satellite of the Monastery of St Katherine (see pp126-7). It has a nice chapel and the corpse of an old monk called Father Gregory. Wisps of hair and the 'last gasp' dying expression are still seen on his face. It's thought he lived in St Katherine in the 19th century, retiring here for warmer climes in his old age. The monastery (9am-noon, except Fri and Sun, public and Christian holidays) is at the seafront, not far from the Coptic Church.

Hot springs are found in palm groves at **Hammam Musa (Moses's Pool)**. They're good for bathing and one theory goes this is the Biblical site of Elim (where the Israelites camped). They're about 7km out of town so get a taxi (LE15-20). Entry tickets cost LE25.

PRACTICAL INFORMATION
Orientation
El Tur has a simple grid layout. There's just one important street to know about (still unnamed in 2013). At one end is the East Delta bus station; at the other, some banks. A few hundred metres up the road from the bus station, near Maka Hotel, is a cluster of

cafés. These are a reference point for other things, including minibuses to Wadi Feiran and St Katherine.

Getting around
The grid system makes navigating easy. Taxis are most useful for reaching outlying places like Hammam Musa. The official ones are orange and white but plain cars operate too. None of them has a meter so negotiate before you leave.

Services
Most things are on the main city street, including **Banque Misr** and the **National Bank of Egypt** (both Sat-Thur, 8am-2pm). They have ATMs and you should stock up on cash if you're going inland (especially to Wadi Feiran, which has no banks).

The main **post office** (Sat-Thur, 8am-2pm) is near the East Delta bus station. The **hospital** is next door (open 24 hours).

Internet can sometimes be used in the basement of the city's Coptic Church. It costs LE1/hr (very cheap) but has unreliable opening hours. Other cafés open and close quickly so ask around.

Visa renewals
The visa office (Sat-Thur, 8am-3pm) is at the end of the road from the banks to the seafront. Taxis from East Delta bus station cost about LE10; just say 'visa'. For more details see p18.

El Tur
(Tur Sina)

0   100   200   300m

To Wadi Feiran
& St Katherine

East Delta
bus station

Hospital

Main
Post Office

Maka
Hotel

Cafés

High Jet
ticket office

Coptic church
(internet sometimes
available)

To Hammam Musa &
Moses Bay Hotel

Minibuses to Wadi
Feiran/St Katherine

Banque
Misr

National
Bank of Egypt

Service taxi
station

Post
Office

Delmon
Hotel

Monastery of
St George

To Sharm
el Sheikh

trailblazer

Visa office

Where to stay and eat

Few like Tur enough to **stay** but there are options. *Delmon Hotel* (☎ 069-377 1060) is near the Coptic Church. It's a one-star option but not too bad; rooms have a/c and att, with singles LE130 and doubles LE170.

More upmarket is *Moses Bay Hotel* (☎ 069-377 4343, 💻 www.mosesbayhotel .com), a few kilometres out of town (singles €30/LE255 and doubles €40/LE340).

The **cafés** near Maka Hotel do snacks. The huge haul of fish piled onto plates in Sharm comes mostly from Tur, but few local restaurants look appealing.

Moving on

Tur has regular buses to Sharm, Dahab and Cairo and minibuses to Wadi Feiran and St Katherine. Be warned: catching the minibus can be tricky. Departure times can vary and seats aren't guaranteed.

By public bus East Delta runs the following services: Sharm, 11 buses, 12.30pm-1am (LE9, 1½hrs); Dahab, 3am, 7.30am, 3.30pm, 4.30pm, 5.30pm (LE20-30, 2½-4hrs); Nuweiba, 3am (LE20, 3-5hrs); Taba, 9am (LE30, 4-6hrs); Cairo 14 buses, 8.45am-1am.

High Jet and MCV also have buses to Cairo. The ticket office is amongst the cafés near Maka Hotel.

By minibus Minibuses go to Wadi Feiran at 2pm and 8pm (LE10-15, 1-1½hrs) and St Katherine at 2.30pm and 8.30pm (LE15-20, 2-2½hrs). The St Katherine services can be used for Wadi Feiran, but you might have to pay a St Katherine fare.

Both minibuses go from an obscure street corner: from the café area near Maka Hotel take a road between the Alekhas phone shop (which has a big red sign) and Layaly el Helmya café next to it. Follow this down over three blocks/streets and stop at the third. The minibuses wait on a corner directly opposite a mobile phone shop with a red 3G sign outside.

Important note: these buses can go late and early and they're often full with people returning inland after travelling out in the morning. They're best for individuals. Try and arrive 45 minutes early, ideally for the 2pm buses, where you'll have two options. Evening buses are more unreliable.

Service taxis There's a service taxi station where minibuses go to Sharm (LE10), Suez (LE25) and Cairo (LE30). These are small and cramped so buses are better.

By private taxi Taxis can be hired for long-distance trips. Aim for the following fares: LE150-200 to Sharm, LE150-200 to Wadi Feiran and LE350-400 to St Katherine.

GATEWAY TOWNS

❏ **Mounting a camel, Isabella Bird,** *A pilgrimage to Sinai* **(1886)**
Isabella Bird travelled to St Katherine in the 19th century. She was one of the most adventurous women of her day but like many never quite mastered the art of mounting a camel: 'When I can walk no farther my camel, with much difficulty and many objurgations, is made to lie down. Hassan stands at one side and the Sheikhs on the other, and with Hassan's help I attempt to take a flying leap into the middle of the saddle. Sometimes this is successful the first time, and if it is Hassan puts an arm in front of me and the Sheikh puts an arm behind me, and the dreaded moment arrives, which I am more cowardly about each time. The camel, with a jerk that might dislocate one's neck, jumps on his knees, nearly throwing me backwards, then another violent jerk brings him to his haunches, and would throw me over his head but for Hassan's arm, then, the forward movement is arrested by another jerk which sets him on his four legs and leaves me breathless on the lofty elevation of his hump. This process is reversed as one dismounts, and is repeated six times daily!'

6   TRAIL GUIDES & MAPS

Using this guide

TRAIL MAPS

Scale and walking times

The maps are drawn to an approximate scale of 1:30,000 (1cm to 300m). There's an exception for a small mountain called Jebel el Deir: this is shown on a single map with the scale doubled to roughly 1:15,000 (1cm to 150m).

Walking times are shown between small black triangles in the side bars of each map. These are only approximations and they vary widely in the Sinai: you, your guide, your camels, the season and time of day you're walking all have a big effect. The times refer to walking time; rest stops aren't included.

Up or down?

The trail is a dotted line. An arrow on it indicates a moderate slope: a double arrow shows that it's steep.

If you were walking from A (at 1000m) to B (at 1200m) and it was steep it would be shown thus: A—->>—-B. The arrows point to the higher parts of the trail.

Place names

There is no standard for transliterating Arabic into English; the Sinai's place names are spelt in many different ways. The most common one is usually used here and for places that aren't named anywhere else they're written phonetically. In all cases a soft 'J' is substituted for the hard Egyptian 'G', reflecting the names as they're pronounced in the native Bedouin dialect.

Water sources

Key water sources are marked. Where plenty are clustered together, just one is shown. The trek descriptions give further notes on getting water.

❏ **Routes and guides**

The trail guides are designed to give you as much independence as you want on any given route. This isn't to suggest you should go without a guide: they're important in many areas other than navigation and tribes stipulate you take them. For clarity, text about places that are trekked to on different trails is repeated rather than having page references.

❏ **Useful words for the trail**
The following words feature in trek descriptions and conversations on the trail. Have a quick read before you get started:

Bir (*beer*) – well
Darb – track, trail
Ein – spring
Farsh – basin, depression
Gimma – peak, summit
Hajar – rock
Jebel – mountain
Karm – garden
Kineesa – church, monastery
Moiyet – water source

Naqb – pass, route between places
Ras – summit, promontory, headland
Rojom – pile of stones to mark the way
Sed – dam, plunge pool or waterfall
Shellal – waterfall
Seil – mouth of wadi, or village here
Shegeef – gully
Shejera – tree
Tareeg – way, path
Wadi – valley, watercourse

Overlaps
The High Mountain Region is criss-crossed with trekking routes and some maps overlap. Only useful overlaps or those which help you go from one route to another are depicted. Minor and unnecessary ones aren't shown.

Other features
The maps don't mark every garden, peak, cliff and other feature on a trek. They'd become too cluttered as such: only those features most pertinent to navigation are depicted. See Map key p274.

GPS WAYPOINTS

These are given at key points such as trailheads, junctions and summits. For landscapes with tricky route finding, more waypoints are given. Odd points, such as a hidden historical site or obscure spring, are always marked.

Each trekking route has its own numbered set and the list is on pp279-84. GPS accuracy won't always be precise in the Sinai: it can vary depending on the quality of satellite reception you have.

High Mountain Region

The High Mountain Region is an area of red granite peaks around St Katherine. Egypt's highest summits are found here, with some looking to both Africa and Asia. The landscapes resonate with Biblical fable and ancient Christian ruins stand scattered across the mountainsides. It's the most-popular trekking region in the Sinai but that's not to say it's crowded; far from it.

Mount Sinai aside, trekkers only come in the hundreds every year and most stick to the best-known trails. On some treks you won't see any other trekkers

TRAIL GUIDE & MAPS

at all. Even if you don't make this area the focus of a trip you should at least spend a bit of time here. You'd miss out otherwise.

TRIBES AND TREKKING

High Mountain Region

The High Mountain Region is **Jebeleya territory** and every guide must be a local tribesman. There's a special guide-rotation system here, known as the *dor*. Each guide has a place; he waits his turn, does his job, then goes back to wait again. The system chooses the guide — not you. To take your own you're supposed to pay twice over: the one you take and the one who was scheduled to work.

Some trumpet this system as a model of fairness, but it's not. First of all, it's a bad deal for trekkers. It's reasonable to expect a choice in something you pay for; especially something as important as a guide (and not least when guides often cost more here than elsewhere). It's frustrating for guides too. It stops them working when they're in demand and hinders the building of long-term relationships with trekkers. Furthermore, all guides are rewarded equally; the guides who burn the midnight oil to learn a language and read up on history, culture and wildlife get the same as those who don't care a jot.

Whispers of discontent have become a steady chorus of protest in recent years and Jebeleya Sheikhs are well aware of the problems. Change is said to be coming and some Bedouin camps are already starting to use their own guides (eg Desert Fox Camp). Hopefully, it'll be replaced in 2013.

Finding a guide

First of all, ask for the latest on the *dor* (see above). If you still have to use it the chances are you'll get a guide you're happy with. It's run by the Sheikh Mousa Mountain Tours Office at the Bedouin Camp and Guesthouse. Go through this or any other agency to arrange. An industry has grown up 'outside this system' too and guides can be found on a casual basis. These guides are as good as any and you can choose your own and pay less. It might be preferable

---

❑ **The Jebeleya tribe**

The Jebeleya ('Mountain People') are a small tribe from the High Mountain Region. They're something of an oddity for the Sinai – or anywhere in the Middle East – claiming an ancestry quite distinct to most Bedouin.

One of the tribe's biggest divisions – the Aulad Jindi ('Children of the Soldiers') – traces its roots to a group of European Christian soldiers, dispatched to guard the Monastery of St Katherine in the 6th century. Some other divisions also claim non-Arab roots. The Jebeleya look much like other tribes today but their roots are betrayed by their bond with the monastery.

Many tribesmen work for the monks and the Monastery Fathers and Sheiks remain close. Even the ancient vow of protection is honoured. When the police force collapsed across the Sinai during the revolution the young men of the Jebeleya armed themselves and kept a vigil, guarding the monastery day and night.

in many ways but it's not advisable. If caught you can get into trouble with the tribe and it'll be an even bigger problem for your guide.

Remember you can still take a guide by working within the system. The following are a few of the many good ones worth tracking down:

● **Faraj Ahmed** (mob ☎ 0122-678 9869) Experienced guide, good English and excellent knowledge of local plants and wildlife.
● **Ahmed Saaleh Awad** (mob ☎ 0122-351 4898, 🖳 sinaigold@yahoo.com) Expert in herbal medicine with good English.
● **Nasr Mansour** (mob ☎ 0122-930 6533) Experienced guide, good English.
● **Ramadan Musa Saalih Abu Ghalaba** (mob ☎ 0100-820 3221, 🖳 www.sinai mylove.com) Young but good, experienced guide with fluent English.
● **Metowah Abu Musaad** (mob ☎ 0109-590 3269, 🖳 metaw2005@hotmail .com). Another young guide with superb English. Based in Dahab.
● **Mohammed Eid** (mob ☎ 0100-977 3329). Speaks good English.
● **Suliman el Henehy** (mob ☎ 0100-914 1766, 🖳 suliman3020@yahoo.com). Experienced, affable guide with excellent English.
● **Salema Eid** (mob ☎ 0100-735 9622). Excellent guide who loves to explore new places. Divides his time between St Katherine and Slovenia.

Jebel Umm Shomer
Jebel Umm Shomer is in **Aulad Said territory** and it's best to use their guides and cameleers. A few tribesmen live in St Katherine but they're hard to track down (the best place is the Mohammed Salem Cafeteria, mid-morning, see box p130). Even if you find one, few speak English and this trek is thus always best organised through a local agency.

Trekking agencies
Guides and treks are best organised through local camps or agencies. They're listed on p11 and should charge the rates on the following page.

Trekking costs
Jebeleya costs vary but reckon on paying LE100-150 a day for basic guide fees: prices rise as routes get longer or more difficult. On top of this there's a Sheikh's permission fee, usually about LE80-100 a day, meaning the basic cost will be around LE180-250 per day. Camels are LE80-120 a day when needed. These prices won't always include food so factor extra in for this.

Through an agency, **Aulad Said** fees are about the same (but usually LE120-150 per day if you do it independently). For the Jebel Umm Shomer route you usually have to pay for jeeps both ends of the trek. Guides might ask for an extra day's pay for the return trip at the end too.

ST KATHERINE

St Katherine ('Katreen') nestles at the heart of the High Mountain Region and is the highest town in Egypt. The area has an ancient Christian history but the town itself is a mostly modern creation, developed from the 1970s. It has a strong Bedouin feel and makes an excellent trekking base.

TRAIL GUIDE & MAPS

Most trailheads start out of town and it's an important service hub for the interior, having at least one of all the main services you need.

What to see and do
The Golden Calf (El Bagara) The Israelites made the Golden Calf as an idol when Moses was on Mount Sinai. He smashed the Tablets of Law in anger when he returned to see them worshipping it (the second commandment expressly forbid idol worship). There's a rock shaped like a calf (see map p128) on the road between the monastery and town which monks say was used to make the idol. Look out for a small black pothole in the rocks. This is the calf's eye and the rest of its form unfolds easily thereafter.

St Katherine Protectorate Visitor Centre This small, EU-funded initiative is one of South Sinai's few museums. It has superb exhibitions on the local environment and culture, each housed in its own stone hut. A caretaker takes you round to unlock them. Free trail guides are available for walking routes around town too, all well worth picking up. The centre (see Map 1, p128; 9.30am-1.30pm, except Fri and Sun; admission free) is just off the main road out of town.

The Blue Mountain (or Blue Desert) Belgian artist Jean Verame painted outcrops blue here to celebrate Egypt's historic peace with Israel (it took two years to get the go-ahead, then ten tons of paint). They're dotted across the beautiful Plain of Sened, like a gigantic, open-air art installation. Many Bedouin preferred it as it was before, but it's still worth a look. The site is about 10km out of town and a jeep costs LE200-300. You can also hire a guide and walk over the low pass of Naqb Dhirwa, from Wadi Sebaiya.

Have a swim The Catherine Plaza (see map p128) lets non-guests use its pool for LE40 and it's great for a plunge after a long summer trek.

The Monastery of St Katherine The monastery (daily 9am-noon excl Fri & Sun, public holidays and Christian festivals) dates from the 6th century and is a UNESCO World Heritage Site. It's said to be the oldest working Christian monastery in the world (though monks at the Monastery of St Anthony in Egypt's Eastern Desert would disagree). No visit to St Katherine would be complete without a trip here and it works well after the Mount Sinai trek.

The **Katholikon ('Church of the Transfiguration')** is the main church, dating back to 542AD. It was built on the site of an earlier chapel that some say was founded by the Emperor Constantine's mother, Helena, in the 4th century. Here is a run-down of its most interesting features:

The outer doors of the **Narthex (entry porch)** were made by 11th century Crusaders and their graffiti is still seen: shields, coats of arms, crosses and cherubs. The next doors lead into the main church area and date from the 6th century, when the monastery was founded. They're made from Lebanese cedar wood and show the birds and flowers of paradise.

There are 12 columns in the **Nave (main church area)**, and each represents a month of the year. Icons above each column show the month's special saints. The screen at the end of the nave is called the iconostasis. It's made of carved, gold-plated wood and dates from 1612. Down the **side aisle** on the left there's a small wooden shrine with a bone in it. Monks say this is the toe bone of St Katherine, found with the rest of her remains in the 9th century.

The **Mosaic of the Transfiguration** decorates the ceiling behind the iconostasis and is perhaps the most celebrated mosaic in the Eastern Orthodox Church. Jesus is in the middle with Moses standing to his left and Elijah his right. The *Transfiguration* was the event in which Jesus is said to have appeared divinely radiant on a mountain. The sun strikes his golden face through the windows every morning, re-creating the fabled scene.

The **Apse** has the church altar and St Katherine's gold-plated sarcophagus. The monks sometimes open it to show her relics to Orthodox Christians. Nearby is the Chapel of the Burning Bush, around which the monastery was originally built. This is the holiest spot in the Sinai and entry isn't usually permitted.

● **Other things to see** The Katholikon is just a small part of the monastery complex. The rest is mostly closed but there are still a few things to see.

Skulls, hands and shin bones of monks stand piled high in the **ossuary (skull house)**. Burial space was limited in the rocky ground so bodies were left to decompose before being exhumed and replaced with new ones. Unfortunately, this was closed to the public recently, but it might open again.

The monastery escaped the ravages of European iconoclasm and now has the finest collection of icons anywhere in the world. They're displayed in the **monastery museum** along with relics such as ivory staffs, silver croziers, holy chalices and a copy of the pledge of security it's said the Prophet Mohammed gave the monks in the 7th century (see p67).

There's a **bush** that people mill around near the Katholikon. This isn't the Burning Bush itself, but monks say it was planted from original cuttings. The lower branches are usually stripped bare by tourists.

❏ **Codex Sinaiticus**
The *Codex Sinaiticus* – or Book of Sinai – was one of the most important Christian Bibles ever made. Before the 4th century, Christianity's scriptures were scattered around in separate volumes. The Codex took the step of transcribing them into a single book for the first time, becoming the Bible upon which all others were based.

Four separate scribes worked on the transcription, driving towards a single style. This push for consistency meant each scribe had to change the language and, sometimes, the theology of the original scriptures they copied. Further to this each went over the work of the others, making corrections and re-writing lengthy passages.

These editorial changes are probably the most interesting part of the Codex. Whereas the Bible has traditionally been regarded as the unalterable Word of God, the Codex manuscript clearly demonstrates the role of the human hand.

It was stored in the Monastery of St Katherine's library (the biggest Christian library outside the Vatican). German Biblical scholar Constantine von Tischendorf secured it on loan for the Czar of Russia in the 19th century but never returned it. Its pieces are now scattered in four institutions – one of them being the British Library in London. The monks regard it as a stolen treasure and campaign for its full return.

There's also a small, makeshift **mosque**. One story goes the monks hobbled it together themselves, after hearing Caliph al Hakim was racing for the monastery in a destructive frenzy, having sacked the Church of the Holy Sepulchre in Jerusalem. They hoped that in consecrating the ground for Muslims, they'd avoid his wrath. Actually, its history is uncertain; it was probably built in less-dramatic circumstances, on the request of Hakim's successor, Caliph el Afdal, in the early 12th century.

PRACTICAL INFORMATION
Orientation and arrival
St Katherine has three districts. **El Milga** is the main town area, with the mosque, post office, bank and shops. The neighbouring district, **Shamaya**, has more shops, hotels and a hospital. **El Rasees** is a mostly residential area straddling both.

East Delta buses terminate outside the mosque in El Milga. If you're staying at the Monastery of St Katherine, or Desert Fox Camp, get off before. Stop at the first, small roundabout on the edge of town, near the gate of Hotel Wadi Raha. Drivers should know it. If not just say 'El Deir' (The Monastery) or even better 'Fox' (ie Fox Camp), and you should be dropped here. It's over 1km to the monastery (a long walk with heavy bags) but a short way to the camp. St Katherine airport started handling flights again in 2013 (see p14). This airport is about 20km out of town and a taxi costs about LE80. Book taxis ahead.

Services
There's a branch of Banque Misr (Sun-Thur, 8am-2pm) in El Milga – the only **bank** in the interior of South Sinai. It does foreign exchange and there's an ATM outside; this can break so play it safe and get cash when you can.

The **post office** (see map opposite; Sat-Thur, 8am-2pm), near the mosque in El Milga, handles poste restante. Next door there's a **telephone centrale** (Sat-Thur, 8am-4pm).

A few Bedouin camps have **internet** and there's a good café called Orabi Services (noon-2am, LE5/hr) in Shamaya.

The **hospital** (see map below; 24hrs) is in Shamaya and doctors do GP-style

St Katherine

To Abu Seila

To Kharazeen,
St Katherine
Visitor Centre,
Mt Sinai Ecolodge/
Wadi Sebaiya,
The Blue Mountain
& airport

El Wady el
Mouquaduss

Hotel Wadi
Raha

● Hospital

Catherine
Plaza

Monastery
roundabout

0   200   400m

Hardware store

SHAMAYA

Daniela
Village

Moonland

See 'St Katherine Centre' map

Shahrazad
Restaurant

Desert Fox
Camp

Golden
Calf

To Monastery of
St Katherine
& Mount Sinai

To Wadi Tlah &
Jebel Abbas Basha

EL·MILGA

Internet
Café

Bedouin Camp
& Guesthouse

EL·RASEES

Medicinal
Plant Association
(greenhouses)

★ trailblazer

Sheikh
Sina office

Police
Station

To Wadi Arbain,
Mount Sinai &
Jebel Katherina

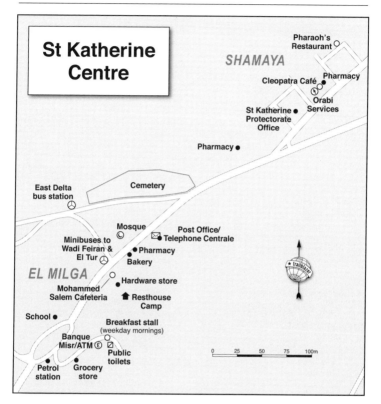

St Katherine Centre

SHAMAYA

Pharaoh's Restaurant

Pharmacy

Cleopatra Café

Orabi Services

St Katherine Protectorate Office

Pharmacy

East Delta bus station

Cemetery

Mosque

Post Office/ Telephone Centrale

Minibuses to Wadi Feiran & El Tur

Pharmacy

Bakery

EL MILGA

Hardware store

Mohammed Salem Cafeteria

Resthouse Camp

School

Breakfast stall
(weekday mornings)

Banque Misr/ATM

Public toilets

Petrol station

Grocery store

0   25   50   75   100m

★ trailblazer

consultations and emergency treatment. A smaller hospital opened recently in Wadi Sebaiya. **Pharmacies** are dotted up the main road, opening until about 10pm.

There's a **police station** in El Milga but often it's better to speak to the Bedouin (the owners of Desert Fox camp are well-connected). Things are dealt with more effectively within the tribe.

For **trekking equipment** a hardware shop near Mohammed Salem Cafeteria sells shemaghs, candles, string and other oddments. There's another one in Shamaya.

For **equipment repairs** see if a local Bedouin woman can help.

The Medicinal Plants Association sells **local produce** like herbs and honey.

Where to stay

Bedouin camps These are grounded in the local trekking scene and thus the best places to stay. *Desert Fox Camp* (☎ 069-347 0344, 🖳 www.sinaidesertfox.com) is first on the way into town. It's a friendly place with a traditional Bedouin tent rigged up in the courtyard and it's the best place to organise treks. It has internet access and does simple rooms, with singles for LE30-40 and doubles LE60. Tents can be pitched in the olive garden for LE20.

Up the road towards town is *Moonland* (mob ☎ 0100-658 9550), with simple but decent rooms from LE30 to LE60. It's a quiet place and, whilst this might be an attraction in itself, it can also feel dead and lacking in atmosphere.

Resthouse Camp (mob ☎ 0111-759 8464) is a new camp in El Milga, by Mohammed Salem Cafeteria. The rooms are clean and comfortable, they have a/c and are good value at LE60-80. It also puts you at the heart of town, useful for getting early buses.

Bedouin Camp and Guesthouse (☎ 069-347 0457, 🖥 www.sheikmousa.com) is a good, long-running camp with singles from LE55 to LE85 and doubles from LE100 to LE150. It's another excellent place to organise treks and has free wi-fi for guests.

The Monastery of St Katherine
The *Monastery of St Katherine* (☎ 069-347 0353) has been hosting travellers for centuries and its guesthouse is going strong today. The melée subsides in early afternoon and staying here gives you a feel for monastery life. Singles with a/c and bathrooms are LE200 and doubles LE360. Prices include an excellent Greek-style dinner and breakfast. Book ahead as it gets busy with pilgrims and tour groups.

Expensive hotels
These are really for tourists doing Mount Sinai and they leave you isolated for trekking. Even so they're good for a night of comfort after a tough week in the mountains.

The best is *Daniela Village* (☎ 02-3748 6712, 🖥 www.daniela-hotels.com). It's a quiet, family-run place with chalet-style rooms; singles start at €36 (LE305) and doubles €44 (LE370).

El Wady el Mouquaduss (☎ 069-347 0225) is next door, with singles for LE80-120 and doubles LE150-200. The rooms have fridges, TVs and telephones and are about the best value in this range.

Other options are *Catherine Plaza* and *Hotel Wadi Raha*, but with singles from US$60 (LE360) and doubles US$80 (LE475), the prices are higher than the quality.

Gardens and eco-lodges
Bedouin gardens (see box p52) are good places to stay but the best ones are on the trail. Details are given in the trek descriptions.

There's an EU-funded **eco-lodge** about 7km out of town in Wadi Sebaiya called *Mount Sinai Ecolodge* (☎ 069-347 0880, 🖥 info@sheikhsina.com). Though built with good intentions, this maroons you in a remote wadi with little to recommend it. There's a better one on the trek to Jebel Banat (Al Karm Ecolodge, see p137).

Where to eat
St Katherine doesn't have a vibrant eating scene but the food is filling, tasty and cheap. Bedouin camps serve food but you could also try the following.

Local cafés *Shahrazad Restaurant* in Shamaya is a popular breakfast option with good taameya sandwiches (LE1-2) and lentil soup (LE5). A *street stall* does similar fare outside the bank on weekday mornings (sandwiches LE1-2). *Mohammed Salem Cafeteria* serves food from lunchtime, giving generously sized meals of chicken or kofta with rice (LE20-30).

Pharaohs Restaurant in Shamaya does kofta and kebab dishes for LE25-30 in the evening. *Cleopatra Café* is the best place to get a coffee and shisha. It's also the evening entertainment hub: which is to say it's where locals gather to play backgammon whilst watching soaps, football and belly dancing.

Hotel buffets and bars Bigger hotels have buffets that cater to non guests. *Catherine Plaza* has one at 7pm for about

---

❏ **Mohammed Salem Cafeteria**

Mohammed Salem Cafeteria, opposite the mosque, is the social hub of town: everyone from the Bedouin to the plain clothes police gather here through the day. It's a good place for finding drivers and guides and for getting the latest about minibuses, camel races etc. Ask in the kitchen or the shop near the road.

LE45. Most hotels serve (overpriced) alcohol and there's a 24hr bar in the Plaza.

Self-catering Minimarkets and fruit and vegetable shops are in El Milga. There's a government bakery near the post office that does five pieces of flat bread for LE2-3 in the morning (arrive before 10am).

Moving on
Public transport goes west but services to the east are limited. The only option is the so-called Bedouin Bus, a traveller-focused service going every other day.

● **By public bus** There's an East Delta bus to Cairo at 6am (LE55, 7-8 hrs). It can also be used for Wadi Feiran (45 mins, LE10-15) or anywhere up the west coast between Feiran and Suez.

If you miss the bus to Cairo get one of the minibuses mentioned below to El Tur and pick up an onward service there. The bus station is near the mosque and opens just 15 minutes before departure.
● **By public minibus** There are two minibuses to El Tur: 6.30am and 2.30pm (LE15-20, 2-2½hrs). Both can be used for getting to Wadi Feiran (LE10-15, 45 mins). Another goes to Suez at 6am (LE50, 3-4hrs) but it's crowded and overpriced so use the

East Delta service (this goes through Suez on the way to Cairo).

The Bedouin Bus goes to Dahab on Tuesdays and Fridays (11am, LE50) and Nuweiba on Wednesdays and Sundays (8am, LE50). Both Dahab and Nuweiba services can be used for the desert trailheads of Wadi Arada, the Nawamis village and Ein Hudera (see p229).

Minibuses go from outside the mosque/Mohammed Salem Cafeteria. Check times ahead.
● **In a shared taxi** People often want to get back to the east coast after doing Mount Sinai. The monastery car park is the best place to look, especially between 10am and midday. It's always quieter on Fridays and Sundays.
● **By private taxi** Taxis can be used to go anywhere at these approximate rates: Wadi Feiran, LE60-90; Dahab, LE200-220; Nuweiba, LE200-220; Sharm, LE350-400; Taba, LE350-400; El Tur, LE350-400; Cairo LE650-800.

Try one of the following Bedouin drivers as a taxi: Hamid Mohammed (mob ☎ 0100-310 6228), Hamid Farhan (mob ☎ 0100-571 6099) and Salah Mahmoud (mob ☎ 0120-472 3492). If all are busy arrange another through a Bedouin camp.

NORTHERN PEAKS CIRCUIT (2-3 days)
Practicalities
● **Difficulty and scheduling** This is a moderate trek whose summits are all optional. You could finish in two days but three would be more comfortable.
● **Camels** Water is lacking in the first section and you might need a camel. Discuss this before you go as it will affect where you camp.
● **Links with other treks** This can be linked with the Galt el Azraq (p142) or Jebel Abbas Basha and Jebel Katherina (p153) treks.

Kharazeen to Jebel el Ojar [Map 1]
Start at the small settlement of **Kharazeen** (GPS 1). It's opposite the St Katherine Protectorate Visitor Centre on the main road out of town. Jebel Suna towers clearly up to the north. You ascend to the big pass just right of it.

Look for a reddish house with blue shutters and a tree outside; it's to the right of the settlement's main jeep track. Just right from here there's a **black dike** in the mountainside, with a big boulder at the bottom. Move up the slopes behind the house and veer gradually onto the dike higher up.

❏ **Leopard traps (Nosret el nimr)**

Leopards once roamed widely in the Sinai and the Bedouin built traps to catch them. In mountainous regions they were usually sited on high, windy passes that the leopards used as natural thoroughfares.

Each trap had a chamber and doorway and a live goat kid was put inside, with a string tied from its leg to a stone over the door. It would try to run instinctively as the leopard entered, jerking the stone down to seal it inside. The leopards here – Arabian leopards – were smaller than their African counterparts, as you'll see from the modest size of the traps. They were often modified to catch other animals too.

The trail becomes more visible around here, but that's not to say it's easy to follow. Its markers are just the odd *rojom* or side line of stones. It takes unexpected turns and often fades completely so look carefully. It becomes better-trodden higher up, veering to the pass right of the peak (GPS 2).

On the other side is a wide, open basin called Farsh Suna. The mountain at the far end is Jebel el Ojar and a U-shaped pass separates it from some high ground to the right. Look out for the elongated heap of stones on the pass: this is an **old leopard trap** (see box above). You'll find more traps in the northern mountains than anywhere else, suggesting it was once prime big cat country.

Climbing **Jebel Suna** is optional: if you just have the energy for one peak do Jebel el Ojar. For Jebel Suna go down from the pass and veer gradually left, skirting round the northern crags of the mountain. You rise on steep, bouldery ground, emerging at a high point where you can scramble left up ledges to the top (GPS 3). Allow 15-25 minutes up and a little less back down.

To continue, head straight out across **Farsh Suna**. There's a **big gully** between Jebel el Ojar's summit and a smaller, subsidiary peak on the left. Leave the trail and head for the bottom of the gully, moving straight up its boulder-choked course. Move right from the top for the summit (GPS 4).

Jebel el Ojar is rarely climbed and has a wild feel; the view from the top is one of the finest in the High Mountain Region. Mount Sinai, Jebel Katherina and Jebel Abbas Basha all stand out clearly in the southern distance, each with a little building on top. Looking north you can gaze out to the distant escarpment of Jebel Tih: the Biblical 'Wilderness of the Wanderings'.

It's possible to descend Jebel el Ojar from the top of the gully, going down the other way to the north. You have to veer gradually right – or east – to join Wadi Anshil Essutia. It's faster but there are no trails and finding your way through the crags can be tricky. It's safest to go back the same way to Farsh Suna, continuing as described from there.

Jebel el Ojar/Farsh Suna to Wadi Abu Zeituna [Maps 1-2]

Head north through the U-shaped pass from Farsh Suna and follow **Wadi Anshil Essutia** down the other side. There's a trail in places but it's rough and untrodden in others. Just keep going in the bottom as best you can. Further down there's a **big enclosure** with walls on both sides of the wadi. After this there's a sharp right bend to a **rocky junction** (GPS 5). *(Cont'd on p136)*

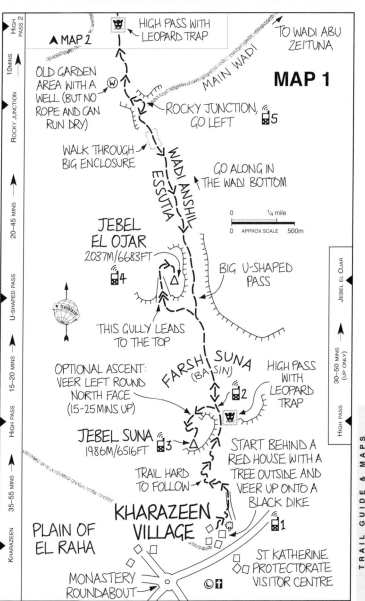

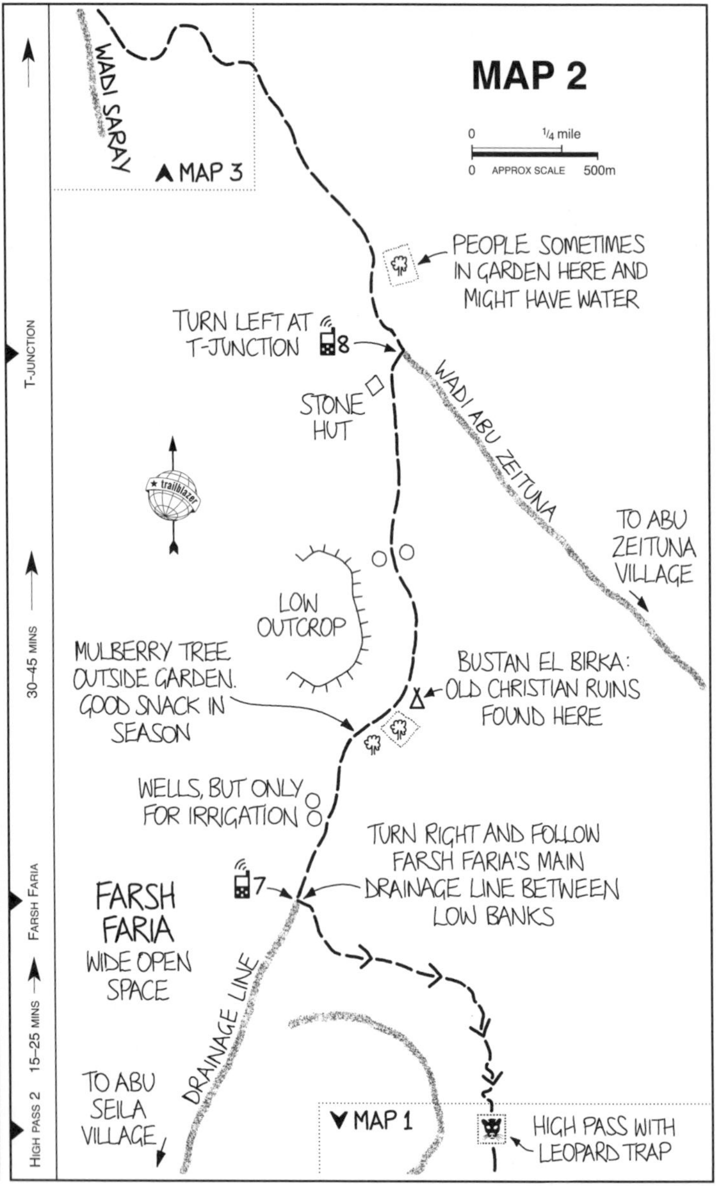

MAP 2

0 — ¼ mile
0 — APPROX SCALE — 500m

WADI SARAY

▲ MAP 3

PEOPLE SOMETIMES IN GARDEN HERE AND MIGHT HAVE WATER

TURN LEFT AT T-JUNCTION 📱8

WADI ABU ZEITUNA

STONE HUT

TO ABU ZEITUNA VILLAGE

LOW OUTCROP

★ trailblazer

MULBERRY TREE OUTSIDE GARDEN. GOOD SNACK IN SEASON

BUSTAN EL BIRKA: OLD CHRISTIAN RUINS FOUND HERE

WELLS, BUT ONLY FOR IRRIGATION

TURN RIGHT AND FOLLOW FARSH FARIA'S MAIN DRAINAGE LINE BETWEEN LOW BANKS

📱7

FARSH FARIA WIDE OPEN SPACE

DRAINAGE LINE

TO ABU SEILA VILLAGE

▼ MAP 1

HIGH PASS WITH LEOPARD TRAP

TRAIL GUIDE & MAPS

T-JUNCTION

30-45 MINS

FARSH FARIA

15-25 MINS

High Pass 2

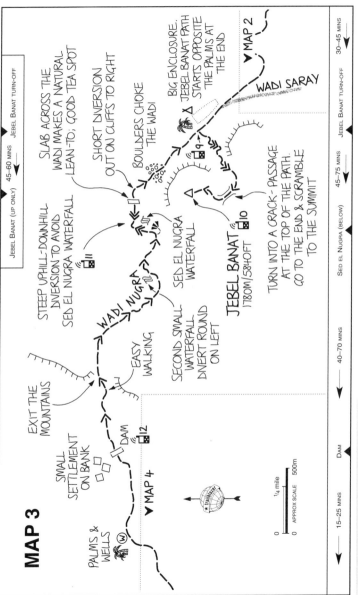

MAP 3

SLAB ACROSS THE WADI MAKES A NATURAL LEAN-TO; GOOD TEA SPOT

SHORT DIVERSION OUT ON CLIFFS TO RIGHT

BIG ENCLOSURE. JEBEL BANAT PATH STARTS OPPOSITE THE PALMS AT THE END

► MAP 2

WADI SARAY

BOULDERS CHOKE THE WADI

STEEP UPHILL-DOWNHILL DIVERSION TO AVOID SED EL NUGRA WATERFALL

SED EL NUGRA WATERFALL

JEBEL BANAT 1780M/584-OFT

TURN INTO A CRACK-PASSAGE AT THE TOP OF THE PATH. GO TO THE END & SCRAMBLE TO THE SUMMIT

WADI NUGRA

SED EL NUGRA WATERFALL

SECOND SMALL WATERFALL DIVERT ROUND ON LEFT

EASY WALKING

EXIT THE MOUNTAINS

SMALL SETTLEMENT ON BANK

DAM

► MAP 4

PALMS & WELLS

0   ¼ mile
0   APPROX SCALE   500m

trailblazer

> ❏ **Mulberry trees** *(toot)*
> Mulberry trees were introduced in Byzantine times. There are seven in the High
> Mountain Region and each belongs to the Jebeleya tribe. You're welcome to pick the
> fruit. It looks a bit like a blackberry and ripens between May and July.

(Cont'd from p132) Turn into the **small wadi** on the left and follow its course
up. There are old enclosures in its lower parts. The well here might hold water
in wetter months but it doesn't always have a rope. It's about ten minutes up here
to the **top of a pass** (GPS 6): it has a leopard trap and views back to Jebel el Ojar.

Continue down on a decent trail. This soon bends left into the wide open
spaces of **Farsh Faria** (GPS 7). This is pronounced 'Farsh *Furair*'. Turning left
here would take you in a southerly direction, then over a low pass to the village
of Abu Seila (where you finish later). However, turn right and follow the main
watercourse along, going between low banks. There are a few wells further up
but water is pumped out for the gardens; it's not used for drinking.

Look out for the **mulberry tree** (see box above) beside a garden wall soon
after the wells. It's one of just a few in the High Mountain Region and provides
a good snack in season. The area here is known as **Bustan el Birka** and it was
an important settlement site for early Christians. You'll find a few ruins if you
explore and it can be a campsite if you arrive late.

Carry on until you reach the T-junction with **Wadi Abu Zeituna** (GPS 8).

Wadi Abu Zeituna to Jebel Banat [Maps 2-3]
Turn left and follow Wadi Abu Zeituna, going past a few gardens. There are
sometimes people here in cooler months so ask to **refill your water bottles**. The
next guaranteed source is near Al Karm Ecolodge, a few hours past Jebel Banat:
if you're sleeping at the mountain, it'll be the second day.

Further ahead the wadi twists sharply before entering a straight stretch
where Jebel Banat comes into view. There's a **big walled enclosure** here with
a few palm trees at the end; one is notably taller than the others. The ascent path
to Jebel Banat starts directly opposite (GPS 9).

Camping on Jebel Banat The enclosure is a good spot to camp on the first
night. You could always sleep on the peak too, getting a beautiful sunset and
sunrise. Carry water, food and enough warm clothes.

Jebel Banat: the ascent [Map 3]
Jebel Banat means 'Mountain of the Girls'. It's nearly 1000m lower than Jebel
Katherina but some say its views are even more impressive; 1½-2½ hours is
enough for the ascent, allowing you a bit of time on top.

It's a strenuous hike up the steep, stony slopes from the wadi. Rojoms dot
the way but route finding is easy anyway. When you reach the top of this steep
stretch a rocky landscape opens on the right. Go into a **crack-passage** that cuts
through this and follow it straight up to the end.

The **smooth summit mass** of Jebel Banat stands to the right and you have
to scramble. The rock is mostly sloping granite and the lack of handholds can

be uncomfortable. Explore and find the best way up, remembering it for the way down.

The summit is marked by **two big boulders** (GPS 10). Looking south there's a wide panorama of the High Mountain Region. To the north are the desolate expanses of Elwa el Ajrameya. Jebel Tih stands far out in the distance. Looking west the big hulk of Jebel Serbal is also visible.

Jebel Banat to Al Karm Ecolodge [Maps 3-4]

Carry on down the wadi from the palms: it becomes known as **Wadi Nugra** here. Big boulders soon choke its course; weave and scramble through. Not far along a **rough cliff trail** runs out on the wadi's right side, bypassing a more difficult stretch in the bottom. Rojoms mark the start so look carefully. It's just a short diversion and you soon drop back to the bottom. A gigantic slab lies slanted across the wadi here; it's an excellent **lean-to shelter**.

The wadi soon bends sharply left and drops over **Sed el Nugra**: a sheer, 30m waterfall cliff. There's no way down here.

To bypass it, strike out at the very point the wadi begins to bend left, following a trail up its steep side (GPS 11). You reach a high point looking out to Jebel Banat's mighty north face. The descent begins immediately after, on steep, loose ground. It's longer, because of the big drop in the wadi.

Turn left and walk up to see Sed el Nugra from below. A big tongue of mossy sediments hangs down from the cliff, dripping with water. Wadi Nugra drains almost all the northern massif and Sed el Nugra turns from a drip to a raging torrent during storms (it's no place to be during rain).

The wadi soon drops over a **second waterfall**. This is smaller but still an awkward scramble. Follow a path around its left side. You can scramble back to the bottom, continuing in the wadi without interruption. You'll see a few wells with solar panels along here, but they don't always have ropes.

You emerge in open lowland country. Continue in the lower drainage line of the wadi, crossing a small dam (GPS 12). A bit further on are some palms and wells. The wadi veers gradually left now, going through a short rocky section and soon running past a few Bedouin gardens to *Al Karm Ecolodge* (GPS 13; see box below). This area is known as Wadi Gharba.

Al Karm Ecolodge to Naqb Abu Seila [Maps 4-5]

Walk up the low hills behind Al Karm Ecolodge, heading south. There's a big gap in the mountains to the left: this is the **Naqb el Hawa** pass and the way back to St Katherine. *(Cont'd on p140)*

❏ **Al Karm Ecolodge**

This is an EU-funded, sustainable tourism initiative with solar-heated showers and composting toilets. Candles give the only light at night. You could stay here if you're doing the trek more slowly. It costs LE70-90 per person and LE30 to pitch a tent. It's also an excellent spot to buy souvenirs; Bedouin women come from the nearby village of Sheikh Auwad in the morning to sell their handicrafts.

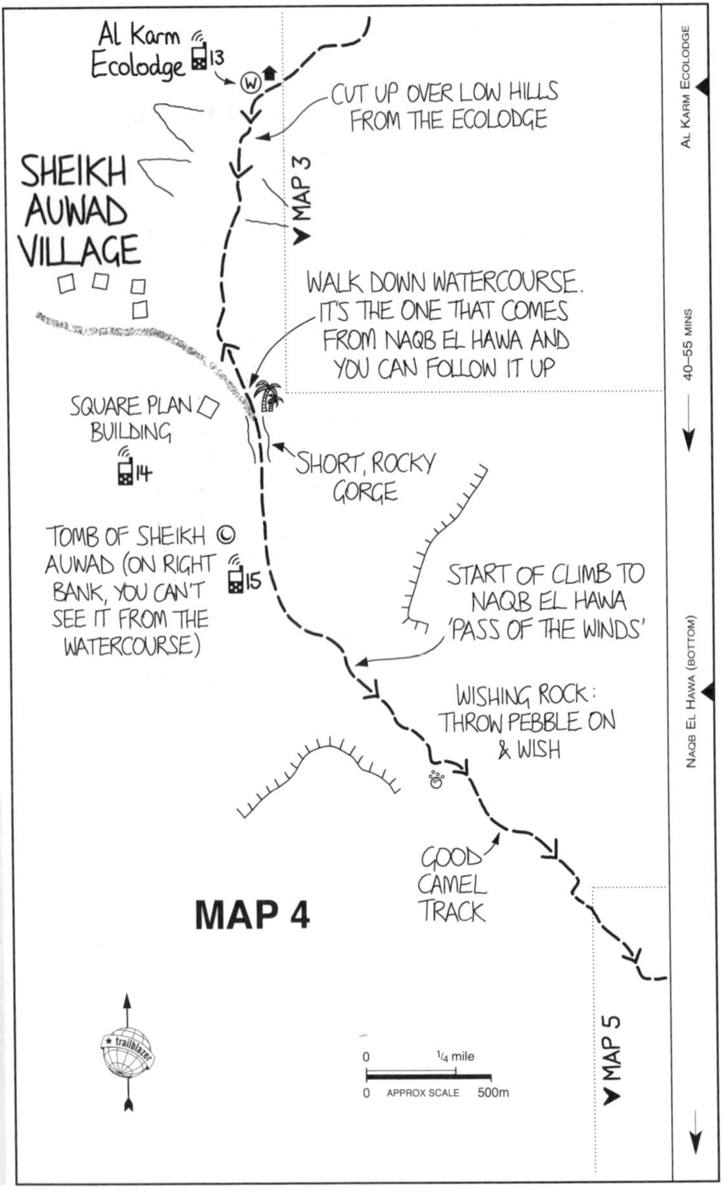

Al Karm Ecolodge 🔋13

CUT UP OVER LOW HILLS FROM THE ECOLODGE

▼ MAP 3

SHEIKH AUWAD VILLAGE

WALK DOWN WATERCOURSE. IT'S THE ONE THAT COMES FROM NAQB EL HAWA AND YOU CAN FOLLOW IT UP

SQUARE PLAN BUILDING 🔋14

SHORT, ROCKY GORGE

TOMB OF SHEIKH © AUWAD (ON RIGHT 🔋15 BANK, YOU CAN'T SEE IT FROM THE WATERCOURSE)

START OF CLIMB TO NAQB EL HAWA 'PASS OF THE WINDS'

WISHING ROCK: THROW PEBBLE ON & WISH

GOOD CAMEL TRACK

MAP 4

▼ MAP 5

0   ¼ mile

0   APPROX SCALE   500m

AL KARM ECOLODGE

40-55 MINS

NAQB EL HAWA (BOTTOM)

TRAIL GUIDE & MAPS

MAP 5

PALMS & WELL-
SOMETIMES
PADLOCKED

WELL/CISTERN WITH A RED
METAL LID. POOL FOR CAMELS.
LOOK BACK FOR VIEWS OF
JEBEL ZIBB RUB'I

TOP OF NAQB
EL HAWA 📱16

▼ MAP 7

LEAVE THE MAIN TRAIL &
VEER RIGHT TO THE PASS
OF NAQB ABU SEILA

ABU SEILA
VILLAGE

NAQB ABU SEILA

📱19

📱18
WALK OR
SCRAMBLE

◎ MOSQUE 📱17

TO
KHARAZAT
SHAGG

SCHOOL

WADI TLAH

📱20
GARDEN OF
DR AHMED

PLAIN OF
EL RAHA

▼ MAP 6

MORE
BOULDERY
HERE

TO TOWN OF
ST KATHERINE

0   ¼ mile
0   APPROX SCALE   500m

MAP 4

75-105 MINS FROM NAQB EL HAWA (BOTTOM) (MAP 4)

NAQB EL HAWA (TOP)

20-40 MINS

WADI TLAH

TRAIL GUIDE & MAPS

(Cont'd from p137) You pass the small village of **Sheikh Auwad** before reaching the line of a watercourse. This comes down from Naqb el Hawa. Go down, turn left and follow its bottom course along.

A **small rocky gorge** soon enlivens the walking (GPS 14). The tomb of Sheikh Auwad, a revered Jebeleya saint, stands on the right bank after the gorge, but you have to cut out to see it. It's an easy walk from here to the bottom of Naqb el Hawa (GPS 15), marked by a lone acacia tree.

Naqb el Hawa ('Pass of the Winds') was once the last leg of the ancient pilgrim road to Mount Sinai. A big camel path runs up it today, giving a nice, gentle ascent. Look out for an unusual wishing rock (see box p164) just right of the trail in the first section: you throw pebbles on top of most wishing rocks, but you aim them into smooth hollows on the side of this one.

The trail is dotted with Bedouin gardens and a few wells. The wells don't always have ropes but there's a cistern with good water further up (it has a red metal lid and a camel pool next to it). Look back to see a rocky pinnacle capped with an upstanding cuboid here. This is **Jebel Zibb Rub'i**; some say it's named after a Bedouin ibex hunter gored to death by his prey.

Continue to the top of Naqb el Hawa (GPS 16). The **Plain of el Raha** unfolds in splendid view from the top. It's said the Israelites stayed here as God gave Moses the Ten Commandments on Mount Sinai (part of the mass at the far end of the plain). You can follow the main trail to the village of **Abu Seila** ahead, finishing the trek early (GPS 17). Ask around for a car; it's about LE15-25 to St Katherine. Walking on the road takes about 45-60 minutes.

To continue, go down the path and look for a small trail that **veers off the main one to the right** (there are actually a couple of trails – it doesn't matter which one you take). Follow it down to a big gap in the rocky ranges to the right.

This is an important pass known either as **Naqb Abu Seila** or **El Buggiyah** (GPS 18). El Buggiyah means 'The Hornpipe', as the pass is said to blow like a horn as wind rushes through it.

Naqb Abu Seila to St Katherine [Maps 5-6]

Naqb Abu Seila has an easy walking trail on its right side. A more adventurous option is to scramble straight down the bottom. There are small waterfall cliffs and some sloping walls, but nothing too tricky.

Either way you soon reach **Wadi Tlah**, entering near some palms and enclosures (GPS 19). You can camp here if you're arriving late. To link this trek with Galt el Azraq turn right and see p154 and Map 7. To continue back to St Katherine turn left (south-east) and follow the wadi.

Wadi Tlah is a beautiful wadi lined all along with Bedouin gardens. About five to ten minutes up one garden has some outbuildings in the walls by the trail (GPS 20). This belongs to **Dr Ahmed Mansour**. He's one of the Sinai's most eminent Bedouin herbalists and knows how to use every plant on the peninsula. He's friendly, hospitable and will always offer a cup of tea.

Follow a trail along the right of the wadi. Further up a bouldery stretch makes it tricky to see. The **Chapel of St John Klimakos** is high on the right of the wadi around here but is only seen in glimpses. The best views are had by

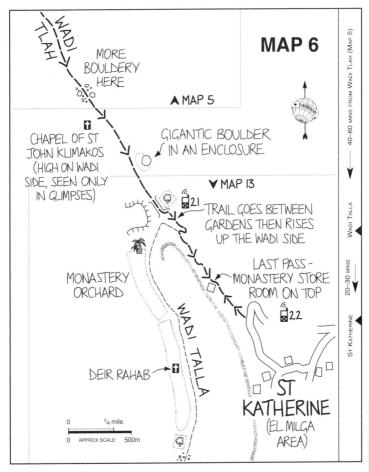

MAP 6

WADI TLAH

MORE BOULDERY HERE

▲ MAP 5

trailblaze

40–60 MINS FROM WADI TLAH (MAP 5)

† CHAPEL OF ST JOHN KLIMAKOS (HIGH ON WADI SIDE, SEEN ONLY IN GLIMPSES)

GIGANTIC BOULDER IN AN ENCLOSURE

▼ MAP 13

📱21

TRAIL GOES BETWEEN GARDENS THEN RISES UP THE WADI SIDE

LAST PASS – MONASTERY STORE ROOM ON TOP

📱22

WADI TALLA

20–30 MINS

ST KATHERINE

MONASTERY ORCHARD

WADI TALLA

DEIR RAHAB → †

0   ¼ mile
0   APPROX SCALE   500m

ST KATHERINE (EL MILGA AREA)

looking back further up (a path runs back to it). St John Klimakos, a Syrian ascetic, lived on the chapel site in the 6th and 7th centuries. He wrote a book called *The Ladder of Divine Ascent* outlining the rungs of the spiritual ladder leading to heaven. It was a sensation with early desert ascetics.

The **rocky jaws of Wadi Talla** open on the right: walk past and follow the trail as it zigzags up the side of the wadi ahead (GPS 21). Further up is a pass capped with a **monastery storeroom** (GPS 22): it's a short walk down **Wadi Quweiz** to town. To link this trek with the Jebel Abbas Basha and Jebel Katherina trail take the path that doubles back into Wadi Talla, just after you come out of the bottom of Wadi Tlah. See p154 and Map 13.

TRAIL GUIDE & MAPS

GALT EL AZRAQ (3-4 days)

Practicalities

● **Difficulty and scheduling** This has a few strenuous sections and bits of scrambling but nothing too tricky. You could get round in two very long days, but it wouldn't give you time to enjoy anything and guides would be reluctant to do it this fast. It's best done in three or four days. You only need about half a day on the first day: it takes about this long to get to a good campsite.

● **Camels** Use a camel to carry food and bags. You can meet it at the end of each day, walking with a small daypack in between.

● **Links with other treks** You can link this onto the end of the Northern Peaks Circuit (see p131). At the other end it joins the Jebel Abbas Basha and Mount Katherina route: you could do either peak or both (see p153).

Abu Seila to Kharazat Shagg   [Map 7]

Start at the small village of **Abu Seila**, about 4km north-west of St Katherine. Walk along the tarmac road in 45-60 minutes or get a taxi for LE15-25. The road ends at a small mosque by a school, with a jeep track continuing after (GPS 1). Go down the track to where it bends sharply right, then press straight ahead over blackened ground between some houses. Veer gradually left, going down past a few walled enclosures to Naqb Abu Seila (GPS 2).

This is an impressive pass that cuts down through rocky ranges. Some Bedouin call it El Buggiyah ('The Hornpipe') saying it blows like a horn as the wind rushes through it. You can take an easy walking trail on the right or scramble down the rocky bottom (nothing too tricky). Either way you come out in **Wadi Tlah**, entering near some palm clusters and enclosures (GPS 3).

Turn right and follow the wadi ahead. **Wadi Shagg** opens on the left about 10 minutes along, with enclosures and palms on both sides (GPS 4).

Turn in and walk past a few gardens. Look for a path up the left, about 150m after the last garden (GPS 5): it's hard to spot but easy to follow once you're on it. It joins a better trail higher up the wadi side. Turn right and continue along; it soon **drops back** to the wadi bottom.

It's narrow and shadowy here, with the feel of a gorge. You'll soon reach a feature like a garden wall: it's actually a **small ramp/walkway** up to the next part of the wadi. Directly below it on the left is a **spring under a boulder**. It's seen as a pool after rain and often holds water until May.

The trail soon runs steeply up the left, bringing you out in a watercourse below the pools of **Kharazat Shagg** (GPS 6). Don't scramble straight up to the pools here (it's tricky and hazardous). Go up a rocky rib to the right to emerge at some palm trees above them. You can go back down from here. One of the pools is permanent, holding water through the hottest summers. This water isn't used for drinking but you can have a paddle or bathe.

Kharazat Shagg to Wadi Abu Tuweita   [Maps 7-8]

Follow the wadi round a sharp left bend from Kharazat Shagg. It's known as **Wadi Tinya** and has a few abandoned gardens and the odd disused well.

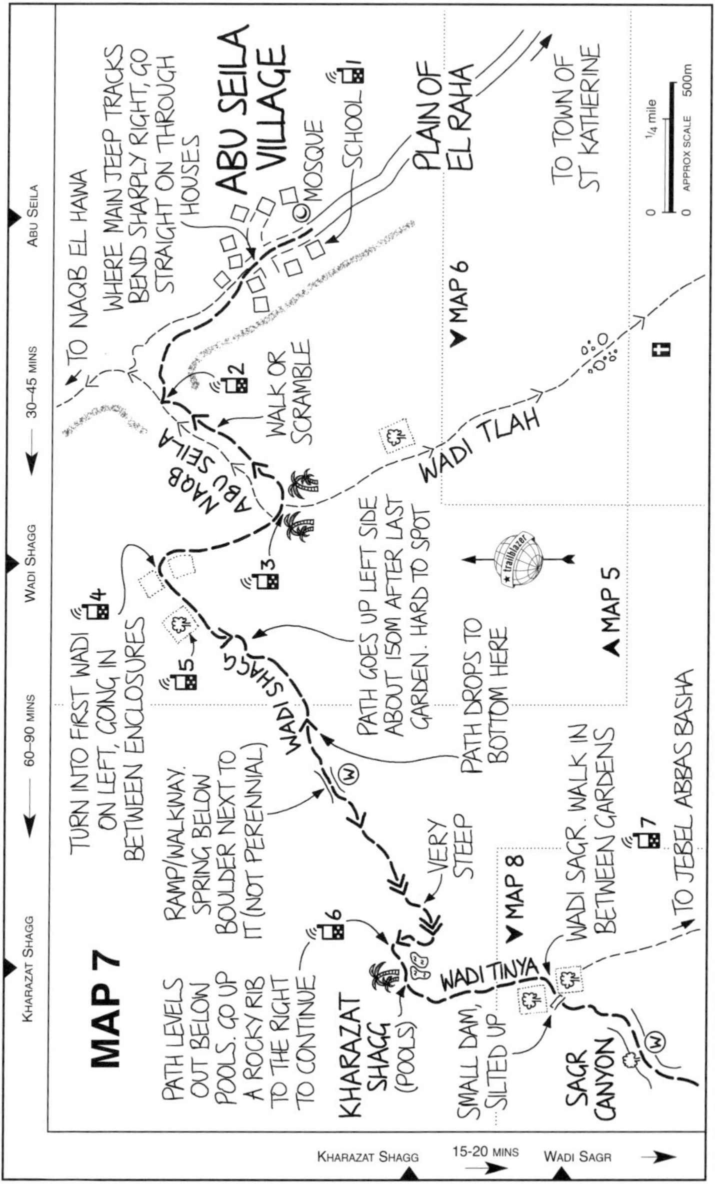
MAP 7
Abu Seila
30–45 mins
Wadi Shagg
60–90 mins
Kharazat Shagg
15-20 mins
Wadi Sagr
TO NAQB EL HAWA
WHERE MAIN JEEP TRACKS BEND SHARPLY RIGHT, GO STRAIGHT ON THROUGH HOUSES
ABU SEILA VILLAGE
MOSQUE
SCHOOL
PLAIN OF EL RAHA
TO TOWN OF ST KATHERINE
APPROX SCALE
0
1/4 mile
0
500m
MAP 6
WALK OR SCRAMBLE
NAQB ABU SEILA
WADI TLAH
TURN INTO FIRST WADI ON LEFT, GOING IN BETWEEN ENCLOSURES
PATH GOES UP LEFT SIDE ABOUT 150M AFTER LAST GARDEN. HARD TO SPOT
MAP 5
WADI SHAGG
RAMP/WALKWAY. SPRING BELOW BOULDER NEXT TO IT (NOT PERENNIAL)
PATH DROPS TO BOTTOM HERE
VERY STEEP
MAP 8
WADI SAGR. WALK IN BETWEEN GARDENS
TO JEBEL ABBAS BASHA
PATH LEVELS OUT BELOW POOLS. GO UP A ROCKY RIB TO THE RIGHT TO CONTINUE
KHARAZAT SHAGG (POOLS)
WADI TINYA
SMALL DAM, SILTED UP
SAGR CANYON

Wadi Sagr ('Wadi of the Falcon') opens on the right about 15-20 minutes later (GPS 7): it's a small wadi with two gardens outside. Turn in between the gardens and cross a small dam in the first section – whose reservoir is now filled with sediments – following the wadi up. It makes slight twists before narrowing into the shadowy confines of the **Sagr Canyon**.

Scramble up a low, rocky wall to enter the canyon. Just a short way in there's a wild fig tree and a small drip spring on the cliff next to it. The pool catches a perennial trickle and holds water throughout the year. It's an important drinking source so have a gulp and top up your bottles.

Further up there's another short scramble. The canyon ends after this and a **landscape of low rocky outcrops** comes into view ahead. Follow a faint trail that veers left through these outcrops, heading south-west: it's just a few hundred metres across this area to the bigger course of **Wadi Abu Tuweita** ('Valley of the Mulberries') (GPS 8).

Wadi Abu Tuweita to Galt el Azraq [Map 8]

Turn right and follow the wadi. A minute or two along you'll reach a nice **Bedouin garden** with several *arishas*, a deep well and a composting toilet. It's owned by Bedouin brothers called Ahmed and Saad Salah and makes a good camp. The alternative is a couple of boulder shelters about 20-40 minutes ahead. Whatever you decide, get all the water you need before you leave as the well here is the last good source for about half a day.

Carry on in Wadi Abu Tuweita and switch from the right to the left side, going between the gardens. Further up, there's a stone room built into the wall next to the trail (on the right). Turn left to exit here (GPS 9).

Go up the rocky wadi side to emerge in a higher, flat basin known as **Farsh Umm Sila**. Further ahead a broad rocky ridge divides this basin into **two separate branches**. Trails run through both and join again further ahead. You can follow either, but the one to the right is better.

The trail rises gradually up the side of the ridge into an area of low outcrops. Follow it across this area and look out for a fine **boulder shelter** with a little doorway. The trail —which is faint — veers progressively left, passing a gigantic rock known as **Hajar Nimr** ('Leopard Rock'). There's a shady hollow under this where it's said a fearsome leopard once lived.

You soon emerge in a more open area, joining the other trail from Farsh Umm Sila. Both continue as one now, running off to the right past a collection of **rock patterns** (GPS 10). There are spirals, hearts and other shapes, mostly made by Israeli trekkers a few decades back.

The trail runs through a narrowing in low bluffs, bringing you out high on the side of **Wadi Talla** (GPS 11). This is a gigantic wadi that drains a huge swathe of the mountains; it's sometimes called **Wadi Talla Kibeera** ('Big Wadi Talla') to distinguish it from a smaller wadi of the same name nearer St Katherine (Maps 6 and 13). Galt el Azraq lies far below, surrounded by flashes of green (GPS 12). A steep trail runs down, veering to the left of the pool near the bottom. There's a short, steep scramble at the very end.

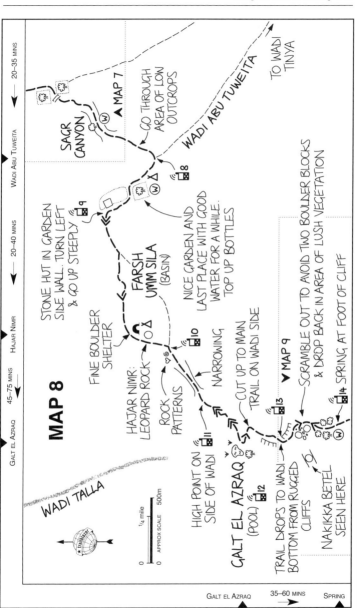

TRAIL GUIDE & MAPS

Galt el Azraq means 'The Blue Pool' and springs keep it at least four metres deep all year. Marsh plants, bushes and trees grow in profusion; amongst them a *Rubus Sanctus* – the species immortalised as the Burning Bush of the Bible. It's great for a swim after a hot trek but don't dive in (it's not as deep as it looks) and be warned – it's cold! It would be a superb camp site but animals drink here at night so it's always best to move on.

Galt el Azraq to Farsh Rummana   [Maps 8-9]

You now follow Wadi Talla Kibeera south towards Farsh Rummana. Clamber back out the same way from Galt el Azraq and move up the wadi side: there are various ways up. Whatever way you go, continue until you meet a trail along the wadi 30-40m higher. Look carefully so you don't overshoot it.

Follow this to the right and you'll soon reach a **rugged stretch of cliffs**. Its line sometimes disappears on hard rock but rojoms appear to mark out the route. It's not far along before it drops to the wadi bottom (GPS 13).

Further ahead you have to divert round several **obstacles in the wadi**. The first is a small boulder jam. Bypass this by scrambling up the cliffs on the left: they're smooth and sloping immediately above the block and it's safer higher up. Don't drop back down too soon; there's another boulder block shortly after the first. Continue along the cliffs. Look to the other side of the wadi and you'll see a canyon with a boulder jammed halfway up its course. This is **Nakikka Betel** ('Berry Canyon') and it's sometimes used as an adventurous scrambling route to Jebel Bab el Dunya (it runs into Wadi Zuweitar on Map 10 – just before Ein Najila). The rare, endemic Sinai rose is said to grow in the canyon.

You can soon scramble back to the wadi bottom, emerging in an area of thick shrubs and trees. This is called **Abu Habak** ('The Father of Mint'). Look carefully on the right side near the end; there's a **spring at the foot of a cliff** (GPS 14). A single, spiky hawthorn tree stands next to it and grasses and ferns pinpoint its more precise whereabouts. It's a good spot to top bottles up – but don't overload: there's more water at Farsh Rummana.

Whether you can continue in the wadi bottom here depends on how rains have altered the sediments. Deep dips can form below boulders, blocking progress. If it's like that, scramble out on the left again, dropping down further ahead. The wadi becomes wider, flatter and easier to follow now. There are plenty of enclosures and the odd gigantic boulder and palm.

Farsh Rummana ('Basin of the Pomegranates') (GPS 15) is further along. Camels wait here and it's a good campsite. Water is available and you can sleep in a garden or a big boulder shelter with two rooms. There's an empty stone building too (often used by trekking groups).

Farsh Rummana to Ein Najila   [Maps 9-10]

Farsh Rummana is at the bottom of **Naqb Bahriya**: a wadi that cuts into rocky ranges to the west. Enter and scramble over big boulders in the bottom: it's easiest on the right side. About halfway up, there's a diversion out on the cliffs to the right; this avoids a more difficult stretch in the bottom (GPS 16). Rojoms guide you and you can soon drop back to the bottom.

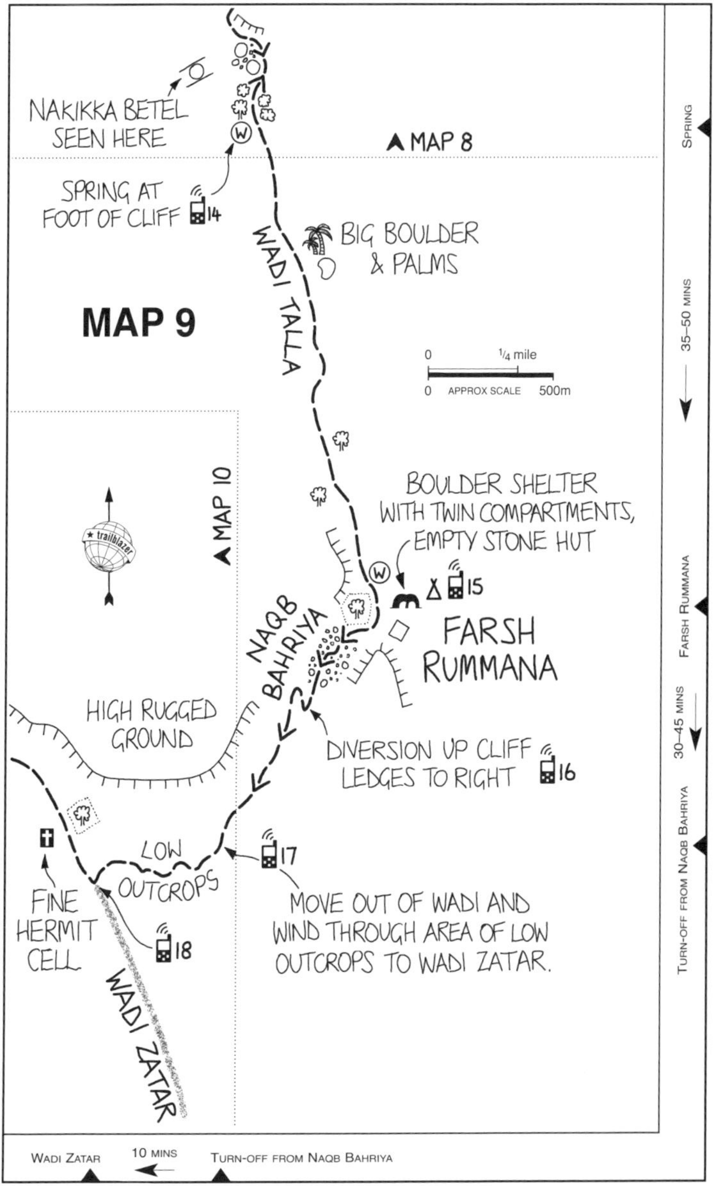

NAKIKKA BETEL
SEEN HERE

SPRING AT
FOOT OF CLIFF ⏚14

▲ MAP 8

SPRING

BIG BOULDER
& PALMS

MAP 9

WADI TALLA

0   1/4 mile

0   APPROX SCALE   500m

35–50 MINS

▲ MAP 10

BOULDER SHELTER
WITH TWIN COMPARTMENTS,
EMPTY STONE HUT

△ ⏚15

FARSH
RUMMANA

FARSH RUMMANA

NAQB BAHRIYA

HIGH RUGGED
GROUND

DIVERSION UP CLIFF
LEDGES TO RIGHT ⏚16

30–45 MINS

FINE
HERMIT
CELL

LOW
OUTCROPS

⏚17

⏚18

MOVE OUT OF WADI AND
WIND THROUGH AREA OF LOW
OUTCROPS TO WADI ZATAR.

WADI ZATAR

TURN-OFF FROM NAQB BAHRIYA

WADI ZATAR ←10 MINS TURN-OFF FROM NAQB BAHRIYA

TRAIL GUIDE & MAPS

The wadi is flat and straight in its upper section. Further along the high, rocky ground to the right gives way to an area of **lower cliffs and outcrops**. You have to move through here now but the turn-off is tricky to spot; it's marked only by a small rojom. Help others and add a stone (GPS 17).

Once you've got it, follow a twisting westerly line through this rockscape, going deliberately from one rojom to the next until you reach the small course of **Wadi Zatar** (GPS 18). Turn right and follow it along.

There's a **garden** with a **hermit cell** opposite here. It has a porch and inner chamber, accessed by a wooden door with its own metal knocker. It's one of the finest in the area and would make a superb sleeping spot.

After this, you enter the big, wide course of **Wadi Zuweitar** (GPS 19). This runs right (north) to Wadi Talla Kibeera, ending at the **Nakkika Betel** canyon passed earlier. Go the other way, veering left and heading south. You soon reach a sharp right bend: a little wadi rises off here to the south, which is where you'll go later. Ignore it now and follow the bend the full way round.

This brings you to **Ein Najila** ('The Spring of Grass') (GPS 20). A permanent cliff trickle creates rock pools in the wadi bottom here (though they evaporate in hotter months and they're not good for drinking).

A **ruined church** is just a short walk away. This was once a two-storey building and its fruit pits, wine press and chapel can still be seen. It served a thriving community of ascetics until the 8th century (a day of exploring here will uncover many hidden hermit cells). Jebel Bab el Dunya towers up directly to the west.

Jebel Bab el Dunya: the ascent [Map 10]
Jebel Bab el Dunya is a frontier summit and one of the Sinai's true gems. The Bedouin often call it **Jebel Bab** but – to be absolutely correct – this is a different summit in the same massif (the next one to the north).

Bab el Dunya is climbed in about 1½-2½ hours, there and back. There's a steep scramble to the main summit ridge, but it's not too tricky. Getting to the highest point is more difficult but you don't have to do it.

A trail winds from Ein Najila to the peak; you'll see cairns on its high points as you go. Turn left when you reach a **little fork** near the bottom of the mountain and follow a trail up its bouldery lower slopes. The terrain becomes rockier halfway up and rojoms guide you on a steep scramble.

You come out on the top of the summit ridge. To continue go left from where you first emerged on the ridge; you'll reach the **top of a gully**. This cuts down the west side of the mountain; descend 5-10m then scramble out on the left. Veer gradually left here, rising to the summit (GPS 21).

Jebel Bab el Dunya means 'Door to the World' and the summit vista is arguably the best in the Sinai. The mountain directly west is Jebel Madsus and the one to the north-west is Jebel Tarbush. These peaks are rarely seen in such good profile. The jagged summits of Africa are often seen over the Gulf of Suez. Jebel Katherina lies south-east. The flat-topped Jebel Tih – the Biblical 'Wilderness of the Wanderings' – lines the northern distance.

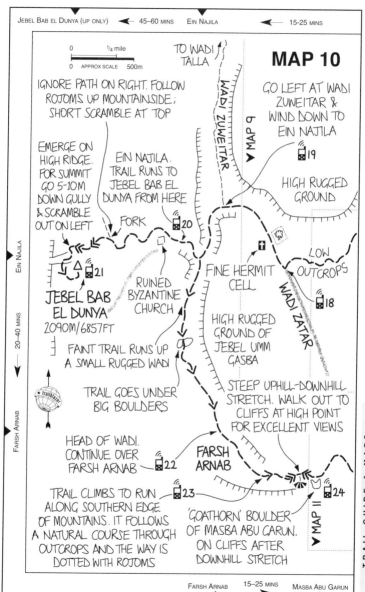

JEBEL BAB EL DUNYA (up only) ◄— 45–60 MINS   EIN NAJILA   ◄— 15–25 MINS

MAP 10

0 ____ ¼ mile
0 ____ APPROX SCALE ____ 500m

TO WADI TALLA

GO LEFT AT WADI ZUWEITAR & WIND DOWN TO EIN NAJILA

IGNORE PATH ON RIGHT. FOLLOW ROJOMS UP MOUNTAINSIDE; SHORT SCRAMBLE AT TOP

WADI ZUWEITAR

► MAP 9

📱19

EMERGE ON HIGH RIDGE. FOR SUMMIT GO 5-10M DOWN GULLY & SCRAMBLE OUT ON LEFT

EIN NAJILA. TRAIL RUNS TO JEBEL BAB EL DUNYA FROM HERE

HIGH RUGGED GROUND

FORK

📱20

LOW OUTCROPS

EIN NAJILA

📱21

JEBEL BAB EL DUNYA
2090M/6857FT

RUINED BYZANTINE CHURCH

FINE HERMIT CELL

WADI ZATAR

📱18

20–40 MINS

FAINT TRAIL RUNS UP A SMALL RUGGED WADI

HIGH RUGGED GROUND OF JEBEL UMM GASBA

TRAIL GOES UNDER BIG BOULDERS

trailblazer

STEEP UPHILL-DOWNHILL STRETCH. WALK OUT TO CLIFFS AT HIGH POINT FOR EXCELLENT VIEWS

FARSH ARNAB

HEAD OF WADI. CONTINUE OVER FARSH ARNAB

📱22

FARSH ARNAB

TRAIL CLIMBS TO RUN ALONG SOUTHERN EDGE OF MOUNTAINS. IT FOLLOWS A NATURAL COURSE THROUGH OUTCROPS AND THE WAY IS DOTTED WITH ROJOMS

📱23

📱24

► MAP 11

'GOATHORN' BOULDER OF MASBA ABU GARUN. ON CLIFFS AFTER DOWNHILL STRETCH

TRAIL GUIDE & MAPS

FARSH ARNAB   15–25 MINS   MASBA ABU GARUN

Ein Najila to Naqb Umm Siha   [Maps 10-11]

Go back to the bend before Ein Najila and turn right, following the smaller wadi rising off to the south. This rugged wadi skirts round the bottom of a mass of high, rocky land to the left: Jebel Umm Gasba. A trail remains faint – but visible – at all times. This brings you to a high point at the **head of the wadi** (GPS 22); look back for a last view of the Bab el Dunya ranges.

Follow the trail south-east over a flat expanse called **Farsh Arnab** ('Basin of the Rabbit'). It veers sharply left at the far end (GPS 23) cutting up through low crags to run along the southern edge of the mountains. It follows a natural easterly course through low bluffs and outcrops: the way unfolds easily as you go and it's dotted with rojoms all along.

About five to ten minutes along there's a steep uphill-downhill stretch. Walk out at the highest point to a cliff-edge with spectacular views: **Jebel Masba Abu Garun** (GPS 24). The cliffs drop hundreds of metres and the vertical difference with some wadis is over a kilometre. It was through this rugged wilderness that monks once travelled to Jebel Umm Shomer – one of the high peaks to the south – but it's one of the most untrodden parts of the Sinai today.

Walk out to the cliff edge again at the very bottom of the downhill stretch. This is the site most properly known as **Masba Abu Garun** ('The Father of Horns'). A boulder stands on a high precipice here, cleft into two sharp, upstanding pieces – the legendary horns in the name.

Follow the trail ahead, continuing between low bluffs and outcrops. It soon starts a sustained downhill stretch, running down to **Wadi Umm Siha** (GPS 25). Turn left and follow the wadi to the top of a pass called **Naqb Umm Siha**. There's a big boulder with an overhang on its top section here. Views extend over Wadi Jibal from this pass, which is where you go next.

Naqb Umm Siha to Wadi Zawatin   [Maps 11-12]

Go down the other side of Naqb Umm Siha to a wadi crossroads below (GPS 26). The wadi to the left goes to Farsh Rummana. The smaller one on the right is called Wadi Maza. Continue ahead in **Wadi Jibal**, following a good camel trail. You pass the odd **garden** and there's an especially nice one, belonging to a man called Salem Faraj, about 15-25 minutes along; it has a bamboo screen toilet on its side wall (GPS 27). It has fig, pomegranate and other fruit trees, and a deep well, and is a good spot to *camp* in if you're arriving late.

Further along a **Byzantine well** has steps down to the water level – but it's not suitable for drinking. The trail rises into the open flatlands of **Rehabit Nada**. Legend has it Nada was a tribesman who carried a rock the length of this area every morning (it's not clear why). You can still see it today; it's a **small, light-coloured boulder**, and it'll be somewhere next to the trail. Try carrying it a few metres and you'll see why Nada was deemed worthy of eternal association with the spot. There's a **small cemetery** at the very far end of Rehabit Nada but it's easy to miss. This site fell out of use decades ago.

The trail runs down the small pass of **Naqb Zawatin**, bringing you into **Wadi Zawatin** ('Wadi of the Olives'). You enter between the walls of two gardens, opposite a **small arisha** (GPS 28). Wadi Zawatin is a nice place to stay

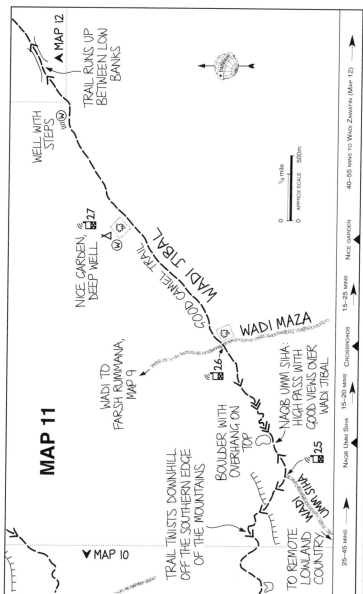

MAP 11

▼ MAP 10

◀ MAP 12

TRAIL RUNS UP BETWEEN LOW BANKS

WELL WITH STEPS Ⓦ

NICE GARDEN, DEEP WELL Δ Ⓦ ⌂27

GOOD CAMEL TRAIL

WADI JIBAL

WADI TO FARSH RUMMANA, MAP 9

WADI MAZA

⌂26

BOULDER WITH OVERHANG ON TOP

NAQB UMM SIHA: HIGH PASS WITH GOOD VIEWS OVER WADI JIBAL

⌂25

WADI UMM SIHA

TRAIL TWISTS DOWNHILL OFF THE SOUTHERN EDGE OF THE MOUNTAINS

TO REMOTE LOWLAND COUNTRY

★ Trailwater

¼ mile
0
0   500m
APPROX SCALE

| 25–45 MINS | NAQB UMM SIHA | 15–20 MINS | CROSSROADS | 15–25 MINS | NICE GARDEN | 40–55 MINS TO WADI ZAWATIN (MAP 12) |

TRAIL GUIDE & MAPS

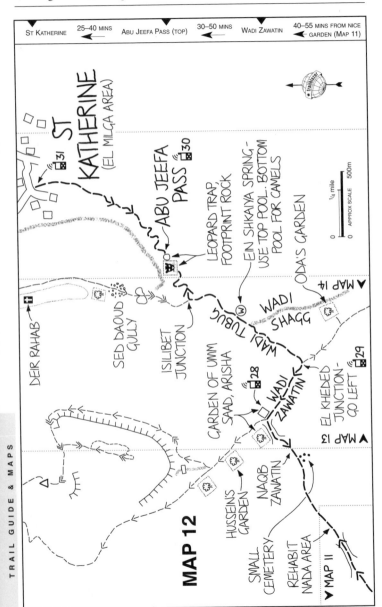

St Katherine ◄ 25–40 MINS ◄ Abu Jeefa Pass (top) ◄ 30–50 MINS ◄ Wadi Zawatin ◄ 40–55 MINS FROM NICE GARDEN (Map 11)

ST KATHERINE (EL MILGA AREA)

📷31

ABU JEEFA PASS 📷30

LEOPARD TRAP, FOOTPRINT ROCK

EIN SHKAIYA SPRING – USE TOP POOL. BOTTOM POOL FOR CAMELS

ODA'S GARDEN

▼ MAP 14

DEIR RAHAB

SED DAOUD GULLY

ISILIBET JUNCTION

WADI SHAGG

WADI TUBUG

GARDEN OF UMM SAAD, ARISHA

📷28

WADI ZAWATIN

EL KHEDED JUNCTION – GO LEFT 📷29

▼ MAP 13

HUSSEIN'S GARDEN

NAQB ZAWATIN

SMALL CEMETERY

REHABIT NADA AREA

▼ MAP 11

MAP 12

¼ mile

0 — APPROX SCALE — 500m

TRAIL GUIDE & MAPS

❏ **Bedouin footprint rocks**

The Bedouin once used rocks to propose marriage. If a man saw a woman he wanted to marry, he'd scratch an outline of his foot on a nearby rock. If the woman agreed, she'd scratch hers next to it (adding the feet of any children if she'd been married before). If the marriage was approved by her family, the father would encircle both footprints. The rocks are found widely and each tells its own story: you'll see footprints alone, footprints together, and most with no circles around.

---

and several Bedouin gardens offer accommodation – see p159 for options. To link up with the Jebel Abbas Basha or Jebel Katherina trek go to Map 14 and p156. You can go straight to either mountain or do both.

Wadi Zawatin to St Katherine   [Map 12]

Turn right and walk down the wadi. Jebel Katherina towers up ahead and you pass a few Bedouin orchards. This stretch of Wadi Zawatin is often called **El Kheded** (GPS 29). Follow the main path as it bends left into **Wadi Tubug** and look out for a **mulberry tree** (see box p136) below on the right. It's one of the biggest in the region and probably dates from Byzantine times. Jebeleya law gives it protected status but you can still pick the fruit (if others haven't polished it off before). A nearby walnut tree offers alternative grazing.

   Wadi Shagg soon opens on the right. **Ein Shkaiya** – a famous spring – is just after. Two pools catch a perennial cliff trickle here and it's an important drinking source. Use the top pool as the bottom one is for watering camels. Purify what you collect as birds can still use the top one.

   Follow the path down to a junction called **Isilibet**. Wadi Tubug continues to a gully called **Sed Daoud** ('David's Dam'). Ignore it and ascend the **Abu Jeefa** pass on a good, zigzag trail (GPS 30). There's an old leopard trap (see box p132) on top. A bit further down on the other side is a rock with **footprint scratchings** (see box p164) – one of the biggest in the area. The scratchings face away from you so glance back. The town of **St Katherine** (see pp125-31) is in good view below and it's an easy walk back (GPS 31).

JEBEL KATHERINA AND JEBEL ABBAS BASHA (2-3 days)

Practicalities

● **Difficulty and scheduling**   These are the two highest peaks in the St Katherine area and both involve strenuous ascents with bits of scrambling. You can finish in two days but it's worth bivvying on Jebel Katherina to make it three. You get the sunset, sunrise and a spectacular night view from the top and there's a little hut for shelter (take candles and warm clothes). You might also consider climbing Jebel Ahmar, a mountain on the way.

● **Guides**   Guide fees are normal for Jebel Abbas Basha but higher for Jebel Katherina. Reckon on upwards of LE250 for the ascent day. The descent day is usually cheaper if you stay on top but you'll have to discuss and haggle. To add Jebel Ahmar, your guide will want more.

❏ **Jebel Katherina in the snow – E H Palmer, *Desert of The Exodus*, 1871**
'The wind blew bitterly cold, and the road lay over a smooth white expanse of snow, which instead of being firm as it appeared, was a mere trap to let one down knee-deep, amidst sharp slippery stones, imperilling one's limbs at every step. It was a most exasperating walk; our legs had entirely their own way, and one or other of us was constantly disappearing between some concealed boulders, or slipping gracefully down the slope and having to begin again. One of the Arabs flatly refused to go on, but as I insisted, and old Salem offered to show him the way, the poor shoeless vagabond started off again with the theodolite on his shoulders.

For my part, having slipped back again to my starting-point for the sixth time, I had arrived at the conclusion that life was not worth having under the circumstances, and was about to lie down and perish, when I suddenly caught sight of one of my companions struggling on a little ahead of me. His evidently intense physical suffering cheered me with the thought that I was not alone in my misery; and after a series of startling gymnastics I succeeded in reaching the summit, perfectly exhausted and frozen.'

● **Links with other treks** You can link this onto the Galt el Azraq (see p142) or Northern Peaks Circuit (see p131) treks. You could also do either Jebel Abbas Basha or Jebel Katherina as a peak in its own right.

St Katherine to Wadi Tubug [Map 13]

This trek starts in **Wadi Quweiz**; an easy walk from the Bedouin Camp and Guesthouse in **El Milga**. Follow the tarmac road as it bends uphill through a housing district; Wadi Quweiz is on the left about ten minutes up. It has a jeep track and a few houses up its lower stretch. Follow it up to a low pass capped with a **monastery storeroom** (GPS 1).

There's a good view back to St Katherine here: Jebel Rabba towers high with Wadi el Arbain to the left (where the trek ends later). Carry on down the other side on a good trail. Five to ten minutes along there's a **fork** where one branch of the path zigzags down to the wadi bottom, running off between two gardens into **Wadi Tlah** (GPS 2). Ignore this and take the one ahead at a higher level. This veers left into the **rocky jaws of Wadi Talla**.

The path soon runs alongside a **big orchard**. This belongs to the Monastery of St Katherine and produces hundreds of kilos of fruit and nuts for the monks every year. Wadi Talla is taken over almost entirely by monastery gardens – another big one starts a little way up. This one's filled with olive groves and there's a building in the middle called **Deir Rahab** ('Monastery of Cosmas and Damianos'). It commemorates a pair of Christian twins who practised medicine in 3rd century Syria. They treated the needy and – according to legend – performed the world's first successful leg transplant. They soon became the victims of their own success though: the Romans heard about their clinic and killed them when they refused to renounce Christianity. They remain especially popular martyrs in the Orthodox Church today.

Continue to the end of Wadi Talla. The path becomes more rugged and you pass a **Bedouin garden** before reaching the bottom of a big, rocky gully. This

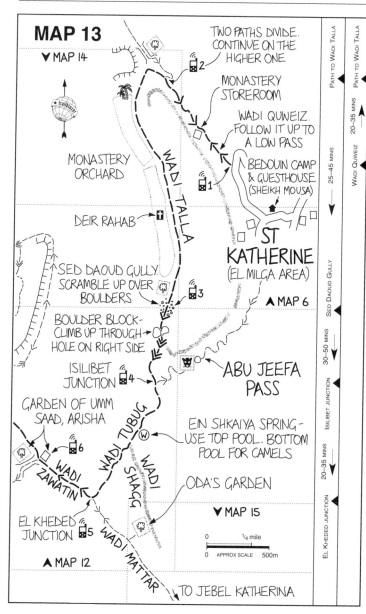

MAP 13

▼ MAP 14

TWO PATHS DIVIDE.
CONTINUE ON THE
HIGHER ONE

📱2

MONASTERY
STOREROOM

WADI QUWEIZ.
FOLLOW IT UP TO
A LOW PASS

BEDOUIN CAMP
& GUESTHOUSE
(SHEIKH MOUSA)

MONASTERY
ORCHARD

WADI TALLA

📱1

DEIR RAHAB

ST
KATHERINE
(EL MILGA AREA)

▲ MAP 6

SED DAOUD GULLY.
SCRAMBLE UP OVER
BOULDERS

📱3

BOULDER BLOCK-
CLIMB UP THROUGH
HOLE ON RIGHT SIDE

ABU JEEFA
PASS

ISILIBET
JUNCTION 📱4

GARDEN OF UMM
SAAD, ARISHA

📱6

WADI TUBUG

EIN SHKAIYA SPRING-
USE TOP POOL. BOTTOM
POOL FOR CAMELS

WADI
ZAWATIN

WADI
SHAGG

ODA'S GARDEN

▼ MAP 15

EL KHEDED 📱5
JUNCTION

WADI MATTAR

▲ MAP 12

0   1/4 mile
0   APPROX SCALE   500m

TO JEBEL KATHERINA

PATH TO WADI TALLA | PATH TO WADI TALLA | 20–35 MINS | WADI QUWEIZ | 25–45 MINS | SED DAOUD GULLY | 30–50 MINS | ISILIBET JUNCTION | 20–35 MINS | EL KHEDED JUNCTION

TRAIL GUIDE & MAPS

is known as **Sed Daoud** ('David's Dam'); its name comes from a Bedouin legend the Biblical King David once drank here (GPS 3).

The trail runs up the left side of the gully but tapers out. Drop down and
scramble up the bouldery bottom course: route finding is trial and error. About
halfway up there's a gigantic **boulder block**; the only way to pass is by scrambling up through a hole on the right. It's a short, vertical climb and a bit of a
squeeze, so ditch your rucksack and get someone to pass it up. The gully soon
flattens and you can walk out of its upper stretch to a junction called **Isilibet**
(GPS 4). On the left a big zigzag trail goes to the top of a pass. This is called
Abu Jeefa and it's the most important camel route between St Katherine and
these parts of the mountains. The name means 'Father of the Corpse' – perhaps
after the camels that slipped and died.

Wadi Tubug to Wadi Zawatin   [Maps 13-14]
Wadi Tubug is a small wadi lined with luxuriant Bedouin gardens – amongst
the most productive in the region. Follow a big path ahead. **Ein Shkaiya** soon
appears on the left: this is a **spring** where two pools catch a perennial trickle
from the cliffs. The bottom one is for watering camels, so use the top one. Even
here, purify what you collect as it can be used by birds.

The rocky mouth of **Wadi Shagg** opens after the spring. Continue in Wadi
Tubug and look for a mulberry tree below the path on the left. Some say it dates
from the 7th century and Jebeleya law accords it special protection. You can still
pick the fruit, but you'll be lucky to find any. Others pick it soon after it ripens.
A nearby walnut tree might offer an alternative. Wadi Tubug soon runs into **El
Kheded** (GPS 5) – a junction at the bottom of **Wadi Zawatin**.

The trail up the slope to the left leads to Jebel Katherina: to go there now
move onto p159 and Map 15. For Jebel Abbas Basha, turn right and continue up
the wadi, following a good trail past some Bedouin gardens. About five to ten
minutes up there's a **small arisha** on the right (GPS 6).

Directly opposite is a gap between **two garden walls**: a trail leads through
and up a pass known as Naqb Zawatin – the most common route to Farsh
Rumanna, Jebel Bab el Dunya and Galt el Azraq.

Continuing up Wadi Zawatin you can walk between the gardens or take a
trail above them on the right (easier). Further up – before the very last garden
in the wadi – you'll see the mouth of a **smaller wadi** on the right (GPS 7).

It's directly below the southern buttress of Farsh Abu Mahshur: a gigantic
mass of sheer, smooth granite cliffs. Turn off here for **Farsh Abu Mahshur**.

Going this way involves plenty of steep, strenuous scrambling. For an easier walking alternative continue up Wadi Zawatin to **Sharafat Sakikriyeh** – a
saddle (GPS 12). Turn right here and follow a clear zigzag trail north-east to the
top of the peak (GPS 11). Allow about 50-70 minutes.

Wadi Zawatin to Jebel Abbas Basha   [Map 14]
Leave the main path and enter the small wadi. There's a **little dam** on the left a
short way in. **Don't go towards this**: veer right on a rough trail, rising up
through rocky bluffs to a **low pass**. A rugged wadi stretches out before you – go
down and follow it ahead; its line stays clear as it runs round the bottom of the

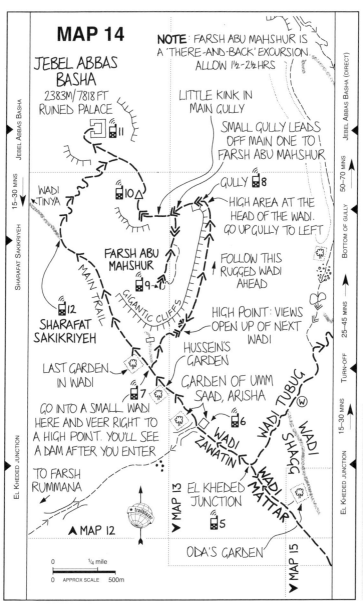

MAP 14

JEBEL ABBAS BASHA
2383M/7818 FT
RUINED PALACE

NOTE: FARSH ABU MAHSHUR IS A 'THERE-AND-BACK' EXCURSION. ALLOW 1½-2½ HRS

LITTLE KINK IN MAIN GULLY

SMALL GULLY LEADS OFF MAIN ONE TO FARSH ABU MAHSHUR

GULLY

HIGH AREA AT THE HEAD OF THE WADI. GO UP GULLY TO LEFT

WADI TINYA

FOLLOW THIS RUGGED WADI AHEAD

FARSH ABU MAHSHUR

MAIN TRAIL

GIGANTIC CLIFFS

HIGH POINT: VIEWS OPEN UP OF NEXT WADI

SHARAFAT SAKIKRIYEH

HUSSEIN'S GARDEN

LAST GARDEN IN WADI

GARDEN OF UMM SAAD, ARISHA

GO INTO A SMALL WADI HERE AND VEER RIGHT TO A HIGH POINT. YOU'LL SEE A DAM AFTER YOU ENTER

WADI ZAWATIN

WADI TUBUG

WADI SHAGG

WADI MATTAR

TO FARSH RUMMANA

MAP 13

EL KHEDED JUNCTION

ODA'S GARDEN

MAP 15

▲ MAP 12

0   ¼ mile
0   APPROX SCALE   500m

JEBEL ABBAS BASHA

SHARAFAT SAKIKRIYEH

EL KHEDED JUNCTION

JEBEL ABBAS BASHA (DIRECT)

BOTTOM OF GULLY

TURN-OFF

15-30 MINS

25-45 MINS

50-70 MINS

15-30 MINS

TRAIL GUIDE & MAPS

gigantic cliffs to the left. Further up a better trail emerges, rising up steep, rugged slopes to a **high, flat area** at the wadi's head (GPS 8).

Looking directly left you'll see a **gully in the cliffs**. It's a wide, shallow one; better defined higher up. The bottom is a mass of smooth, sloping rocks. Scramble in and follow the gully upwards. A **smaller gully** soon cuts into the cliffs on the left; several trees grow up its boulder-choked course. Turn in and scramble up here to emerge in a high basin. Cross to a gap on its far right side, where a **small natural passageway** begins. Follow this down in a more or less straight line through the rockscape before you.

The basin of **Farsh Abu Mahshur** (GPS 9) comes into good view below. 'Mahshur' means a place that's enclosed or difficult to get to – and you'll see why. There are two options. You can press straight on in the passageway, which soon becomes a **steep crack**. This is the standard route, but it's exposed and best avoided if you don't like scrambling. Alternatively, walk out over the back of the **big, broad granite ridge** on the left. You can follow it the length of the basin to cut down a series of wide, easy ledges at the far end. Follow the rojoms carefully so you don't wander into dangerous places.

Farsh Abu Mahshur was a Christian hideaway and the foundations of an **early church** stand near a few trees. Just south of this spot a **narrow passageway** starts in the bluffs, running down to a lower portion of the basin. There's a ruined Byzantine dam here, which trapped sediments, enabling the Christians to cultivate cereals. After Abu Mahshur, return to the main gully.

Continuing up there's a point that might be mistaken for a **fork**; a small bouldery branch rises ahead/to the left. Follow the main gully round a very slight kink to the right. A bit further up it cuts through rocky ground as a narrower crack (take the bigger crack on the left – not a more minor one on the right). This brings you to the top and it's a simple walk to the summit, marked by a large cairn (GPS 10). In past ages this peak was known as Jebel Tinya, but it's usually just called Jebel Abbas Basha today. Correctly, **Jebel Abbas Basha** is its sister peak, crowned with a large, square-shaped palace (GPS 11). A trail connects both and you can enter the palace.

The Ottoman Viceroy Abbas Basha ordered its construction in the mid 19th century, wanting a sanatorium for his chronic tuberculosis. He hoped to build it on Mount Sinai, but apparently changed his mind when monks told him the air was cleaner, and that meat rotted more slowly here (of course, a ruse to protect their holy mountain). Hundreds of Bedouin were pressed into service, with many dying on the job. Construction halted when Abbas died in 1854: some say he was murdered by a servant who was having an affair with a lady of his harem.

Jebel Abbas Basha to Wadi Ahmar   [Maps 14-15]

Pick up the big trail halfway between the two peaks and follow it down to the saddle of **Sharafat Sakikriyeh** (GPS 12). Wadi Tinya runs off to the right

> ❑ **Pasha**
> Note that Pasha is an honorary Turkish title spelt with a P. With Arabic having no P sound locals use the nearest equivalent: B. The peak is written how it's said – Abbas *Basha*.

❏ **Camping in Wadi Zawatin**
Wadi Zawatin has beautiful Bedouin orchards. **Hussein Abu Towarah** has a garden
in the upper parts; it has a deep well, a composting toilet and a stone shelter for cold
nights. Further down, near the arisha, is the garden of a Bedouin woman called **Umm
Saad** (also known as **Ammreya**). It's a bit more basic but the welcome is warm.
There are others too – ask and you'll find good alternatives. A little further on from
Wadi Zawatin is the garden of **Oda Mohammed** (see below).

(north-west), leading a few kilometres down to the pools of Kharazat Shagg, on
the Galt el Azraq trek (see Map 7, p143). Go the other way, moving back down
Wadi Zawatin (see box above) to El Kheded.

Continue from El Kheded, following a trail up a gentle slope towards Jebel
Katherina. This brings you into **Wadi Mattar** ('The Wadi of Rain'). Follow the
trail ahead here. About five minutes along you can see part of **Wadi Shagg**
through some low bluffs on the left. There's a small stone building just before
it and the tops of some trees are visible in a garden beyond.

This belongs to **Oda Mohammed** and it's another good place to stay. Even
if you don't stay you can always get a cup of tea or some water, and fresh apricots are sometimes available in late April and May.

Continue in Wadi Mattar and keep a good lookout on the left about five to
ten minutes along (when you pass two enclosures). Camouflaged in the bluffs
is an **unusual hermit cell**. Most cells have an entrance but this one is completely walled up. One story goes the hermit's companions blocked it when he
died, turning his favourite spiritual spot into a tomb.

Just after this there's a **mulberry tree** with a ring of stones around it –
another possible snacking spot. It stands outside a walled enclosure and marks
the point you have to **veer left** through a **line of low rocky outcrops**. The small
mouth of **Wadi Ahmar** ('Red Wadi') opens up on the other side (GPS 13).
Gardens are seen left and right before you enter: the last spots for water until
after Jebel Katherina. Top up with everything you need and remember it's higher than other peaks – more exertion means more water. Also check you have
enough warm clothes and, if possible, take a few candles for the summit hut.

Wadi Ahmar to Farsh Umm Sila   [Map 15]

You can climb Jebel Katherina and get back to town in a day. To sleep on top
you'll need about half a day; aim to arrive at least an hour before sunset as it's
always spectacular. You could set off later or climb a mountain called **Jebel
Ahmar** on the way. A pointer is given but it's not marked on the map – you'll
have to rely on your guide. Go into Wadi Ahmar and follow it ahead. There's a
small **rectangular building** about five minutes up – probably an early monastic retreat. Scramble up some wide rocky ledges behind it and continue in the
wadi bottom. It soon straightens and rises gently to a wide, V-shaped pass.
Ignore a faint trail up the right of the wadi here – this is a different route to Jebel
Katherina – and continue directly ahead.

TRAIL GUIDE & MAPS

Follow the rojoms as they guide you along the left side of the wadi, squeezing and ducking between boulders. A **big pass** soon opens on the right. Jebel Katherina's summit **pokes up above it** and you go here next. For Jebel Ahmar, carry on up the wadi – ask your guide.

Cross Wadi Ahmar where a **single tree stands below a huge boulder** (GPS 14). Under the boulder is a shady hollow with graffiti. Enter the pass to the south, rising on a bouldery trail. It levels out in a rugged rockscape. There are no good trails so follow the rojoms carefully. Jebel Katherina is an obvious reference to the south. Also useful is the highest rocky ground to your left (east). You skirt round the foot of this all the way – let its general line guide you.

A small trail soon joins from the right: this is the one that left Wadi Ahmar earlier. Afterwards is a **small wire enclosure** (GPS 15). From here, rise through a gap between the highest ground on the left and some slightly lower bluffs to the right. The route finding becomes easier here and you soon reach a **bigger wadi** (GPS 16). It drains out of a small rocky gorge and marks the place red rock is replaced by black (the red is some 570 million years older).

Veer left on a clear trail rising south-east to the saddle of **Farsh Umm Sila** (GPS 17). **Wadi Shagg Musa** ('The Cleft of Moses') runs north, with Mount Sinai in splendid profile at the end. You go this way later. Jebel Katherina is south, with a chapel on top.

Jebel Katherina   [Map 15]

A good zigzag trail leads up the mountain and two separate summits come into view where it levels out at the top. **Jebel Katherina** is the first on the right (GPS 18). Its chapel dates from the early 20th century and marks the spot it's said angels laid St Katherine's body after her martyrdom in Alexandria (see p77). The peak further south has two radio masts on top. It's often grouped with Jebel Katherina and called by the same name but – to be absolutely correct – this is **Jebel Zebir** (GPS 19). It's about five metres higher than Jebel Katherina and is Egypt's highest point at 2642m.

Both peaks stand about 250m higher than any others around St Katherine. You're at the **crossroads of Africa and Asia** here – the biggest continents on earth – and on a good day you can see both. The deserts around Ein Hudera are visible to the north-east and Jebel Tih ('the Wilderness of the Wanderings') to the north. Jebel Umm Shomer and Jebel Rimhan are the jagged-looking

---

❏ **Things that go bump in the night**
Ghost stories are in wide circulation around Jebel Katherina. It's said to be haunted by *jinn* or **ghosts**, including that of a monk who froze one night in the chapel. Clattering is common and some report whispering in strange tongues. Don't worry: the noise is created by all the litter. Wind blows it about and mice roll it around. As for the voices – if they really do occur – an engineer trekker suggested to me the radio masts might have something to do with it. Apparently, they work with an AM signal which – unlike an FM signal – can be amplified roughly by pieces of metal debris to create the sort of trailing, diffuse sounds reported.

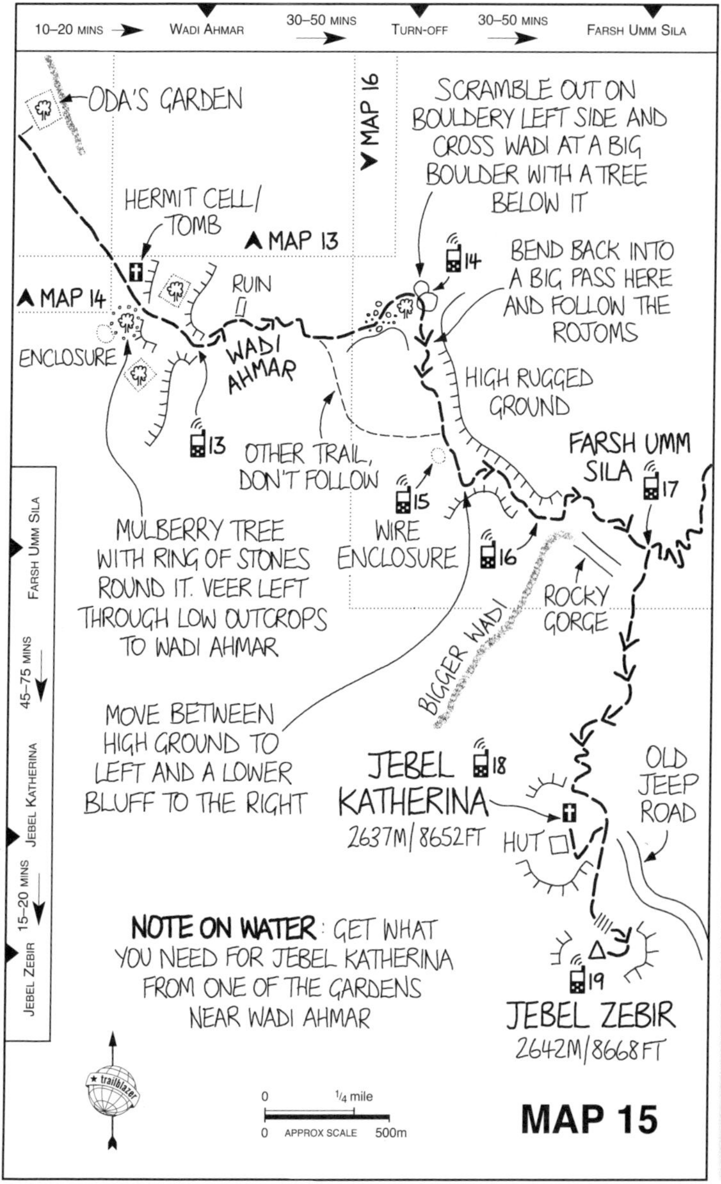

MAP 15

mountains to the south. Camping out is well worth it. Along with sunset and sunrise, ships glitter on the Gulf and faraway towns and cities glow.

You can sleep in an **empty room** below the chapel but it's basic and you have to sleep on floorboards (watch out for splinters).

The only disappointing thing about Jebel Katherina is the amount of rubbish. Trekkers are responsible for their fair share but most dates from the **Egypt–Israel wars** – this was once a military stronghold and you can see the road soldiers used to drive up here (it snakes up from Wadi Rutig, south of St Katherine). To descend, return to **Farsh Umm Sila** (GPS 17).

Farsh Umm Sila to St Katherine   [Map 16]

Turn right into **Wadi Shagg Musa** and follow a good trail down: Mount Sinai looms ahead all the way. Further down, a trail runs off the main one to the right. It crosses a small walkway to **Ein Shanir** ('Spring of the Partridges') (GPS 20). This catches a perennial trickle from the cliffs and is an important drinking source. Legend has it a flock of partridges guided monks here when they were bringing St Katherine's remains down in the 9th century.

Carry on down to **Wadi el Arbain**. You enter near the garden of a Jebeleya tribesman called **Ramadan Musa Abu Said** and it's worth dropping in (GPS 21). There are boulders with Nabataean graffiti here and he keeps a thriving colony of rock hyrax (see p63). It's awash with tea and hospitality and there's *accommodation* too. A cosy stone room costs about LE50 a night (food is available) and you can pitch your tent for LE30.

Deir el Arbain ('Monastery of the Forty Martyrs') is next to Ramadan's garden. It dates from about the same time as the Monastery of St Katherine and there are contrasting accounts over its name. Some say it honours the Forty Martyrs of Sebaste: a group of Roman soldiers killed for professing Christianity in the 4th century. Another story suggests it commemorates a massacre of monks in these parts by early, pre-Islamic desert peoples.

To connect this trek with Mount Sinai, see p164 and Map 17. Otherwise, a clear trail runs down Wadi el Arbain to St Katherine. The wadi is notable for its rocks: many have **Nabataean, early Christian and Bedouin footprint graffiti** (see p153).

Further along – standing partly in the enclosure of a small chapel – is the **Rock of Moses**. There are twelve niches in its side that it's said flowed springs when Moses struck it with his staff. Look out for a **big wishing rock** below the trail near the end of the wadi. It's one of the most important in the area (see p163). The trail ends at the main road in the El Rasees area (GPS 22).

MOUNT SINAI/JEBEL MUSA (1-2 days)

Practicalities

● **Guides** Guides should cost LE120-150 – no other fees – and they charge about LE85-120 to go up the Steps of Repentance or Camel Path.

● **Difficulty and schedule** This is mostly a moderate trek but Jebel Safsafa involves an exposed scramble (optional). It's possible to finish in a day, catching

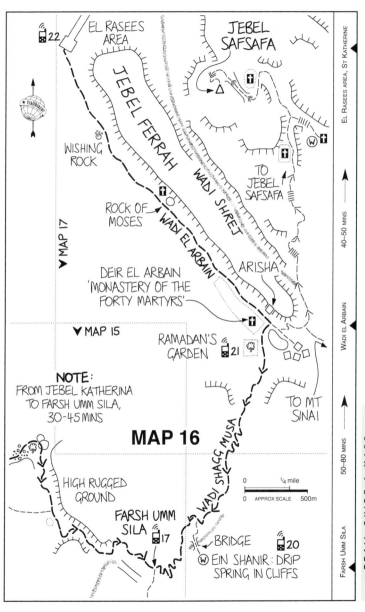

EL RASEES
AREA

JEBEL
SAFSAFA

trailblazer

JEBEL FERRAH

WADI SHREJ

WISHING
ROCK

ROCK OF
MOSES

WADI EL ARBAIN

ARISHA

DEIR EL ARBAIN
'MONASTERY OF THE
FORTY MARTYRS'

RAMADAN'S
GARDEN

TO
JEBEL
SAFSAFA

TO MT
SINAI

NOTE:
FROM JEBEL KATHERINA
TO FARSH UMM SILA,
30-45 MINS

MAP 16

HIGH RUGGED
GROUND

WADI SHAGG MUSA

FARSH UMM
SILA

BRIDGE

EIN SHANIR: DRIP
SPRING IN CLIFFS

0   1/4 mile
0   APPROX SCALE   500m

MAP 17

MAP 15

EL RASEES AREA, ST KATHERINE

40-50 MINS

WADI EL ARBAIN

50-80 MINS

FARSH UMM SILA

TRAIL GUIDE & MAPS

> ❏ **Jebeleya wishing rocks**
> The Jebeleya believe throwing a pebble on top of a rock gets you a wish. The pebble
> has to stay on top and it can't be any old rock; it has to be a designated wishing rock.
> These usually acquired their special status because of a lucky association in the past,
> though most are forgotten today. The rocks are common on major thoroughfares and
> you'll spot them easily for their scatterings of pebbles.

the sunset on top and coming down in twilight. Even so, most sleep out to see
the sunrise, then visit the Monastery of St Katherine in the morning.
● **Links with other treks** This can be linked on to the end of the Jebel
Katherina and Jebel Abbas Basha trek (p153). You could tag an ascent of Jebel
el Deir on the other end (p169).

Town of St Katherine to Deir el Arbain   [Map 17]

Walk to the end of the road in **El Rasees** (GPS 1). Follow a good, paved foot-
path into the course of **Wadi el Arbain** here. About ten minutes along, there's
a big boulder below the path on the right. It's usually heaped with small pebbles
and is the most famous **Jebeleya wishing rock** (see box above) in the area.

Hajar Musa ('Rock of Moses') is further along. It's built into the wall of a
chapel enclosure and has 12 distinct fissures in its side. According to legend,
each babbled water when Moses struck it with his staff. Monks add their own
footnote, claiming it rumbled after the Israelites as a makeshift water barrel on
their wanderings, returning when they reached the Promised Land.

Wadi el Arbain has lots of **other interesting rocks**, including ones with
Nabataean, early Christian and Bedouin footprint graffiti (see box p153).
They dot the trail, but most face away from you.

The trail runs alongside a garden of olive trees – all many centuries old.
They belong to **Deir el Arbain** ('Monastery of the Forty Martyrs'), further up.
This is one of the Sinai's **oldest monasteries**, dating from about the same time
as the Monastery of St Katherine. Some say its honours the Forty Martyrs of
Sebaste; a group of Roman Christian soldiers killed in 4th century Turkey.
Others, that it commemorates a massacre of monks around here by pre-Islamic
desert peoples. This monastery was once especially hallowed for the Bedouin.
They said its grounds had special healing powers and that mountain spirits held
nightly revels, whirling to the sound of divine fantasias.

A **small arisha** gives shelter on the trail by the monastery. Alternatively,
drop in on the garden of a Jebeleya tribesman called **Ramadan Musa Abu
Said**. It's round the other side of the monastery and tea, water and hospitality
are always in good supply. He keeps a thriving colony of **rock hyrax** (see p63),
always hard to spot in the wild.

Deir el Arbain to Jebel Safsafa Chapel   [Map 17]

From the arisha, the path runs up gentle slopes to the left. You soon reach a **fork**
where you have to turn left (GPS 2). There are actually a few forks here – some

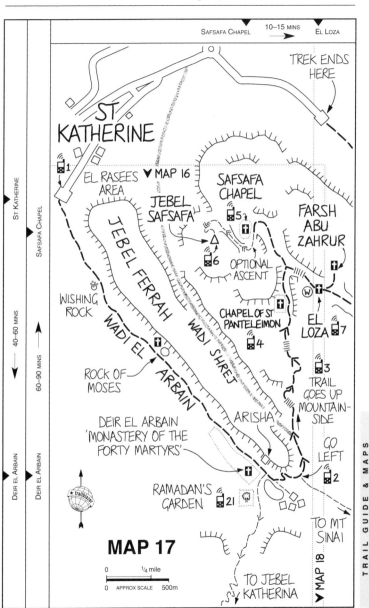

SAFSAFA CHAPEL → 10–15 MINS → EL LOZA

TREK ENDS HERE

ST KATHERINE

EL RASEES AREA   ▼ MAP 16

SAFSAFA CHAPEL

JEBEL SAFSAFA

FARSH ABU ZAHRUR

OPTIONAL ASCENT

JEBEL FERRAH

WADI EL ARBAIN

WADI EL SHRET

WISHING ROCK

CHAPEL OF ST PANTELEIMON

EL LOZA

ROCK OF MOSES

TRAIL GOES UP MOUNTAINSIDE

DEIR EL ARBAIN 'MONASTERY OF THE FORTY MARTYRS'

ARISHA

GO LEFT

RAMADAN'S GARDEN

TO MT SINAI

▼ MAP 18

MAP 17

0   ¼ mile
0   APPROX SCALE   500m

TO JEBEL KATHERINA

★ trailblazer

St Katherine

Safsafa Chapel

40–60 MINS

60–90 MINS

Deir el Arbain

St Katherine

Safsafa Chapel

Deir el Arbain

TRAIL GUIDE & MAPS

of them more minor than others – but their paths all converge in the same basic place higher up: take whichever one you want.

Veer progressively left up steep slopes to the flat upper stretch of **Wadi Shrej** (sometimes called **Wadi Ferrah**). Look for a path that runs out on the right of the wadi here, rising up the rocky side of Jebel Safsafa (GPS 3). This is sometimes called **Darb el Shrej** and it's a paved path with steps up steeper sections. Some claim it's the route Moses took up the mountain.

Higher up, this levels out, running between low bluffs into an open basin (GPS 4). The **Chapel of St Panteleimon** stands here.

Move through a **small pass** in the bluffs behind the chapel. An ancient **paved trail** starts on the other side; this is the main path on the mountain. Turn left and follow it ahead; this leads you round to the **Safsafa Chapel** ('Chapel of the Holy Girdle of the Virgin Mary') (GPS 5).

To climb **Jebel Safsafa** (GPS 6) go left from where you first reached the chapel. Scramble along the rocky bluffs directly above its enclosure to the southern end of the basin. Head straight up a **big bouldery gully** on the right: a fine view of the **Plain of el Raha** opens from the top. Legend has it the Israelites stayed here when Moses spent his 40 nights on Mount Sinai.

Go left and scramble up rocky walls to the higher parts of the mountain. Just below the summit you have to traverse a sloping ledge over a dizzy drop. Most trekkers are content to stop here: if you attempt it **extreme care** is needed. Remember you have to come down this way too – that's always harder.

Jebel Safsafa chapel to Farsh Elias [Maps 17-18]
Go back on the same path you came along to the chapel. This soon rises into a small basin known as **El Loza**. The name means 'The Almond', after an ancient tree still here today. **Kineesit el Loza** ('Chapel of St Gregory of Sinai') is nearby, along with a **deep well of cool water** – the best on the mountain. Help yourself, but note it's used heavily by guides and often runs dry.

Turn left through a gap in the rocks just after the chapel and walk into **Farsh Abu Zahrur**. The **Chapel of St John the Baptist** stands here by a cluster of hawthorn (*zahrur*) trees. If you clamber up the southern bluffs of the basin you'll find a dam. This was built to stop mountain torrents shooting on to the Monastery of St Katherine. The crags to the east offer a famous – and near vertical – 400m view down on the monastery. There are plenty of passages and peaks around here exploring around here too.

These parts of Jebel Safsafa were the most heavily settled in the whole of the Sinai. It's thought about 100 monks once lived here, each with his own spot. Their ruins still dot unlikely hollows of the mountain today.

Go back and join the main trail. Turn left and follow it ahead; it soon leads uphill, bending right through rocky bluffs into **Farsh Elias** ('Elijah's Basin') (GPS 8). Legend has it the **Prophet Elijah** spoke with God here and there's a small chapel in his honour. Nearby is a dam and a courtyard with some cypress trees. If you explore further afield you'll find the **Chapel of St Stephen**. It's next to the hermit cell where he lived 1500 years ago.

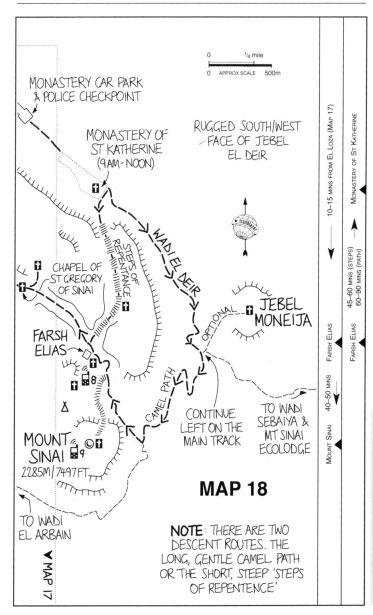

MONASTERY CAR PARK & POLICE CHECKPOINT

MONASTERY OF ST KATHERINE (9AM-NOON)

RUGGED SOUTH/WEST FACE OF JEBEL EL DEIR

0   ¼ mile
0   APPROX SCALE   500m

10-15 MINS FROM EL LOZA (MAP 17)

MONASTERY OF ST KATHERINE

WADI EL DEIR

STEPS OF REPENTANCE

CHAPEL OF ST GREGORY OF SINAI

FARSH ELIAS

JEBEL MONEIJA

OPTIONAL

CAMEL PATH

45-60 MINS (STEPS)
60-90 MINS (PATH)

FARSH ELIAS

CONTINUE LEFT ON THE MAIN TRACK

TO WADI SEBAIYA & MT SINAI ECOLODGE

40-50 MINS

MOUNT SINAI 2285M / 7497FT

MOUNT SINAI

MAP 18

TO WADI EL ARBAIN

▼ MAP 17

NOTE: THERE ARE TWO DESCENT ROUTES. THE LONG, GENTLE CAMEL PATH OR THE SHORT, STEEP 'STEPS OF REPENTENCE'

TRAIL GUIDE & MAPS

Farsh Elias is home to a Bedouin café doing hot food all night. Protectorate authorities request trekkers camp somewhere in the basin rather than on Mount Sinai itself. The hundreds of visitors put extra heavy strain on its facilities and it's hard to control the waste. You'll also sleep better. Crocodiles of tourists lumber up here from the early hours, making an almighty racket. If you want to bivvy on a summit, there are nice peaks around Farsh Abu Zahrur.

Farsh Elias to Mount Sinai   [Map 18]

Mount Sinai's sunrise is world-famous but sunset is better – if only for the peace and quiet. A trail zigzags up from the basin and a flight of solid-hewn steps begins higher, with about 750 to reach the top (GPS 9). The **Chapel of the Holy Trinity** stands on the summit, marking the spot it's said God gave Moses the Ten Commandments. Close by, a **small mosque** stands over the **cave** where legend has it Moses sheltered. Both the chapel and mosque were built partly from the ruins of an **early Byzantine church**.

The summit has excellent views. The dark heights of Jebel Katherina loom up to the south-west. Jebel el Ojar stands to the north, with a distinctive U-shaped pass to the right of it. The table-topped Jebel Tih escarpment lines the northern distance.

Farsh Elias to the Monastery of St Katherine   [Map 18]

The Monastery of St Katherine closes at midday so get down with an hour or two to look around (it's closed on Fridays and Sundays). There are two options: the long, circuitous **Camel Path**, or the steep, direct **Steps of Repentance**.

The camel path starts above Farsh Elias, running through a narrow cutting in the rock. This was blasted away under the Ottoman Viceroy Abbas Basha, who wanted to build a palace on Mount Sinai (see p158 for the full story). The path is easy to follow. The only point of potential error comes when you pass **Jebel Moneija**, a little peak with a chapel on top. Follow the main path to the left here. Other trails go right, leading down to a settlement in Wadi Sebaiya. People often mistake this for St Katherine, especially in poor light.

The **Steps of Repentance** start by the dam in Farsh Elias and there are about 3000. They were started in the 4th century and – it seems probable – finished with a flurry of activity in the 6th century. There are two arches in the first section. The first is the **Gate of Elijah**; the second, the **Gate of Forgiveness**. Both have Byzantine inscriptions, made by pilgrims.

Further down is the small **Chapel of the Virgin of the Economos**. One story suggests it marks a delivery of food to the monastery during a time of famine. Another, that it marks the miraculous extirpation of fleas from its grounds (which some quip is a miracle that needs repeating).

The steps soon end and you come into the big course of Wadi el Deir. At the southern end of the valley is **Jebel Moneija**, crowned with the **Chapel of St Theodore of Tyro and St Theodore the Recruit**. The **Monastery of St Katherine** (see pp126-8) is directly ahead (GPS 10). A track runs back to a car park, from where you can follow the road to town. For Jebel el Deir move onto the next map.

JEBEL EL DEIR (1-2 days)

Practicalities

● **Difficulty and scheduling** This route involves more scrambling than any in the book. The holds are good and there's no serious exposure, but you need to feel comfortable moving on rocky terrain. It's possible to finish in a day but it's nice to sleep out too. Start later on the first day if you'll be camping and take all your water as there's none on the mountain.

● **Guides** Jebel el Deir is little trodden. Few guides know it well, but you still have to take one (follow this description if they don't know it).

● **Links with other treks** This links onto the end of Mount Sinai.

Monastery of St Katherine to Farsh Jamaam [Map 19]

Note: the scale on the map is roughly double that used elsewhere.
Start at the **Monastery of St Katherine** (GPS 1). Go past the main entrance of the monastery, towards its last south-east tower. Turn left and strike up Jebel el Deir's low, rocky flanks in a northerly direction.

There are no trails so take your own line, aiming for the bottom of a **steep ravine** in the mountainside ahead (GPS 2). Two trees grow in its lower section, but they can look like one from a distance (and they won't be green or so obvious without leaves in winter). Don't confuse the ravine with a wide, bouldery rake that rises gently up bluffs to the left before it.

To begin, go up the **right side** of the ravine: there are wide, easy ledges. Immediately after the two trees there's a boulder jammed in the ravine. Cross over here and scramble up its **left side**. Continue until you pass another boulder block further up. Drop down now and go up the bottom.

You soon reach a **fork**: take the left branch. There's a **second fork** shortly after but it's more minor. The main feature is a shadowy crack on the left; go right, scrambling up steep rocky walls and veering left at the top.

You exit the ravine and emerge in the more **open spaces of Jebel el Deir's west face** (GPS 3). It's about 1885m; a 300m vertical gain from the monastery.

Traverse the west side of the mountain, rising up rocky ledges in a northerly direction. Rojoms dot the way.

Veer sharply to the right as you approach the far west shoulder of the mountain, moving up steeper ground to a **high flat basin** (GPS 4). There are good views back to Mount Sinai, Jebel Safsafa and the gigantic Plain of el Raha ('The Plain of Rest') from here.

Cross the basin to a gap on its far side. Big views open up of a new part of the mountain. The highest ground to the east is the **main summit ridge**. Scanning the ground around the bottom you might just be able to pick out a small building. This is a **ruined Byzantine church**.

Follow a rough trail down towards the church. Looking right the perspective of the mountain changes, with a **broad rocky buttress** coming into profile. This stands parallel to the main summit ridge and you need to veer towards it. There's a very rough trail in places and a few rojoms dot the way; but nothing is obvious so it's good to use major landmarks for orientation.

> ❏ **Hermit cells**
>
> Hermit cells are dotted across the mountains. Most were made by blocking up hollows under boulders. Many date from Byzantine times, when ascetics scattered out for spiritual solitude. A few go back even further and remain the haunting legacy of the Roman persecutions, when thousands fled here to escape the bloodshed.

Scramble down a rocky wall to a little wadi that runs down the side of the **broad rocky buttress** (GPS 5). There are Byzantine ruins here, including several old buildings and a dam, though the reservoir is now filled with sediments. Further up the wadi is a **hermit cell** (see box above) that offers a possible sleeping spot.

Go back past the point you first entered this little wadi, following it round a bend to the right. There's a steep section with little flights of **Byzantine steps** (just small, rough stones in a line). These were once part of a trail that linked the last buildings with the bigger **church** (GPS 6).

The church is reached by cutting over a low rocky spur. It's one of a few buildings here. This is actually one of the biggest Byzantine complexes in the region and it's thought up to 20 monks once lived here.

The church lies in a **steep gully** below the main summit ridge. Follow this gully up, scrambling over big boulders. From the top you can follow a natural passageway straight through the bluffs to **Farsh Jamaam** (GPS 7).

Farsh Jamaam stands about 2010m high on the west face of Jebel el Deir. You can look down on the Monastery of St Katherine from a ravine on its western side. There's another ravine on its southern side. This is sometimes used as a descent route but there's a tricky section halfway down (you have to climb down a gap below a boulder on a rickety ladder). Farsh Jamaam is a good spot to camp, with a beautiful spectacle of Mount Sinai at sunset.

Farsh Jamaam to the summit of Jebel El Deir [Map 19]

A **big crack** cuts into the summit ridge where you first entered Farsh Jamaam, giving a direct scrambling route to the top. Look out for the small Byzantine dam at the bottom, taking care not to damage it. About halfway up there's a rock jammed in the crack. It's hard to get good handholds; do it by bracing yourself on the walls (or get a leg-up). There's a small basin at the top of the crack; walk up smooth granite slabs from here to the **summit** (GPS 8).

Jebel el Ojar stands north with a U-shaped pass next to it. The beautiful, flat-topped Jebel Tih stretches across the horizon beyond. The main peak to the east is Jebel Umm Alawi. You get a very rarely seen view of Mount Sinai with Jebel Katherina beyond it here too.

Jebel el Deir to the Monastery of St Galaktion & St Episteme [Map 19]

Walk north along the back of the summit ridge to where it rises up in a small mass of knobbly boulders at the very end. Immediately before this, a **gully** cuts steeply down to the right (GPS 9) – follow it down.

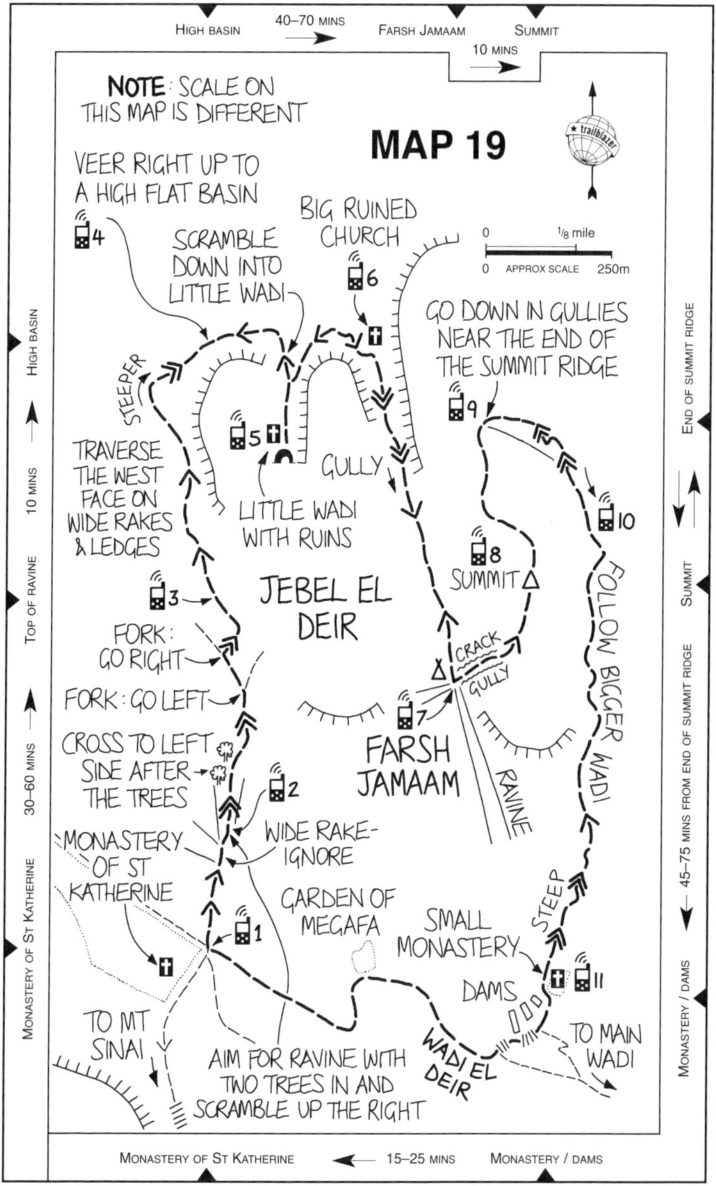

MAP 19

NOTE: SCALE ON THIS MAP IS DIFFERENT

40–70 MINS
HIGH BASIN → FARSH JAMAAM   SUMMIT
10 MINS →

VEER RIGHT UP TO A HIGH FLAT BASIN
📱4

SCRAMBLE DOWN INTO LITTLE WADI

BIG RUINED CHURCH
📱6 †

GO DOWN IN GULLIES NEAR THE END OF THE SUMMIT RIDGE
📱9

0   1/8 mile
0   APPROX SCALE   250m

STEEPER

TRAVERSE THE WEST FACE ON WIDE RAKES & LEDGES

📱5 †
LITTLE WADI WITH RUINS

GULLY

📱10

HIGH BASIN

10 MINS

TOP OF RAVINE

30–60 MINS

MONASTERY OF ST KATHERINE

📱3

FORK: GO RIGHT
FORK: GO LEFT
CROSS TO LEFT SIDE AFTER THE TREES

MONASTERY OF ST KATHERINE

📱2
WIDE RAKE– IGNORE

GARDEN OF MEGAFA

JEBEL EL DEIR

SUMMIT
📱8 △

△ CRACK
GULLY
📱7
FARSH JAMAAM

RAVINE

FOLLOW BIGGER WADI

END OF SUMMIT RIDGE

SUMMIT

45–75 MINS FROM END OF SUMMIT RIDGE

📱1

TO MT SINAI †

AIM FOR RAVINE WITH TWO TREES IN AND SCRAMBLE UP THE RIGHT

SMALL MONASTERY
DAMS

STEEP

† 📱11

WADI EL DEIR

TO MAIN WADI

MONASTERY / DAMS

MONASTERY OF ST KATHERINE ← 15–25 MINS → MONASTERY / DAMS

TRAIL GUIDE & MAPS

Walk straight over a basin at the bottom to another gully that drains out of its far side. Scramble down and turn right at the bottom, moving south through a gap in the rocks to a **bigger wadi** (GPS 10). Follow this wadi along, going parallel to the summit ridge. This soon steepens into a ravine.

It's an easy one with traces of a rough foot or goat trail and it leads directly down to the **Monastery of St Galaktion and St Episteme** (GPS 11). Another ravine runs in at exactly the same point from the right here. This is the one that dropped from the southern end of Farsh Jamaam earlier.

The monastery is said to be the oldest in the Sinai. It takes its name from two Christians who lived here in the 3rd century. It's said they led a community of ascetics before being captured by Roman troops and killed in Alexandria. The building is used as a retreat by local monks wanting to get away from the daily tourist hubbub at the Monastery of St Katherine.

Back to the Monastery of St Katherine   [Map 19]

There are **three dams** below the monastery. These stop flash floods or 'seils' tearing down to the bigger Monastery of St Katherine (it has been damaged by plenty through the ages). There's a small building above the top dam and it has a cistern with a metal lid in its porch. This is usually left without a padlock and water is sometimes available in the wetter months.

Follow a paved path down past the dams. The **Garden of Megafa** is lower down. This is another retreat for monks and there's an original hermit cell in its grounds. It's just a short way back to the Monastery of St Katherine, from where you can move on easily back to town.

JEBEL UMM SHOMER (3 days)

Practicalities

● **Getting to the trailhead** This trek starts in Wadi Zeituna, about 20km south of St Katherine. You can walk, or ride a camel, but most trekkers organise 4x4 transport for LE300-500. The track is one of the worst in the mountains and especially in a pick-up truck (which is how the Bedouin usually drive it). A jeep will be safer and is recommended. An empty storeroom gives a sleeping spot at the trailhead (take candles). There's a deep well in a nearby garden, but it isn't always full and it doesn't have a rope. There's a bigger one on the jeep track a few hundred metres before where you can get water up in a bucket.

● **Guide issues** This trek is in Aulad Said territory; it's best to use their tribesmen as guides and cameleers. A few live in St Katherine but they're hard to find; it's best to organise through a local agency (see p124-5). Guides and cameleers may want an extra day's pay for the return trip.

● **Camels** These are essential for water and bags. There are good stretches for riding on the last two days, so consider one per person. Doing the trek like this, you could always ride in on the first day too.

● **Difficulty** The first day is strenuous with sustained scrambling on Jebel Umm Shomer (holds are good and there isn't too much exposure). The last two days are an easy, downhill wadi walk all the way to the coast.

❏ **Thunder on the mountain**
Jebel Umm Shomer was long said to boom out deafening rolls of thunder. The
Bedouin, monks and explorers all heard it. It led some to believe Umm Shomer was
the real Mount Sinai of the Bible – with its thunder, lightning and divine trumpets –
but the British Ordnance Survey team devised a more plausible theory. They put it
down to earth tremors – which still rumble the Sinai today – dislocating gigantic
weathered blocks, which crashed down to the wadis below.

Zeituna to Jebel Abu Shajara [Map 20]

Walk up the small wadi from the trailhead, following it around a hairpin bend
to the left and continuing in a straight stretch. Five to ten minutes along there's
a slight kink where a watercourse runs in from the right (GPS 2). **Strike out to
the right** here, heading up the wadi side to the south-west. There are no good
trails but you soon reach the crest of a ridge.

It's a dividing ridge that splits the last small wadi from a bigger one to the
west. A better trail starts here; follow it along the other side of the ridge towards
the **head of the new wadi** (GPS 3). This is actually a saddle that separates it
from another new wadi to the south. Good views extend all the way down to a
mountain called **Jebel Rimhan**. Jebel Umm Shomer stands just to the right of
this —its sister peak — though it's still out of view.

The high, rugged ground of **Jebel Abu Shajara** stands west. Head up its
steep slopes, veering gradually left to the south-west. The trail is faint and you
have to look carefully. Help trekkers who follow by making the odd rojom. It
levels off higher up and becomes easier to follow (GPS 4).

There are good views of Jebel Rimhan again and sometimes even the Hejaz
mountains of Arabia stand up in the distance. Jebel Umm Shomer edges gradually into view and you soon reach a **high point** (GPS 5) where it stands directly opposite, over on the far side of a **big, natural saddle below**.

Wadi Zeraigiyeh is to the right of the saddle; to the left is **Wadi Rimhan**.
Jebel Umm Shomer appears as a series of jagged peaks. You climb it in a ravine
cutting straight up between the two highest peaks on the right.

Jebel Umm Shomer: the ascent [Maps 20-21]

Jebel Umm Shomer is the Sinai's second highest summit at 2586m. It's a strenuous 500 vertical metres from the saddle to the summit and the same back
down. There's a scramble at the top but it's not too difficult.

Follow a steep, loose trail down to the **saddle** and cross to its far side. Look
out for a pile of stones here. This looks like an old leopard trap but it's smaller
than most other specimens. It might have been a trap adapted for a different animal or just a normal one more heavily ruined (GPS 6).

The trail starts behind this, going up the **lower left side of the ravine** (it
does this to avoid a steep, smooth waterfall cliff). Further up it **switches to the
right side**, before leading into its main course. A continuous line of rojoms
emerges here, dotting the rocks to keep you on track. *(Cont'd on p176)*

TRAIL GUIDE & MAPS

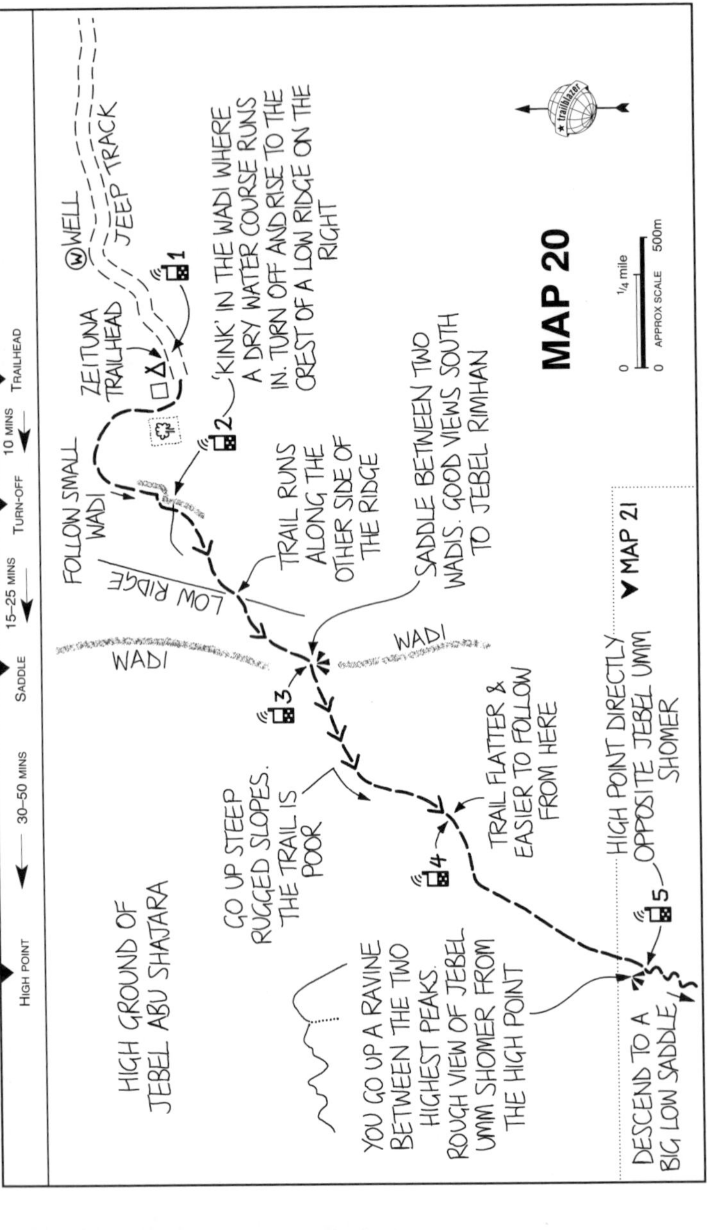

MAP 20

TRAIL GUIDE & MAPS

High Point — 30–50 MINS — SADDLE — 15–25 MINS — TURN-OFF — 10 MINS — TRAILHEAD

0 — ¼ mile — 0 — 500m — APPROX SCALE

ZEITUNA TRAILHEAD

WELL

JEEP TRACK

'KINK' IN THE WADI WHERE A DRY WATER COURSE RUNS IN. TURN OFF AND RISE TO THE CREST OF A LOW RIDGE ON THE RIGHT

FOLLOW SMALL WADI

TRAIL RUNS ALONG THE OTHER SIDE OF THE RIDGE

SADDLE BETWEEN TWO WADIS. GOOD VIEWS SOUTH TO JEBEL RIMHAN

LOW RIDGE

WADI

WADI

TRAIL FLATTER & EASIER TO FOLLOW FROM HERE

MAP 21

HIGH POINT DIRECTLY OPPOSITE JEBEL UMM SHOMER

HIGH GROUND OF JEBEL ABU SHAJARA

GO UP STEEP RUGGED SLOPES. THE TRAIL IS POOR

YOU GO UP A RAVINE BETWEEN THE TWO HIGHEST PEAKS. ROUGH VIEW OF JEBEL UMM SHOMER FROM THE HIGH POINT

DESCEND TO A BIG LOW SADDLE

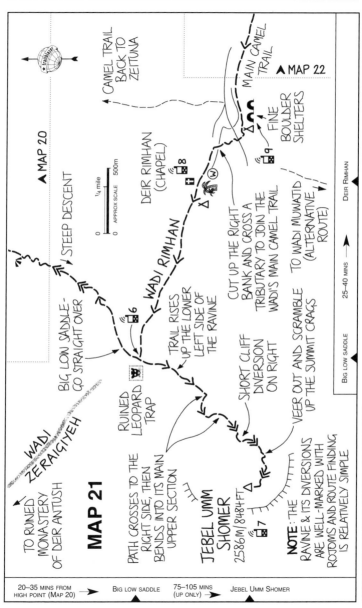

CAMEL TRAIL BACK TO ZEITUNA

MAP 22 ▲

MAIN CAMEL TRAIL

FINE BOULDER SHELTERS

MAP 20 ▲

STEEP DESCENT

DEIR RIMHAN (CHAPEL)

8 ▦ ✚

⚑ 9

W

△

CUT UP THE RIGHT BANK AND CROSS A TRIBUTARY TO JOIN THE WADI'S MAIN CAMEL TRAIL

TO WADI MUWATID (ALTERNATIVE ROUTE)

DEIR RIMHAN →

BIG LOW SADDLE — GO STRAIGHT OVER

WADI ZERAIGIYEH

TO RUINED MONASTERY OF DEIR ANTUSH

RUINED LEOPARD TRAP ▣

6 ⚑

WADI RIMHAN

TRAIL RISES UP THE LOWER LEFT SIDE OF THE RAVINE

SHORT CLIFF DIVERSION ON RIGHT

VEER OUT AND SCRAMBLE UP THE SUMMIT CRAGS

25–40 MINS

BIG LOW SADDLE ▶

MAP 21

PATH CROSSES TO THE RIGHT SIDE, THEN BENDS INTO ITS MAIN UPPER SECTION

JEBEL UMM SHOMER
2586m/8484ft

△

7 ▦

NOTE: THE RAVINE & ITS DIVERSIONS ARE WELL-MARKED WITH ROTOMS AND ROUTE FINDING IS RELATIVELY SIMPLE

0   ¼ mile
0   500m
APPROX SCALE

20–35 MINS FROM HIGH POINT (MAP 20) →   BIG LOW SADDLE   75–105 MINS (UP ONLY) →   JEBEL UMM SHOMER

(Cont'd from p173) There's another **diversion** out on wide cliff ledges higher up, but it's a short one. The summit section soon comes into view on the right. It's a gigantic mass of knobbly boulders and round, bulging cliff faces.

Many early travellers – including the celebrated explorer John Lewis Burckhardt – turned back at this point. Nowadays you can just follow the rojoms, going deliberately from one to the next through the crags. The only difficult part comes when you reach a crack jammed with small rocks. Even this isn't too bad though – especially not with a leg up. It's just a short way from here to the top, marked by a big boulder cleft down the middle.

Jebel Umm Shomer has one of the finest views in the Sinai. The jagged peaks of Egypt rise beyond the Gulf of Suez. The summits of the High Mountain Region are away to the north. Jebel Rimhan rises in the south and 15km beyond is Jebel Thebt, the third highest peak in the Sinai at 2439m.

Have a scout around the summit. One boulder bears the inscriptions of the first climbers: T E Yorke and the Reverend T J Prout. Both were British and ascended in 1862. Correctly, they were the first Western climbers: the Bedouin had been up here before. A Byzantine crucifix suggests Christians had summitted earlier too. Also look for **Hajar el Bint** (see box below): a rock that protrudes on the west side of the peak. It looks as if it had a crack that was filled up with another stone. It has a legend attached to it, but it's little known today.

Follow the rojoms back down to the saddle, going the same way you came. **Wadi Rimhan** runs off to the right (south-east). Before continuing you could consider an excursion in the wadi on the other side too.

Excursion to Deir Antush

Deir Antush is a ruined monastery about 3km down Wadi Zeraigiyeh. It's made of big, solid blocks of stone and has six hermit cells and other buildings around it. Amongst them is a ruined mosque, converted from the monastery's old winery (its *mihrab* is still visible). It was the last outlying monastery to be abandoned, probably at the end of the 1700s. You'd need a good 3-4 hours given the descent and ascent involved. There's not a lot left to see and the chances are you won't have the time. Even so – if you do – it's there.

❏ **Hajar el Bint (The Girl's Rock), E H Palmer, *Desert of The Exodus*, 1871**
Hajar el Bint was once so famous Jebel Umm Shomer was known only by its name. The 19th-century British explorer Edward Henry Palmer records its legend as thus: 'Long ages ago there dwelt upon Umm Shomer a fairy who used to fascinate stray travellers by the exquisite strains which she could elicit from her flute of reeds. She was beautiful beyond mortal loveliness and her only covering was the long streaming hair which flowed in rich waves over her neck. One day a Bedawi hunter, while pursuing his game in the mountains, came suddenly upon the damsel, who entertained him with pleasant discourse and left him completely enamoured of her charms. In the morning he determined to seek again the mysterious beauty and to bring her back with him by force or stratagem. But, when he came to a point in the road where the path lay through a narrow cleft in the rock, he found that the fairy maiden had anticipated him, and baffled his evil designs by miraculously closing up the fissure in the rock as we behold it in the present day. Since that time she has never again been seen'.

Jebel Umm Shomer to Deir Rimhan [Map 21]

Wadi Rimhan is a big wadi running all the way to the coastal plain. Its lower stretch is known as Wadi Isleh but it's the same basic wadi from start to finish. Follow a good trail down from the saddle. Further ahead on the left is the church of **Deir Rimhan** (GPS 8), a modern satellite of the Monastery of St Katherine. This site was occupied on and off until the 8th century and crucifixes and inscriptions of pilgrims are still found on nearby rocks. Guides always use the garden below as a campsite; it has dead wood and a few wells. Alternatively, there are a couple of boulder shelters 10-15 minutes away (see below).

Alternative route to Wadi Isleh

Jebel Umm Shomer and Jebel Rimhan are separated by a big pass. Wadi Muwajid begins on the other side, running down to Wadi Isleh. Guides might suggest this as an alternative to the camel trail in Wadi Rimhan; it takes about 4-7 hours, bringing you out on Map 25, before the beautiful gorge. It's good if you're short on time but you'll have to carry all your water and meet your camel later.

Explorers found monastic ruins around the head of the wadi in the 19th century, but they're well-hidden and tricky to find now. The best ones are in the wadi's lower stretch.

Deir Rimhan to Wadi Isleh [Maps 21-23]

Continue down the wadi, looking for a faint trail up its **right bank** a bit further down. This crosses a small tributary to lead you onto the main right bank of Wadi Rimhan, where the **camel trail** begins. There are two **boulder shelters** at the start (GPS 9). Both have small doorways and they'd be excellent, cosy spots to shelter in, in bad weather. Follow the camel trail down the wadi.

Further down there's a ruined house just left of the trail and another short-ly afterwards. After this the **path drops** to the wadi bottom, entering near an enclosure (GPS 10). A bit further down another obscure camel trail runs out on the right bank. This bypasses a rocky stretch in the bottom. It's a short diversion and you soon re-enter the wadi again. Without a camel, go in the bottom.

The wadi makes sharp bends as it begins to cut a more southerly course, soon **narrowing between low rocky walls**. Further ahead is **Moiyet Zilega**, where palms grow amongst patches of pink granite (GPS 11). Water was once available in abundance but it's been mostly drained off by the gardens today.

Wadi Tarfa opens on the left after Moiyet Zilega: this runs back to Wadi Rahaba (near where the trek started). There are **steep slabs of granite** in the wadi bottom around here; lead your camels down carefully.

About 10-15 minutes after this a solid, paved **Byzantine path** rises out on the left side of the wadi. This runs up to Wadi Tarfa and is one of several old camel roads that ran between Mount Sinai and Raithu (modern-day El Tur). This became the main trail to the Monastery of St Katherine after the Islamic Conquest, replacing the route through Wadi Feiran: traders, travellers, monks and pilgrims all followed it (some still use it today).

Wadi Thebt soon joins Wadi Rimhan and both continue as a single, bigger wadi. This is where it becomes **Wadi Isleh** (GPS 12). *(Cont'd on p180)*

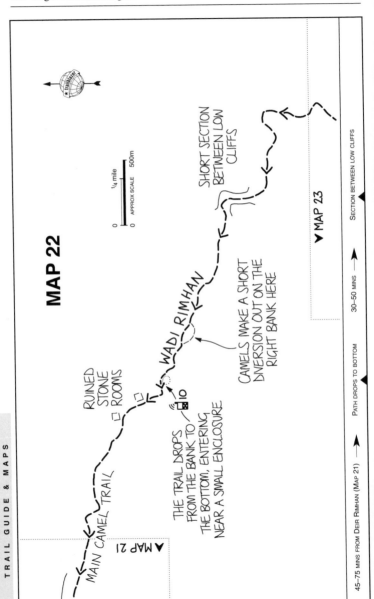

MAP 22

¼ mile
0 — 500m
0 APPROX SCALE

RUINED STONE ROOMS

MAIN CAMEL TRAIL

▼ MAP 21

WADI RIMHAN

THE TRAIL DROPS FROM THE BANK TO THE BOTTOM, ENTERING NEAR A SMALL ENCLOSURE

CAMELS MAKE A SHORT DIVERSION OUT ON THE RIGHT BANK HERE

SHORT SECTION BETWEEN LOW CLIFFS

▼ MAP 23

45–75 MINS FROM DEIR RIMHAN (MAP 21) ⟶   PATH DROPS TO BOTTOM ⟶   30–50 MINS ⟶   SECTION BETWEEN LOW CLIFFS

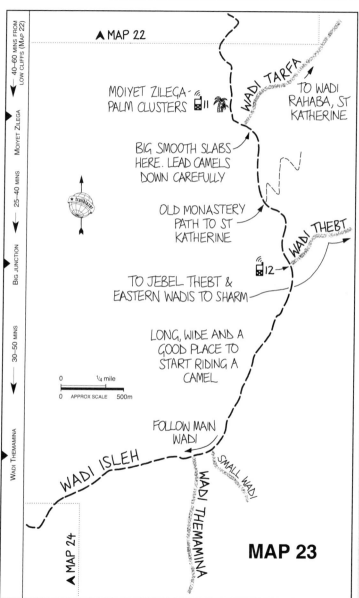

40–60 MINS FROM LOW CLIFFS (MAP 22)

◀ MAP 22

MOIYET ZILEGA-
PALM CLUSTERS 📱11 🌴

WADI TARFA

TO WADI
RAHABA, ST
KATHERINE

BIG SMOOTH SLABS
HERE. LEAD CAMELS
DOWN CAREFULLY

MOIYET ZILEGA   25–40 MINS

★ trailblazer

OLD MONASTERY
PATH TO ST
KATHERINE

WADI THEBT

BIG JUNCTION

📱12

TO JEBEL THEBT &
EASTERN WADIS TO SHARM

30–50 MINS

LONG, WIDE AND A
GOOD PLACE TO
START RIDING A
CAMEL

0   ¼ mile
0   APPROX SCALE   500m

FOLLOW MAIN
WADI

WADI THEMAMINA

WADI ISLEH

SMALL WADI

WADI THEMAMINA

MAP 23

◀ MAP 24

TRAIL GUIDE & MAPS

Wadi Isleh to Wadi Muwajid [Maps 23-25]

Wadi Isleh is wide, flat and good for riding camels. Up ahead, a wadi rises through the mountains to a high V-shaped pass. This is **Wadi Themamina**, a pretty wadi sometimes used as an alternative route to the coast.

Look out for the vegetation change in Wadi Isleh: the climate is milder and the first acacias and succulents begin to appear.

Further down, the wadi **narrows between high walls** (GPS 13). A pinnacle of high, smooth granite comes into clear view on the left after you get through. This might be called **Jebel Zebribi**. Look for the **huge boulders** in the wadi bottom below (GPS 14): they look as if they crashed down directly from its summit and their biggest bulk is probably buried underground.

There are plenty of gardens in the wadi from here. They're usually occupied in cooler months, and people will always give you water.

Wadi Muwajid joins from the right (GPS 15). This begins from the pass between Jebel Umm Shomer and Jebel Rimhan and makes an excellent camp on the second night. Even if you don't camp, go and explore. There are clusters of palms, dense bamboo thickets and ruined monastic buildings. Look out for the ziziphus tree (p64) at the mouth of the wadi: it has a small cherry-sized fruit, sometimes called 'Chinese Sour Date'. It's a bit dry, but not a bad snack for the trail. There's sometimes a creek around here where you can get water too.

Wadi Muwajid to the Plain of Qa [Maps 25-26]

About 15-20 minutes down from Wadi Muwajid is an area of dense vegetation (GPS 16): grasses, marsh plants, bamboos and palms all grow thickly and a creek flows through the greenery in wetter months. The wadi narrows between high, sheer walls, becoming a **fine gorge**. It's rocky underfoot and there are often small waterfalls; camels should be led along. The Bedouin say this gorge can fill to the brim with water during the heaviest storms.

The wadi widens at the end of the gorge; just follow its course ahead. Further along there's a sharp hairpin bend; make sure you go round its whole length. A smaller wadi runs off the bend to the south-east and can look deceptively like a continuation of its main course (GPS 17).

The wadi runs between high, narrow walls again but it's nothing as spectacular as before. After this you spill out of the wadi's rocky jaws onto the **Plain of Qa**. Cut up the right bank of Wadi Isleh's lower drainage line after exiting to reach the small Bedouin settlement of **Seil Isleh** (GPS 18). Ask around and you'll find someone with a pick-up truck. Getting to El Tur (see pp119-21) costs about LE150-300.

> ❏ **Walking from St Katherine to Wadi Feiran**
> You can walk between St Katherine and Wadi Feiran. Follow Naqb el Hawa down to the village of Sheikh Auwad (see Maps 4 and 5, pp138-9). **Wadi Solaf** runs to Feiran from here, bringing you out near the Furrah village area. There are good views of Jebel Serbal and a few Nawamis tombs towards the end, but it's mostly a monotonous wadi slog. It can be done in a long day but two would be more comfortable.

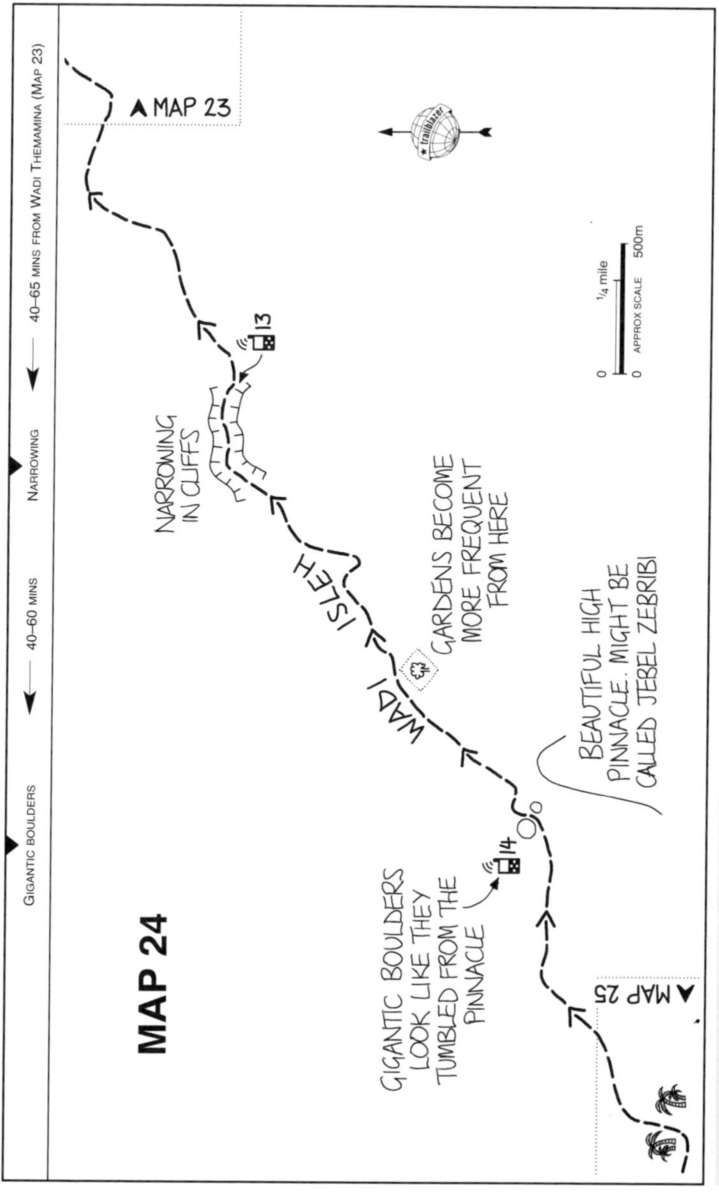

40–65 MINS FROM WADI THEMAMINA (MAP 23)

NARROWING

40–60 MINS

GIGANTIC BOULDERS

MAP 24

▲ MAP 25

APPROX SCALE

0   ¼ mile

0   500m

NARROWING
IN CLIFFS

WADI ISLEH

GARDENS BECOME
MORE FREQUENT
FROM HERE

BEAUTIFUL HIGH
PINNACLE. MIGHT BE
CALLED JEBEL ZEBRIBI

GIGANTIC BOULDERS
LOOK LIKE THEY
TUMBLED FROM THE
PINNACLE

13

14

TRAIL GUIDE & MAPS

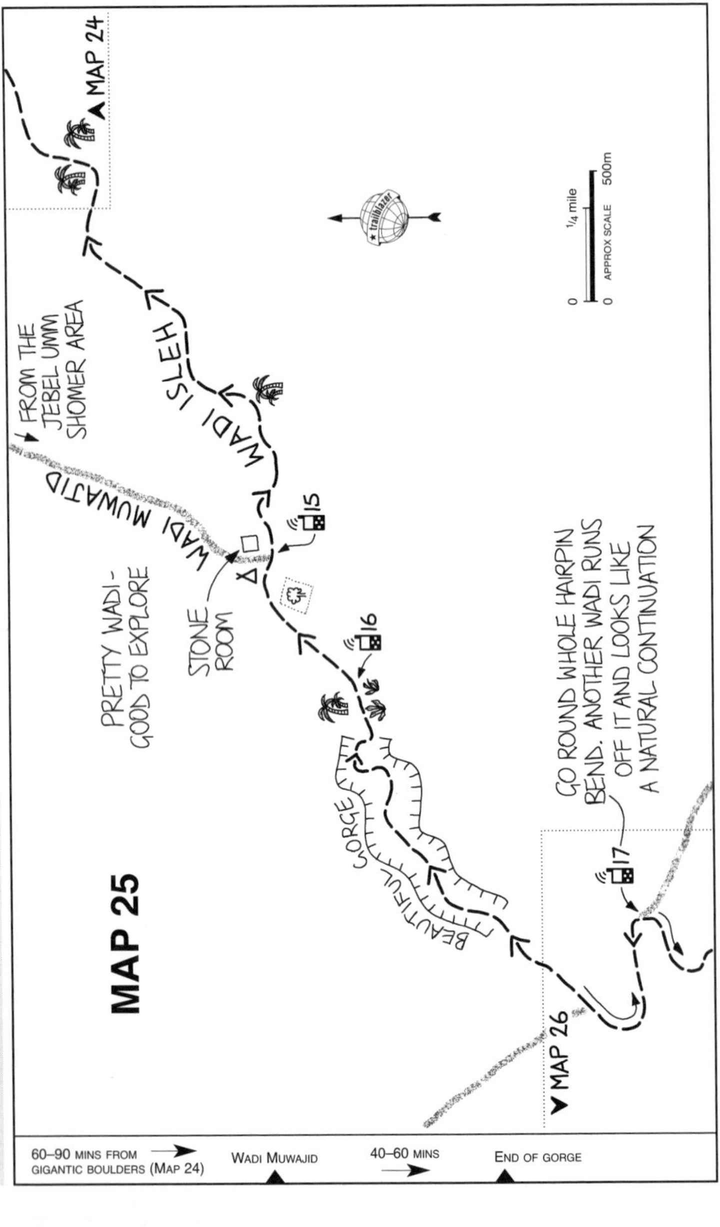

MAP 25

MAP 24

FROM THE
JEBEL UMM
SHOMER AREA

WADI ISLEH

WADI MUWAJID

PRETTY WADI-
GOOD TO EXPLORE

STONE
ROOM

15

16

BEAUTIFUL GORGE

GO ROUND WHOLE HAIRPIN
BEND. ANOTHER WADI RUNS
OFF IT AND LOOKS LIKE
A NATURAL CONTINUATION

17

MAP 26

APPROX SCALE
0 — ¼ mile
0 — 500m

60–90 MINS FROM
GIGANTIC BOULDERS (MAP 24)   WADI MUWAJID   40–60 MINS   END OF GORGE

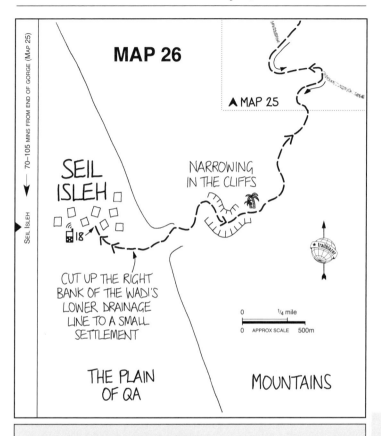

MAP 26

▲ MAP 25

SEIL ISLEH

NARROWING IN THE CLIFFS

📱18

CUT UP THE RIGHT BANK OF THE WADI'S LOWER DRAINAGE LINE TO A SMALL SETTLEMENT

THE PLAIN OF QA

MOUNTAINS

70-105 MINS FROM END OF GORGE (MAP 25)

SEIL ISLEH

★ trailblazer

0	¼ mile
0	APPROX SCALE 500m

❏ **The Sinai: cradle of the alphabet**
The early 20th century saw the discovery of an unrecorded script in the mines of Serabit el Khadem. Written left to right, it had about 30 characters. Most were a copy of an Egyptian hieroglyph – or at least a close derivative – but, crucially, each represented a sound in the language of the Sinai's native miners (a Semitic language). It was the first sound of whatever the hieroglyph showed – but as it was said in the local tongue. The hieroglyph for an ox was translated *aleph*, and thus took the 'a' sound, for example. The hieroglyph for home was said *beth,* so it became 'b' etc. The script is called Proto Sinaitic and it's thought to date from about 1800-1500BC. Many scholars regard it as having made the critical departure from hieroglyphics to a proper, phonetic alphabet. It's from this that most other alphabets – from Phoenician to Old Hebrew, Nabataean, Greek, Latin, Arabic and Ge'ez – are said to be derived. Some raise caution owing to the small number of the samples; but if the theory is correct the world and its literature owe much to a group of slaves in a forgotten corner of the Sinai desert.

TRAIL GUIDE & MAPS

Wadi Feiran

Wadi Feiran opens on the west coast, winding inland through progressively high, rugged mountain ranges. It's home to a gigantic palm grove that early travellers knew simply as the 'Pearl of Sinai'. Tourism bypasses it almost completely today and the region has the feel of a frontier: you're always on the edge of a great adventure. With no actual hotels, cafés or other tourist facilities, and with English almost non-existent, it's a difficult place to trek; but some will find its wild side the most rewarding. Take a generous supply of hard cash.

TRIBES AND TREKKING

The Gararsha
Wadi Feiran is home to Bedouin of every Towarah tribe – including plenty of the Jebeleya – but it's firm Gararsha territory. Only Gararsha guides and cameleers can be used for trekking. Guides are a flat-rate LE200 per day and camels (or donkeys) are about the same. Find guides in one of the local Bedouin gardens. Hamid Hassan Salem's (see p186) is the best.

Gararsha guides are competent but few speak English. **Ismaieel Abaid Atwa** (mob ☎ 0128-010 8413) and **Salah Abaid Atwa** (mob ☎ 0127-907 3309) are two brothers from a well-known guiding family and both are recommended.

The Serabit el Khadem trek
This trek crosses three Bedouin territories from start to finish. The first part takes place in Gararsha territory. About halfway through come the lands of the Hamada. Towards Serabit el Khadem everything becomes Alegat/Muzeina. If you're just one or two people it's often possible to go all the way with a Gararsha guide, but it depends. Bigger groups will usually have to swap: tribes will push for their share of the business. It's easy enough to swap along the way. Full notes are given in the trek description.

WADI FEIRAN

What to see and do
Jebel Tahuna is a small hill opposite Deir Banat, the convent, and some say it's where Moses saw the Battle of Rephidim. It was used as a necropolis in early Christian times and the tombs of old monks still scatter its slopes. The ruins of a 1500-year-old oratory crown the summit. There's a trail up from an Arabic sign near an acacia tree, but it's poor and often disappears (allow about 30-45 minutes to the top). There's a good view south to Jebel Serbal but the rugged face of Jebel Banat (see p200) looks even more beautiful to the north.

Wadi Feiran was home to the Sinai's first episcopal city: **Pharan**. Its crumbling walls, altars and stairways stand on a neck of land near Deir Banat, known as El Maharrad (some of its relics were unfortunately looted in the revolution). Other ruins stand scattered all over the wadi. The hollows in the yellowish alluvial cliffs are ancient tombs or hermit holes.

Sheikh Shebib was a Gararsha holy man and his **tomb** stands in the palm grove. He was once greatly revered; locals believed his ghost dwelt in the mountains, helping Gararsha brethren in need. The 19th-century explorer E H Palmer reports a miraculous happening before he arrived. Apparently, the ghost rescued an ibex hunter who'd broken his leg in the mountains, spiriting him safely home before returning a few days later – in true local style – to demand an extortionate sum of baksheesh.

PRACTICAL INFORMATION
Orientation and arrival

Wadi Feiran is lined with development but the hub is **Seil Aleyat**. There's a convent called Deir Banat (see p186) here, along with a Bedouin settlement and a small mosque. A big **palm grove** starts further up the road and has two good Bedouin gardens where you can sleep (see Where to stay).

A few kilometres further up is a village area called **Furrah** (pronounced Fur-*agh*, from deep in your throat). It has a few services and shops but little else. When approaching on public transport tell the driver where to stop. Most know Deir Banat and Bedouin drivers know the gardens. Driving between them takes less than a minute; walking about ten.

Getting around

Flag down a pick-up truck and jump in the back for Furrah. Everywhere else is walkable in around 10-15 minutes.

Services

Furrah has a few services including a post office and a hospital. Everything's basic though. The **post office** is just a man with a rickety old set of scales; the **hospital** is staffed by one overworked doctor who only does first-aid.

Only Mobinil mobiles (see p50) beginning 0122, 0128 (and occasionally 0127) work in Furrah. You can buy a SIM in Feiran. Otherwise, use the **telephone centrale** (Sat-Thur, 8am-3pm).

Two shops in Seil Aleyat sell **food**. Deir Banat, the convent, sells oranges,

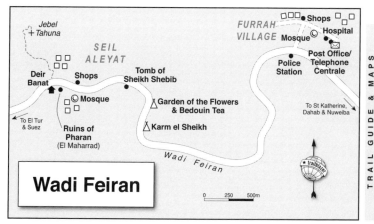

Wadi Feiran

grapefruits and other fruit from its orchard in season. Bedouin gardens grow herbs, vegetables, dates, fresh tobacco and other produce, which might be sold.

Where to stay

Working institutions provide accommodation: either the convent or a Bedouin garden.

Deir Banat (**Convent of Feiran**; ☎ 069-385 0071, ✉ sinai.oasisfaran@yahoo .gr) is a satellite of the Monastery of St Katherine, and is home to four nuns. It's a tranquil spot with cypress, blossom and orchard trees: a stark contrast to the dusty wadi outside. The rooms have a bed, shower and a/c and they're clean and comfortable. Singles are €40 (LE340) and doubles €60 (LE510) and prices include Greek food, cooked by the sisters. The nuns can sometimes find something cheap in the outhouses if you look utterly destitute.

Bedouin gardens These keep you close to the Bedouin and they're good for organising treks. Everything is basic but the gardens have their own tranquil charm.

The nicest one is owned by Hamid Hassan Salem and has a sign outside reading *The Garden of Flowers and Bedouin Tea*. Tea and bread are given freely, but buy your own food from the shops (and always be courteous, offering to share).

The next garden up the road is *Karm el Sheikh* (*karm* means garden, a wordplay on *Sharm el Sheikh*). It's not as nice but the owner is one of the few locals to speak English, which is useful. Negotiate before you stay, and expect to pay about LE15-25 a night at either place.

Moving on

Nothing makes scheduled stops so stand on the open road and flag it down. Most services originate elsewhere, picking up delays.

By public bus East Delta has a bus to Cairo at 6.45am (LE50, 6-7hrs). It starts in St Katherine and is usually on time. Another goes to St Katherine at 5-6.30pm (LE10-15, 45 mins). This starts in Cairo at 11am so expect delays.

By minibus Four minibuses go to El Tur at 7am, 7.15am, 2pm and 3.15pm (LE10-15, 1-1½hrs). Two go to St Katherine, with services at 3pm and 10pm (LE10-15, 45 mins). There's another minibus to Suez at 6.45-7am (LE40), coming from St Katherine. Minibuses can come early or late and you should always arrive at least 15 minutes before the noted times. Recruit local help to point them out as they have no markings to distinguish one from another.

By private taxi Find taxis by asking around. Expect to pay the following: St Katherine, LE70-100; El Tur, LE150-200; Sharm, LE250-350.

JEBEL SERBAL CIRCUIT (3-4 days)

Practicalities

● **Difficulty and scheduling** This is an extremely strenuous trek, with steep ascents, descents, and plenty of scrambling throughout. Trails are poor and sometimes non-existent and the terrain is often loose and uncomfortable. You'll have to be an experienced trekker and in good shape to attempt it. It's easiest in winter and spring, when water is most available. In summer, it's better to consider the early exit option outlined opposite. You can get round in three days, but four is better: this gives you time to explore and – with Jebel Serbal so beautiful and deserted – there's little point in rushing.

● **Camels** This trek is tough enough with a daysack, let alone a backpack, and it's best to use a camel — though this isn't always straightforward. The camel trail up the mountain is poorly maintained. Even if you *can* take a camel on the first half, the treacherous terrain means it won't be able to accompany you on the second. You have to arrange for another one to meet you later, carrying everything you need in between (the first camel will go back down Wadi Rimm; the second one will meet you near Wadi Mileihim). If you have to do parts unsupported – it'll usually be the first half – travel light and leave extra room in your bag for water. Donkeys can sometimes be used instead of camels, but it depends: discuss everything with your guide.

● **Early exit option** If you have concerns about the whole trip, make an easy exit halfway around. Go down Wadi Rimm, just before the most difficult part of the trek starts. You'd need 2-3 days to do this shorter option and just one camel (or, alternatively, a donkey).

● **Links with other treks** Jebel Salla (see p200) can be tagged onto the end, but it'd be a strenuous sting in the tail of an already tiring trek.

Seil Aleyat to Naqb Shahrani [Maps 27-28]

Start at the Bedouin settlement in **Seil Aleyat** (GPS 1). It's next to Deir Banat and has a small white mosque amongst the houses. Walk through and enter **Wadi Aleyat** behind, following a trail along its left side. This beats out across the middle section further up, but boulders make it tricky to spot.

There are a few **abandoned houses** here; only Bedouin shepherdesses and the odd wayfarer use these today. Further on, there's a large natural fork where the wadi divides into two branches around a low ridge (GPS 2). Continue along the branch to the **right**. The left one leads to the Wadi Shineinir ravine: an ascent route for Jebel Serbal in the 1800s, but one rarely used today.

This trek has **excellent views** to Jebel Serbal, arguably the best from any-where, and you can get an idea of where to aim for. It's a mass of big pinnacles, with the ones on the left (east) bigger than those on the right (west). You go up a ravine called **Naqb Shahrani**, directly below the last big pinnacle across from the left (ie between this and the first smaller one on the right). You can't see the ravine clearly yet; but it comes into better profile later. *(cont'd on p190)*

❏ **A legend of treasure – by E H Palmer, *Desert of The Exodus*, 1871**
'A Bedawi was walking one day in Cairo when a man whom he had never seen before accosted him and invited him into his house. After hospitably entertaining him, the stranger, a Maghrabi of course, informed him that his magic arts had revealed the existence of an immense treasure in Wadi Aleyat, and offered to share it with him if he would conduct him to the spot.

They set out together, found the treasure as it had been described, and, having laden their camel with gold, were returning home, when the Bedawi conceived the idea of murdering the benefactor and appropriating all the spoil. But the magician was too subtle for him, and just as the Arab's finger was upon the trigger of his matchlock he suddenly threw a little dust behind him, and the traitor fell to the ground blinded. On his way back to Suez, however, the Maghrabi repented, and not only sent back a remedy which restored the other's sight, but is said to have taken the unnec-essary trouble of writing over the Bab en Nasr (one of the old gates of Cairo) the words 'Cursed be he who blinds a Bedawi'.
Note: a Maghrabi is a Western Arab.

TRAIL GUIDE & MAPS

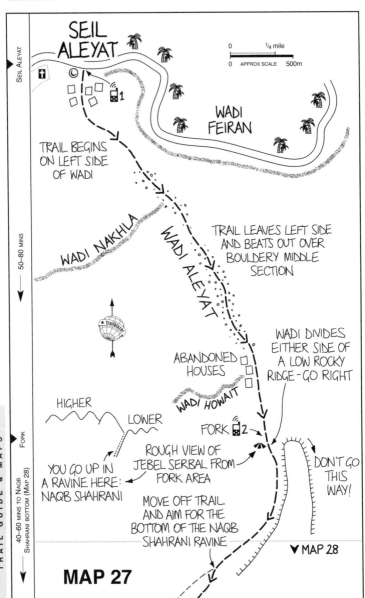

SEIL ALEYAT

SEIL ALEYAT

WADI FEIRAN

0   ¼ mile
0   APPROX SCALE   500m

TRAIL BEGINS
ON LEFT SIDE
OF WADI

50–80 MINS

WADI NAKHLA

WADI ALEYAT

TRAIL LEAVES LEFT SIDE
AND BEATS OUT OVER
BOULDERY MIDDLE
SECTION

WADI DIVIDES
EITHER SIDE OF
A LOW ROCKY
RIDGE – GO RIGHT

ABANDONED
HOUSES

WADI HOWAIT

HIGHER

LOWER

FORK

FORK 2

ROUGH VIEW OF
JEBEL SERBAL FROM
FORK AREA

DON'T GO
THIS
WAY!

YOU GO UP IN
A RAVINE HERE:
NAQB SHAHRANI

40–60 MINS TO NAQB
SHAHRANI BOTTOM (MAP 28)

MOVE OFF TRAIL
AND AIM FOR THE
BOTTOM OF THE NAQB
SHAHRANI RAVINE

▼ MAP 28

MAP 27

TRAIL GUIDE & MAPS

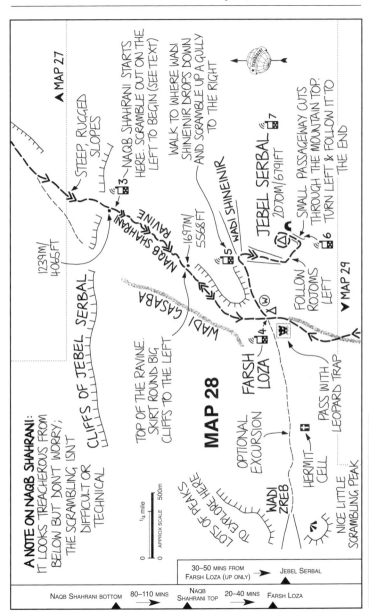

MAP 28

▲ MAP 27

STEEP, RUGGED SLOPES

3 — NAQB SHAHRANI STARTS HERE. SCRAMBLE OUT ON THE LEFT TO BEGIN (SEE TEXT)

WALK TO WHERE WADI SHINEINIR DROPS DOWN AND SCRAMBLE UP A GULLY TO THE RIGHT

1239M/ 4065FT

CLIFFS OF JEBEL SERBAL

NAQB SHAHRANI RAVINE

1697M/ 5568FT

WADI GASABA

WADI SHINEINIR

5

JEBEL SERBAL 2070M/6791FT

7

SMALL PASSAGEWAY CUTS THROUGH THE MOUNTAIN TOP. TURN LEFT & FOLLOW IT TO THE END

6

FOLLOW ROTOMS LEFT

▼ MAP 29

W

△

4

FARSH LOZA

TOP OF THE RAVINE. SKIRT ROUND BIG CLIFFS TO THE LEFT

OPTIONAL EXCURSION

PASS WITH LEOPARD TRAP

HERMIT CELL

WADI ZREB

LOTS OF PEAKS TO EXPLORE HERE

NICE LITTLE SCRAMBLING PEAK

A NOTE ON NAQB SHAHRANI:
IT LOOKS TREACHEROUS FROM BELOW BUT DON'T WORRY; THE SCRAMBLING ISN'T DIFFICULT OR TECHNICAL

0   ¼ mile
0   APPROX SCALE   500m

| | 30–50 MINS FROM FARSH LOZA (UP ONLY) ▶ | JEBEL SERBAL ▲ |

| NAQB SHAHRANI BOTTOM ▲ | 80–110 MINS ▶ | NAQB SHAHRANI TOP ▲ | 20–40 MINS ▶ | FARSH LOZA ▲ |

(Cont'd from p187) Follow a trail along the left side of the wadi. Strike off closer to Jebel Serbal, heading up its rough footslopes for the bottom of Naqb Shahrani (GPS 3). The turn-off isn't marked and you can go at various points: faint trails and the odd rojom are found, but there's nothing well-established, so just head the best way you see. Look back for good views over the wadi.

Naqb Shahrani to Farsh Loza [Map 28]
Naqb Shahrani looks daunting from below but it's the most popular ascent route and there isn't too much to worry about. Look out for some patches of rugged red rock in the lower stretch; they're shot through with thin black dikes. **Scramble up on the left side** here, walking on big, sloping slabs. This avoids trickier obstacles in the bottom, including a smooth waterfall cliff. Drop back to the bottom further up – just beyond the waterfall – and continue straight up.

There are no route-finding difficulties in Naqb Shahrani: a natural 'way of boulders' unfolds easily as you go. The exertion is rewarded by spectacular cliff scenery. It's a privilege to walk in high places like this and there's usually enough dead shrubbery for a tea break halfway up.

The ravine narrows at the top. At the highest point you're at about 1700m; 1000m higher than where you started in Wadi Feiran. From the bottom to the top of the ravine it's about 500 vertical metres. Looking ahead (south-west) you can see new parts of Jebel Serbal's north face and the upper section of a deep ravine called **Wadi Gasaba** ('Wadi of the Canes'). This comes up from the same wadi below. It's another route up the mountain but, being regularly damaged by flash floods, is much tougher. Only the odd hardy ibex hunter ever treads there today. From the top of the ravine, follow a trail round the bottom of the gigantic cliffs to the left. Go down a short, steep section, ascending an equally steep stretch immediately afterwards. The gradient soon eases off and you veer gradually left into the basin of **Farsh Loza** (GPS 4).

Farsh Loza [Map 28]
Farsh Loza ('Basin of the Almond') is a **key crossroads** on Jebel Serbal; routes join it on the four big compass points. There's an abandoned enclosure in the middle and a low shelter around the bottom of a boulder over on the left. Next to it is a cluster of trees and a **natural spring** below a boulder. This is the only perennial source on the mountain. It often runs low and becomes greenish in summer so filter and flavour it to improve the taste.

Camping on Serbal The Bedouin always camp at the shelter in Farsh Loza. It's where pack animals arrive and it has shelter, water and other odds and ends. Alternatives include a summit boulder shelter or a hermit cell in a basin west of Farsh Loza (both could sleep one or two people). A few other boulder shelters can be found, including some in Farsh Loza, if you scout around.

Farsh Loza to Jebel Serbal [Map 28]
Jebel Serbal's summit is seen east from Farsh Loza; a high mass of smooth, rounded granite. About 1½-2½ hours should be enough to get up and down, with a bit of time on top. It's a beautiful sunset or sunrise spot.

Follow a small wadi east from the shelter in Farsh Loza. Go all the way to its natural end, where Wadi Shineinir drops down as a ravine. This is the one you would have reached if you'd gone the other way in Wadi Aleyat.

There's a **gully in the cliffs** to the right here (GPS 5): it's a minor, shallow one and a fan of small boulders spills down the slope below it. Tufts of shrubbery grow amongst them. Follow this gully up. It's easiest on the rocky left side; boulders choke the bottom. Jebel Serbal's summit towers up on the left.

When you reach the top of the gully, look left; a **rockscape** of slabs, bulging cliffs and big boulders opens up. Move left (south-east) across this rather than heading straight for the highest summit ground: you won't be able to get up the final cliffs this way. There are rojoms and the odd line of stones placed as steps (all ancient) as you go across: follow them carefully.

In less than five minutes you reach a **small, straight passageway** (GPS 6). This cuts through the summit section of Jebel Serbal; turn left (north-east) and follow it all the way up to the end.

There's a small **boulder shelter** here. Just before it there's another boulder covered in **Nabataean graffiti**. There's more graffiti on the wall of the passageway directly opposite. It probably dates back around 2000 years and it records the earliest-known mountaineering in the Sinai.

Go left for the summit. There's a rock arrangement like a **maze** here. It was noted by travellers in the 19th century but little is known of its origins. The ruins of a little square building stand nearby. This was once called **El Madhawwa** and some said it was a tower in a beacon chain used to transmit fire signals across the peninsula (there was another one at Ein Hudera). Modern archaeologists have suggested it was actually a Nabataean temple.

The highest point is marked by a **small cairn** (GPS 7); there's a summit book hidden in the rocks here. Magnificent views open up on every side. Wadi Feiran lies north, with the flat-topped Jebel Tih ('The Wilderness of the Wanderings') across the distance beyond. The Plain of Qa and Gulf of Suez are to the west, with Egypt's Red Sea Mountains rising up behind. One jagged summit stands out above all others here; this is known as Jebel Gharib. The High Mountain Region of St Katherine is south-east.

Jebel Serbal: the high parts [Map 28]

Jebel Serbal is usually deserted and it's worth spending a good part of the second day wandering round its high parts. You could have lunch here and then take a leisurely stroll down to the campsite at Hajar Imbardia later.

A big basin west of Farsh Loza is worth a look; follow a little wadi out towards it. There's a hermit cell (see box p170) on its left (south) side. Over on the far west a ravine called **Wadi Zreb** drops away. The little peak to the left of this gives views of its spectacular cliffs. You can look over Wadi Mileihim from here too; you'll tackle this wadi later in the trek. The bigger peak to the right (north) of Wadi Zreb can also be scrambled. There are lots of other possibilities, including the huge pinnacle that towered above Naqb Shahrani. This is on the other side of the wadi running east from Farsh Loza to Jebel Serbal.

TRAIL GUIDE & MAPS

Farsh Loza to Hajar Imbardia [Maps 28-29]

This section involves traversing the southern side of Jebel Serbal. It's a gradual descent that involves veering progressively left between minor wadis. This is the camel trail on the mountain but it's not always obvious or well-beaten so stay aware of major landscape features along the way.

Think about water before you leave Farsh Loza. It's usually available in Wadi Sigillia during wetter months but the next guaranteed spot will be, courtesy of your second camel (if you have one), at the end of the wadi. Remember, pack animals used on the first half of the trek have to go back down Wadi Rimm – so load up with all you need.

Exit Farsh Loza from a low pass on its southern side. There's an old **leopard trap** (see box p132) on the top here. Continue down the other side, following a clear trail along the wadi ahead. It runs along the right side to begin with, **crossing to its left bank** a short way down.

The trail stays faint but visible, skirting gradually round the bottom of Jebel Serbal's high cliffs to the left. Further on, a low rocky outcrop stands just off the bottom of these high cliffs to the right; the trail goes through the **gap between them** (GPS 8). Look to the wadi bottom just before you go through; there's a hairpin bend with a few old agricultural plots around it.

A **small rocky wadi** opens on the other side. Go down a short way and look for a trail on its **left side**; it's faint and tricky to spot. This keeps you at a higher level as the wadi bottom cuts down. A bit further along you'll see the fork where it runs in to meet the main wadi below — the one you started in.

Just after passing this fork you enter another minor wadi; the trail is hard to see again. Looking ahead, there's a big rocky hill with smooth faces of granite on its high right side. Veer left through the pass that separates this from the higher mass of Jebel Serbal (GPS 9). There's another **leopard trap** here.

Continue down a **bigger wadi**. Over on the left is a gigantic boulder called **Hajar Imbardia** (GPS 10). It's a well-used natural shelter and the roof of its main compartment is blackened from all the fires. There are some old garden plots below it, with a trough that might hold water a week or two after rain. This is the best *campsite* if you're arriving late on the second day.

Hajar Imbardia to Wadi Rimm [Map 29]

Continue down from Hajar Imbardia to a **single palm tree**. This stands at the top of a ravine called Wadi Beartheran (sometimes used as an alternative descent route to Wadi Sigillia). A faint trail moves left here, rising on rocky bluffs. It continues to veer gradually left, giving spectacular views: the Gulf of Suez is visible to the west and the peak that dominates the foreground is Jebel Umm Takha (pronounced 'Jebel Umm *Tarkha*'). The trail soon leads down to a mass of land capped with gigantic slabs of smooth granite.

It turns sharply left just before this mass, running through a wide natural passageway in the rocks. There's a **hermit cell** just right of the trail.

Views of **Wadi Rimm** open up; veer right to its head (GPS 11). There's a boulder shelter with twin compartments here.

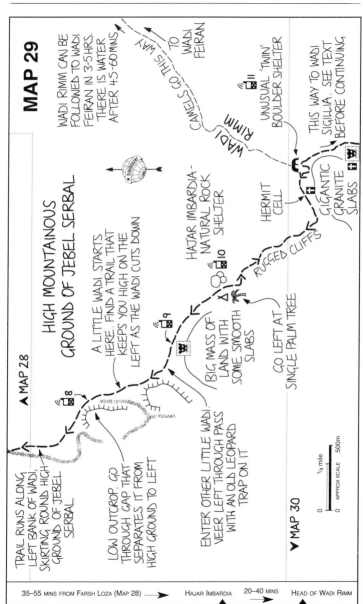

MAP 29

WADI RIMM CAN BE FOLLOWED TO WADI FEIRAN IN 3-5HRS. THERE IS WATER AFTER 45-60 MINS.

TO WADI FEIRAN

CAMELS GO THIS WAY

WADI RIMM

UNUSUAL 'TWIN' BOULDER SHELTER
⌂▦11

THIS WAY TO WADI SIGILLA. SEE TEXT BEFORE CONTINUING

HERMIT CELL
☩

GIGANTIC GRANITE SLABS
☩▦

▲ MAP 28

HIGH MOUNTAINOUS GROUND OF JEBEL SERBAL

A LITTLE WADI STARTS HERE. FINDS A TRAIL THAT KEEPS YOU HIGH ON THE LEFT AS THE WADI CUTS DOWN

HAJAR IMBARDIA - NATURAL ROCK SHELTER
△ ⌂▦10

RUGGED CLIFFS

⌂▦9

▦

BIG MASS OF LAND WITH SOME SMOOTH SLABS

GO LEFT AT SINGLE PALM TREE

TRAIL RUNS ALONG LEFT BANK OF WADI, SKIRTING ROUND HIGH GROUND OF JEBEL SERBAL

⌂▦8

LOW OUTCROP. GO THROUGH GAP THAT SEPARATES IT FROM HIGH GROUND TO LEFT

ENTER OTHER LITTLE WADI. VEER LEFT THROUGH PASS WITH AN OLD LEOPARD TRAP ON IT

▼ MAP 30

0   ¼ mile
0   500m
APPROX SCALE

35–55 MINS FROM FARSH LOZA (MAP 28) ——▶   HAJAR IMBARDIA   20–40 MINS ——▶   HEAD OF WADI RIMM

TRAIL GUIDE & MAPS

Finishing down Wadi Rimm Wadi Rimm runs all the way down to Feiran, joining near the village of Furrah. There's a path down the upper parts. Where it tapers out lower down, just follow the wadi ahead. The walk takes 3-5 hours and there are wells 45-60 minutes down (they don't have ropes). If you don't have enough water or supplies, or if you're having difficulties with what you've done so far, go back. Things get harder here and it's tricky to turn back.

Continuing in Wadi Sigillia Many Bedouin regard Wadi Sigillia as one of the three most beautiful wadis in the Sinai (the others being Wadi Isleh and Wadi Hebran). Continuing this way makes a bigger circular trek of Jebel Serbal but be warned: it's tough. Camels have to turn back and you won't see the next one for at least 3-5 hours. This means you'll carry extra weight on one of the most difficult stretches, so pack everything non-essential back to Feiran.

Water in Wadi Sigillia Wadi Sigillia often has a creek in wetter months. People might be in the wadi with water at this time too. Discuss it with your guide as he'll know best for the time of year. If in any doubt, carry everything you need until you'll see your next camel (at least 3-5 hours ahead). If running low, remember there's a well down Wadi Rimm, but you'll have to go and come back (about a laborious two hours' return).

Wadi Rimm to Wadi Sigillia [Maps 29-30]

Walk the opposite way to Wadi Rimm, heading to the south between big bluffs. There's another **leopard trap** to the right of the trail along here; further beyond is a ruined **Byzantine church**. You soon reach the top of a **ravine** that drops a few hundred metres down to Wadi Sigillia; this is where you descend (GPS 12).

An ancient stairway runs down the ravine here which the Bedouin call **Abu Selim** ('Father of Steps'). It dates back to Byzantine times and was once part of a trail that linked the episcopal city in Feiran with some monastic retreats in Wadi Sigillia. Apart from the Steps of Repentance on Mount Sinai, it's the most significant stairway on the peninsula.

The stairway is well-preserved in the upper section. Where the steps begin to break up lower down, go down the **left side** of the ravine. You'll see stretches of the steps again but don't try to join them: they're unstable and prone to collapse. Even going down the left side has its hazards; the ground is loose and uncomfortable so take extra care. Let your Bedouin guide scout the way. The safest route can change from one year's flash floods to the next.

Wadi Sigillia is seen at the bottom of the ravine. There are a few options for continuing. You can go down and turn right to follow the wadi in the bottom, but this involves negotiating big boulders (unnecessarily difficult). You could go to the bottom and cross the wadi to join a paved path starting on its opposite side. This is a continuation of Darb Abu Selim and the Bedouin say it leads to a ruined church called Deir Sigillia (part of a bigger Byzantine complex). You could do this as an excursion; allow about 1½-2½ hours.

The last alternative – and the one most guides choose – is to take a path out on the right side of the ravine about 100m before the bottom (GPS 13). This runs along the high side of Wadi Sigillia and gives easier walking. It's hard to

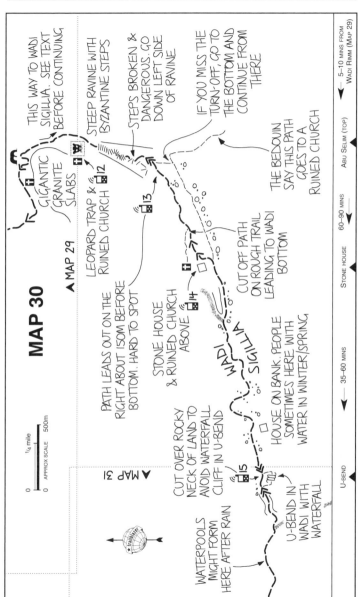

MAP 30

▲ MAP 29

▲ MAP 31

0   ¼ mile
0   APPROX SCALE   500m

THIS WAY TO WADI SIGILLIA. SEE TEXT BEFORE CONTINUING

STEEP RAVINE WITH BYZANTINE STEPS

STEPS BROKEN & DANGEROUS. GO DOWN LEFT SIDE OF RAVINE

IF YOU MISS THE TURN-OFF, GO TO THE BOTTOM AND CONTINUE FROM THERE

GIGANTIC GRANITE SLABS

LEOPARD TRAP & RUINED CHURCH 12

13

THE BEDOUIN SAY THIS PATH GOES TO A RUINED CHURCH

PATH LEADS OUT ON THE RIGHT ABOUT ISOM BEFORE BOTTOM. HARD TO SPOT

CUT OFF PATH ON ROUGH TRAIL LEADING TO WADI BOTTOM

STONE HOUSE & RUINED CHURCH ABOVE 14

WADI SIGILLIA

CUT OVER ROCKY NECK OF LAND TO AVOID WATERFALL CLIFF IN U-BEND

15

HOUSE ON BANK. PEOPLE SOMETIMES HERE WITH WATER IN WINTER/SPRING

U-BEND IN WADI WITH WATERFALL

WATERPOOLS MIGHT FORM HERE AFTER RAIN

← 5–10 MINS FROM WADI RIMM (MAP 29)

ABU SELIM (TOP)

← 60–90 MINS

STONE HOUSE

← 35–60 MINS

U-BEND

TRAIL GUIDE & MAPS

spot the path at first, but easy to follow once you're on it. This is actually another continuation of Darb Abu Selim, with some stone foundations in parts. It leads to an **old ruined church** but becomes more tricky towards the end. Cut off on a rough trail about 10-15 minutes along. This leads down to a **stone house** on a lower bank of the wadi (GPS 14). It's directly below the ruined church you'd have got to anyway and you can clamber back up to have a look.

Wadi Sigillia to Sed Sigillia   [Maps 30-31]
Go to the bottom of Wadi Sigillia and turn right. You have to scramble over big boulders all the way and progress is slow. Further down there's a little house on a high bank of the wadi to the left. It's easy to miss from the bottom and is only of note as there are sometimes people here with water.

Further down, there's a sharp **U-bend** in the wadi. A small waterfall cliff gives a tricky scramble halfway round this so don't follow it. Instead, cut straight up over the rocky neck where the wadi begins to bend and descend on the other side (GPS 15). You re-enter the wadi just below the waterfall.

The wadi goes through a **narrow stretch** after this. A bit further on from here you might see big pools in wetter months. There's often a creek too. The water is typically greenish, but you can still purify and drink.

Further down there's a **stone house** on the right bank of the wadi. It has a boulder with a dwelling built around it in the garden. This is where camels usually wait. If you're pushing round fast it can be a good place to stay on the second night too. The next decent camp is about two hours ahead.

Wadi Sigillia runs between lower sides here. **Wadi Ramuz** is seen on the left and **Wadi Maganees** on the right. After this is **Sed Sigillia** (GPS 16). A waterfall runs down smooth granite slabs here in wetter times. Wadi Sigillia becomes known as Wadi Jeba after this and runs to the coastal plain (there's a difficult scramble to get out and a long walk afterwards: not recommended).

Wadi Mileihim to Wadi Ajela   [Maps 31-32]
From Sed Sigillia take a northerly route back to Wadi Feiran. Two major wadis are followed on the way: the first is **Wadi Mileihim** (Wadi Mileihim is marked Wadi *Umm Lahm* on some maps) and the second **Wadi Ajela**. Wadi Milehim opens directly above the Sed Sigillia waterfall slabs, but it's awkward to clamber straight in. A path rises into the wadi more easily a few metres before the waterfall begins. This runs along the high right side of the wadi before dropping down to the bottom. A bit further along you see **Wadi Aloga** to the right. Take a faint trail up the left bank of the wadi about five minutes after this. It brings you to some old agricultural plots, where the trail continues more easily ahead (GPS 17). Don't worry if you miss it; continue in the wadi bottom and you'll still get to where you need to go.

Jebel Serbal's south face towers up in good view here. Immediately left of it is the **big pass** you go through later. A bit further up the wadi there's an old stone house where you can sometimes camp if you're arriving late.

Continue up Wadi Mileihim to the big pass (GPS 18). A **second, higher pass** comes into clear view from the top. *(Cont'd on p200)*

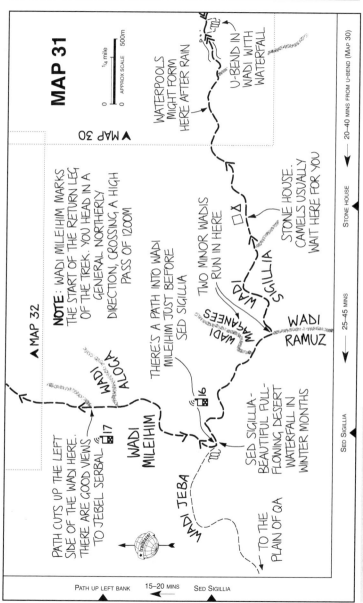

MAP 31

0 — 1/4 mile
0 — 500m
APPROX SCALE

▼ MAP 30

NOTE: WADI MILEIHIM MARKS THE START OF THE RETURN LEG OF THE TREK. YOU HEAD IN A GENERAL NORTHERLY DIRECTION, CROSSING A HIGH PASS OF 1200M

▲ MAP 32

WATERPOOLS MIGHT FORM HERE AFTER RAIN

U-BEND IN WADI WITH WATERFALL

PATH CUTS UP THE LEFT SIDE OF THE WADI HERE. THERE ARE GOOD VIEWS TO JEBEL SERBAL 17

WADI ALOCA

THERE'S A PATH INTO WADI MILEIHIM JUST BEFORE SED SIGILLIA

WADI MILEIHIM

TWO MINOR WADIS RUN IN HERE

WADI MATANEES

WADI SIGILLIA

STONE HOUSE. CAMELS USUALLY WAIT HERE FOR YOU

16

WADI RAMUZ

SED SIGILLIA- BEAUTIFUL FULL- FLOWING DESERT WATERFALL IN WINTER MONTHS

WADI JEBA

TO THE PLAIN OF QA

★ trailblazer

20-40 MINS FROM U-BEND (MAP 30)

STONE HOUSE ◀

25-45 MINS

SED SIGILLIA

PATH UP LEFT BANK   15-20 MINS   SED SIGILLIA

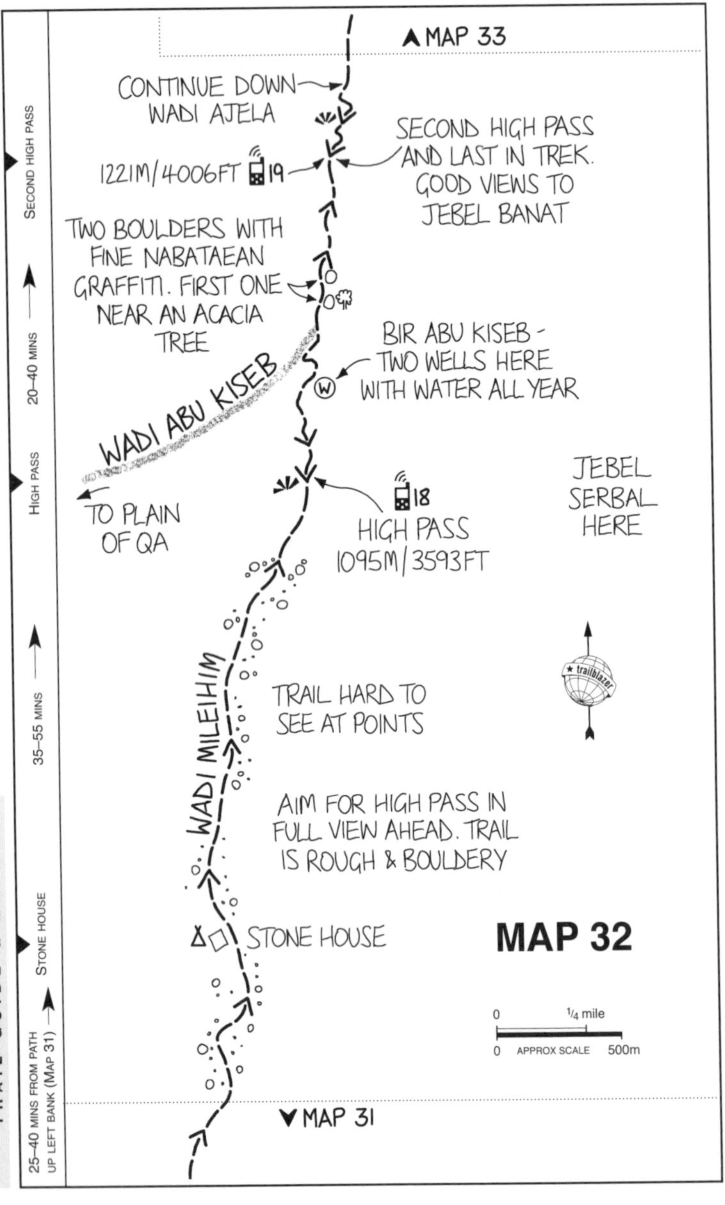

▲ MAP 33

CONTINUE DOWN → WADI AJELA

SECOND HIGH PASS AND LAST IN TREK. GOOD VIEWS TO JEBEL BANAT

1221M/4006FT 📱19

TWO BOULDERS WITH FINE NABATAEAN GRAFFITI. FIRST ONE NEAR AN ACACIA TREE

BIR ABU KISEB - TWO WELLS HERE WITH WATER ALL YEAR

WADI ABU KISEB

TO PLAIN OF QA

📱18

JEBEL SERBAL HERE

HIGH PASS 1095M/3593FT

WADI MILEIHIM

TRAIL HARD TO SEE AT POINTS

AIM FOR HIGH PASS IN FULL VIEW AHEAD. TRAIL IS ROUGH & BOULDERY

△◻ STONE HOUSE

MAP 32

0   1/4 mile
0   APPROX SCALE   500m

▼ MAP 31

SECOND HIGH PASS — 20-40 MINS ↑ HIGH PASS ← 35-55 MINS — STONE HOUSE ◄ 25-40 MINS FROM PATH UP LEFT BANK (MAP 31)

TRAIL GUIDE & MAPS

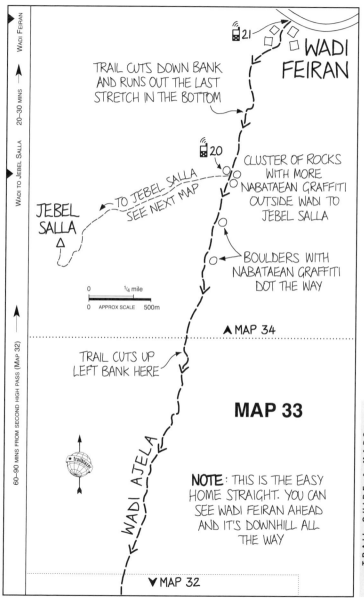

(Cont'd from p196) A trail links both passes and **Bir Abu Kiseb** is about halfway between. Two wells are sunk in a rocky bank to the right of the trail here. They're perennial but the shafts are uneven and it's always tricky getting water. Filter anything you collect as it's often laced with sediments stirred about when pulling it up. Directly opposite, **Wadi Abu Kiseb** cuts between low ranges to the Plain of Qa. The Gulf of Suez is visible in the distance.

Carry on to the second pass (GPS 19). Look out for two boulders with **Nabataean graffiti** on the final uphill stretch. The first is near a spindly acacia tree and it shows old script. The second is a bit higher and it depicts an ibex hunt: the ibex have huge, exaggerated horns and it shows just how long the history of hunting them stretches back here in Feiran.

Views extend over Wadi Ajela from the pass. It runs straight down to Wadi Feiran and you can see the road at the end. Rising up behind is the big, beautiful mountain of Jebel Banat (see box below).

Wadi Ajela to Wadi Feiran   [Map 32-33]
Everything is simple from here: it's the home straight and you just have to follow the wadi ahead. About halfway down, the path switches over to run along the bank on the left (west). Look out for boulders with Nabataean graffiti; there's a large cluster around a small wadi on the left (GPS 20).

This wadi leads to the high, sugarloaf dome of **Jebel Salla** and if you have the time and energy you could tag an ascent on (see p202, Map 34). Otherwise, it's an easy walk back to Wadi Feiran (GPS 21). Turn right to walk back to Seil Aleyat or hitch.

JEBEL SALLA (½ day)

Practicalities
● **Guides** This is a half-day trip but guides still expect the full LE200. Camels won't be used so pack all your water (about 2-3 litres).
● **Difficulty and schedule** This is a short, strenuous ascent. It mixes walking and easy scrambling and there's brief (but avoidable) exposure on the top.
● **Links with other treks** This can be tagged onto the end of the Jebel Serbal trek but it would be strenuous way to finish.

> ❏ **The legend of Jebel Banat**
> Jebel Banat is the major peak on the northern side of Wadi Feiran. It means 'Mountain of the Girls' and legend has it it's named after two sisters who fled here when their father tried to marry them against their will. They remained in hiding until their father learned of their whereabouts and came in pursuit.
>
> Seeing him coming from afar, they climbed the mountain, braided their hair together and threw themselves to their deaths. The story is often told but it's often mistakenly attributed to another mountain called Jebel Banat near St Katherine. Jebel Banat can be ascended easily in a day, starting from Wadi Nefuz. You go up round the back of it to climb the more gentle slopes on its northern side, from an area called Farsh Tibeina.

Wadi Feiran to Hajar Salla [Map 34]

Start from the small Bedouin settlement in **Wadi Ajela** (GPS 1). Get there by following the road from Seil Aleyat or just hitch. **Jebel Salla** is in clear view from the road: it's the high dome of smooth, exfoliated granite on the right side of the wadi. It has a distinctive light shading.

Follow the trail up Wadi Ajela. About 10-15 minutes along it **cuts up a steep alluvial bank** on the right, continuing at a higher level. The wadi is wide, rugged and dotted with green acacias. It rises to a high pass ahead. Jebel Serbal is the mountain to the left; Jebel Serabil, the one to the right.

A **wadi on the right** soon offers clear, unobstructed views to Jebel Salla (GPS 2). Small rocks with **Nabataean graffiti** are clustered around its mouth; this area is sometimes referred to as **Hajar Salla**.

Hajar Salla to Jebel Salla [Map 34]

Jebel Salla looks more like a peak for climbers than trekkers, but don't worry; there are no real difficulties. The holds are good where you have to scramble and there's only a brief stretch of exposure on top. Turn right into the wadi from Hajar Salla and follow it up to where it **divides around a broad rocky ridge** (GPS 3). Ignore both branches and strike straight up the ridge itself, going up the back of it. There are no trails but route finding is always straightforward.

Go directly up towards the dome; it's a mix of walking and easy scrambling. When you reach the bottom of the dome veer left onto a **wide bouldery rake** that rises gently across its east face (GPS 4).

This brings you to the southern end of the dome, where you can double back to scramble up the last rocky heights. It's difficult to get up the highest part of the south face so veer left around its **west side** (GPS 5). There's some brief exposure here but you can limit it with your route.

Monastic ruins crown the summit, including an old church. There are other buildings on the west and north faces. You'll also see banks of stones piled on sheer precipices, which have long puzzled observers.

The 19th-century British Ordnance Survey team thought Jebel Salla was a **fortress peak** Christians retreated to when under siege, suggesting the stones were there to dislodge as missiles. This seems a bit implausible: it's unlikely they'd have marooned themselves on an obvious peak without water given the numerous other places they could scatter to. Others have suggested the stones were assembled as walkways of faith around the mountain. Whatever the case all these ruins are an impressive testament to the exploration and industry of early Christians in these high, difficult parts of the Sinai.

Jebel Salla has good views of the surrounding peaks. There's an especially striking view to Jebel Banat (see box opposite) in the north. There's also a pretty peak to the south-west called Jebel Abura. Jebel Salla is one of the few places from which this is ever seen in such good profile.

Return to Wadi Feiran the way you came. There are other wadis that can make it into a circular route but they're either unnecessarily circuitous with little merit in themselves, or too precipitous and dangerous.

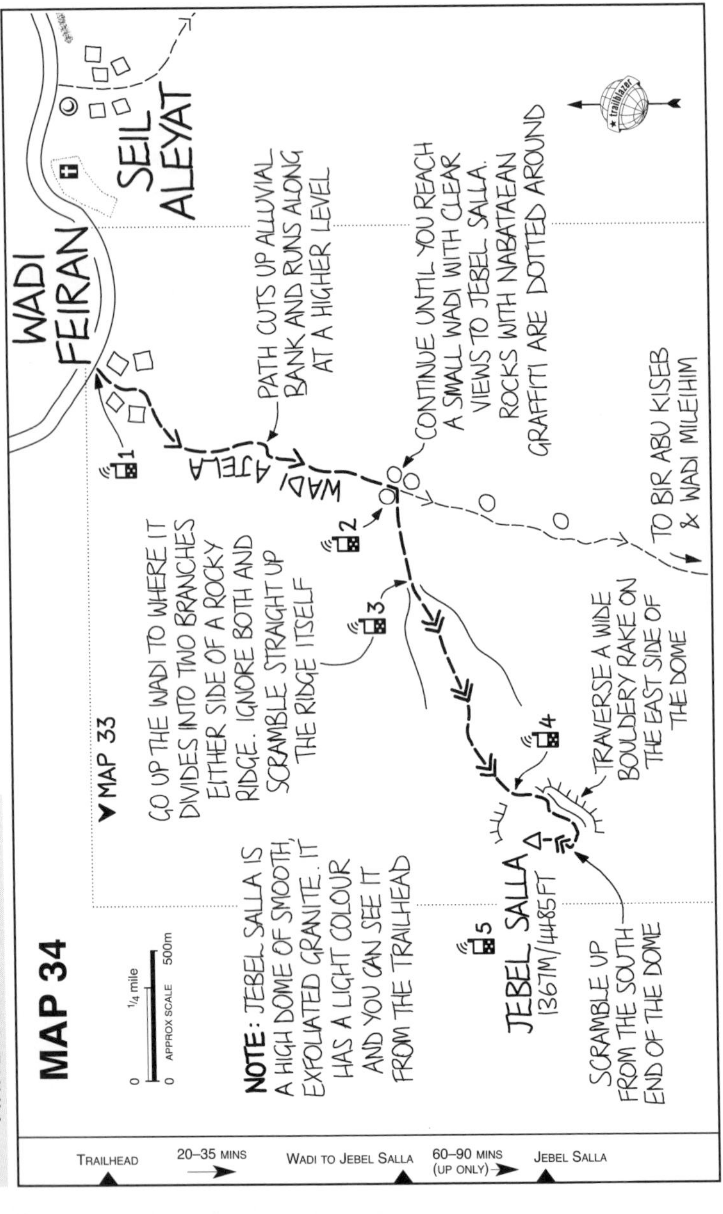

MAP 34

0 ———— 1/4 mile
0 ———— 500m
APPROX SCALE

NOTE: JEBEL SALLA IS A HIGH DOME OF SMOOTH, EXFOLIATED GRANITE. IT HAS A LIGHT COLOUR AND YOU CAN SEE IT FROM THE TRAILHEAD

▼MAP 33

GO UP THE WADI TO WHERE IT DIVIDES INTO TWO BRANCHES EITHER SIDE OF A ROCKY RIDGE. IGNORE BOTH AND SCRAMBLE STRAIGHT UP THE RIDGE ITSELF

WADI FEIRAN

SEIL ALEYAT

PATH CUTS UP ALLUVIAL BANK AND RUNS ALONG AT A HIGHER LEVEL

WADI ATELA

CONTINUE UNTIL YOU REACH A SMALL WADI WITH CLEAR VIEWS TO JEBEL SALLA. ROCKS WITH NABATAEAN GRAFFITI ARE DOTTED AROUND

TO BIR ABU KISEB & WADI MILEIHIM

TRAVERSE A WIDE BOULDERY RAKE ON THE EAST SIDE OF THE DOME

JEBEL SALLA
1367M/4485FT

SCRAMBLE UP FROM THE SOUTH END OF THE DOME

TRAIL GUIDE & MAPS

| TRAILHEAD | 20–35 MINS → | WADI TO JEBEL SALLA | 60–90 MINS (UP ONLY) → | JEBEL SALLA |

WADI FEIRAN TO SERABIT EL KHADEM (2½-3 days)

Practicalities

● **Difficulty and scheduling** This is a moderate route done mostly on gentle trails or jeep tracks. The exception is a mountainous part on the second day. Everything is at lower altitude on this route too, which means it's uncomfortable in hotter months and best done in winter. Allow 2½-3 days.

● **Shorter options** To avoid the first day of trekking, 4x4 transport can be arranged to Wadi Maghara. To do the last part at Serabit el Khadem, go to Abu Zenima (see p221) and find onward transport there.

● **Getting to the trailhead** This is about 20km west on the main road from Seil Aleyat. Cars cost around LE50, but hitching is usually easy too.

● **Organisation and guides** Few agencies work here and it's better to organise yourself. The trek passes through several tribal territories, so there's more to think about. The first part is in Gararsha territory and you need a Gararsha guide. Halfway along it becomes Hamada: one or two people can usually continue with a Gararsha guide but bigger groups will often need a new one.

Serabit el Khadem is in Alegat and Muzeina lands and local guides might have to be employed. Hamada and Alegat/Muzeina guides are about LE100-150. Route descriptions indicate the points where new guides are needed.

● **Does the guide know the way?** Most of this trek is familiar to the Bedouin but one section remains little-known. It's the part between Wadi Maghara and the settlement of Sheikh Saadan, usually done on the second day.

Most guides go via a place called Sheikh Hashash. This is close to Sheikh Saadan but reached on a different – and less impressive – route. Go through the route to see if your guide knows the way. If not, you can follow the description, but it's recommended you have a GPS. The trails are poor and the terrain tricky.

● **Camels** It's difficult to use camels to cover the whole of this route and as long as you're prepared to rough it – you can go without. You can set off with half the food you need, stocking up in a village halfway along (there's a shop, though it'll be closed at the weekend). For water, you can rely on people in settlements.

Wadi Mukattab to Seih Sidreh [Maps 35-36]

This trek starts in **Wadi Mukattab**, about 20km west of Seil Aleyat. It's a wide wadi that opens up on the north side of the road.

The small Bedouin settlement of Seil Mukattab is on its east side. Over on the west is a **low, yellowish escarpment**; you start more on this side.

Pick up the main jeep track here and follow it straight up the wadi (GPS 1). It runs parallel with the escarpment before bending left around an outcrop near its far end. It winds up through low, broken terrain to a **wide, open area** (GPS 2). It feels more like a plain than a wadi here but this is still Wadi Mukattab. Looking north-west you'll see **Jebel Abu Alaqa**; a low mountain with an impressive geological fold in its side. This appears at various junctures in the trek and is a good, large-scale reference point to keep in mind. *(Cont'd on p206)*

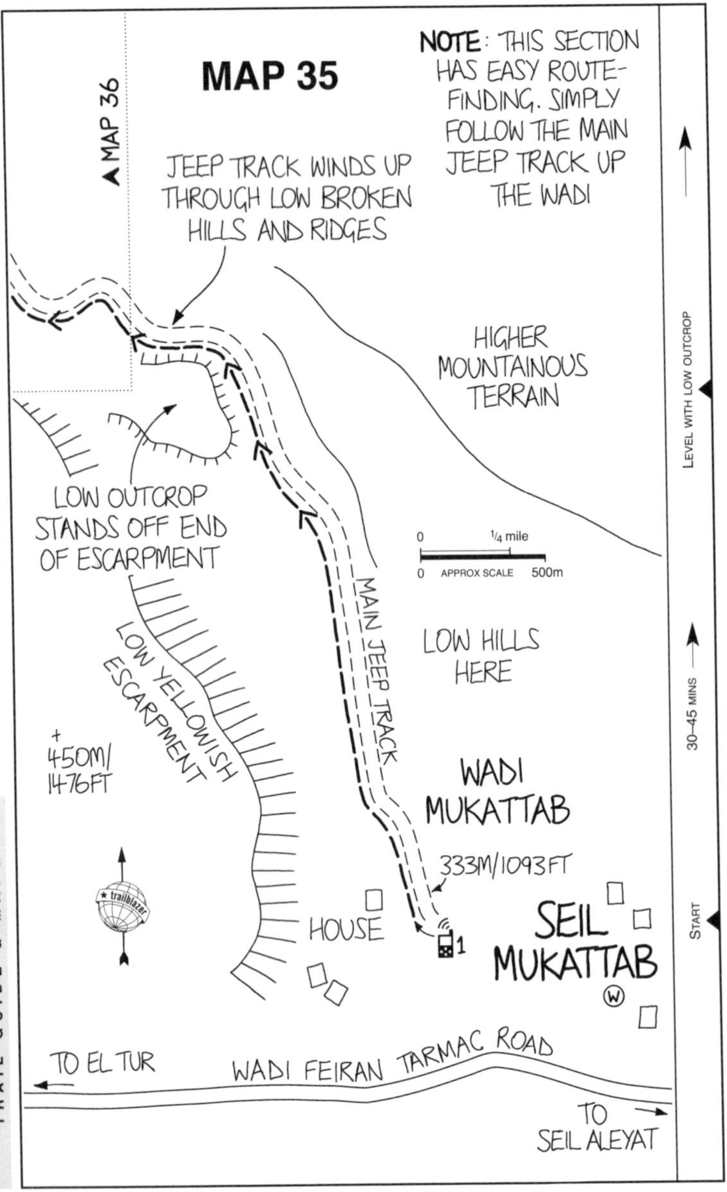

MAP 35

◄ MAP 36

JEEP TRACK WINDS UP
THROUGH LOW BROKEN
HILLS AND RIDGES

NOTE: THIS SECTION
HAS EASY ROUTE-
FINDING. SIMPLY
FOLLOW THE MAIN
JEEP TRACK UP
THE WADI

HIGHER
MOUNTAINOUS
TERRAIN

LEVEL WITH LOW OUTCROP

LOW OUTCROP
STANDS OFF END
OF ESCARPMENT

LOW YELLOWISH
ESCARPMENT

+
450M/
1476FT

★ trailblazer

MAIN JEEP TRACK

0   1/4 mile
0   APPROX SCALE   500m

LOW HILLS
HERE

WADI
MUKATTAB

333M/1093FT

30-45 MINS

HOUSE

SEIL
MUKATTAB
Ⓦ

1

START

TO EL TUR

WADI FEIRAN TARMAC ROAD

TO
SEIL ALEYAT

TRAIL GUIDE & MAPS

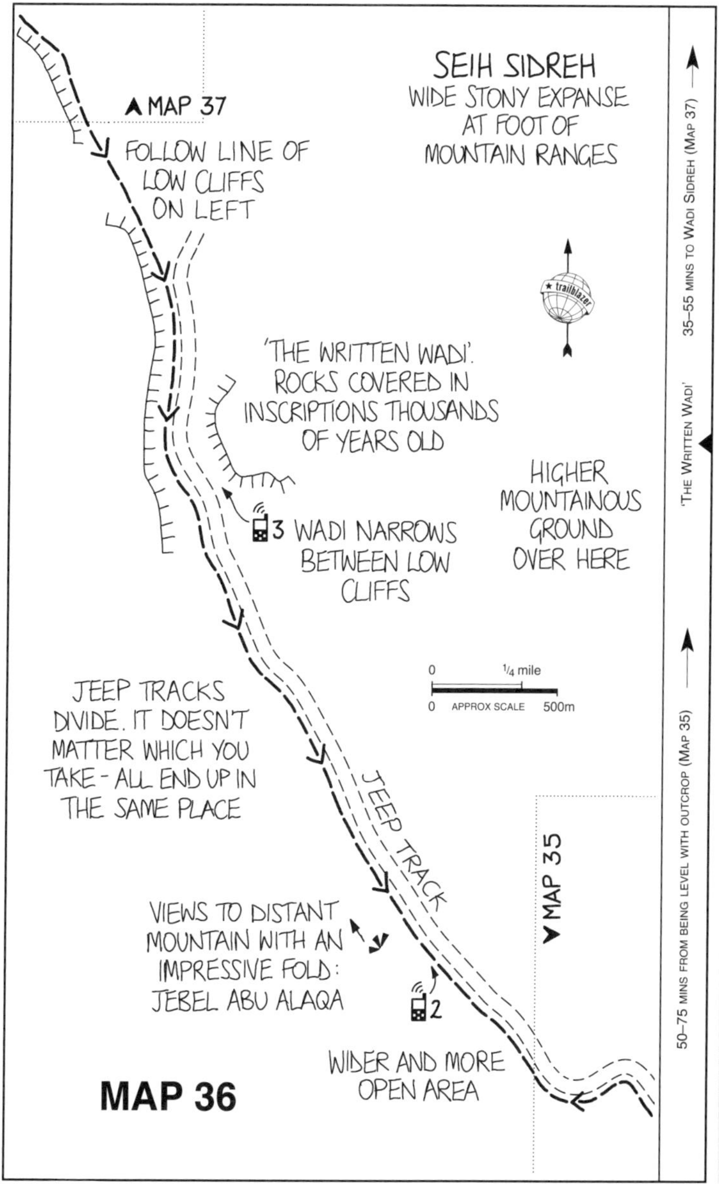

SEIH SIDREH
WIDE STONY EXPANSE
AT FOOT OF
MOUNTAIN RANGES

▲ MAP 37

FOLLOW LINE OF
LOW CLIFFS
ON LEFT

'THE WRITTEN WADI'.
ROCKS COVERED IN
INSCRIPTIONS THOUSANDS
OF YEARS OLD

HIGHER
MOUNTAINOUS
GROUND
OVER HERE

3 WADI NARROWS
BETWEEN LOW
CLIFFS

JEEP TRACKS
DIVIDE. IT DOESN'T
MATTER WHICH YOU
TAKE - ALL END UP IN
THE SAME PLACE

0   1/4 mile
0   APPROX SCALE   500m

JEEP TRACK

▼ MAP 35

VIEWS TO DISTANT
MOUNTAIN WITH AN
IMPRESSIVE FOLD:
JEBEL ABU ALAQA

2

WIDER AND MORE
OPEN AREA

MAP 36

35-55 MINS TO WADI SIDREH (MAP 37) ⟶

'THE WRITTEN WADI'

50-75 MINS FROM BEING LEVEL WITH OUTCROP (MAP 35)

TRAIL GUIDE & MAPS

(Cont'd from p203) Follow the jeep track down over this open area. Don't worry about which way to go when tracks split in different directions: they all converge on the same basic line further down.

The wadi soon narrows between low cliffs; this is the part most people mean when they say **Wadi Mukattab** (GPS 3). The name means the **Written Wadi** and graffiti covers its sides. Most is in the Nabataean script and probably dates from about 2000 years ago. There are crucifixes and Christian markings too; mostly made by early pilgrims who mistook the Nabataean script for the writing of the wandering Israelites. Wadi Mukattab ends and you emerge on a flat open floodplain known as **Seih Sidreh**. Far away on the opposite side of this plain is a small building on a little hill: an Egyptian army outpost. The mountains towering up directly behind it separate this area from Serabit el Khadem. They're wild and rugged and you go through the heart of them later.

Seih Sidreh to Wadi Maghara   [Maps 36-38]
The jeep tracks move out into Seih Sidreh here. Leave them and veer gradually left, following a line of low cliffs round. Further around, some more cliffs rise up on the right to form a more obvious wadi (GPS 4). This is **Wadi Sidreh** (or sometimes, Wadi Seih); follow its course ahead. Jebel Abu Alaqa – the mountain with the fold – is seen at points along here.

Further up there's a **Bedouin settlement**; the first place to get water. It's also the last until mid way through the second day so stock up with whatever you need. There are no shops and you'll have to ask people in the houses.

Further on Wadi Sidreh narrows between higher walls and you reach the small white tomb of **Sheikh Suleiman** (GPS 5). Most say he was a Gararsha holy man; though some of the Hamada tribe claim him as one of theirs. Directly opposite this tomb is the mouth of **Wadi Maghara**.

Wadi Maghara   [Map 38]
Follow Wadi Maghara up, going past some **empty houses**. These are used if there's a festival at the Sheikh Suleiman tomb. Look carefully on the left side after passing these; an angular boulder sits perched on the low wadi bank, supported by a smaller stone. There are **ancient Egyptian hieroglyphics** on the underside of this, just a bit bigger than handwriting size. You'll also find the neatly made inscription of an explorer: this is dated 1850, making it about 4500 years older than the hieroglyphics. There's a fork in the wadi after this (GPS 6). The branch to the right is **Wadi Iqne**, where you continue on the second day. The one on the left is still Wadi Maghara and it's where the old archaeological sites are found.

Wadi Maghara means Wadi of the Caves, after the old Egyptian turquoise mines along it. They're dotted high on the left side of the wadi and most date back to the Old Kingdom, around 2700BC. It's said they have bits of miners' graffiti inside; some of it, apparently, in the proto-Sinaitic script, which is said to be the foundation stone of most modern alphabets (see box p183). The odd bit of 19th-century explorers' graffiti is scattered about too. Twelve **bas-relief carvings** were once found in Wadi Maghara, each showing the Pharaoh under which a particular mine was worked. Most have been cut away and taken to the

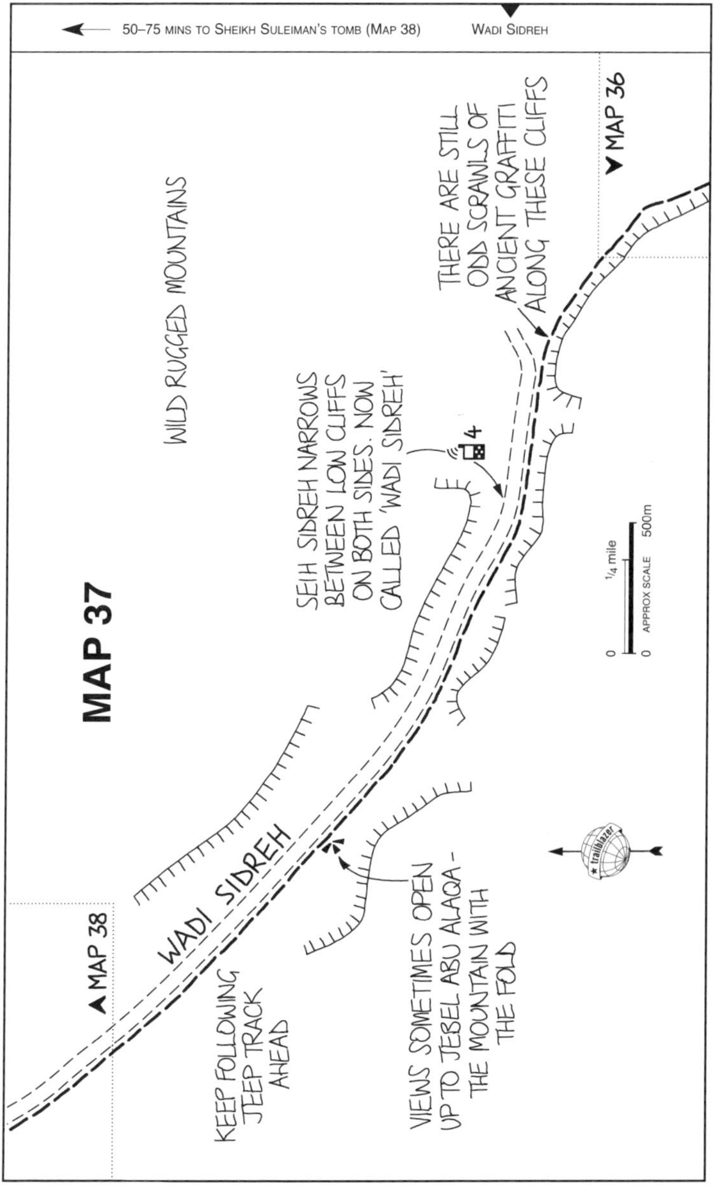
MAP 37
50–75 MINS TO SHEIKH SULEIMAN'S TOMB (MAP 38)
WADI SIDREH
MAP 36
MAP 38
THERE ARE STILL ODD SCRAWLS OF ANCIENT GRAFFITI ALONG THESE CLIFFS
WILD RUGGED MOUNTAINS
SEIH SIDREH NARROWS BETWEEN LOW CLIFFS ON BOTH SIDES. NOW CALLED 'WADI SIDREH'
4
WADI SIDREH
KEEP FOLLOWING JEEP TRACK AHEAD
VIEWS SOMETIMES OPEN UP TO JEBEL ABU ALAQA - THE MOUNTAIN WITH THE FOLD
0
1/4 mile
0
APPROX SCALE
500m
trailblazer

❑ Demons of the desert
The Bedouin once believed in desert demons, the most fearsome of which were female spirits called *ghulah*. They lived in high mountain caves, preying on lone male travellers or young boys straggling at the back of camel caravans. Victims were snatched away and devoured, only ever to be seen again as a pile of bones. If a Bedouin man suspected a ghulah of being in the area he was honour-bound to hunt her down and kill her. This word might be the root of the English term 'ghoul'.

Egyptian Museum in Cairo, but there's still one left to see. To get there, walk up the wadi from the fork until you see a **small metal sign** with Hebrew writing: the carving is on a cliff about 100 vertical metres up the left side of the wadi (GPS 7). A trail leads up but splits into several different branches higher up. Take the trails that veer more to the left near the top (there's a bit of a scramble) and be warned: the carving is small and the same colour as the rock. A guide or a GPS will save time looking.

The figure shown is a Pharaoh called **King Sekhemkhet**, who reigned about 2650BC. Little is known about him and his only other relic is an unfinished step pyramid at Saqqara, just outside Cairo. There are three different representations of him: he's seen in classic Pharaoh pose in the one in the left, smiting a captive with his mace. He's wearing the white crown of Upper Egypt in the next one along and in the last he's donning the red crown of Lower Egypt. Parts of the carving have been cut away by tomb robbers.

High on the cliffs here you can look down on the hill that splits Wadi Maghara and Wadi Iqne. This is where the miners once lived and their ruined dwellings are still visible on top. There are also good views out to the rugged massif you'll go through on the next day. This is a superb spot for sunset.

Camping options Wadi Maghara is a peaceful spot to camp. If the weather's bad, sleep in the empty houses. The caves give excellent shelter and you can sleep in these too, although not every guide will want to join you.

Wadi Iqne to Wadi Amran   [Maps 38-39]

This stage involves cutting through the massif between here and Serabit el Khadem. It's little-known – even to the Bedouin – and if your guide doesn't know the way you'll have to be extra-vigilant. It's recommended you take a GPS as there are sometimes no trails and the landscape is tricky.

Enter **Wadi Iqne** from the fork in Wadi Maghara. It's dotted with pretty green acacias and runs between low banks. Follow its main course towards the mountains: they appear in a beautiful panorama and you go towards a middle section that looks slightly

---

❑ Place names and water
The **place names** were supplied by two Bedouin guides. They aren't listed on maps and can't be given with the same certainty as elsewhere.

The next guaranteed spot for **water** is Sheikh Saadan (more than five hours ahead). If you don't have enough walk back to the village in Wadi Sidreh and fill up there.

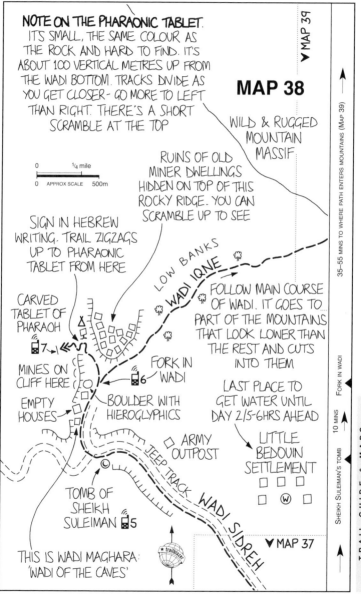

NOTE ON THE PHARAONIC TABLET. IT'S SMALL, THE SAME COLOUR AS THE ROCK AND HARD TO FIND. IT'S ABOUT 100 VERTICAL METRES UP FROM THE WADI BOTTOM. TRACKS DIVIDE AS YOU GET CLOSER - GO MORE TO LEFT THAN RIGHT. THERE'S A SHORT SCRAMBLE AT THE TOP

▼ MAP 39

MAP 38

WILD & RUGGED MOUNTAIN MASSIF

35-55 MINS TO WHERE PATH ENTERS MOUNTAINS (MAP 39)

0   ¼ mile
0   APPROX SCALE   500m

RUINS OF OLD MINER DWELLINGS HIDDEN ON TOP OF THIS ROCKY RIDGE. YOU CAN SCRAMBLE UP TO SEE

SIGN IN HEBREW WRITING. TRAIL ZIGZAGS UP TO PHARAONIC TABLET FROM HERE

LOW BANKS

WADI IQNE

FOLLOW MAIN COURSE OF WADI. IT GOES TO PART OF THE MOUNTAINS THAT LOOK LOWER THAN THE REST AND CUTS INTO THEM

CARVED TABLET OF PHARAOH 📱7

MINES ON CLIFF HERE

EMPTY HOUSES

FORK IN WADI 📱6

BOULDER WITH HIEROGLYPHICS

LAST PLACE TO GET WATER UNTIL DAY 2/5-6HRS AHEAD

FORK IN WADI ◀

10 MINS

LITTLE BEDOUIN SETTLEMENT

ARMY OUTPOST

JEEP TRACK

WADI SIDREH

TOMB OF SHEIKH SULEIMAN 📱5

SHEIKH SULEIMAN'S TOMB

THIS IS WADI MAGHARA: 'WADI OF THE CAVES'

★ trailblazer

▼ MAP 37

TRAIL GUIDE & MAPS

lower than the rest. You reach the mountains about 35-55 minutes along and the wadi soon **begins to cut in through their rocky outer walls** (GPS 8). Continue ahead as it twists between increasingly high sides shot through with dikes. Further up there's a **big junction** where different wadis run in. It's essential to stay alert with route finding here (GPS 9). Where Wadi Iqne ends, one wadi rises off gently to the right (south-east). Wadi Shigg opens almost directly opposite (east): it has a big rocky mouth and is the major wadi in this massif. Ignore both and take a left to follow **Wadi Nakhla** ahead in a northerly direction. About 10 minutes along another rocky wadi opens on the right: this is **Wadi Amran** (GPS 10). You need to get into this but you can't do it here: a steep waterfall cliff blocks progress halfway round its first bend. Cut over the rocky shoulder that separates it from where you are now in Wadi Nakhla.

Start by going up the steep alluvial bank between the lower drainage lines of Wadi Nakhla and Wadi Amran. From the top you'll see a **patch of lightish coloured granite** on the rocky hillside ahead (just to the right). There's a **black dike** directly behind it. Walk ahead, until you're level with the dike.

Here a **shallow gully** cuts up the rocky slopes on the dike's basic line; turn in and follow it straight up to the top of a small notch-pass (GPS 11). This looks out over Wadi Amran. Have a glance back and you'll see some gigantic dikes in the mountainside opposite. Jebel Abu Alaqa – the mountain with the fold – is also glimpsed for the last time. Continue down to Wadi Amran, entering near a **dead, headless palm tree**.

Wadi Amran to Sheikh Saadan [Maps 39-40]

Go ahead in the bouldery bottom. A short way along a small branch of the wadi bends left through a narrow, slanted opening in the rocks; **don't go this way**. Continue ahead, rising past a stone house with some small terraces below (GPS 12). There are a few ziziphus trees (see p64) here that might give a snack in season: it has a dry, cherry-sized fruit, sometimes called Chinese Sour Date.

The wadi narrows into a steep, V-shaped ravine ahead, known as **Wadi Abu Dees**. Big boulders choke its course and there are bits of scrambling.

Further up there's a **fork** where one branch of the ravine goes left and a more minor one right (GPS 13): **go left**. There's a **little dam** at the bottom of this branch that often holds water after rain. It might be greenish but you can still purify. The gradient of the ravine soon eases and, a little higher, it flattens and straightens out. Follow its main course ahead. A bit further up there's a small left bend where a spindly acacia tree stands on the wadi's right bank (GPS 14). This is a turn-off for Wadi Umm Retem – an important wadi which you'll join later – but don't go this way now.

Carry on in the same wadi, as it becomes ever-smaller and rises in a northerly direction to a pass known as **Naqb Shaieer** (GPS 15). One of the most abrupt **geological changes** in the Sinai becomes visible around here. The granite scenery of the mountain massif gives way to a mostly sandstone landscape of isolated peaks with flattish, plateau-like tops. This extends up to Serabit el Khadem: it doesn't have the same drama, but it has its own plain beauty.

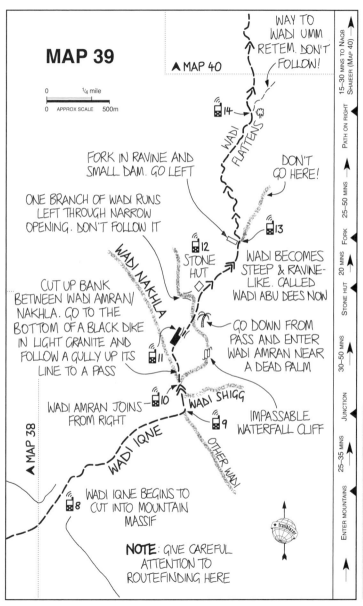

MAP 39

0 ___ 1/4 mile
0 APPROX SCALE 500m

WAY TO WADI UMM RETEM. DON'T FOLLOW!

▲ MAP 40

WADI FLATTENS

14

FORK IN RAVINE AND SMALL DAM. GO LEFT

DON'T GO HERE!

ONE BRANCH OF WADI RUNS LEFT THROUGH NARROW OPENING. DON'T FOLLOW IT

12
STONE HUT

13

WADI BECOMES STEEP & RAVINE-LIKE. CALLED WADI ABU DEES NOW

WADI NAKHLA

CUT UP BANK BETWEEN WADI AMRAN/ NAKHLA. GO TO THE BOTTOM OF A BLACK DIKE IN LIGHT GRANITE AND FOLLOW A GULLY UP ITS LINE TO A PASS

GO DOWN FROM PASS AND ENTER WADI AMRAN NEAR A DEAD PALM

11

WADI AMRAN JOINS FROM RIGHT

10

WADI SHIGG

9

IMPASSABLE WATERFALL CLIFF

WADI IQNE

OTHER WADI

▲ MAP 38

8

WADI IQNE BEGINS TO CUT INTO MOUNTAIN MASSIF

NOTE: GIVE CAREFUL ATTENTION TO ROUTEFINDING HERE

trailblaze

15–30 MINS TO NAQB SHAIEER (MAP 40)

PATH ON RIGHT   25–50 MINS   FORK   20 MINS   STONE HUT   30–50 MINS   JUNCTION   25–35 MINS   ENTER MOUNTAINS

TRAIL GUIDE & MAPS

Looking north the peak of **Jebel Ajayz Hassan** dominates the foreground. **Wadi Hafir** cuts down its left (west) side with **Wadi Hamra** on the right (east). Follow the trail from the pass towards Wadi Hamra.

There are views of a twin-peaked mountain in the north as you go along here: it's called **Jebel Umm Rejlairn**. The name means 'Mother of Legs'; each peak is said to be one of its two legs. It's up near Serabit el Khadem and you'll see it a few more times in the trek after this.

A trail runs high above Wadi Hamra on the left, but it's more fun to go in the wadi itself. Drop in and follow it down. Wadi Hamra means 'The Red Wadi'. It's red granite in an otherwise sandstone area (though note the red rock becomes more visible further down the wadi). The granite is the oldest rock in the Sinai; the sandstone was laid down on top when the peninsula was under a shallow sea. This wadi is just one place where the pattern of erosion has exposed their juxtaposition.

You soon have to scramble down a rocky bank. Wadi Hamra becomes more narrow and enclosed after this and has the odd boulder with **Nabataean graffiti**. Further ahead it joins the bigger course of **Wadi Umm Retem** (GPS 16).

Turn left and follow it ahead. There's a cluster of palms a little way along and an old dry well called **Bir Melha** ('The Salty Well'). Wadi Umm Retem soon leads into the bigger course of **Wadi Sahu**.

Turn right and walk to the small white tomb of **Sheikh Saadan** (GPS 17). He was a holy man of the Hamada and this area takes its name from him.

Sheikh Saadan There is a small settlement with a couple of shops here, but they're both obscure so ask a local. To push on to Serabit el Khadem you'd need about three to five hours. If you're arriving late you could camp back in Wadi Umm Retem or around Wadi Sahu. The people will show you somewhere to stay and might even invite you into their garden or house. To fill some time you could go to the tomb of Sheikh Hashash (see box below).

Guide issues Wadi Sahu is Hamada territory and you need to check the situation on guides. If you're alone people won't care so much but in a bigger group they'll want a cut of the business. Your current guide will be able to check. If you take a Hamada guide to Serabit el Khadem pay about LE100-150. One that comes recommended is **Ibrahim Abu Yasser**. He only speaks Arabic but he's a good, knowledgeable guide, and is well worth asking around for.

❏ **Sheikh Hashash**
The tomb of Sheikh Hashash is about 2km up Wadi Sahu to the north-east, left of where you first entered. He's often thought to belong to a local tribe – the Hamada, Alegat or Sowalha, for example – but he was actually a Jebeleya tribesman from St Katherine. Local legend has it that strong gusts of wind swept the funeral shroud off his body, carrying it high into the sky. It blew all the way across the Sinai before coming down in Wadi Sahu. The Bedouin believed this was where his spirit wanted to settle and built the tomb where it landed. Other tombs and a large cemetery stand alongside it; it's one of the biggest Sheikh burial sites in the region.

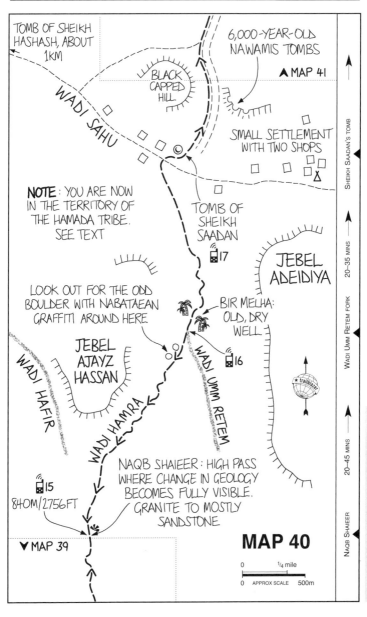

TOMB OF SHEIKH HASHASH, ABOUT 1KM

6,000-YEAR-OLD NAWAMIS TOMBS

▲ MAP 41

WADI SAHU

BLACK CAPPED HILL

SMALL SETTLEMENT WITH TWO SHOPS

NOTE: YOU ARE NOW IN THE TERRITORY OF THE HAMADA TRIBE. SEE TEXT

TOMB OF SHEIKH SAADAN

📱17

JEBEL ADEIDIYA

LOOK OUT FOR THE ODD BOULDER WITH NABATAEAN GRAFFITI AROUND HERE

JEBEL AJAYZ HASSAN

BIR MELHA: OLD, DRY WELL

📱16

WADI HAFIR

WADI HAMRA

WADI UMM RETEM

📱15
840M/2756FT

NAQB SHAIEER: HIGH PASS WHERE CHANGE IN GEOLOGY BECOMES FULLY VISIBLE. GRANITE TO MOSTLY SANDSTONE

▼ MAP 39

★ trailblazer

MAP 40

0   ¼ mile

0   APPROX SCALE   500m

SHEIKH SAADAN'S TOMB

20-35 MINS

WADI UMM RETEM FORK

20-45 MINS

NAQB SHAIEER

TRAIL GUIDE & MAPS

Sheikh Saadan to Wadi Lahian [Maps 40-42]

There are various routes to Serabit; this one involves following a big, easy jeep track to the north. Start from the tomb of Sheikh Saadan and join the track that runs to the right (east) side of the blackish hill ahead. There are some **Nawamis tombs** (see box p246) on a rocky spur to the right in the first stages. These are around 6000 years old, pre-dating even the Pharaonic sites of the route. They were built by early mining peoples and are found widely in the region.

There's a high pass further up (GPS 18). On the right side is a low band of reddish rocks with modern graffiti. On the left are rocks with more interesting **Nabataean graffiti**. It's unlike any other piece in the Sinai, showing peculiar patterns and footprints with individual toes marked out in them.

Carry on down the jeep track: the high escarpment of **Jebel Tih** – the Biblical 'Wilderness of the Wanderings' — stands out ahead. Look out for two spindly acacia trees on the right side about 5-10 minutes down (GPS 19). You can turn off to enter the upper course of a small wadi on the left here, following it down to meet the jeep track again further ahead. Going this way is just a more interesting alternative: there are boulders with Nabataean graffiti and some have **Bedouin footprint graffiti** (see box p153). There's a short scramble about halfway down the wadi but it's nothing too tricky.

Turn left when you re-join the jeep track (GPS 20). Further along is a **fork** where another track rises gently on the left (GPS 21). Take the one ahead, going at a lower level. This is the start of **Wadi Lahian** and it's dotted with the odd gigantic acacia tree. Further up there's a **Bedouin settlement** where some Hamada and a few Alegat and Muzeina families live. You might notice a few more Nawamis tombs on the low cliffs to the left here.

Wadi Lahian to Wadi Bala [Map 42]

Jebel Hasaani is a big ridge that runs down the right (east) side of Wadi Lahian, and Serabit el Khadem is over the other side. This section involves cutting over the ridge to get there. Carry on up Wadi Lahian and look for two stone huts on the right side. The first is heavily ruined and has an acacia tree within its walls. The second is a bit further on, with a **dead and fire-blackened acacia** outside it. Turn right into **a small watercourse** on the slopes of Jebel Hasaani just afterwards, following a faint trail up its left side (GPS 22).

This veers left to cross a small ridge dividing this watercourse from the next one along. The trail becomes better in this new watercourse and further up, veers out on the left, running north along the upper parts of Jebel Hasaani.

This soon bends right, taking you through a little notch in a reddish band of rock, and cutting over the crest of the ridge (GPS 23).

Good views open up and **Wadi Bala** is seen down below. Another big ridge like Jebel Hasaani rises up on its far side. This is the Serabit el Khadem highland. If you look closely you'll see the paved path up the side. The two-legged mountain Jebel Umm Rejlairn (see p212) is visible too.

Follow a faint trail down Jebel Hasaani to Wadi Bala (GPS 24). It can be tricky to follow in places but if you go off track it's not too hard to find your own way down. Turn left in the wadi, following it around a sharp bend to its

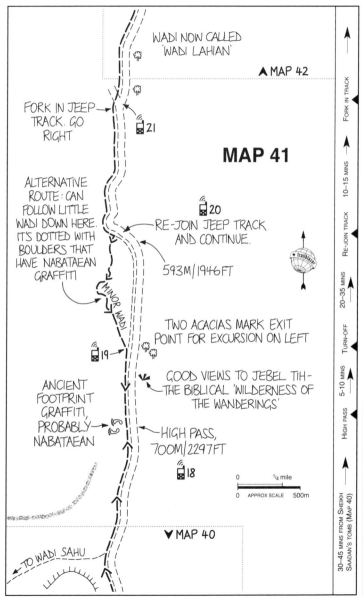

WADI NOW CALLED
'WADI LAHIAN'

▲ MAP 42

FORK IN JEEP
TRACK. GO
RIGHT

📱 21

MAP 41

ALTERNATIVE
ROUTE: CAN
FOLLOW LITTLE
WADI DOWN HERE.
IT'S DOTTED WITH
BOULDERS THAT
HAVE NABATAEAN
GRAFFITI

📱 20

RE-JOIN JEEP TRACK
AND CONTINUE.

593M/1946FT

MINOR WADI

TWO ACACIAS MARK EXIT
POINT FOR EXCURSION ON LEFT

📱 19

GOOD VIEWS TO JEBEL TIH-
THE BIBLICAL 'WILDERNESS OF
THE WANDERINGS'

ANCIENT
FOOTPRINT
GRAFFITI,
PROBABLY
NABATAEAN

HIGH PASS,
700M/2297FT

📱 18

0   ¼ mile

0   APPROX SCALE   500m

▼ MAP 40

TO WADI SAHU

FORK IN TRACK   10-15 MINS   RE-JOIN TRACK   20-35 MINS   TURN-OFF   5-10 MINS   HIGH PASS   30-45 MINS FROM SHEIKH
SAADAN'S TOMB (MAP 40)

TRAIL GUIDE & MAPS

natural end: the paved trail to Serabit el Khadem starts here (GPS 25). You'll also find the tarmac road to the village of Serabit (sometimes called 'Barakat'). If you're arriving late on the second day, **Wadi Bala** is the best spot to wild camp. The village has a small camp but it's not always open.

Guide issues You're now in the territory of the Alegat tribe but a few Muzeina families live here too. If you're arriving with a Hamada guide from Wadi Sahu you can usually continue as you are. If you are coming from Abu Zenima, intending to do the ruined temple hike, you need an Alegat/Muzeina guide from the Serabit village.

Serabit el Khadem [Maps 42-44]

Serabit el Khadem is home to the best-preserved Egyptian temple outside Africa. It was once a mining colony rich with turquoise and the name means Heights of the Slave, probably after the native miners who worked here. The hike is a well-established one with big trails until the last section. You can do it in a circle, starting in Wadi Bala and looping round to the village area.

Join the paved trail at the end of Wadi Bala. About halfway up is **Rod el Air**, where Egyptian hieroglyphics cover the rocks. Most date from the Middle and New Kingdoms. There are drawings of the sailing vessels that shipped turquoise back to Egypt, along with depictions of ibex, gazelle and more exotic animals such as cranes, ostriches and giraffes: they were clearly drawn by those with a mainland African – rather than a Sinai – experience.

You soon emerge on top of the Serabit highland. Good views open up all around: Jebel Umm Rejlairn is south and the Jebel Tih escarpment lines the distance to the north. Looking north-west you might see a little settlement and a mosque in the desert; this is on the way to Abu Zenima.

Further along there's a **double signpost** with Arabic writing. The path to the left (north-east) goes a short way to the mines of **Magharat el Teleha** (GPS 26). These were worked about 1990BC in the Middle Kingdom, 700 years after the mines in Wadi Maghara. One mine has early miners' graffiti in the proto Sinaitic script and you can still see chisel marks in places. The air is still and stale and you can just imagine what it must have been like slaving here in the heat (see box below). *(Cont'd on p220)*

❏ **An inscription from the mines, E H Palmer, *Desert of The Exodus*, 1871**
One short inscription from the mines was made by Harura, a superintendent who came to Serabit in the New Kingdom. His words might give some idea of what it was like to be in these parts a few thousand years ago: 'When I came to this land, I began to labour strenuously. Behold me how I tarried there after I had left Egypt; my face sweated, my blood grew hot, I ordered the workmen working daily, and said unto them, there is turquoise in the mine and the vein will be found in time. And it was so; the vein was found and the mine yielded well. The troops came and occupied it so that none escaped therefrom. My face grew not frightened at the work, I toiled cheerfully; I brought abundance upon abundance of turquoise and obtained yet more in my search. I did not miss a single vein'.

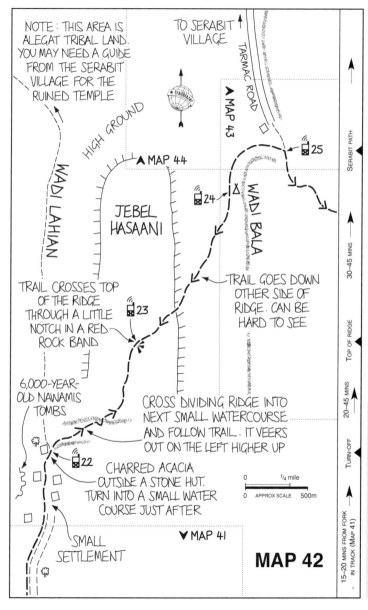

NOTE: THIS AREA IS ALEGAT TRIBAL LAND. YOU MAY NEED A GUIDE FROM THE SERABIT VILLAGE FOR THE RUINED TEMPLE

TO SERABIT VILLAGE

TARMAC ROAD

▲ MAP 43

📱 25

▲ MAP 44

HIGH GROUND

WADI LAHIAN

JEBEL HASAANI

WADI BALA

📱 24

TRAIL CROSSES TOP OF THE RIDGE THROUGH A LITTLE NOTCH IN A RED ROCK BAND

TRAIL GOES DOWN OTHER SIDE OF RIDGE. CAN BE HARD TO SEE

📱 23

6,000-YEAR-OLD NAWAMIS TOMBS

CROSS DIVIDING RIDGE INTO NEXT SMALL WATERCOURSE AND FOLLOW TRAIL. IT VEERS OUT ON THE LEFT HIGHER UP

📱 22

CHARRED ACACIA OUTSIDE A STONE HUT. TURN INTO A SMALL WATER COURSE JUST AFTER

0 ¼ mile
0 APPROX SCALE 500m

▼ MAP 41

SMALL SETTLEMENT

MAP 42

SERABIT PATH

30–45 MINS

TOP OF RIDGE

20–45 MINS

TURN-OFF

15–20 MINS FROM FORK IN TRACK (MAP 41)

TRAIL GUIDE & MAPS

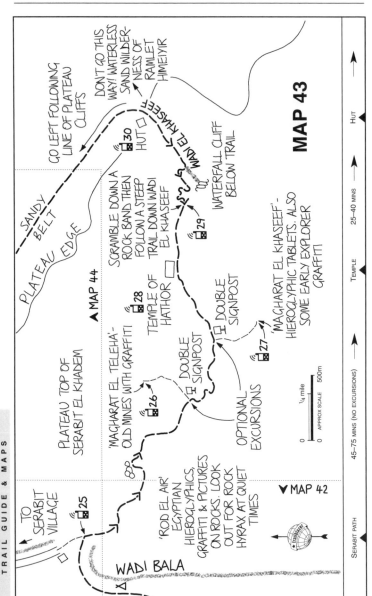

MAP 43

DON'T GO THIS WAY! WATERLESS SAND WILDERNESS OF RAMLET HIMEIYIR

GO LEFT FOLLOWING LINE OF PLATEAU CLIFFS

SANDY BELT

PLATEAU EDGE

30

HUT

HUT

WADI EL KHASEEF

WATERFALL CLIFF BELOW TRAIL

SCRAMBLE DOWN A ROCK BAND THEN FOLLOW A STEEP TRAIL DOWN WADI EL KHASEEF

▲ MAP 44

29

28

TEMPLE OF HATHOR

DOUBLE SIGNPOST

'MAGHARAT EL KHASEEF' - HIEROGLYPHIC TABLETS. ALSO SOME EARLY EXPLORER GRAFFITI

27

PLATEAU TOP OF SERABIT EL KHADEM

'MAGHARAT EL TELEHA' - OLD MINES WITH GRAFFITI

26

DOUBLE SIGNPOST

OPTIONAL EXCURSIONS

0   ¼ mile
APPROX SCALE
0   500m

TO SERABIT VILLAGE

25

'ROD EL AIR' EGYPTIAN HIEROGLYPHICS, GRAFFITI & PICTURES ON ROCKS. LOOK OUT FOR ROCK HYRAX AT QUIET TIMES

▼ MAP 42

WADI BALA

TRAIL GUIDE & MAPS

SERABIT PATH   45-75 MINS (NO EXCURSIONS)   TEMPLE   25-40 MINS   HUT

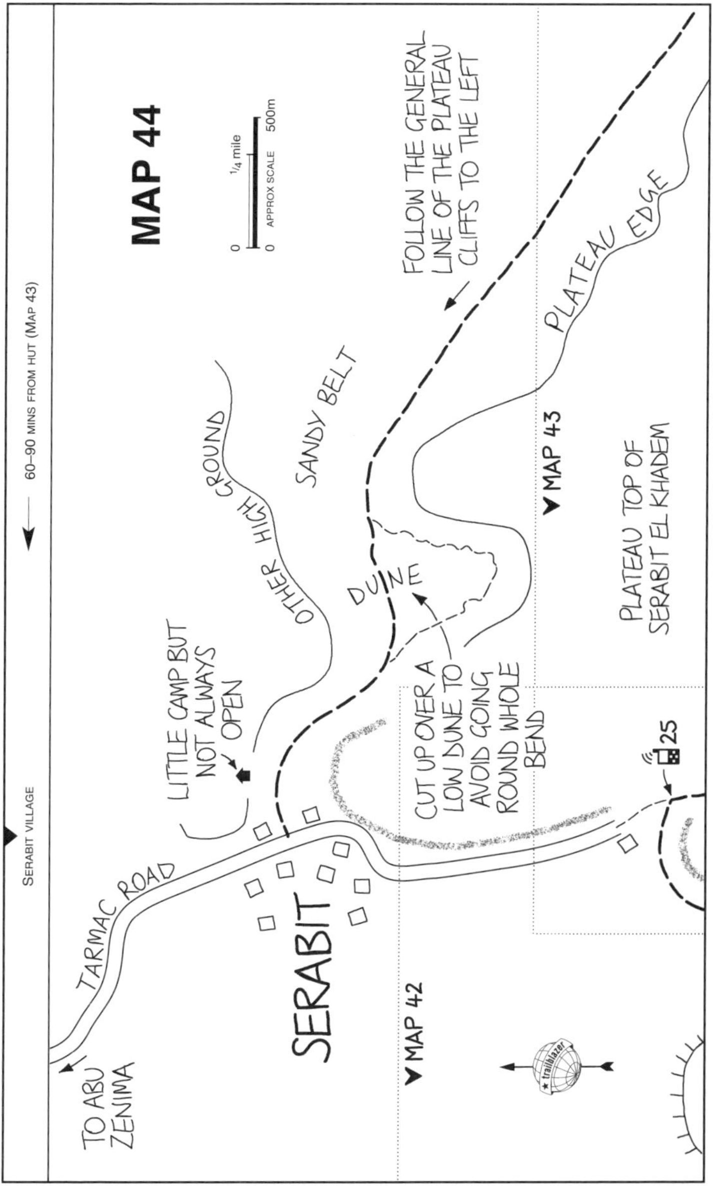

MAP 44

60–90 MINS FROM HUT (MAP 43)

SERABIT VILLAGE

FOLLOW THE GENERAL LINE OF THE PLATEAU CLIFFS TO THE LEFT

PLATEAU EDGE

OTHER HIGH GROUND

SANDY BELT

DUNE

▼ MAP 43

PLATEAU TOP OF SERABIT EL KHADEM

LITTLE CAMP BUT NOT ALWAYS OPEN

TARMAC ROAD

CUT UP OVER A LOW DUNE TO AVOID GOING ROUND WHOLE BEND

25

SERABIT

TO ABU ZENIMA

▼ MAP 42

0   ¼ mile
APPROX SCALE
0   500m

TRAIL GUIDE & MAPS

(Cont'd from p216) Continue on the main path until you reach **another double signpost**. A very faint trail goes right here, heading south-west to some other mines (GPS 27). These are sometimes called **Magharat el Khaseef** and one has an impressive hieroglyphic tablet. A few metres away a low cliff drops down, with more tablets on its face. There's a piece of graffiti from a traveller in 1825 too.

Return the same way to the signpost and continue along the main trail to the **Temple of Hathor** (GPS 28). Hathor was Serabit's patron goddess: she was believed to guide the miners to new veins and keep them safe. Her temple started as a rock-hewn cave in the Middle Kingdom around 1900BC; it's at the eastern end of the complex. Next door (south) is a cave dedicated to Ptah, the creator God of Memphis. It was later re-dedicated to Hathor and other deities, including Soped: 'Lord of the Eastern Desert Lands'. The Pharaoh Ramesses IV built himself a 'Temple of Millions of Years' close by around 1155BC.

The temple expanded gradually west from these caves. Little sanctuaries were built consecutively and a long row gradually emerged. Each was associated with its own divine or royal cult and processional ways went along them. They were followed by priests to celebrate the daily cults and other special occasions. The stones with curved tops are funerary stelae.

Follow the main trail east from the temple. Excellent views extend out over **Ramlet Himeiyir**: the great red sand wilderness at the foot of Jebel Tih. The heights of Jebel Serbal are in the distance to the right.

You soon get to the plateau edge, where you have to scramble down a short, steep rock band (GPS 29). The trail zigzags down high ledges after this, descending directly above the deep course of **Wadi el Khaseef**. You'll see an impressive vertical waterfall cliff below. The trail soon straightens, running down to the wadi bottom. Walk on to its mouth, where there's a **small stone hut** (GPS 30). A big belt of sand opens here and it's **vital to turn left** (north-west). Going right would take you into the waterless sands of Ramlet Himeiyir.

Walk along the sandy belt to the north-west, **following the line of the Serabit el Khadem highland on the left**. It's a simple case of skirting around the bottom of this all the way to the village. This area is sometimes called **Wadi Suwig**. There are jeep tracks but the walking is often better higher up, where the sand is harder. There's a sharp bend at the end of the belt but you can cut over a low dune to avoid walking its full length. At the end of the belt is a camp (not always open). After this is the Serabit village (GPS 31).

Getting out of Serabit A pick-up truck to Abu Zenima is about LE200-300; just ask around (see opposite for more on Abu Zenima). There are more interesting ways to leave if you can stretch to a jeep (LE500-800 per day). One route goes through the sand wilderness of Ramlet Himeiyir to Jebel Fuga; a field of natural rock columns. Another goes back via the old manganese mines of Umm Bojma. Either route takes you back to Wadi Mukattab and then to Wadi Feiran.

Jebel Tih ('The Wilderness of the Wanderings') You can trek to Jebel Tih. It's a remote area with beautiful vistas of the mountains, virtually never visited. Ramlet Himeiyir and Jebel Fuga, mentioned above, are alternatives. For a longer trip you could take a camel along the bottom of Jebel Tih to Ein Hudera.

There are also ways to St Katherine. One downside is it's expensive. Negotiating here can start at LE600-700 (€80) a day; prices come down, but not by much. **Mohammed Radwan** is a well-known Muzeina guide and you'll find him easily by asking around.

ABU ZENIMA

Abu Zenima is halfway up the Sinai's west coast. It's a small, dusty backwater dominated by the belching chimneys of the Sinai Manganese Company. It's not a place to stay; the only question is whether you do a short excursion to **Hammam Faraun (Baths of the Pharaoh)** before you go. This is a hot spring about 20km north of Abu Zenima. Legend has it the Egyptian king drowned chasing the Israelites across the Red Sea here. Some say you can still hear his gurgled cries today. There are two geothermal caves in the cliffs; both natural saunas. One has steps up to it and becomes a narrow, winding passageway a little way in. There's only one passage and it ends in a cul-de-sac – so don't worry about getting lost – but it's hot, pitch-black, and you have to stoop and fumble, so take a torch. Once done, dip off in the sea; the hot springs trickle to the shore.

Get a taxi in Abu Zenima by asking around in shops or cafés. Pay about LE70-100 return and expect the driver to wait for an hour.

Getting there and away
Abu Zenima is served by buses going both ways along the west coast – just ask the driver to stop. To catch buses from Abu Zenima itself, you'll have to flag them down, but they won't all stop. Get a taxi 15km south to Abu Rudeis, which has a proper East Delta bus station. Find one by asking around and pay LE30-40.

Getting from Abu Zenima to Serabit
To do the short trek around Serabit el Khadem (pp216-220, Maps 42-44), find transport in Abu Zenima, asking around with locals. Someone with a pick-up truck will have to take you as it's off-road part of the way. Pay about LE200-300.

ABU RUDEIS

Abu Rudeis is a bigger, nicer town than Abu Zenima but there's still little to keep you. The East Delta **bus station** is the real reason to come. You can go south to El Tur (LE10, 1½-2½hrs) and Sharm (LE20, 2½-3½hrs). There's a bus to St Katherine at 4pm (LE15, 1-1½hrs) but it leaves Cairo at 11am and often picks up delays. Buses also go to Cairo (LE40, 5-6 hrs).

❏ **Walking from Wadi Feiran to St Katherine**
You can follow **Wadi Solaf** from Wadi Feiran to St Katherine. It starts near the village of Furrah and leads to Sheikh Auwad. This is a village at the bottom of the Naqb el Hawa pass, which can be followed up to Abu Seila and from there to town (see Maps 4 and 5, pp138-9). There are Nawamis tombs in Wadi Solaf but the walk is done mostly between low, unremarkable ranges and has little merit in itself. Allow a long day, or do it in two.

The Desert

This stretches over the eastern side of the Sinai and is best known for its twisting canyons, shimmering oases and towering outcrops. Its mountains are mostly sandstone peaks, different in appearance – and in climbing – to those of the high granite districts. As much as the scenery, trekking feels different here because of the camels. They stay with you the whole trek. Travelling like this gives the best feel for the old, wandering ways of the Bedouin. If there's a downside it's that it can get busy with jeeps, but don't let this put you off. Most of the time you'll still be firmly away from it all in the wilderness.

TRIBES AND TREKKING

The Muzeina and Tarabin tribes hold lands here. The Muzeina have everything around the Ein Hudera area, where most treks are set. The Tarabin territory stretches about halfway down between Ras Shaitan and Ein Hudera.

Trekking policies

Tribes are generally more relaxed here than in the mountains. The Muzeina allow Bedouin of any tribe to work on their lands. The Tarabin attitude works on a simple mirror basis. The Muzeina are free to work as they allow the Tarabin to do the same. Tribesmen of the Jebeleya, Gararsha and some other tribes are usually prohibited on the same grounds.

Trekking costs

These vary depending on where you organise a trek. In a coastal town like Nuweiba it'll be about LE250-450 per day for everything: guide, camel, food and water. Each extra camel will cost about LE100-200 per day. At a desert trailhead such as Ein Hudera, the Nawamis village or Wadi Arada it'll be cheaper; usually about LE150-250 for the full package and LE80-120 per extra camel.

NUWEIBA

Nuweiba is 85km up the coast from Dahab with a similar setting: rugged mountains and beautiful views to the Hejaz. It has seen change: it was a Bedouin fishing village (see box below) a few decades ago, then a thriving moshav in the Israeli period ('Neviot'). Today it's an international port town and the third biggest tourist centre in the Sinai. Despite this it still has a provincial air and the

> ❑ **Fish with the Bedouin**
> Nuweiba is a traditional fishing village and it can be fun to go out and fish with the locals. Camp chefs will usually cook what you catch. Zoola Beach (see p226) can be a good place to find a local fisherman.

Bedouin presence is more noticeable than in Sharm or Dahab. It's a good place to stay for a night; there's accommodation for every budget, guides are easy to find and you're near the trailhead for the Ras Shaitan to Ein Hudera trek.

PRACTICAL INFORMATION
Orientation

Nuweiba is a gigantic headland divided into three areas. On the southern side is the port, with the ferry terminal for Jordan. On the north is Nuweiba City; actually, still mostly a city of empty blocks waiting to be filled in. Further north, Tarabin stretches up a sandy coastline. It's called 'Tarabin' as this is where Tarabin territory begins. Further south it's all Muzeina. East Delta buses arrive near the port. If coming from the north it is best to get off early (you'll only have to get a taxi back otherwise). Ask the driver to pull over in Tarabin (say 'Soft Beach' to be dropped in about the right place). Walk the last few hundred metres, from the highway to the seafront strip.

Getting around

Taxis are essential here – but pricey. Expect to pay about LE20-30 from Nuweiba City to the port. Between Nuweiba City and the northern end of Tarabin, LE5-10 (or just walk along the beach in about half an hour). The taxis here aren't colour coded; ask around and someone with a car will usually take you. Or organise one through a camp.

Services

Branches of Banque Misr and the National Bank of Egypt are opposite the port (Sun-Thur, 8.30am-2pm). Both **banks** change major currencies including Jordanian Dinars and they also have **ATMs**. The Banque Misr ATM does 24hr foreign exchange. Banque Misr in the Hilton is always useful as it's open daily (9am-9pm) and non-guests can use it. In Nuweiba City there's an ATM on the main town street and another in the Helnan lobby.

Nuweiba Central Hospital (☎ 069-350 0302) does GP-style consultations throughout the day and emergency treatment 24hrs. There's a **pharmacy** in Nuweiba City and a couple of others at the port.

The main **post office** (Sat-Thur, 8am-2pm) is near the hospital. There's a smaller one near East Delta bus station, at the port (same hours). For **internet** try Al Mostakbal Café (8am-2am, LE5/hr) in Nuweiba City. The Online Center (noon-midnight, LE5/hr) is between Nuweiba City and Tarabin.

There's a **newspaper shop** selling *Al Ahram* on the main street in Nuweiba City. You can usually get *Egypt Today* as well. It's a good spot to stock up on fresh reading material.

There's a **laundry** in Tarabin, charging LE2-5 per piece.

Where to stay

Nuweiba has suffered with the collapse of the Israeli market and more recently with the slump since the revolution.

Some of the budget camps below were opening on and off in 2012, struggling to make ends meet. Things may change and options will be more limited than normal, but you'll always find something.

The best value comes in the mid-price bracket here. Hotels that'd cost more in Sharm and Dahab drop prices to bring business to a lesser-known area.

Budget accommodation There are two main areas of budget accommodation. The best known is Tarabin, where camps run up the beach in a line. The other is between Nuweiba City and the port, in an area dubbed 'The Duna'. Camps are more idyllic here, if a bit out of the way. The budget scene is based mostly on beach huts. These get hot and muggy and mosquitoes are active all year. A tent will give more comfortable sleeping quarters. The cleanliness of the bedding can also be questionable in places.

Tarabin (see map p225) is entered through a Disneyland-style castle gate. There's not much to choose between the camps but of the basic, hut-based ones, *Sababa* (mob ☎ 0122-057 7989, 🖳 sababa-camp.blogspot.co.uk) is the nicest. It has free wi-fi, spotless huts and a warm welcome.

(Cont'd on p226)

TRAIL GUIDE & MAPS

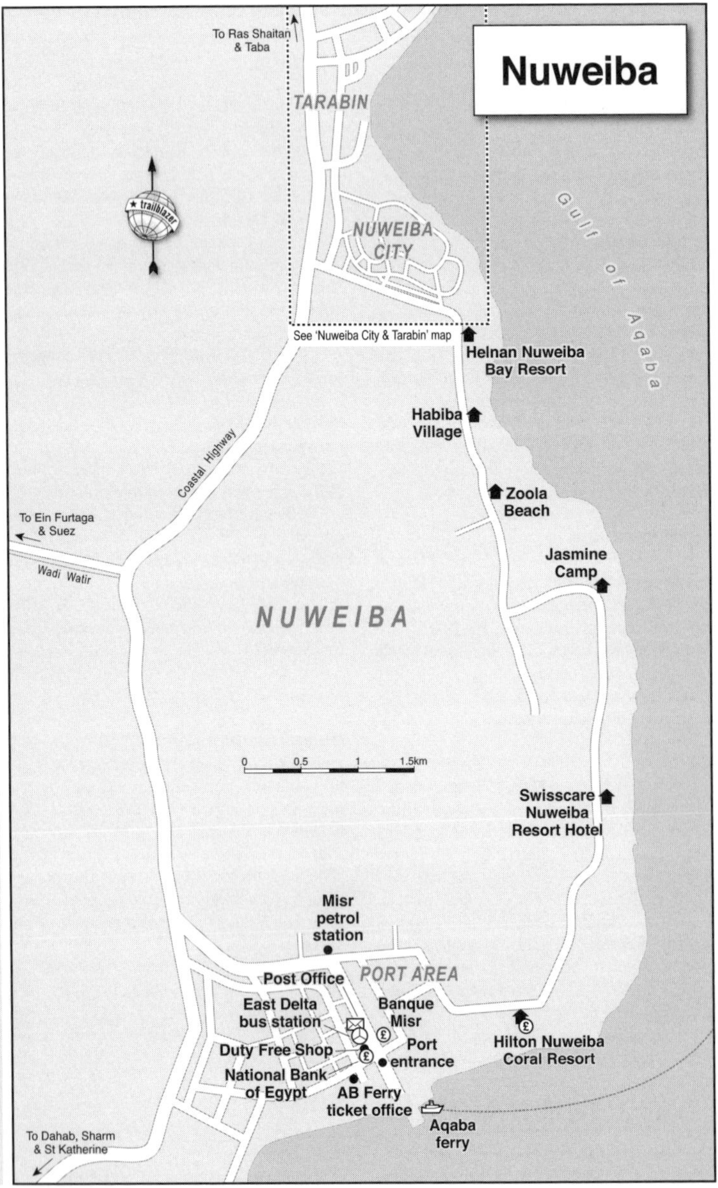

Nuweiba

To Ras Shaitan & Taba

TARABIN

NUWEIBA CITY

Gulf of Aqaba

See 'Nuweiba City & Tarabin' map

Helnan Nuweiba Bay Resort

Habiba Village

Coastal Highway

To Ein Furtaga & Suez

Wadi Watir

Zoola Beach

Jasmine Camp

NUWEIBA

0   0.5   1   1.5km

Swisscare Nuweiba Resort Hotel

Misr petrol station

Post Office   PORT AREA

East Delta bus station   Banque Misr

Duty Free Shop   Port entrance

National Bank of Egypt   Hilton Nuweiba Coral Resort

AB Ferry ticket office

Aqaba ferry

To Dahab, Sharm & St Katherine

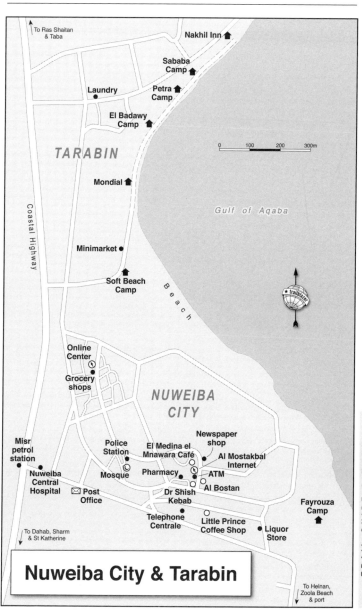

Nuweiba City & Tarabin

(Cont'd from p223) **Petra Camp** (mob ☎ 0100-472 2001), further south, is another good choice; hammocks swing on the beach and the whole place has an easy feel. The huts have a/c and start from LE40.

El Badawy (mob ☎ 0106-525 4115, 🖳 elbadawycamp.dk) is a friendly place offering proper rooms with a/c and bathrooms. Singles start from LE90 and doubles LE120. There's also **Mondial** (mob ☎ 0122-796 3385), with decent rooms from LE70 (single) and LE100 (double).

Soft Beach (☎ 069-350 0010, 🖳 www .softbeachcamp.com), at the very southern end of Tarabin, was once a favourite but standards of service have slipped lately. One thing that hasn't slipped are the breakfasts: they are still top-notch. Single huts are LE50 and doubles LE100.

Between Nuweiba City and the port (see map p224) The best option is **Zoola Beach**, in a traditional Bedouin part of Nuweiba. It's set amidst beach dunes and has an island castaway feel. You can sleep in huts or hammocks and the Bedouin go out of their way to make your stay a good one. It's a 40-minute walk from Nuweiba City and a sign marks the turn-off from the road. A track leads through a grove of trees: go right at the first fork.

Another option is **Jasmine Camp**, further down the road towards the port. It has a nice beach, easy-going staff and huts are LE20.

The only camp in **Nuweiba City** (see map p225) is **Fayrouza Camp**. Clean, comfortable huts are LE40 with doubles LE50. It's a nice option and very conveniently located for services.

Mid-price Nuweiba (see map p224) has some of the best hotels in this range. **Swisscare Nuweiba Resort Hotel** (☎ 069-352 0640, 🖳 www.swisscare-hotels.com) is perhaps the best value, with a good beach, reef and spacious, multi-room suites. Singles start from US$45 (LE270) and doubles US$60 (LE360).

Habiba (mob ☎ 0122-217 6624, 🖳 www.habibavillage.com) is a camp-style option with a second-hand library, nice beach and restaurant. The rooms have a/c but they're overpriced at US$30 (LE190) and US$45 (LE290).

Nakhil Inn (see map p225; ☎ 069-350 0879), at the very northern end of **Tarabin**, is perhaps the nicest of all. It's a family-run place offering beach bungalows with high tree-house-style sleeping platforms. There are standard-style rooms as well: all accommodation has a/c and att with singles US$48 (LE285) and doubles US$60 (LE360).

Expensive There are really only two options (see map p224). **Hilton Nuweiba Coral Resort** (☎ 069-352 0320, 🖳 www.hilton.com) is near the port with singles from US$80 (LE475) and doubles US$100 (LE595). **Helnan Nuweiba Bay Resort** (☎ 069-350 0401, 🖳 www.helnan.com) is in Nuweiba City. This has singles from US$125 (LE745) and doubles from US$160 (LE950). Both are nice, but if you're staying somewhere like this, it's better to do it in Sharm or Dahab.

Where to eat
Most camps have restaurants but there are other places if you're out and about.

Budget food Nuweiba is the sort of provincial town where budget eating should be easy, but it's not: it's easier to eat cheaply in Sharm. The best option in Nuweiba City is **El Medina el Mnawara** (see map p225). It's round the back of the main street and opens at breakfast, serving sandwiches (LE1-2) until late.

There are **budget cafés** near the port, offering sandwiches from LE2 upwards.

Restaurants and cafés (see map p225) **Dr Shish Kebab** is a long-running favourite in Nuweiba City: meat grills, seafood and pizza are on the menu.

Little Prince Coffee Shop (mob ☎ 0122-471 8011) is nearby; it's a small, friendly café with backgammon boards and traditional Arab décor. It does good homemade ice cream and snacks. Bigger meals are always good, but call ahead. They're specially prepared and slow-cooked over several hours.

Al Bostan, on the main street, is an open-air café. It's a good place to shoot the breeze with a shisha and coffee in the evening.

There's sometimes a **stall** selling sugar-cane juice outside the entrance from about 8pm.

Guides in Nuweiba

Nuweiba is a safari hub and most desert treks can be arranged here. The Ras Shaitan to Ein Hudera trek is always best organised here as the choice of guide is better than in Ras Shaitan. Work to a next-day basis as it's a longer trip and camels have to be trotted 15km north to Ras.

Find guides by asking in the camps. Zoola Beach is a favoured Bedouin haunt and always a good place to begin.

Farag Soliman (mob ☎ 0100-188 1852, 🖳 farag_soliman2003@yahoo.com) is a local Muzeina guide; fluent in English, with an excellent knowledge of the landscape, culture and history. He always travels with another Bedouin for safety and keeps a good, amenable set of camels. He's the only guide who can be vouched for personally. However, the following are very knowledgeable and also speak good English: **Rashid Hamd Rashid** (mob ☎ 0106-138 8257), Tarabin; and **Musallem Abu Faraj** (mob ☎ 0102-290 7022), Tarabin.

Moving on

Transport isn't so frequent and there's a gap on the route to St Katherine. The only cheap option is the twice-weekly Bedouin Bus (see p115).

● **By public bus** East Delta runs the following buses: Taba, 9am, midday, 3pm (LE11, 1-1½hrs); Cairo, 9am, 3pm (LE60-70, 8-9hrs); Dahab, 6.30am, 4.30pm (LE11, 1-1½hrs); Sharm, 6.30am (LE25, 2½-3½ hrs); El Tur, 6.30am (LE25, 4-6 hrs).

The bus to Taba can be used to go anywhere up the coast, including Ras Shaitan. Wait on the highway and flag it down; it usually arrives 15-30 minutes after departure.

In late 2012 the Nuweiba–Cairo bus, which crosses central Sinai, was closed to

---

❏ **Diving and snorkelling in Nuweiba**
Nuweiba's dive sites aren't as impressive as the ones further south in Sharm and Dahab but they're at least quieter.

● **Abou Lou Lou** This is the Hilton Nuweiba Coral Resort reef, known for its lionfish. The LE200 access fee is steep compared to elsewhere.

● **Swisscare Nuweiba Reef** This pretty reef is visited by eagle rays and giant turtles. You can snorkel for a reasonable LE50 per day.

● **The Pipeline** Two underwater pipes from an old Israeli desalination plant are found here. It's an interesting hybrid of the man-made and natural, and coral has colonised the pipes. It's too deep for snorkellers.

● **The Sinker** A weighted mooring buoy is pulled 12m down below here. One story goes the Israeli Navy botched their depth calculations before dropping it. Its attraction is similar to the pipeline.

● **Angelfish Reefs** There are several reefs here, all known for their small seahorses. The Magana Beach camp, south of Ras Shaitan, is the best place to go from and it charges LE30 for beach use.

Diving companies Nuweiba's dive scene isn't policed as carefully as it is in Sharm or Dahab and illegal operators have sprung up since the revolution. The dive companies of bigger hotels should be fine and the following can be recommended. For more on diving safely, read the box on p97.

● **African Divers** (mob ☎ 0122-311 0505, 🖳 www.africandiversnuweiba.com).

TRAIL GUIDE & MAPS

foreigners. Ask around and if it's off limits go via Sharm.

● **By minibus** The Bedouin Bus (see p115) goes to St Katherine on Wednesdays and Sundays. It leaves from the hospital at 2pm or opposite the East Delta bus station at 2.30pm. Tickets are LE50. Check 🖥 www .bedouinbus.com.

● **By ferry AB Maritime Company** (🖥 www.abmaritime.com, ☎ 069-520 0472) runs one daily ferry to Aqaba (3pm, US$60/LE360 one-way, crossing three hours). There are no ferries on Saturdays and departure times can change so check ahead. The ticket office has no sign but it's on the first street corner west of the port entrance, opposite some cafés. Arrive at least two hours before departure, with US$10 for the departure tax (or the Egyptian equivalent).

● **Hitching** Everything runs down the east coast highway and hitching is an option either way. Someone will usually stop (see p41).

● **By private taxi** Taxis are useful with public transport being limited. The following rates are typical: Dahab, LE150-200; Sharm, LE350-400; St Katherine, LE200-220; Ras Shaitan, LE30-40; Taba, LE100-120. You can find taxis by asking around camps or by contacting a local driver such as Subhi Soliman (mob ☎ 0106-138 9060), or Ibrahim Khodair (mob ☎ 0100-537 8810).

RAS SHAITAN

Ras Shaitan ('Devil's Head') is an area of budget beach camps about 15km north of Nuweiba. The camps stretch around a sandy bay in a long line. The vibe ranges from the laid-back to the outright New Age. There's nothing to do as such; it's simply a place to get away from it all. The trek to Ein Hudera starts here and you could stay overnight before meeting your guide at the trailhead the next day. Bring everything you need as there's just one shop in the area (on the opposite side of the highway to Castle Beach).

PRACTICAL INFORMATION
Where to stay
The camp with the widest appeal is *Castle Beach* (mob ☎ 0122-739 8495). It's a simple, clean option with hot showers and a restaurant; huts cost LE180/night with breakfast and dinner included. It's at the southern end of the main bay and all the drivers known it.

Ayash Camp (mob ☎ 0100-444 2147), next door, has huts for LE40.

Something of an oddity in these parts is *Holiday Inn Resort Taba* (see Map 45 p232; ☎ 069-356 0000), at the northern end of the bay. The hotel isn't of much interest but it has an **ATM**; the last place to get cash before you move inland.

Finding a guide
There is no difficulty finding a guide for the Ein Hudera trek; camps will put you in touch with local Tarabin tribesmen. Even so it's recommended you arrange the trek in Nuweiba, for the greater choice available.

Moving on
Flag everything down on the highway. East Delta **buses** arrive 20-40 minutes after leaving Nuweiba (see p227). Coming the other way from Taba they take about 40-60 minutes. **Hitching** becomes important when there are no buses and it's usually easy both ways. For more on the coast up to Taba see pp118-19.

❏ **Snorkelling in Ras Shaitan**
There's a reef at Castle Beach. It's not as spectacular as many others in the Sinai but it's still worth a look. Masks and snorkels can be rented at the camp.

EIN HUDERA

Ein Hudera ('The Green Spring') is perhaps the Sinai's prettiest oasis. Nestling under rugged sandstone cliffs, it has deep wells, thick groves of palm and colourful blossom trees. It has long been a fabled haven for the Bedouin; they once said a secret passage connected it to a paradise at the centre of the earth. Most people visit with jeeps these days, but it's much better to walk. Walking in after a few hard days in the desert means you really appreciate the oasis and why its water, shade, colour and life are so special.

Ein Hudera is a key trekking crossroads. It's crossed by two major routes – the Ras Shaitan to Ein Hudera trek and the Desert Traverse. It's also close to the Haduda Dune trailhead and all can be linked.

PRACTICAL INFORMATION
Where to stay

Ein Hudera has a Garden of Eden feel. Crickets hum, camp fires flicker, and there are big, starry skies.

Several Bedouin gardens offer basic lodgings under palm shelters. The garden of *Rardia Mohammed* is a good one, with a sign reading 'all the comforts of home and more'. Rardia is one of the few women to live alone and she's an attentive host, always on hand with tea. *Sabah Camp*, next door, has a small bathing pool. It's great for a plunge after a long trek.

Expect to pay about LE10-20 to stay in a garden and LE15-25 for an evening meal.

Organising a trek

Guides and camels can be organised in Ein Hudera. Things might take a bit longer, but even if you have to work on a next-day basis staying is never bad.

Onward options include the Haduda Dune and the last two days of the Desert Traverse, to Jebel Mileihis.

To start the Desert Traverse you'd have to get to Wadi Arada, about 12km away on the highway.

Getting to St Katherine highway

Ein Hudera has a deep, secluded desert feel but the highway is less than an hour's walk. Hire a camel if you have heavy bags as it's all done on sand and there's a steep uphill stretch (about LE90).

Walk south to an obvious pass with a whitish colouring. Follow a zigzag camel trail up and you'll see the St Katherine highway across a plain from the top. There's a hut on the road near two high telephone masts: this is **Cafeteria Jomaa**. It's a good place to arrange a pick up (the area has a mobile signal).

There are a couple of historical sites between the pass and the road. Over to the right are said to be the ruined blocks of a Byzantine church called Deir Ein Hudera (or just 'Deir Hudera').

There's also a big rock with Nabataean, Roman and Byzantine inscriptions called Hajar Maktoob ('The Written Rock'), or Hadabat el Hajj ('Hill of the Hajj'), see box below.

Moving on to the other trailheads

From Cafeteria Jomaa it's easy to get to the trailheads and the directions are on p230.

❏ **The lost caravan of the Hajj**
Legend has it an ill-fated Hajj caravan camped at Hadabat el Hajj when returning from Mecca, before getting lost in the Wilderness of the Wanderings. No trace was ever found of the pilgrims, but it's said their last scrawls are still seen on the rock.

TRAIL GUIDE & MAPS

OTHER DESERT TRAILHEADS

There are two other desert trailheads near Ein Hudera. The Haduda Dune trek starts at Nawamis village. The Desert Traverse, at a small hamlet in Wadi Arada. Both are just off the main road between St Katherine and the east coast. It's cheaper to organise treks here than in tourist towns. The daily fees are LE150-250 for a guide and camel (and usually food) and LE80-120 per extra camel. Drawbacks are that both English and the choice of guide are limited. If your trek isn't ready on the same day, sleep in Ein Hudera – see directions below. An alternative is **Nawamis Desert Centre** (📧 nawamiscenter@gmail.com). This was opened by the Makhad Trust (see box p82) in late 2011 to stimulate the Bedouin economy. You can sleep in a Bedouin tent (or pitch your own) for LE20/night or LE50 including breakfast. Book in advance.

Getting to the trailheads
● **Nawamis** This village is 3km west from the Cafeteria Jomaa/Ein Hudera region. A sign marks the turn off on the highway. Walk south a few hundred metres and the village comes into view (see Map 56, p247).
● **Wadi Arada** This wadi is 12km west from Nawamis, on the same highway. The settlement is on the roadside, with a sign to identify it.
● **Ein Hudera** Tell the driver you want 'Sharafat Ein Hudera'. More specifically within this area, 'Cafeteria Jomaa' – a roadside shack (not open as a café now). Use Map 55 on p245, heading north for a whitish gap in low, rocky ground. The oasis is visible from here and the whole walk takes 35-55 minutes.

Transport Use any transport between St Katherine and the east coast. The Bedouin Bus (see p115) is the best option. It goes between Dahab and St Katherine on Tuesdays and Fridays and Nuweiba and St Katherine on Wednesdays and Sundays. Wherever it leaves from – St Katherine, Dahab or Nuweiba – it'll take about 45-60 minutes to get to the trailheads (see Dahab p115, Nuweiba p228 and St Katherine p131 for departure times).

RAS SHAITAN TO EIN HUDERA (3-4 days)

Practicalities
● **Difficulty and scheduling** This is a moderate walk with good stretches for camel riding. It can be finished in three days but four is more comfortable.
● **Links with other treks** From Ein Hudera you can continue with the Haduda Dune trek (p246) or the last part of the Desert Traverse (p254).
● **Other treks in the area** There are other ways to Ein Hudera from the Coloured Canyon (which you usually reach on the second day). One route goes via the 'Rainbow Canyon', before running through one of the biggest drug production districts on the peninsula. The farmers are friendly enough, but it's accessible and vulnerable to attention from the authorities. Guides might also suggest Wadi Let-Hi (pronounced 'Let-hee') but avoid this too; it was mined in the Egypt–Israel wars and its clearance status remains uncertain. The route given is the safest and best until things change elsewhere.

Ras Shaitan to Wadi Wishwashi [Map 45]

This trek starts in **Wadi Melha**, north of the Ras Shaitan bay, and across the highway from the Holiday Inn Resort Taba (GPS 1). It's a big wadi that cuts inland through rugged coastal ranges. About 2.5km along it narrows between high, towering sides (GPS 2). Immediately before this on the left there's an open area where minor wadis run in. Ignore this and press straight through the narrow section. You come out in a wider stretch of Wadi Melha. Look right and you'll see the small, rocky mouth of **Wadi Wishwashi** or the **Whispering Wadi** (GPS 3). This is the way to **Wishwashi Canyon**.

● **Is the narrow section blocked?** Flash floods can shift debris to make it impassable for camels in wetter months. If it hasn't been unblocked by the time you're there, exit in the open area on the left before. A rough trail rises south over a low pass to Wadi Melha Atshana. Turn right and follow it along to join the main route further up (you re-join on Map 46, GPS 9). You miss the early highlights of the trek but it's the only way to continue.

Wishwashi Canyon [Map 45]

Wishwashi Canyon is a short 'there and back' excursion. Follow Wadi Wishwashi up to where it narrows between towering cliffs, scrambling up on the left side. Just after this – and before what looks like a dead-end – the canyon opens on the left. Clamber up to where it ends in a gigantic plunge pool.

Deep pools can form in the canyon after rain, flooding its course (and lying over a month). The only way to continue when it's like this is to swim.

Wadi Melha to Moiyet Melha [Maps 45-46]

Go back and veer right into Wadi Melha. There's another narrow section further up, but it's not as impressive as the last one. Soon afterwards is a **key cross-roads** (GPS 4). The wadi bends sharply right here and there's an acacia in its course. On the left, a small wadi opens in high cliffs. Directly ahead is a **low neck of land**; continue round the back of it. A little watercourse starts here, bending left to some palms below a big, red cliff: **Moiyet Melha** (GPS 5).

There is water here – as the palms show – but it's salty and not for drinking. Moiyet Melha actually means Salty Spring. Water seeps out to wet the cliffs but only birds and other desert wildlife lick it off.

Only a few of the palms are visible. A bigger cluster straddles the cliff to the north and a trail runs along below them. It's worth having an explore.

Moiyet Melha to Farsh Fureh [Map 46]

Turn left from where you first reached the palms, following a zigzag trail up steep, stony slopes. This levels out below a band of low, horizontal cliffs, before veering progressively right. Going around here you can look back down on Wadi Melha again. A big basin soon edges into view: it's swept with light sand and dotted with mounds, outcrops and vegetation. This is **Farsh Fureh**.

The trail runs down to it, entering near a little **cluster of palms** (GPS 6). These stand at the top of the wadi seen left at the previous crossroads. It's through here that the whole of Farsh Fureh drains.

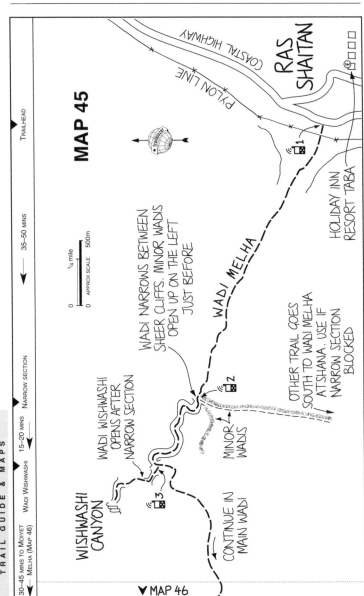

30–45 MINS TO MOIYET MELHA (MAP 46) ◄ WADI WISHWASHI 15–20 MINS ► NARROW SECTION 35–50 MINS TRAILHEAD ►

MAP 45

WADI NARROWS BETWEEN SHEER CLIFFS. MINOR WADIS OPEN UP ON THE LEFT JUST BEFORE

WADI MELHA

PYLON LINE (COASTAL HIGHWAY)

RAS SHAITAN

HOLIDAY INN RESORT TABA

OTHER TRAIL GOES SOUTH TO WADI MELHA ATSHANA. USE IF NARROW SECTION BLOCKED

MINOR WADIS

WADI WISHWASHI OPENS AFTER NARROW SECTION

WISHWASHI CANYON

CONTINUE IN MAIN WADI

▼ MAP 46

0 ¼ mile
0 APPROX SCALE 500m

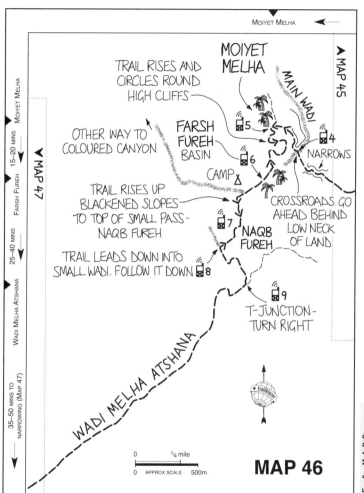

MOIYET MELHA ◀

▲ MAP 45

MOIYET
MELHA

MAIN WADI

TRAIL RISES AND
CIRCLES ROUND
HIGH CLIFFS

📱 5

FARSH
FUREH
BASIN

📱 4

NARROWS

OTHER WAY TO
COLOURED CANYON

📱 6

CAMP △

CROSSROADS. GO
AHEAD BEHIND
LOW NECK
OF LAND

TRAIL RISES UP
BLACKENED SLOPES
TO TOP OF SMALL PASS -
NAQB FUREH

📱 7

NAQB
FUREH

TRAIL LEADS DOWN INTO
SMALL WADI. FOLLOW IT DOWN 📱 8

📱 9

T-JUNCTION -
TURN RIGHT

★ trailblazer

WADI MELHA ATSHANA

MOIYET MELHA
FARSH FUREH 15–20 MINS
25–40 MINS
WADI MELHA ATSHANA
35–50 MINS TO
NARROWING (MAP 47)

◀ MAP 47

0   1/4 mile
0   APPROX SCALE   500m

MAP 46

TRAIL GUIDE & MAPS

Turn right and head for a **second cluster of palms** about 100m away.
Continue past these on the same straight line and you'll be set for some blackish slopes on the south-west side of the basin.
    There are a few separate trails at the bottom, but they all converge on a sin-
gle, well-trodden line higher up. This leads to a low pass called Naqb Fureh,
which is where you go next.

❏ **Wadi Melha Atshana**
This is the second Wadi Melha on the trek: the word *atshana* means thirsty and indicates the wadi has no water. The other Wadi Melha – with the water at Moiyet Melha – sometimes has *royana* tagged on to it, meaning quenched. One wadi wants water, the other drinks its fill. There are other places with names like this in the Sinai: they enabled the Bedouin to twin nearby locations whilst distinguishing them on the most useful practical grounds. For more on Bedouin place names see box p32.

Camping in Farsh Fureh This is the best campsite on the first night and if you arrive early there's plenty to explore. The nicest spot is a secluded corner on the west side of the basin. It has a big acacia tree and a boulder shelter.

Other routes to the Coloured Canyon There are alternative trekking routes from Farsh Fureh. The best-known continues west through a sandy basin with a beautiful small oasis, before heading over a high pass.

Naqb Fureh to Wadi Melha Atshana [Map 46]
Follow the trail to the top of **Naqb Fureh** (GPS 7). Two trails divide and run off over blackened ground ahead; take either. Each veers gradually right, soon cutting down to a **minor wadi** (GPS 8). Turn left here; it goes round a slight kink before straightening down to **Wadi Melha Atshana** (see box above) (GPS 9).

If you had to divert at the first narrowing you'll re-join the main trekking route here. Continue ahead with the route described now.

Wadi Melha Atshana to the Coloured Canyon [Maps 46-47]
Turn right and follow Wadi Melha Atshana. About 2.5km along, it twists between high, narrow walls. Shortly after this narrow section there's a **key junction** (GPS 10). A small rocky wadi opens on the right, giving one possible route to the Coloured Canyon (sometimes called Wadi Mattarsha).

Follow this up a long, straight stretch, turning into the **first major wadi** on the left. Continue round here to a wooden shack (GPS 11). A **small, rocky wadi** opens opposite this on the right, leading to the canyon (GPS 12).

Camels don't usually go this way: they take a different path to an area above the canyon. For the camel route, go past the first wadi, heading towards a pylon on high ground ahead. Turn into the first wadi on the right and follow its rugged course along (GPS 13). Further up you reach a **small sandy basin** (GPS 14). Exit this through a passage on its left side (a big, cuboid-shaped boulder lies in its course). This leads into a **bigger basin** with shacks around its high edges and a trail up its southern side (you go this way later). Turn right and follow a trail of footprints down to a bigger wadi where there's an old shack. Opposite this on the left a **small, rocky wadi** leads to the canyon (GPS 12).

The Coloured Canyon: a circular trail [Map 47]
The Coloured Canyon is named after the reds, yellows and whites in its sides. It's one of the desert's most popular natural attractions and some days see hundreds of visitors flock here (morning and late afternoon are busiest).

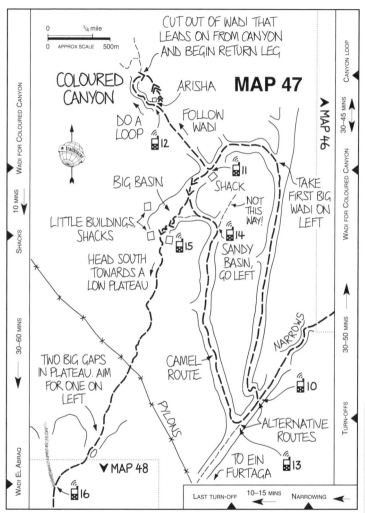

A **steep, bouldery slope** rises into the cliffs next to the canyon's mouth. You'll come back this way later so fix it in your mind as a reference point. At the end of the canyon, the high sides drop away and a minor wadi opens up. Scramble out on its rocky right side a short way along. A few rojoms mark the exit point (if they're not knocked off). Once up follow a southerly trail to the top of the bouldery slope before the canyon and go down. *(Cont'd on p238)*

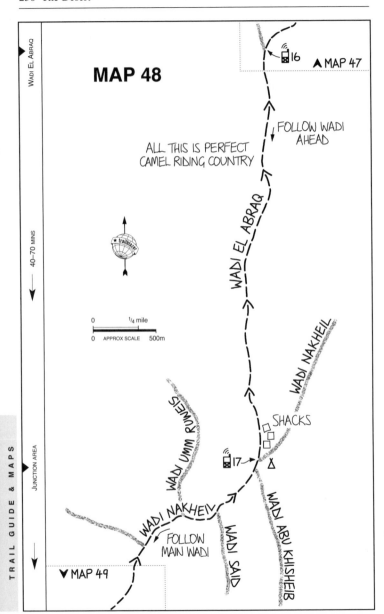

MAP 48

ALL THIS IS PERFECT
CAMEL RIDING COUNTRY

FOLLOW WADI
AHEAD

WADI EL ABRAQ

WADI NAKHEIL

SHACKS

WADI UMM RUWEIS

WADI NAKHEIL

FOLLOW
MAIN WADI

WADI SAID

WADI ABU KHISHEIB

▲ MAP 47

▼ MAP 49

0   ¼ mile
0   APPROX SCALE   500m

trailblazer

WADI EL ABRAQ

40–70 MINS

JUNCTION AREA

TRAIL GUIDE & MAPS

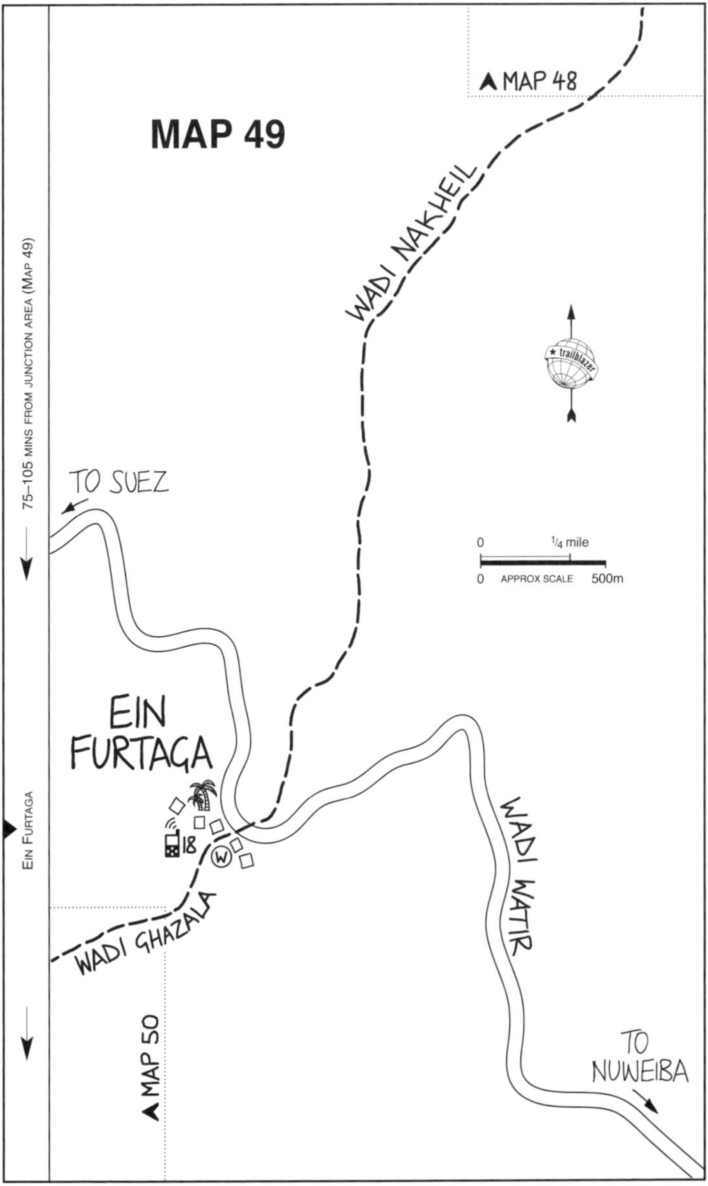

MAP 49

MAP 48

WADI NAKHEIL

75–105 MINS FROM JUNCTION AREA (MAP 49)

TO SUEZ

0   1/4 mile

0   APPROX SCALE   500m

EIN FURTAGA

Ein Furtaga

18

W

WADI WATIR

WADI GHAZALA

MAP 50

TO NUWEIBA

TRAIL GUIDE & MAPS

(Cont'd from p235) Walk out the same way and turn right at the shack. Move up some rugged slopes to a **big basin** and take a zigzag trail up its southern side. This brings you to some more shacks at the top (GPS 15).

The Coloured Canyon to Ein Furtaga   [Maps 47-49]

This point marks the start of a long, southerly wadi trek to Ein Hudera; excellent camel-riding country all the way. Looking south from the shacks you'll see two wadis in a low, blackish plateau. They appear as **big obvious gaps**; head towards the one on the left: **Wadi el Abraq** (GPS 16).

There's a line of electricity pylons about halfway across. Once in the wadi, follow it ahead. About 3km down there's a **junction** where smaller wadis join at staggered intervals around a big bend (GPS 17). The first on the left is Wadi Nakheil and the main wadi takes its name from here.

Wadi el Abraq is thus now called **Wadi Nakheil**. Wadi Nakheil is actually a continuation of Wadi Melha Atshana; it comes from the area where you first turned off for the Coloured Canyon.

Follow the main course of the wadi round, passing all the other ones that run in. Somewhere round here can make a good **camp** on the second night.

About 5km down, Wadi Nakheil ends at **Wadi Watir**. The Nuweiba–Suez highway runs along here. Cross to the oasis settlement of **Ein Furtaga** (GPS 18). A few Tarabin families live here and it's a good spot to re-fill jerry cans – there's no guaranteed water until Ein Hudera.

Ein Furtaga to Wadi Hudera   [Maps 49-52]

Ein Furtaga stands at the mouth of **Wadi Ghazala** ('Wadi of the Gazelles'), which you need to follow ahead. Further along there's a **dam**; behind it is a big water tank. This intercepts debris before it crashes into the dam in flash floods and often holds water for a few weeks after rain. It's usually clouded by sediments: filter anything you collect and let bottles settle before you drink.

About 4.5km along there's a big wadi on the left with an acacia tree outside its mouth (GPS 19). This is **Wadi Mileihis** (**Wadi Umm Lehas** on some maps) and it leads to Jebel Mileihis. Don't go this way now.

Further along there's a **big junction** where minor wadis run in. The first two wadis rise off on the right: the one closest is **Wadi Let-Hi** – pronounced Wadi Let-*hee* – but some maps mark it **Wadi Mikeimin**. This was laid with **landmines** in the Egypt–Israel conflicts and its clearance status remains uncertain. The Bedouin go there today – with some claiming it has been swept – but nothing is sure: **stay well away**. The wadi just beyond it is also called **Wadi Let-Hi**, or sometimes **Wadi Let-Hi** *Agula* to distinguish it from the last one. The wadi on the south-west side of the junction is **Wadi Hullal**.

Follow Wadi Ghazala as it bends south. After 1km it divides around a low black ridge (GPS 20). The branch on the left is the main continuation of Wadi Ghazala leading, in about 11km, to the St Katherine highway. Take the one on the right: this is **Wadi Hudera**, and it leads to Ein Hudera.

Camping on the way to Ein Hudera

Depending on your schedule, you might need to camp somewhere in Wadi Ghazala or Wadi Hudera – Ein Hudera

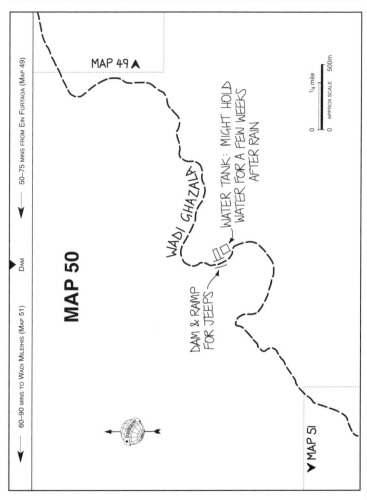

MAP 49 ▲

50–75 MINS FROM EIN FURTAGA (MAP 49)

DAM

60–90 MINS TO WADI MILEIHIS (MAP 51)

MAP 50

WADI GHAZALA

WATER TANK: MIGHT HOLD WATER FOR A FEW WEEKS AFTER RAIN

DAM & RAMP FOR JEEPS

¼ mile
0   500m
0   APPROX SCALE

▼ MAP 51

TRAIL GUIDE & MAPS

is still quite a distance away. Camp anywhere down the wadi sides, finding a secluded alcove and settling down when dusk sets in.

Wadi Hudera to Ein Hudera [Maps 52-54]

This is the home straight; you follow Wadi Hudera all the way to the Ein Hudera oasis. It's sandy underfoot and walking is hard work.

A distinct change in geology comes about in this stretch: the black rock of the coastal ranges gives way to a pretty, red sandstone. *(Cont'd on p244)*

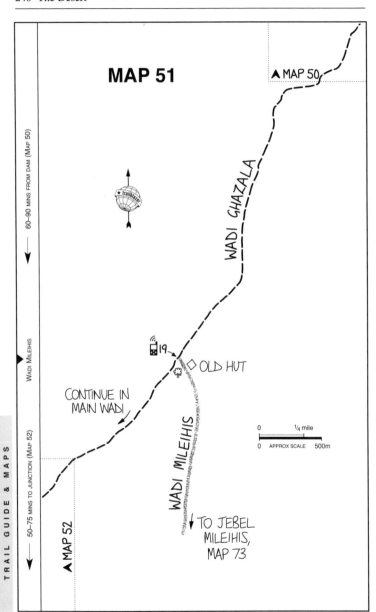

MAP 51

▲ MAP 50

WADI GHAZALA

★ trailblazer

60–90 MINS FROM DAM (MAP 50)

WADI MILEIHIS

50–75 MINS TO JUNCTION (MAP 52)

TRAIL GUIDE & MAPS

📻 19

◇ OLD HUT

CONTINUE IN
MAIN WADI

WADI MILEIHIS

0   ¼ mile
0   APPROX SCALE   500m

▲ MAP 52

↓ TO JEBEL
MILEIHIS,
MAP 73

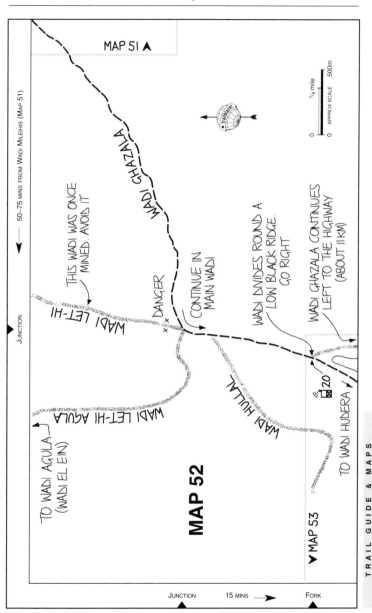

MAP 51 ▲

50–75 MINS FROM WADI MILEIHIS (MAP 51)

APPROX SCALE

¼ mile   500m

JUNCTION

WADI GHAZALA

THIS WADI WAS ONCE MINED. AVOID IT

WADI LET-HI

DANGER

CONTINUE IN MAIN WADI

WADI DIVIDES ROUND A LOW BLACK RIDGE. GO RIGHT

WADI GHAZALA CONTINUES LEFT TO THE HIGHWAY (ABOUT 11 KM)

WADI HULLAL

WADI LET-HI AGULA

TO WADI AGULA (WADI EL EIN)

MAP 52

20

TO WADI HUDERA

▼ MAP 53

JUNCTION   15 MINS ⟶   FORK

TRAIL GUIDE & MAPS

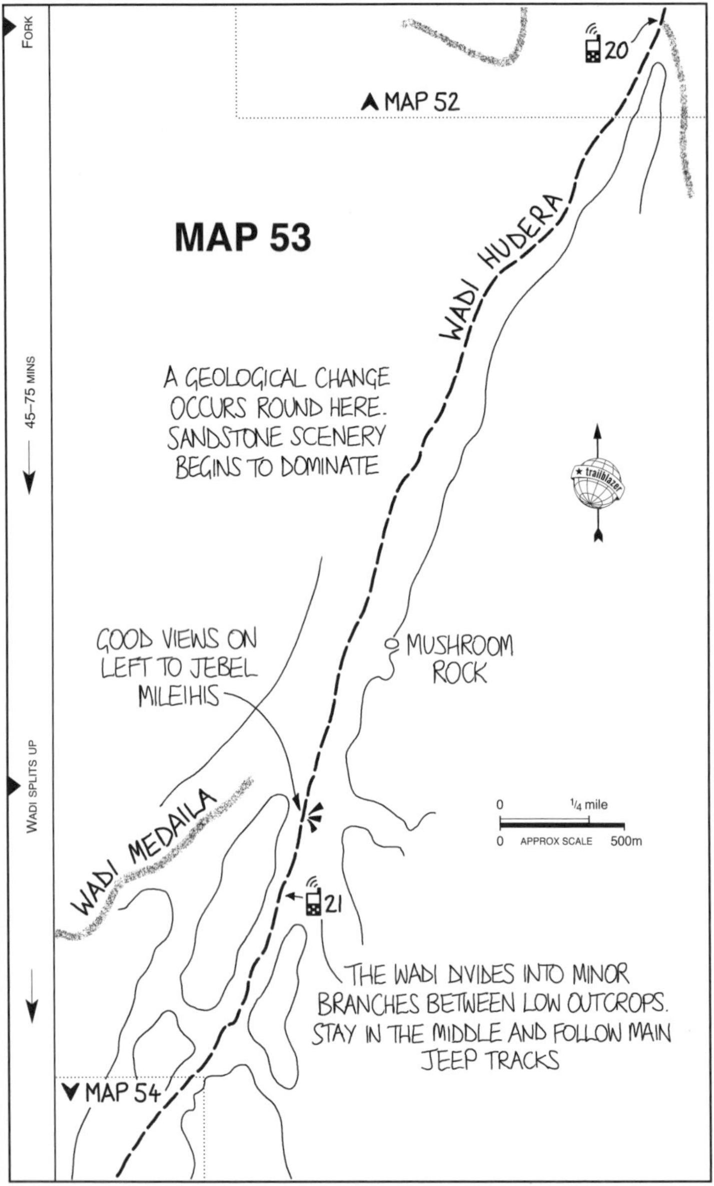
MAP 53
MAP 52
MAP 54
20
21
WADI HUDERA
WADI MEDAILA
A GEOLOGICAL CHANGE OCCURS ROUND HERE. SANDSTONE SCENERY BEGINS TO DOMINATE
GOOD VIEWS ON LEFT TO JEBEL MILEIHIS
MUSHROOM ROCK
THE WADI DIVIDES INTO MINOR BRANCHES BETWEEN LOW OUTCROPS. STAY IN THE MIDDLE AND FOLLOW MAIN JEEP TRACKS
FORK
45–75 MINS
WADI SPLITS UP
0
1/4 mile
0
APPROX SCALE
500m
trailblazer

TRAIL GUIDE & MAPS

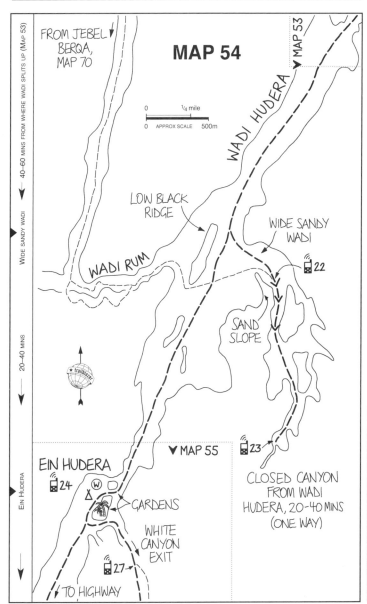

FROM JEBEL BERQA, MAP 70

MAP 54

MAP 53

WADI HUDERA

0   ¼ mile
0   APPROX SCALE   500m

40–60 MINS FROM WHERE WADI SPLITS UP (MAP 53)

WIDE SANDY WADI

LOW BLACK RIDGE

WIDE SANDY WADI

22

WADI RUM

SAND SLOPE

20–40 MINS

★ trailblazer

23

▼ MAP 55

CLOSED CANYON FROM WADI HUDERA, 20-40 MINS (ONE WAY)

EIN HUDERA

24

W

GARDENS

WHITE CANYON EXIT

EIN HUDERA

27

TO HIGHWAY

TRAIL GUIDE & MAPS

(Cont'd from p239) Look for a small rock on the left side of the wadi along here – it's called the **Mushroom Rock** for its distinctive shape.

The left side of the wadi soon lowers and the rugged, table-like peak of Jebel Mileihis comes into view. Rocky outcrops divide Wadi Hudera into several branches here (GPS 21). It looks confusing but don't worry as it's all the same basic wadi. Just continue as much in the middle as you can, following the deepest jeep tracks. If you did stray into another branch it wouldn't be a disaster. Most end in cul-de-sacs and you'd just have to retrace your footsteps (or scramble over the rocky dividing ground) to find your way back.

Further along there's a low black ridge on the right – it stands in front of a wadi called Wadi Rum (blocking the view of its mouth).

Opposite this on the left is a wadi with a **wide sandy mouth** (GPS 22): this is the way to the **Closed Canyon** – see below. It's easy to get to Ein Hudera from here: follow the wadi ahead and you'll be there in 30-45 minutes (GPS 24). For a few more notes on the oasis see p229.

Excursion to the Closed Canyon [Map 54]

The Closed Canyon is well worth the trip. Go into the wide, sandy wadi on the left of Wadi Hudera. This divides into two branches around a rocky block of land; take the one **on the right** – it's a long uphill trudge. Where this levels out a gap emerges in a stretch of low, rocky ground ahead. A pyramid-shaped peak rises in the rocky mass behind.

Go through this gap, turn right and let the wall on this side guide you round to the **mouth of the canyon** (GPS 23). Follow the canyon as it twists between narrow walls, scrambling now and then. You soon reach a plunge pool below a high waterfall chute. This is a natural cul de sac.

Finishing from Ein Hudera [Map 55]

There are **two main ways** to leave Ein Hudera. The quickest one – taking about 45-60 minutes – involves walking to the end of Wadi Hudera and going over a **high pass** (GPS 25). See also p229. The White Canyon takes longer but it's more interesting. Camels can't go in the canyon so if you have one it'll go the long way round and meet you at the end.

The **White Canyon** begins on the doorstep of the oasis, starting as a wadi to the south-east. Cut through the gardens (ask permission) or loop around the outside fences to enter.

Exit the wadi on the right a short way along, following a **rough, whitened trail** up the rocks; it's an obvious one that rises to a **small crack**; edge through and scramble down a low rocky wall.

This is the main stretch of the White Canyon. Follow it to the end and scramble out using a wonky ladder on the cliffs, emerging on a sandy plain dotted with outcrops (GPS 28). One has some Bedouin storerooms built around the bottom and there's a ramshackle *Bedouin café* nearby. There might be someone here in mid morning (don't rely on it though) and tea is usually free.

It's a long walk to the highway, past low mounds and outcrops. It's best to go south-west to a roadside building called **Cafeteria Jomaa** (GPS 26), near two telephone masts — it's not open as a café any more. You can head south too

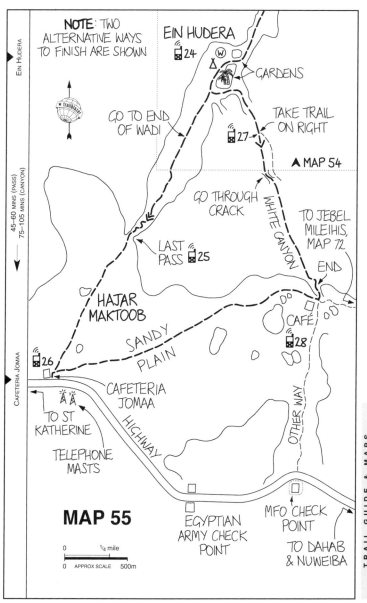

EIN HUDERA

NOTE: TWO ALTERNATIVE WAYS TO FINISH ARE SHOWN

EIN HUDERA

📱24

Ⓦ

GARDENS

GO TO END OF WADI

📱27

TAKE TRAIL ON RIGHT

▲ MAP 54

45–60 MINS (PASS)
75–105 MINS (CANYON)

GO THROUGH CRACK

WHITE CANYON

TO JEBEL MILEIHIS, MAP 72

LAST PASS 📱25

END

HAJAR MAKTOOB

SANDY PLAIN

CAFÉ

📱28

CAFETERIA JOMAA

📱26

CAFETERIA JOMAA

TO ST KATHERINE

TELEPHONE MASTS

HIGHWAY

OTHER WAY

MAP 55

0   ¼ mile
0   APPROX SCALE   500m

EGYPTIAN ARMY CHECK POINT

MFO CHECK POINT

TO DAHAB & NUWEIBA

TRAIL GUIDE & MAPS

but there are **military checkpoints** here (an MFO one and an Egyptian army one) where the soldiers can be awkward.

Links with other treks For the Haduda Dune trek see below and Map 56. For the last part of the Desert Traverse to Jebel Mileihis see p270 and Map 72.

HADUDA DUNE (2 days)

Practicalities

● **Difficulty and scheduling** This is a moderate trek done in two days. Jebel Mutamir has some scrambling but it's not tricky.

● **Links with other treks** Do this after the Ras Shaitan to Ein Hudera trek or as an alternative end to the Desert Traverse, instead of Jebel Mileihis.

● **Getting to the trailhead** This trek starts at a Bedouin village known as Nawamis. It's found off the St Katherine highway, west of the Ein Hudera area. The turn-off is marked by a road sign – marked GPS 1 in this route – and there are a few notes on getting there on p230.

Nawamis village to the tombs   [Map 56]

Nawamis village – marked GPS 2 – is named after a cluster of tombs about 1km away (see box p246). For the tombs head south-west and cut up a **low stony plateau**. The tombs come into good view here. They're small, circular structures and there are 42 in total (GPS 3). Similar tombs are found across the Sinai but none has such a grand desert setting as these.

The tombs to Jebel Mutamir   [Map 56]

Looking south from the tombs you'll see two big masses of sandstone either side of a **wide sandy wadi**: join a rough trail down to the wadi and follow its course ahead.

Further up there's a big break in the sandstone mass on the left. Look to the mass on the right here and you'll see a gently rounded dome or hemisphere. This is the summit of Jebel Mutamir. Go to the area directly below it where drainage channels run down and ascend here (GPS 4).

Jebel Mutamir: the ascent   [Map 56]

Jebel Mutamir (950m high) is a popular scrambling peak. You go up and down the same way and need 45-90 minutes for the return trip. There's a bit of exposure at the top but the worst of it is avoidable.

❏ **Nawamis tombs of the Sinai**
The Nawamis date back about 6000 years and it's thought the Sinai's early mining settlers built them. They're found widely and – with a few exceptions – their doorways always face west. It'll forever remain a mystery why, but it probably had some early significance to do with the sun. *Nawamis* means mosquitoes and the tombs have the name after an old Bedouin legend that the Israelites built them as shelter from a plague of biting insects. Civilisations such as the Nabataeans re-used the tombs, leading some to mistakenly place them much later in the archaeological record.

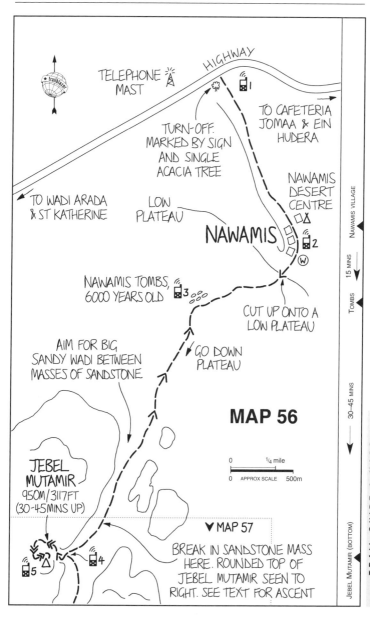

HIGHWAY

TELEPHONE MAST

TURN-OFF. MARKED BY SIGN AND SINGLE ACACIA TREE

TO CAFETERIA JOMAA & EIN HUDERA

TO WADI ARADA & ST KATHERINE

LOW PLATEAU

NAWAMIS DESERT CENTRE

NAWAMIS

NAWAMIS TOMBS, 6000 YEARS OLD

CUT UP ONTO A LOW PLATEAU

AIM FOR BIG SANDY WADI BETWEEN MASSES OF SANDSTONE

GO DOWN PLATEAU

MAP 56

0 ¼ mile

0 APPROX SCALE 500m

JEBEL MUTAMIR 950M/3117FT (30-45MINS UP)

▼ MAP 57

BREAK IN SANDSTONE MASS HERE. ROUNDED TOP OF JEBEL MUTAMIR SEEN TO RIGHT. SEE TEXT FOR ASCENT

NAWAMIS VILLAGE

15 MINS

TOMBS

30-45 MINS

JEBEL MUTAMIR (BOTTOM)

TRAIL GUIDE & MAPS

Start by scrambling up a low rocky wall: a white trail has been roughed out on its face by all the feet. Turn right and follow a gradually rising **rocky rake** below the dome of Jebel Mutamir (it'll be high on your left). About 50m along a **small gap** comes into profile between Jebel Mutamir and another dome immediately to its right. Move up to this gap – clambering up a short, awkward waterfall cliff just below it – and walk straight through.

You emerge in an **open basin** swept with sand. The rocks have strange droops in their surfaces, like they're melting in the sun. Head out across the basin, watching the left side. A **small sandy passage** opens in the rocks about 70-80m along; turn in and scramble up a crack at its far end. The summit of Jebel Mutamir is **directly left** from the top; walk up the smooth dome face (GPS 5). Plates of rock can flake off under your feet so take care.

Impressive views of the desert open up. To the south-east is an isolated sandstone outcrop called Jebel Ikri (pronounced Jebel *Kiri*). You go past this later; it's a good large-scale reference point to keep in mind.

Jebel Mutamir to Jebel Ikri [Maps 56-57]

Continue south in the same wadi from Jebel Mutamir. The sandstone masses soon drop away on both sides; veer round the southern end of the one on the left. Head south-east here – going towards Jebel Ikri in the distance – and you'll soon reach the bottom edge of a **low black plateau**. Turn right and follow this along to enter the course of a **small rocky wadi** (GPS 6).

Follow this wadi as it cuts south-west through the plateau lands. Further down you get to a **small fork** where a minor branch rises on the right. Ignore this and continue in the main branch to the left (GPS 7).

The wadi gets wider and more significant here and you need to continue along. Further on you skirt past the impressive south face of Jebel Ikri. Follow the wadi as it veers gradually right over a crossroads. You come out in a bigger wadi running south; this wadi is sometimes called Wadi Ikri (GPS 8).

Jebel Ikri to Jebel Barqa [Maps 57-59]

This is a long, straight wadi; just follow it ahead. There's a point where you can glimpse Jebel Barqa through a break on the left, but it stays mostly hidden. The high rocky ground seen in the distance —off the end of the wadi to the left — is part of the Jebel Barqa range, but not the summit mass itself.

Continuing down here, look out for an **acacia tree**: it's the only one in this main stretch and it gives a good marker for the exit (GPS 9).

Move out on the left side and veer east through low, broken terrain: there's a faint trail in places but it disappears in others. You soon reach a higher stretch of ground where Jebel Barqa comes into clear view (GPS 10). It stands on the far side of a **big sandy expanse** dotted with low mounds. It's separated from another part of the range to the right by a gap with some **low black hills** in it. Head straight out for this gap, rising gradually all the way.

Once through, veer sharply left round the south-western tip of the mountain. You come out in a sheltered sandy area on its south side: looking up you'll see a shallow gully with a **sandy slope on its left side**. *(Cont'd on p252)*

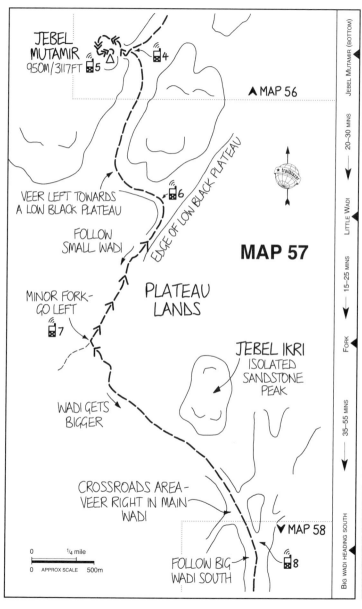

JEBEL MUTAMIR
950M/3117FT 📱5

📱4

▲ MAP 56

EDGE OF LOW BLACK PLATEAU

VEER LEFT TOWARDS
A LOW BLACK PLATEAU

📱6

FOLLOW
SMALL WADI

MAP 57

PLATEAU
LANDS

MINOR FORK-
GO LEFT

📱7

JEBEL IKRI
ISOLATED
SANDSTONE
PEAK

WADI GETS
BIGGER

CROSSROADS AREA-
VEER RIGHT IN MAIN
WADI

▼ MAP 58

📱8

0   ¼ mile
0   APPROX SCALE   500m

FOLLOW BIG
WADI SOUTH

JEBEL MUTAMIR (BOTTOM)   20-30 MINS   LITTLE WADI   15-25 MINS   FORK   35-55 MINS   BIG WADI HEADING SOUTH

TRAIL GUIDE & MAPS

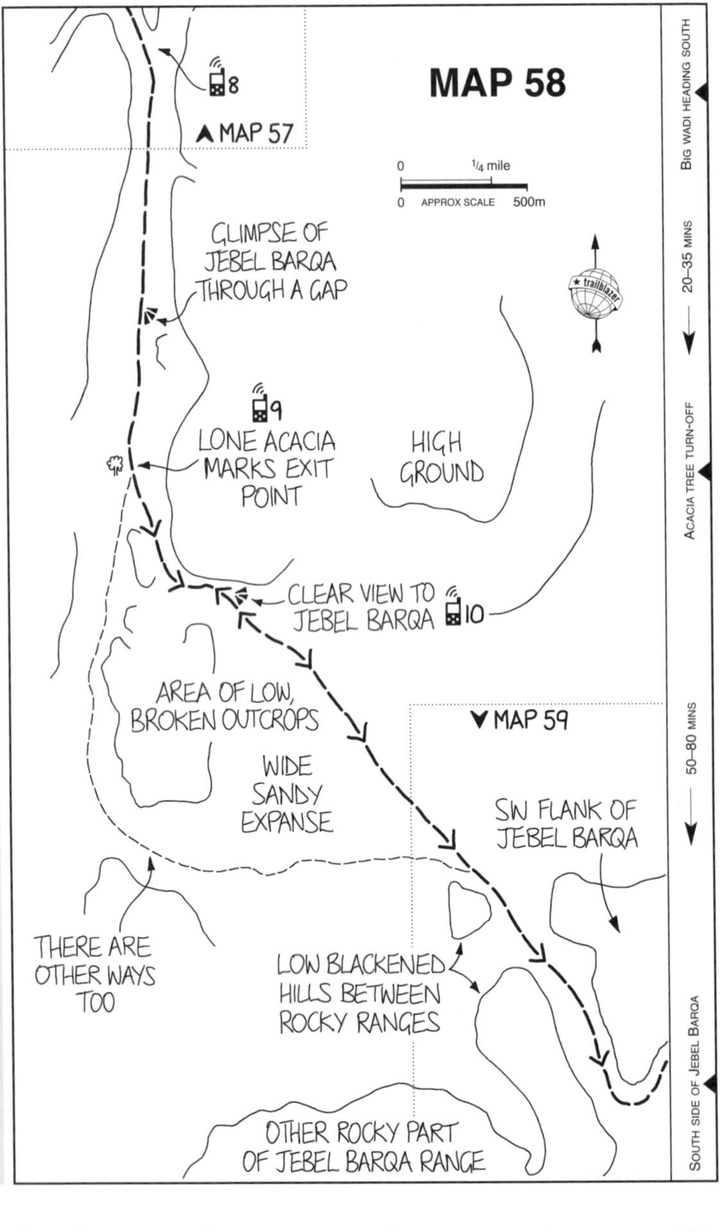

MAP 58

📱8

▲ MAP 57

0   ¼ mile
0   APPROX SCALE   500m

★ trailblazer

GLIMPSE OF
JEBEL BARQA
THROUGH A GAP

HIGH
GROUND

📱9

LONE ACACIA
MARKS EXIT
POINT

CLEAR VIEW TO
JEBEL BARQA 📱10

▼ MAP 59

AREA OF LOW,
BROKEN OUTCROPS

WIDE
SANDY
EXPANSE

SW FLANK OF
JEBEL BARQA

THERE ARE
OTHER WAYS
TOO

LOW BLACKENED
HILLS BETWEEN
ROCKY RANGES

OTHER ROCKY PART
OF JEBEL BARQA RANGE

BIG WADI HEADING SOUTH

20-35 MINS

ACACIA TREE TURN-OFF

50-80 MINS

SOUTH SIDE OF JEBEL BARQA

TRAIL GUIDE & MAPS

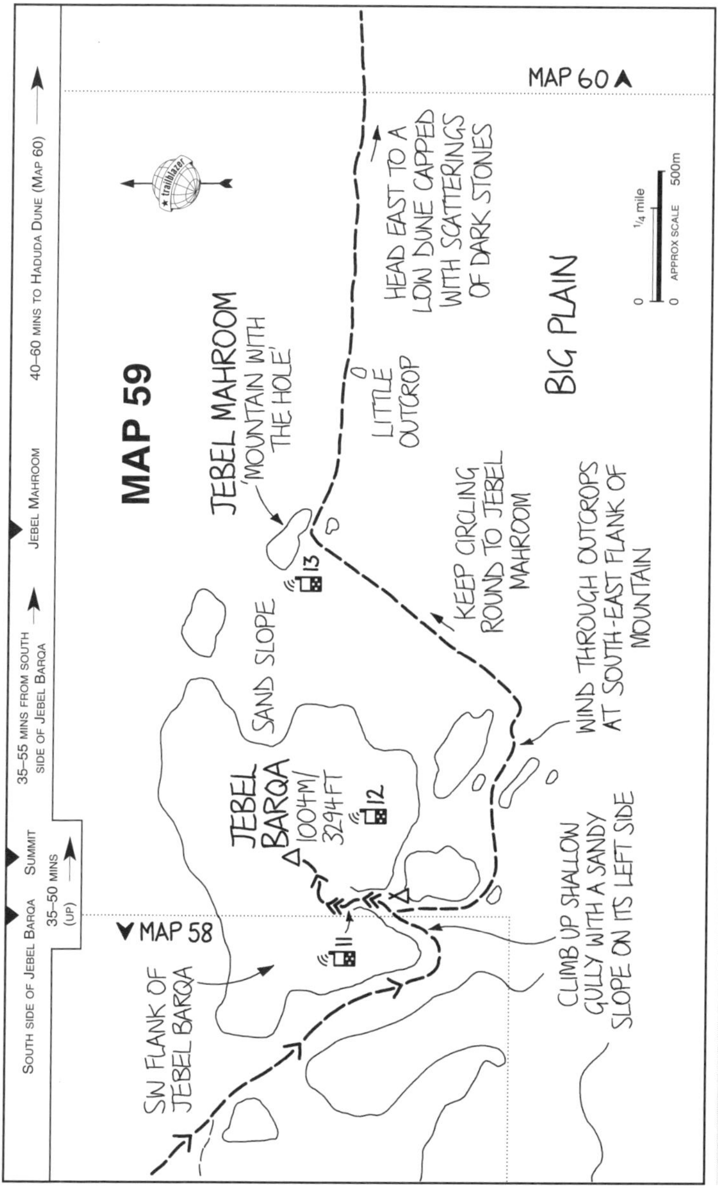

MAP 60 ▲

40–60 MINS TO HADUDA DUNE (MAP 60)

MAP 59

JEBEL MAHROOM
'MOUNTAIN WITH THE HOLE'

HEAD EAST TO A LOW DUNE CAPPED WITH SCATTERINGS OF DARK STONES

LITTLE OUTCROP

BIG PLAIN

35–55 MINS FROM SOUTH SIDE OF JEBEL BARQA

JEBEL MAHROOM

SAND SLOPE

3

KEEP CIRCLING ROUND TO JEBEL MAHROOM

WINDS THROUGH OUTCROPS AT SOUTH-EAST FLANK OF MOUNTAIN

SUMMIT

JEBEL BARQA
100+M/ 394FT

12

▼ MAP 58

SW FLANK OF JEBEL BARQA

11

CLIMB UP SHALLOW GULLY WITH A SANDY SLOPE ON ITS LEFT SIDE

SOUTH SIDE OF JEBEL BARQA

35–50 MINS (UP)

0   ¼ mile

0   APPROX SCALE   500m

TRAIL GUIDE & MAPS

(Cont'd from p248) This is where you begin the ascent to the summit (GPS 11). This area is a good spot to camp on the first night and you can find some nice sheltered spots amongst the rocks.

❑ **Miss the acacia tree?**
Don't worry if you miss the acacia. As long as you cut out over the left side of the wadi when it gets lower and more broken, you'll still get where you need to go.

Jebel Barqa: the ascent [Map 59]
Jebel Barqa is just over 1000m and its position in the middle of a plain gives it an excellent 360° panorama of the desert. Go up the gully with the sandy slope on its side. Head straight up or veer off on a rough trail to the left near the top. Either way it's steep and sometimes loose so tread carefully. Once up it's an easy walk to the summit – marked by a cairn (GPS 12). Remember your tracks or place a few rojoms as it can be tricky finding the top of the gully on the return.

You can look back to Jebel Ikri and Jebel Mutamir to the north-west. The high, flat-topped escarpment of Jebel Gunna dominates the view beyond. Looking east you'll see the Sinai's coastal ranges; behind these, sometimes even the Hejaz of Arabia. The High Mountain Region is south-west.

Jebel Barqa to Jebel Mahroom   [Map 59]
Move around the east side of Jebel Barqa. Its south-east flank is broken into outcrops divided by passageways; wind through however you want (there are lots of interesting places to explore). You soon reach a big open plain, with the small outcrop of **Jebel Mahroom** standing to the far east from Jebel Barqa. It has a hole in its side and you can scramble through. To go to the very top, walk up the sandy gully that starts on its west side.

Jebel Mahroom to Haduda Dune   [Maps 59-60]
The plain around Jebel Mahroom stands about 750m; the Haduda Dune is on its east side. To get there head east from Jebel Mahroom, aiming for some low dunes capped with **scatterings of dark stones** (GPS 14): the face of Haduda falls on the other side. The upper face of the dune is about 50m high and you can run straight down (don't leave anything on top). Veer left where it levels out and join a well-trodden camel trail: this zigzags down the remaining 100m of the sands to **Wadi Haduda** (GPS 15). Turn right and follow the wadi to the highway (GPS 16).

Note: some guides expect you to continue from the dune yourself. Wadi Haduda is sandy and it's tough walking out with a heavy backpack so get the guide to bring the camel down. If you want a car ready at the road the top of the dune usually has a mobile signal (reckon on it being about an hour to the road). Otherwise it's usually easy enough to hitch.

❑ **Nabataean inscriptions?**
Jebel Mahroom and some other outcrops here have odd inscriptions that look Nabataean. Some might be but there are certainly a few fakes about too. They're almost certainly the work of safari companies giving talking props for their guides. Needless to say it's a despicable, profit-driven falsification of the Sinai's rich 2000-year-old historical record.

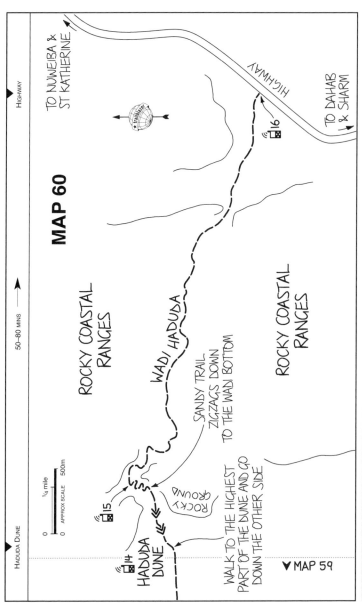

MAP 60

50–80 MINS

HADUDA DUNE

Highway

TO NUWEIBA &
ST KATHERINE

HIGHWAY

TO DAHAB
& SHARM

16

ROCKY COASTAL
RANGES

WADI HADUDA

SANDY TRAIL
ZIGZAGS DOWN
TO THE WADI BOTTOM

ROCKY COASTAL
RANGES

¼ mile
0
0   500m
APPROX SCALE

15

ROCKY
GROUND

WALK TO THE HIGHEST
PART OF THE DUNE AND GO
DOWN THE OTHER SIDE

14

HADUDA
DUNE

▼ MAP 59

TRAIL GUIDE & MAPS

DESERT TRAVERSE (5-6 days)

Practicalities

● **Difficulty and scheduling** This is a moderate trek but there are bits of tricky scrambling in places (all optional). Getting to the top of Jebel Berqa involves a short rock climb for which a rope of about 15m is sensible. You can finish in five days but six is better and some guides might even want seven. It's a good trek for camel riding so consider one per person.

● **Links with other treks** You could cut this route short at Ein Hudera, fore-going Jebel Mileihis for the Haduda Dune trek (p246).

● **Getting to the trailhead** This trek starts at the Wadi Arada hamlet on the St Katherine highway. For notes on getting there see p230.

Wadi Arada to the Arada Canyon   [Maps 61-62]

From the settlement follow **Wadi Arada** north-west between low, broken out-crops (GPS 1). About 10 minutes up it widens into a more **open crossroads area** (GPS 2): head straight over and enter a narrower stretch ahead.

The wadi soon divides around a low, isolated outcrop. A minor branch goes left: take the one on the right, following the main jeep tracks. A bit further along there's a low cliff on the right with some ancient graffiti. This is sometimes called **Hajar Arada** (GPS 3). The graffiti is in the Nabataean style and proba-bly dates back about 2000 years. Camels, hunt scenes and trading vessels are depicted, giving a fascinating glimpse of early life here.

Wadi Arada widens and the high edge of the **Jebel Gunna** escarpment – pronounced more like Jebel *Goona* – comes into view ahead. A bit further on there's an **isolated outcrop** with more inscriptions.

It's best to follow the jeep tracks on the left side of the wadi. These give decent walking and keep you well positioned for the canyon. After about 2km they bend into a **big wadi on the left** (GPS 4). This splits into two separate branches round a rocky block of land: each is a canyon in its own right but they're collectively dubbed the **Arada Canyon** (or 'Double Canyon').

Arada Canyon: circular trail   [Map 62]

The canyons are usually walked as an **anti-clockwise** circular trail, taking 30-45 minutes to complete. Enter the branch on the right: there are bits of easy scrambling along the way. When you get to the top walk south over a **small stony plateau**. This brings you to the upper stretch of the second canyon, more like a little watercourse here; drop down and follow it left.

It soon drops into a **narrow, shadowy crack**. Wedge in and edge a few metres down a steep waterfall chute. Similar obstacles follow but none of them is more difficult than this one. It's an easy walk back to where you started.

Arada Canyon to Farsh Abbeya
[Map 62]

Go back to Wadi Arada and head **north-east**. A lone acacia tree on the far

> ❏ **Scrambling not your thing?**
> If you're not a confident scrambler do the canyons separately, going in and out of each as far as you feel comfortable.

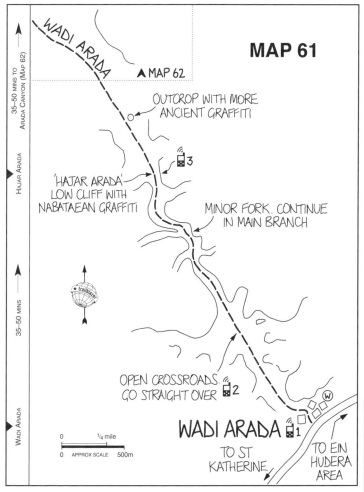

MAP 61

▲ MAP 62

OUTCROP WITH MORE ANCIENT GRAFFITI

📱3

'HAJAR ARADA' LOW CLIFF WITH NABATAEAN GRAFFITI

MINOR FORK. CONTINUE IN MAIN BRANCH

WADI ARADA

35–50 MINS TO ARADA CANYON (MAP 62)

HAJAR ARADA

35–50 MINS

WADI ARADA

★ trailblazer

OPEN CROSSROADS. GO STRAIGHT OVER 📱2

WADI ARADA 📱1

TO ST KATHERINE

TO EIN HUDERA AREA

0   ¼ mile
0   APPROX SCALE   500m

TRAIL GUIDE & MAPS

side of the wadi gives a decent marker to aim for. Looking beyond it you'll see a trail running up the side of Jebel Gunna – follow it up (GPS 5).

It's a good camel trail – always easy to follow – and it zigzags up past colourful bands of rock. It straightens out higher up before bending into a small watercourse draining over the escarpment edge. Follow this watercourse up about 150m, then veer out on the right. There are no good trails but you soon reach a point where you can look out over **Farsh Abbeya** (GPS 6).

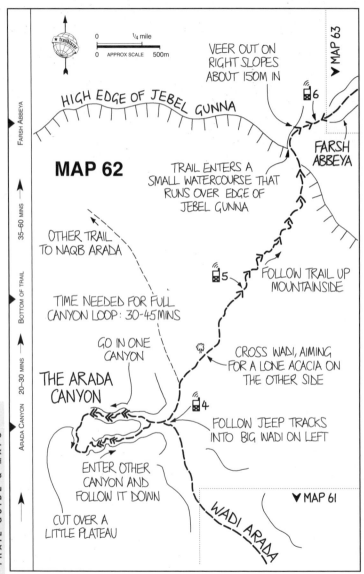

Scale: 0 — 1/4 mile — 0 APPROX SCALE 500m

trailblazer

VEER OUT ON RIGHT SLOPES ABOUT 150M IN

MAP 63

6

HIGH EDGE OF JEBEL GUNNA

FARSH ABBEYA

MAP 62

TRAIL ENTERS A SMALL WATERCOURSE THAT RUNS OVER EDGE OF JEBEL GUNNA

Farsh Abbeya

35–60 MINS

OTHER TRAIL TO NAQB ARADA

5

FOLLOW TRAIL UP MOUNTAINSIDE

Bottom of trail

TIME NEEDED FOR FULL CANYON LOOP: 30–45 MINS

GO IN ONE CANYON

CROSS WADI, AIMING FOR A LONE ACACIA ON THE OTHER SIDE

THE ARADA CANYON

Arada Canyon   20–30 MINS

4

FOLLOW JEEP TRACKS INTO BIG WADI ON LEFT

ENTER OTHER CANYON AND FOLLOW IT DOWN

CUT OVER A LITTLE PLATEAU

MAP 61

WADI ARADA

(Opposite) Top: The Arada Canyon (see Map 62, above). **Bottom**: Building a fire in front of a low cliff reflects the heat, keeping you extra warm on a cold desert night.

Farsh Abbeya is a long, shallow basin or depression on top of Jebel Gunna: it has a lightish colour and it's scattered with shrubbery. Go down and follow its course straight ahead to the north-east. About 1.5km along, the basin's left side gets gradually lower before dwindling down to nothing. The basin is more open now and it soon begins to bend sharply to the right. **Exit just before this bend**: head north into a small watercourse between low, sloping hills (GPS 7).

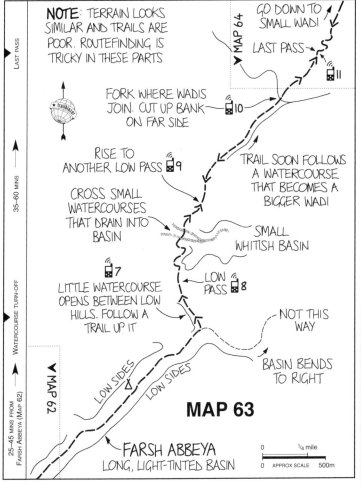

NOTE: TERRAIN LOOKS SIMILAR AND TRAILS ARE POOR. ROUTEFINDING IS TRICKY IN THESE PARTS

GO DOWN TO SMALL WADI

MAP 64

LAST PASS

📱11

FORK WHERE WADIS JOIN. CUT UP BANK ON FAR SIDE — 📱10

RISE TO ANOTHER LOW PASS 📱9

TRAIL SOON FOLLOWS A WATERCOURSE THAT BECOMES A BIGGER WADI

CROSS SMALL WATERCOURSES THAT DRAIN INTO BASIN

SMALL WHITISH BASIN

📱7

LOW PASS 📱8

LITTLE WATERCOURSE OPENS BETWEEN LOW HILLS. FOLLOW A TRAIL UP IT

NOT THIS WAY

BASIN BENDS TO RIGHT

MAP 62

LOW SIDES   LOW SIDES

MAP 63

FARSH ABBEYA LONG, LIGHT-TINTED BASIN

0   1/4 mile
0   APPROX SCALE   500m

LAST PASS

35-60 MINS

WATERCOURSE TURN-OFF

25-45 MINS FROM FARSH ABBEYA (MAP 62)

TRAIL GUIDE & MAPS

(**Opposite**) **Top**: Outcrop, Wadi Arada. **Middle**: Jebel Mileihis (see p270). **Bottom**: Climbing Jebel Mileihis. This is one of the Sinai's best spots for sunset.

Camping in Farsh Abbeya Farsh Abbeya is an excellent camp on the first night. There is plenty of dead wood for fires and good grazing for camels. The next decent campsite is 45-75 minutes ahead, at a place called Bir Umm Hamata (Map 64): it's not as nice but camping here gives a shorter and more manageable walk to Jebel Berqa the next day.

Scheduling to Jebel Berqa You can get to Jebel Berqa on the second day but it's a long, tiring walk and it's unlikely you'll arrive with enough time to climb it. It's best to give the next two full days of the trek to the mountain, going along at whatever pace is comfortable. If you don't make it on the second day you'll get there on the third with time for a comfortable ascent.

Farsh Abbeya to Wadi Umm Hamata [Maps 63-64]
This section involves taking a northerly course over Jebel Gunna, crossing a series of minor passes between basins. The landscape is similar and disorientating and the trail fades completely in places so stay vigilant.

Follow a faint trail up the watercourse from Farsh Abbeya: this brings you to a **minor pass** where there's a small rojom – feel free to add a stone for those who follow (GPS 8). There's a **light-tinted depression** ahead; somewhat reminiscent of Farsh Abbeya. The trail circles round its high left edge – crossing two little watercourses that run into it from the west – before continuing up low hills on the far (north) side. The trail is tricky to follow in places.

It's not far up these hills to the next **minor pass** (GPS 9). Follow the trail down to a **wide greyish expanse** ahead. It runs along in a small watercourse that widens progressively into a bigger wadi.

You soon reach a **natural fork** where another wadi joins from the left (GPS 10): both continue to the right as a single, bigger course. Move straight over the fork and follow a trail that cuts up its far bank. This veers gradually right, rising to the **last minor pass** of this section (GPS 11). Go down into a small wadi ahead. The trail runs along the bottom before cutting out on its left side to avoid a rocky waterfall drop further ahead. It follows the same basic line of the wadi as it runs around the hillside – passing the heads of two small tributaries – before dropping down into a much bigger wadi: **Wadi Umm Hamata** (GPS 12).

Wadi Umm Hamata to Wadi Ghlim [Maps 64-65]
Turn right in Wadi Umm Hamata. Just a short way along a portion of the wadi sinks between low bands of cliffs. This is **Bir Umm Hamata** ('Well of the Wild Figs') (GPS 13). The name refers to an ancient fig tree, still seen here today. There's a spring under the cliffs where they first drop, ie at the upstream extremity. It appears as a surface pool after rain but disappears later. You can still dig down in hotter months but a well in the next wadi might give an easier alternative. Ask your guide – he'll know best. This can be a good spot to camp but do it downstream of the spring to keep the groundwater pristine.

Continue down the wadi from here, following a trail along its right side. About 1.5km along a **low waterfall cliff** cuts across the wadi (GPS 14). Big blocks of rock lie broken below. There are two options here. You can clamber down the cliff and continue in the wadi bottom. This involves scrambling and

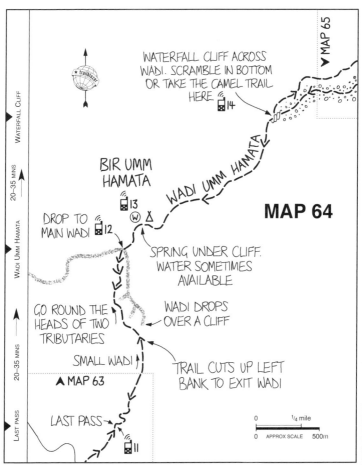

WATERFALL CLIFF ACROSS WADI. SCRAMBLE IN BOTTOM OR TAKE THE CAMEL TRAIL HERE 📱14

▼ MAP 65

trailblazer

WATERFALL CLIFF

20-35 MINS

WADI UMM HAMATA

BIR UMM HAMATA

WADI UMM HAMATA

📱13

MAP 64

DROP TO MAIN WADI 📱12

ⓦ

SPRING UNDER CLIFF. WATER SOMETIMES AVAILABLE

GO ROUND THE HEADS OF TWO TRIBUTARIES

WADI DROPS OVER A CLIFF

20-35 MINS

SMALL WADI

▲ MAP 63

TRAIL CUTS UP LEFT BANK TO EXIT WADI

LAST PASS

LAST PASS

📱11

0   ¼ mile

0   APPROX SCALE   500m

takes longer. Alternatively, a camel trail runs along the left side of the wadi. Either way you come out in another big wadi known as **Wadi Ghlim** (GPS 15). Going right here takes you to Naqb Ghlim and thereafter to the St Katherine highway, near Nawamis village.

Wadi Ghlim to the Berqa Plain   [Maps 65-67]

Turn left in Wadi Ghlim and follow it ahead. About 2km along the wadi sinks between low cliffs, much like at Bir Umm Hamata. This is **Bir Ghlim** (GPS 16). There's a well here that usually holds water in winter and early spring.

(Cont'd on p262)

TRAIL GUIDE & MAPS

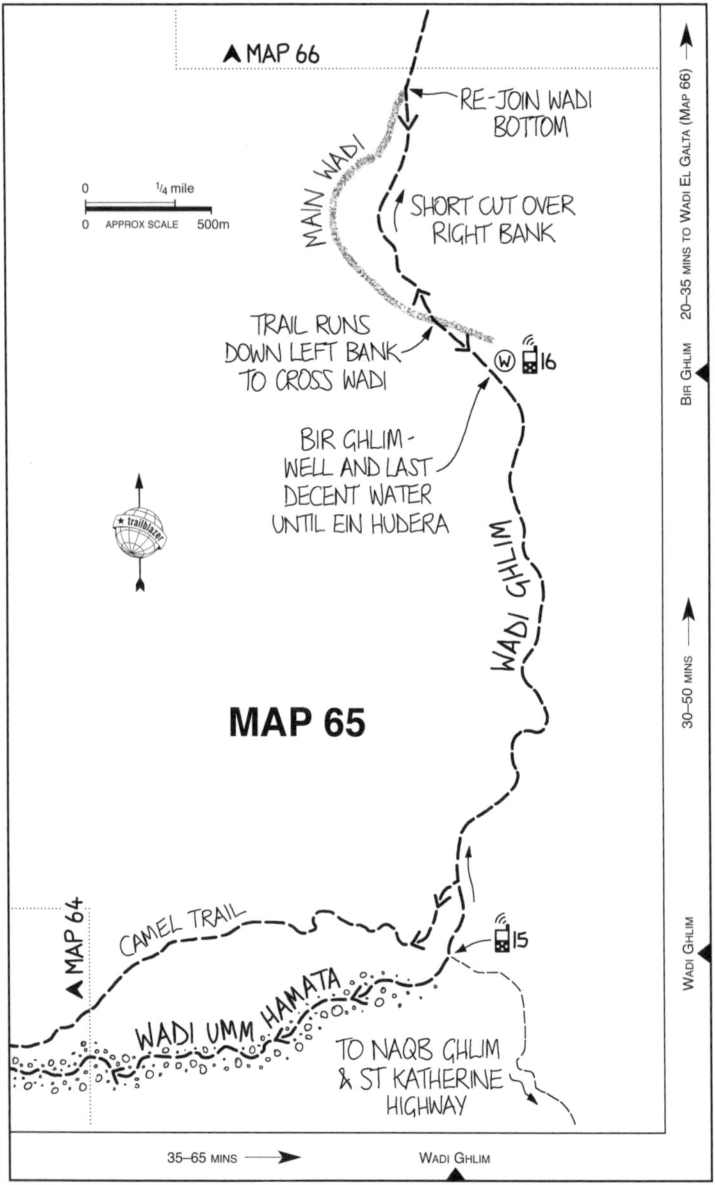

MAP 66

RE-JOIN WADI BOTTOM

SHORT CUT OVER RIGHT BANK

MAIN WADI

0   ¼ mile
0   APPROX SCALE   500m

TRAIL RUNS DOWN LEFT BANK TO CROSS WADI

Ⓦ 📻16

BIR GHLIM - WELL AND LAST DECENT WATER UNTIL EIN HUDERA

★ trailblazer

WADI GHLIM

MAP 65

20-35 MINS TO WADI EL GALTA (MAP 66)

BIR GHLIM

30-50 MINS

CAMEL TRAIL

📻15

WADI GHLIM

MAP 64

WADI UMM HAMATA

TO NAQB GHLIM & ST KATHERINE HIGHWAY

35-65 MINS

WADI GHLIM

TRAIL GUIDE & MAPS

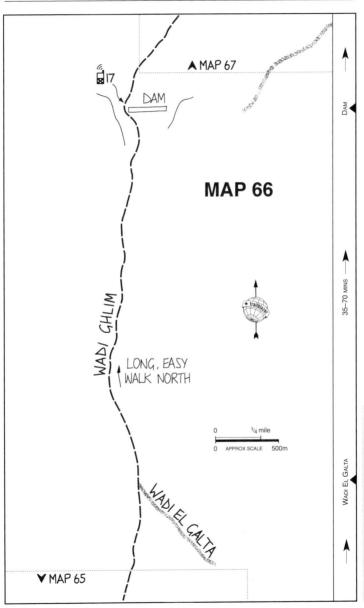

17

DAM

▲ MAP 67

MAP 66

WADI GHLIM

LONG, EASY
WALK NORTH

0   ¼ mile
0   APPROX SCALE   500m

WADI EL GALTA

▼ MAP 65

DAM ◄

◄— 35–70 MINS —►

WADI EL GALTA

TRAIL GUIDE & MAPS

(Cont'd from p259) In hotter months you may have to chimney down the shaft and dig. Check you've got enough water in the jerry can as it's the last place you can get anything decent until Ein Hudera – still 2-3 days away.

The trail cuts down the left bank, then ascends the right one. It continues across the bank here to avoid following the length of a bigger bend in the wadi. It's just a short cut and you soon get back to the wadi bottom.

A big wadi soon runs in from the right: this is **Wadi el Galta** ('Wadi of the Water Pool'); carry on straight past. About 3km further up there's a **big dam** (GPS 17). This marks the end of Wadi Ghlim.

There's a wide expanse after the dam: this is known as Wadi Zeleqa (or Wadi Zaraniq). Move north-east across it now. A **low isolated hill** with a flat-tish top soon comes into profile ahead. Immediately right of it are some low hills with **sandy slopes** on their sides. Go round the east side of the flattish hill, then veer round the back of the hills with the sandy slopes.

A trail leads over them but it's hard to spot (it gets better near the top). Don't worry if you miss it; cut over any way you want and you'll still get where you need to. The trail soon reaches a high point where Jebel Berqa stands visible on the far side of a **wide, sandy plain** (GPS 18). It's one of the desert's most distinctive peaks; its summit is ringed by a rock band that glows like a halo in some lights. To the north a wadi leads a few kilometres off to a big oasis called Ein Umm Ahmed: you can't see it but it's good to know it's there (water).

Onwards to Jebel Berqa   [Maps 67-68]
Go down and head east over the plain; it's a long trudge but is perfect for hon-ing some camel skills. Aim for a **wide, sandy wadi** on the left side of Jebel Berqa (GPS 19). This rises gradually uphill and merges into a **sandy belt** that runs round the northern flanks of the mountain. Circle around in this belt, fol-lowing the general line of the rocky ground on your right. You soon reach a **wide wadi** that runs directly south towards the peak. A **small canyon** opens up at the far end and you start the ascent to the summit here (GPS 20).

Water near Jebel Berqa A conspicuous stretch of vegetation runs across the sandy belt a short way round – mostly big, healthy *retem* bushes (see p64). Follow its line up to the low flanks of the mountain. A small canyon opens in the rocks here with a sandy slope on its left side. Go up the sandy slope and follow a new canyon that opens behind it. There's a natural pool near the end (GPS 23). It's **not permanent** but it usually stays for a couple of months after rain. The desert wildlife uses it heavily, as you'll see by all the tracks, and it's usually a thick, slimy green. Use it to water camels or just keep a bit for an emergency.

Camping around Jebel Berqa Most guides prefer to stay outside the canyon where you climb to the peak but there are plenty of other spots.

Jebel Berqa: the ascent   [Map 68]
At 1167m Jebel Berqa is one of the desert's highest peaks. It's mostly a moder-ate scramble but there's an exposed climb up the top rock band. It's best to take your own rope if you want to try it. You go up and down the same way and you

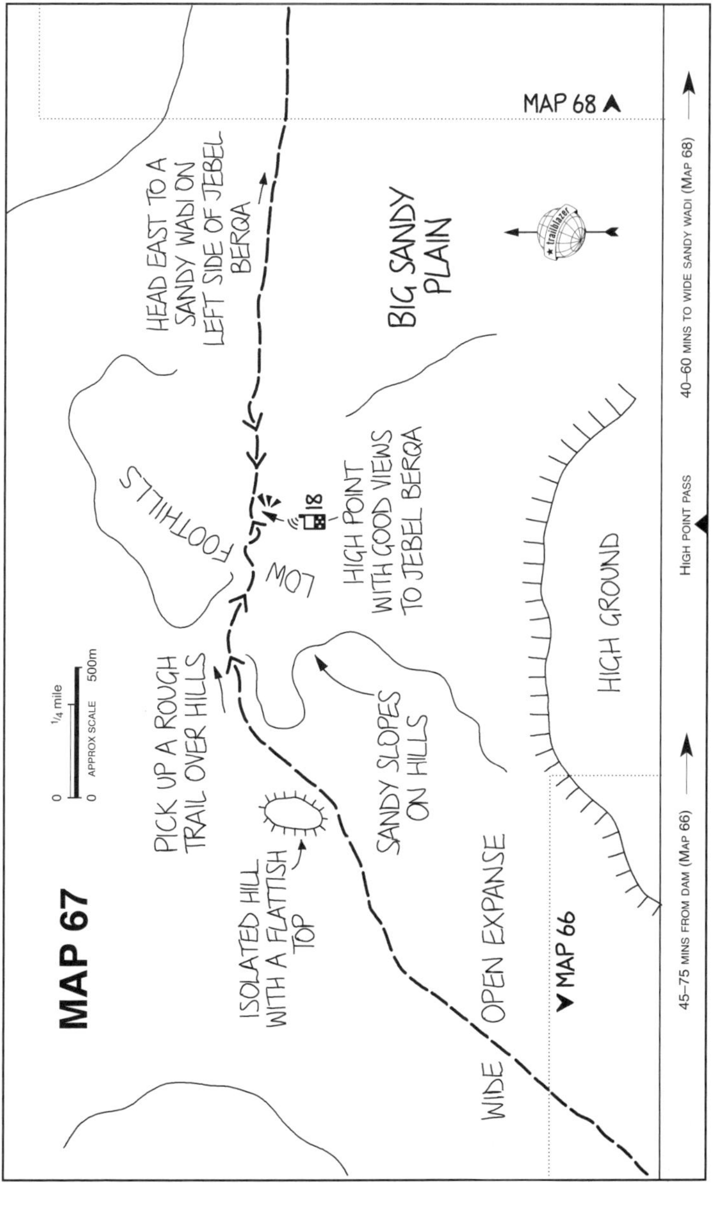
MAP 67
0 ¼ mile
0 APPROX SCALE 500m
WIDE OPEN EXPANSE
MAP 66
ISOLATED HILL WITH A FLATTISH TOP
PICK UP A ROUGH TRAIL OVER HILLS
SANDY SLOPES ON HILLS
FOOTHILLS
LOW
18
HIGH POINT WITH GOOD VIEWS TO JEBEL BERQA
HIGH GROUND
HEAD EAST TO A SANDY WADI ON LEFT SIDE OF JEBEL BERQA
BIG SANDY PLAIN
trailblazer
MAP 68
45–75 MINS FROM DAM (MAP 66)
HIGH POINT PASS
40–60 MINS TO WIDE SANDY WADI (MAP 68)

need 2-3 hours for the return. Sunset and sunrise are spectacular around here and it's worth trying to catch one from the top.

Enter the canyon and follow it ahead. It soon becomes a **steep, bouldery gully** where you have to scramble. Further up there's a natural high point where views extend over the gully's final stretch. Move down and continue straight up. About 40m before the top of the gully you have to scramble out on the left hand side. Look for a place where the rocks have been whitened by all the feet.

Once up here walk along the rocky side of the gully on exactly the same line as its course below. A short, steep scramble above the top of the gully brings you to a **small flat area** capped with a few boulders (GPS 21).

Turn left and follow a steep trail towards the summit. It divides and goes either side of the top rock band: go right, moving south.

You soon reach an obvious point where you can **climb the rock band** – the way has been smoothed out. It's about 10m high, nearly vertical, and above steep, exposed slopes. Bits of loose rock remain on the cliffs, so take extra care. Only try it if you're a good experienced scrambler with your own rope – there are a few anchor stakes hammered in. Don't use ropes rigged on the cliffs. The desert air wears their inner fibres away and they can snap easily.

The peak has magnificent views over the desert (GPS 22). Looking east you'll see the rugged flat top of Jebel Mileihis – the final summit in this route. On a good day the Hejaz ranges stand out beyond. Far away to the north is a peak that looks a bit like Jebel Berqa: this is Ras el Qelb and it stands just north of the Ein Umm Ahmed oasis – which isn't in view.

Moving on from Jebel Berqa There are plenty of interesting spots to explore around Jebel Berqa, including small canyons and some dunes at a wadi called El Brayga (ask your guide). You could stay here, or at least close by, for another night, scheduling to arrive at Ein Hudera later.

Jebel Berqa to Naqb Moehis [Maps 68-69]
Circle back to the big plain before Jebel Berqa. Don't go down the wide, sandy wadi you came up before; take a short-cut behind the outcrop on its southern side. There's an **obvious gap in the rocks**.

Once through, veer back to the plain in a south-westerly direction. Turn left once you reach it and head south (GPS 24). Further along the rocky ground on the left breaks into a more open area scattered with retem bushes. There's an isolated outcrop with a **slight bulge/overhang** in its top right (south) section; the best marker for the start of **Naqb Moehis** (GPS 25).

Naqb Moehis [Maps 69-70]
Naqb Moehis connects this area with the Ein Hudera region. It follows a broad curve, veering progressively south through low, broken terrain. The scenery feels similar and trails are mostly non-existent so – even with a guide – be extra careful with route finding. Skirt past the outcrop with the bulge, heading **straight to the east**. You move through a **narrowing** in the rocks to emerge in a wide open basin (GPS 26). Move out across this, veering slightly right for a stretch of low ground on its far side. (Cont'd on p268)

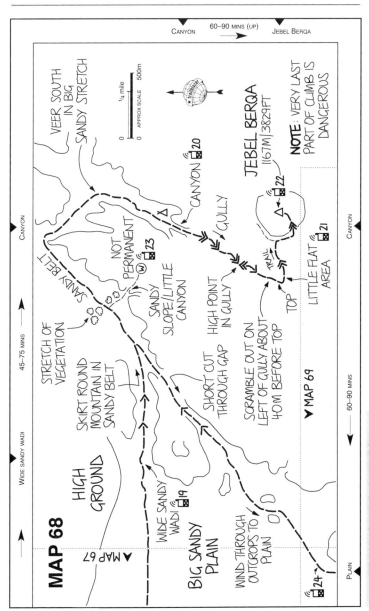

CANYON   60–90 MINS (UP)   JEBEL BERQA

VEER SOUTH IN BIG SANDY STRETCH

¼ mile

500m

APPROX SCALE

0

CANYON

CANYON 20

△

JEBEL BERQA 1161M/3829FT

22

△

NOTE: VERY LAST PART OF CLIMB IS DANGEROUS

CANYON

NOT PERMANENT

13

SANDY BELT

W

SANDY SLOPE/LITTLE CANYON

GULLY

TRAIL

21

LITTLE FLAT AREA

STRETCH OF VEGETATION

SKIRT ROUND MOUNTAIN IN SANDY BELT

HIGH POINT IN GULLY

TOP

45–75 MINS

WIDE SANDY WADI

CANYON

SHORT CUT THROUGH GAP

SCRAMBLE OUT ON LEFT OF GULLY ABOUT 40M BEFORE TOP

▼ MAP 69

60–90 MINS

MAP 68

HIGH GROUND

WIDE SANDY WADI 19

BIG SANDY PLAIN

WIND THROUGH OUTCROPS TO PLAIN

▲ MAP 67

24

PLAIN

TRAIL GUIDE & MAPS

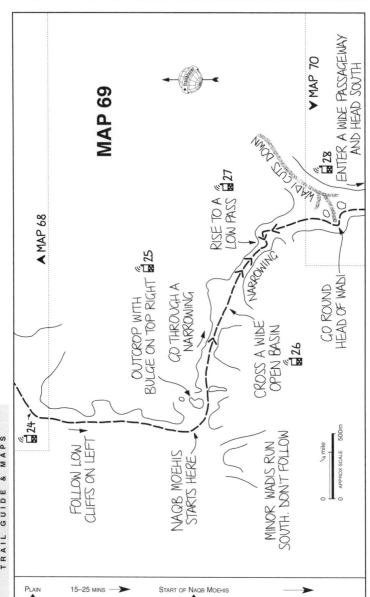

MAP 69

▲ MAP 68

▲ MAP 70

ENTER A WIDE PASSAGEWAY
AND HEAD SOUTH

📷 28

WADI CUTS DOWN

RISE TO A
LOW PASS 📷 27

NARROWING

GO ROUND
HEAD OF WADI

CROSS A WIDE
OPEN BASIN 📷 26

OUTCROP WITH
BULGE ON TOP RIGHT 📷 25

GO THROUGH A
NARROWING

📷 24

FOLLOW LOW
CLIFFS ON LEFT

NAQB MOEHIS
STARTS HERE

MINOR WADIS RUN
SOUTH. DON'T FOLLOW

0   ¼ mile
0   APPROX SCALE   500m

PLAIN   15–25 MINS ➤   START OF NAQB MOEHIS   ➤

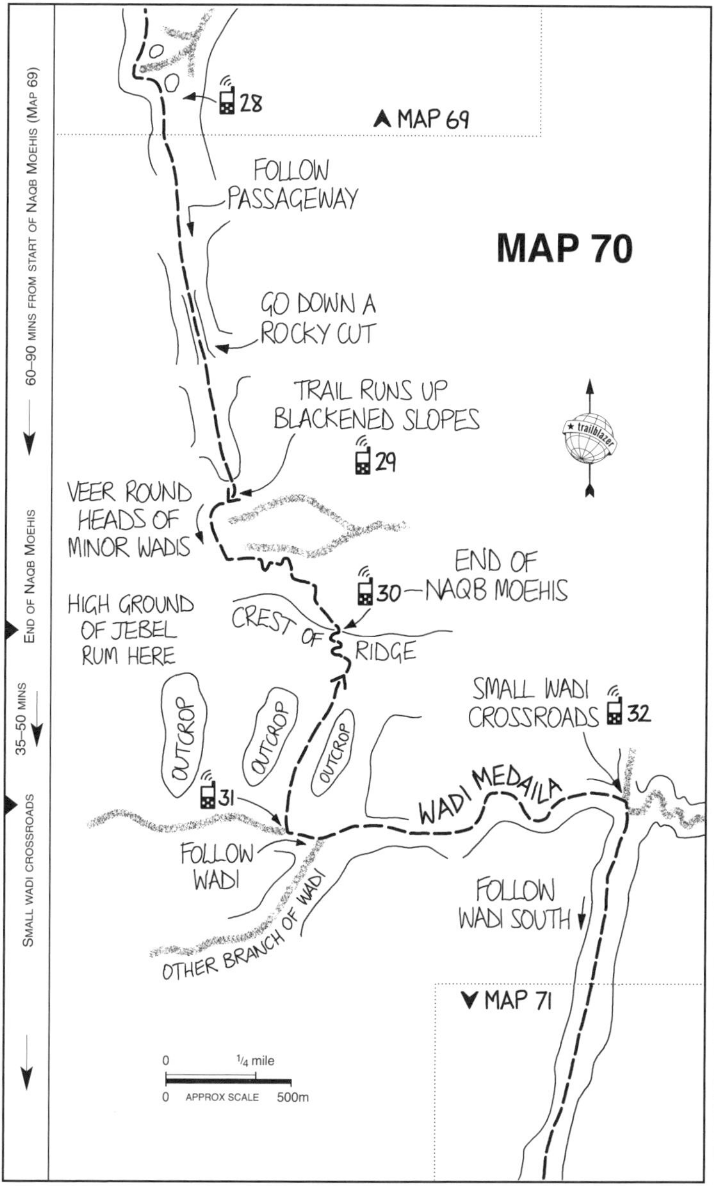

MAP 70

28

▲ MAP 69

FOLLOW
PASSAGEWAY

GO DOWN A
ROCKY CUT

TRAIL RUNS UP
BLACKENED SLOPES

29

VEER ROUND
HEADS OF
MINOR WADIS

END OF
30 — NAQB MOEHIS

HIGH GROUND
OF JEBEL
RUM HERE

CREST OF RIDGE

SMALL WADI
CROSSROADS 32

OUTCROP

OUTCROP

OUTCROP

31

WADI MEDAILA

FOLLOW
WADI

FOLLOW
WADI SOUTH

OTHER BRANCH OF WADI

▼ MAP 71

60–90 MINS FROM START OF NAQB MOEHIS (MAP 69)

END OF NAQB MOEHIS

35–50 MINS

SMALL WADI CROSSROADS

0   1/4 mile

0   APPROX SCALE   500m

TRAIL GUIDE & MAPS

(Cont'd from p264) A natural passage opens in the rocks, rising to a **low pass** (GPS 27). Look carefully as you go up; there's a piece of **Nabataean graffiti** underfoot (showing riding hunters or warriors).

The rugged, table-top summit of Jebel Mileihis is just glimpsed from the top of the pass. Go down to a more open area and veer right. A **deep wadi** cuts into the flat lands ahead – move to its right side and pick up a faint trail. This circles round its head to a **wide natural passageway** on its southern side (GPS 28). It's swept with light sand and runs in a southerly direction (the high black ground in the distance is the last bit of Naqb Moehis).

A trail leads up **black, stony slopes** at the end of the passageway (GPS 29), moving round the heads of two minor wadis before running along the slopes of a high black ridge. Further along it zigzags down the south side of the ridge (GPS 30). This is the end of Naqb Moehis.

Glance back for a beautiful view of Jebel Berqa.

Naqb Moehis to Wadi Hudera [Maps 70-71]

Looking south the high ground of Jebel Rum is to the right: **three isolated outcrops** stand between this and some other rocky ground to the left – each one slightly lower than the next. Go down the zigzag trail and walk between the outcrops ahead. You reach the shallow upper course of a new wadi (GPS 31). Turn left and follow it as it cuts into some cliffs to the east.

This is called **Wadi Medaila** by the Bedouin but it's marked **Wadi Ruethibiya** on some maps. Continue as it twists down to a small crossroads. One wadi goes left here; turn into the one on the right (GPS 32). It's a long, straight wadi that leads south to a T-junction with **Wadi Rum** (GPS 33).

Turn left in Wadi Rum, scrambling down a few rocky walls a short way along. If you want to avoid scrambling, take a camel trail on the right side of the wadi from the T-junction. It drops to the bottom a bit further along.

Wadi Rum runs into **Wadi Hudera** but a **low black ridge** blocks views across it. Turn right and move around its southern tip (GPS 34). Head north-east across Wadi Hudera, aiming for a **wide sandy wadi** on its far side (GPS 35). A sandy slope runs down rocky ground just right of it.

Wadi Hudera to the Closed Canyon [Map 71]

The wadi divides around a rocky mass of land a short way in; take the branch on the right (the one on the left is trickier with route finding). It's a long trudge up deep, soft sand. Where the slope eases off a **small gap** emerges in some rocky ground ahead. **Go through this gap**, turn right and let the wall guide you round to the **mouth of the canyon** (GPS 36). It's a short canyon, but narrow, dramatic and always fun to follow. It ends in a small plunge pool below a high waterfall chute; there's no way ahead. Go back the same way you came.

The area outside the canyon is a good spot to *camp*. For water and a bit more comfort, press on to the Ein Hudera oasis itself.

Onwards to Ein Hudera [Map 71]

Go back to Wadi Hudera and turn left. Ein Hudera is about 30-45 minutes further along (GPS 37). For notes on the oasis see p229.

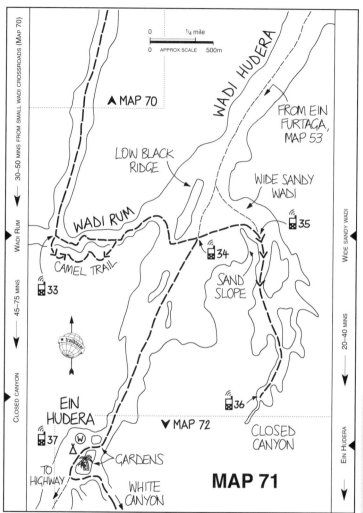

Finishing from Ein Hudera The two options for getting to the St Katherine highway are described on p229 and shown on Map 55.

Links with other treks To forego Jebel Mileihis for the Haduda Dune, first get to the highway. See p230, p246 and Map 56.

TRAIL GUIDE & MAPS

The White Canyon   [Maps 71-72]

The White Canyon gets busy from about 8am. The quietest and most beautiful time is dawn, when the first light gives it an almost ethereal radiance. It starts on the doorstep of the oasis, running south-east as a wide, sandy wadi. Garden owners usually let you cut through their plots but ask permission; otherwise loop around the outside fences. Take a **trail** up the wadi's rocky right side a short way along (GPS 38); it's an obvious one, roughed white by all the feet. It leads up to a **small crack in the rocks**, which you have to edge through. Scramble down a low rocky wall after this to get back to the wadi bottom. You're in the main part of the White Canyon now: it's straight, flat and easy to follow. Use a wonky ladder at the end to scramble out. You emerge on a sandy plain dotted with a few outcrops (GPS 39). One has old storerooms at the bottom and there's a small **Bedouin café** nearby. Someone's often here in mid-morning but don't rely on it. Tea is usually free.

Camels to Jebel Mileihis Camels can't tackle the White Canyon or the Majaaza part of the route to Jebel Mileihis. They go a different way and meet you in Wadi Ghazala, on Map 72, so take a small bag with enough water.

The White Canyon to Jebel Mileihis   [Maps 72-73]

Head east from the end of the canyon, following the line of the cliffs on the left. You soon reach a **gap in the rocky ground** ahead (GPS 40). Go through and scramble down rocky ledges to the top of a **sand-choked gully**. Head down to the bottom and turn left to follow a small, winding course in the rocks. The Bedouin call this area **Majaaza** (sometimes Wadi Majaaza).

This small course soon joins the bigger stretch of **Wadi Ghazala** ('Wadi of the Gazelles') (GPS 41). Looking north-east Jebel Mileihis is clearly visible; head straight out over Wadi Ghazala towards it.

Halfway over you cross a low sandy ridge scattered with stones. Keep going towards Jebel Mileihis and look carefully at the low plateau to the right. A small wadi cuts into it but only comes into clear profile when you get closer: jeep tracks run towards it, giving an additional clue as to its whereabouts.

This is **Wadi Disco** (GPS 42). The name Wadi Disco came about recently: this was once the hub of Bedouin nightlife, famed for its discos or *haflas*. It's not clear what made them legendary enough to have an entire wadi named after them; but whatever the story, the name has stuck.

Wadi Disco is dotted with acacias and there are a couple of shacks halfway up. There are more shacks at the top where you can often get water and a cup of tea (GPS 43). Jebel Mileihis stands in clear view ahead.

Jebel Mileihis   [Map 73]

Jebel Mileihis (Jebel *Umm Lehas* on some maps) is a gigantic sandstone hulk rising to 967m. The ascent makes a great end to the trek. Move round the right side of the mountain to begin, looking carefully for the trail up its lower slopes. It's faint and hard to spot but if you overshoot it you'll find it on the way back – it always stands out better this way (GPS 44).

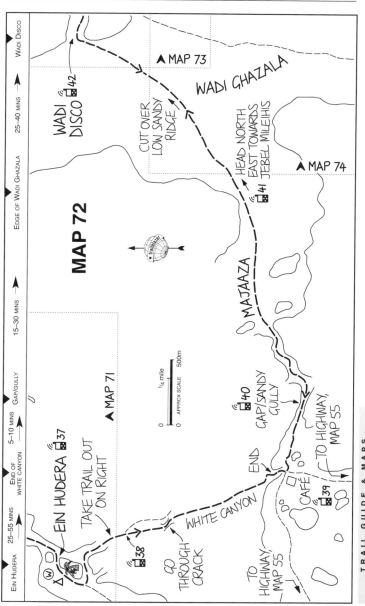

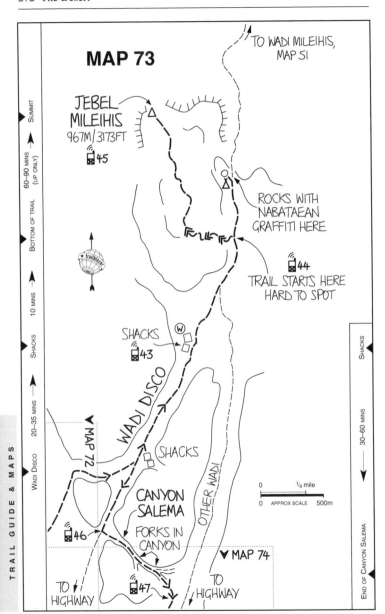

MAP 73

JEBEL MILEIHIS
967M / 3173FT
📱45

TO WADI MILEIHIS, MAP 51

ROCKS WITH NABATAEAN GRAFFITI HERE

📱44
TRAIL STARTS HERE
HARD TO SPOT

SHACKS
📱43

WADI DISCO

SHACKS

CANYON SALEMA

OTHER WADI

FORKS IN CANYON

📱46

📱47

TO HIGHWAY

TO HIGHWAY

▼ MAP 72

▼ MAP 74

0   ¼ mile
0   APPROX SCALE   500m

SUMMIT

60–90 MINS (UP ONLY)

BOTTOM OF TRAIL

10 MINS

SHACKS

20–35 MINS

WADI DISCO

SHACKS

30–60 MINS

END OF CANYON SALEMA

TRAIL GUIDE & MAPS

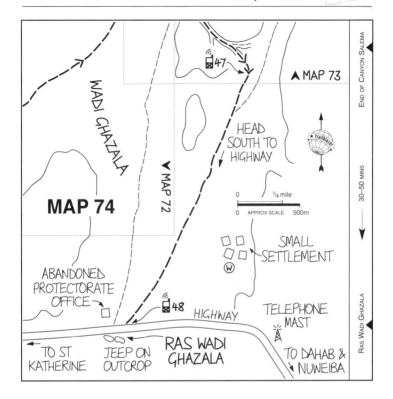

It runs up steep, loose slopes. It's better ascending just off-trail where the rocks haven't been knocked so loose. Further up, the trail **veers sharply right** up a short, steep section, bringing you onto the peak.

Jebel Mileihis has a plateau-like top, dessicated by small watercourses and basins. The true summit is at the **north-western extremity**, marked by a rounded rock on precipitous crags (GPS 45). It's about 1km away.

There's a spectacular 360° panorama here. Almost all of the main desert peaks are in view, including Jebel Berqa to the north-west. The Sinai's coastal ranges are to the east with the Hejaz often visible beyond. The summits of the High Mountain Region are in the distance to the south-west.

Back at the bottom of the mountain, turn left and walk north. There's a sandy corner up here – just left of where a trail rises up some slopes – where you'll find boulders with **Nabataean graffiti**. It makes a good campsite.

Camping on Jebel Mileihis Jebel Mileihis is one of the finest sunset spots in the whole of the Sinai and you could always bivvy on top. Overhangs and hollows give good shelter but the chances are your Bedouin guide won't want to join you at these heights so you'll have to carry everything up.

Jebel Mileihis to Canyon Salema   [Map 73]
To end the trek at Jebel Mileihis you might find a pick-up truck at the shacks near Wadi Disco: pay about LE50-80 to the highway. To walk out, head back down Wadi Disco, but don't bend right to exit where you came in; take another branch straight ahead. A wadi soon opens up on the left here; follow it to where it narrows into a canyon (GPS 46). This is **Canyon Salema**.

Canyon Salema doesn't compare with the other canyons but it's still worth a look. There's a **minor fork** a short way in; a little crack rises up in rocks to the right here, but you need to go left. After this there's a **bigger fork**; go right here. The canyon becomes more open after this; veer up its right side to exit and emerge in the wide spaces of Wadi Ghazala (GPS 47).

Canyon Salema to Ras Wadi Ghazala   [Maps 73-74]
Follow Wadi Ghazala south to the highway. You'll find a camel station at a point known as **Ras Wadi Ghazala** (GPS 48). There's a rusty old jeep on an outcrop here. The Israeli army airlifted it up before they left in the 1980s. There's a mobile signal to call in a taxi but you could also hitch.

Map key

♠	Bank/ATM

♠ Where to stay   ⓔ Bank/ATM   ☑ Public toilet

O Where to eat and drink ⓘ Tourist information   ☐ Building

△ Campsite   ⓢ Internet   ● Other

⊠ Post Office   © Mosque/shrine   ◷◷ Bus station/stop

                         ✚ Church/monastery/   📱08 GPS waypoint
                            hermit cell

⟋ Main trekking path   ⬩⬩⬩ Steps   △ Peak

⟋ Other path   ⟋⟋⟋ Cliffs   Ⓦ Well / water source

⟋⟋ 4 x 4 track   ⟿ Wadi   ▨ Leopard trap

⫽ Road   ⦂⦂ Boulders   ⋒ Boulder shelter

⇗ Slope / steep slope   🌴 Palms / trees   ⚘ Wishing rock

TRAIL GUIDE & MAPS

APPENDIX A: GLOSSARY

Alegat Bedouin tribe (Towarah)
Ammeya spoken, colloquial Arabic
arisha shelter/sun roof
asheera tribe, clan
Aulad Jindi name of clan in Jebeleya
Aulad Said Bedouin tribe (Towarah)
badiya desert wilderness
baksheesh tip, sweetener, backhander
Bani Wassil Bedouin tribe (Towarah)
bedan ibex
Bedawi Bedouin, singular (m)
Bedouin Arabs of wandering descent
Bedu / el Bedu Bedouin (pl)
bir well
cairn pile of summit rocks
chockstone boulder jam
Coptic Egyptian (Orthodox) Christian
crag rugged cliff
darb / darb el hajj road or way/road to
 Mecca, crosses the Sinai
deir monastery, church
dike exposed line of rock, often black
DMS Decompression sickness
dor Jebeleya rotation system for guides
ein spring, water source
escarpment steep slope/cliff separating
 two or more level surfaces
fawanees traditional Ramadan lanterns
farashee Bedouin flatbread
farsh basin, depression
fatla – traditional Egyptian shave, using a
 string
gabeela tribe, tribal confederation
galt water pool, spring-fed
Gararsha Bedouin tribe (Towarah)
ghulah evil female spirit
gimma peak
girbeh big water skin
hafla party, gathering
hajar rock
Hajj pilgrimage to Mecca
halawa sesame-based sweet
Hamada Bedouin tribe (Towarah)
haram forbidden by God
hasheesh marujuana, ie plantation
iftar breakfast or sunset meal in Ramadan
jebel mountain
Jebeleya Bedouin tribe (Towarah)
jelebeya long shirt or robe, traditional
 Arab dress
jinn ghosts

karm garden
keffiyeh Arab head cloth (*shemagh*)
khamsin seasonal springtime wind
kharaza waterpool, rain-fed
khawaja foreigner
kineesa church, monastery
libba thick Bedouin flatbread
Maghrabi in olden times, a Western Arab;
 today, a Moroccan
Masr Egypt
medina city (s) (see also *mudun*)
MFO Multinational Force of Observers
mihrab niche/arch in the wall of a mosque,
 facing Mecca
moiyet water source
moshav An Israeli settlement, usually
 based on co-operative agriculture
mudun cities (pl)
Muzeina Bedouin tribe (Towarah)
naqb pass, route between places
nawamis prehistoric circular tomb
nosret el nimr leopard trap
ofyoon opium
plutons balloon-like masses of molten
 rock, formed deep in the earth
rake wide rocky shelf, ledge
Ramadan Islamic month of fasting
ras headland, promontory, peak
rojom trail-marking stones
sed dam, plunge pool or waterfall
seil flash flood, mouth of wadi, or village
 at mouth of wadi
semzemeeyah – small water skin
shaal Arab headcloth, white
sheikh tribal head, holy man
shejera tree
shellal waterfall
shemagh Arab headcloth, chequered
shibriya traditional Bedouin dagger
shisha hookah / water pipe
simsimiyya traditional stringed instrument
sineeya big plate, tray
Sowalha Bedouin tribe, near Towarah
talla gorge
Tarabin Bedouin tribe, near Nuweiba
tareeg way / path
tiyaha alliance of northern tribes in Sinai
Towarah alliance of southern tribes in Sinai
toot mulberry trees
wadi valley, watercourse, ravine
ziyarah / zoowarah Bedouin holy festival

APPENDIX B: SURVIVAL ARABIC

The more Arabic you speak in the Sinai the better: it's the only language spoken in many trekking areas and wherever you are it'll help. Arabic and English share some sounds but others have no crossover. Arabic can be transliterated into Latin script in many ways and each dictionary has its own rules. These can be numerous and tiresome to remember when you're just trying to get started. This guide gives just four rules and writes everything else as phonetically as possible. There's a lot of slang and what's here won't give word perfect pronunciation or grammar, but you don't need that; you just need to be understood. Practice as soon as you arrive and don't worry about sounding clumsy — everyone does. Mistakes burn the correct words in your vocabulary; gradually you'll see how they can be pieced together into more meaningful phrases and your trip will be all the richer.

NB: pronounce the letters _ai_ like the English word _eye_. The letters _aa_ like the long 'a' in father – every other 'a' you see is short, like 'a' in 'fat'. The letters _ay_ as you name the letter _A_ in the alphabet. The letters _air_, like the English word air (but with a silent 'r').

Greetings

Hello (peace be upon you)	_salem alaykum_
Hello (and upon you too)	_walaykum essalam_
How's it going?	_kayf halak?_
I'm well, glory to God	_alhamdelileh_
What's your name?	_isma-kay?_
My name is...	_ismee..._
Where are you from?	_enta min wayn?_
I'm from…	_ana min…_
Nice to meet you	_forsa saiyeeda_
Welcome	_marhaba_
Bye (farewell with peace)	_maa-salema_

Some basic words

Yes / No	_naam, aywa / lah_
Please	_min fadlak_
Thanks	_shukran_
No thanks	_lah shukran_
You're welcome	_afwan_
Sorry	_airsif_
OK	_mesh / meshee_
Good / not good	_kwaiyis / mish kwaiyis_
Problem / no problem	_mishkilla / mish mishkilla_
Thank God	_alhamdelileh_
God willing	_inshallah_

Some basic questions

How much is / how many?	_bi-kairm / kairm?_
Do you have...?	_andak...?_
Do you want...?	_awz...?_
May I / Is it possible to...?	_mumkin...?_

Who? / When?	_meen? / imta?_
How? / Why?	_izzay? / lay?_
What / What's that?	_ay / ay da?_
Is there? / There is!	_fee? / fee!_
Understand? / Correct?	_fairhim? / sah?_

Further basics

I / You	_ana / enta_
I have / I want	_andee / ana aiyeez_
I understand	_ana fairhim_
I know	_ana aaref_
I speak	_ana atakallim_
I like	_ana uhib_
I go	_ana raiyeh_
I drink	_ana ashrab_
I sleep	_ana anem_
I don't speak Arabic	_Arabee mafeesh / ana ma atakallim arabee_
Do you speak English?	_tata-kallim ingileezee?_

NB: **Negate** by adding _mish_: eg _Ana mish aiyeez_ – 'I don't want', _Ana mish aaref_ – 'I don't know' etc. Even when you don't make grammatical sense it'll be clear you're speaking in the negative. Use _ma_ and _lah_ (both short 'a' sounds) to similar effect.

Organising a trek

Guide / Camel	_daleel / jamel_
Tribe	_gabeela_
Is there a guide here?	_fee daleel hinna?_
I want to go to...	_aiyeez arooah…_
I want to ride a camel	_aiyeez arkab jamal…_

Is there water?	*fee maiya?*
Good water?	*maiya helwa?*
Are there Bedouin?	*fee Bedu?*
Do we have food?	*andeena airkl?*
How many hours?	*kairm say-ah?*
How many days?	*kairm yoom?*

Out on the trail (see also p123)

Come on / let's go!	*yalla / yalla beena!*
Just slowly, bit by bit	*shwaiya shwaiya*
Quickly	*sireeya, bisoora*
Wait / Stop!	*istanna / ogoff!*
I'm hot	*ana haraan*
I'm cold	*ana bardan*
I'm thirsty	*ana atshaan*
I'm hungry	*ana ja-aan*
I'm tired	*ana taaban*
I want a rest	*aiyeez raaha*
Can we have tea?	*mumkin shay?*
Can I take a photo?	*mumkin soora?*

The elements and heavens

Wind / Rain	*hawa / mattar*
Snow, ice / Water	*telj / maiya*
Storm / Sandstorm	*aasifa/ aasifat raml*
Flash flood / Fire	*sayl / naar*
Sea / Sky	*ba-har / samair*
Sun / Cloud	*shams / sahairb*
Dawn	*fajar*
Sunrise	*shroog (ish shams)*
Sunset	*guroob (ish shams)*
Moon / Crescent	*gamar / hilairl*
Planet	*kawkab*
Star / Stars	*nijma / najoom*
Universe / Ghosts	*el kun / jinn*

Trail equipment

Bag / Knife	*shanta / sikeena*
Bottle	*izairza*
Matches / Lighter	*kibreet / wala*
Torch / Candle	*bataraya / shamaa*
Tent / Blanket	*khayma / bataneeya*
Map / Book	*khareeta / kitairb*
Rope / Soap	*habl / saboon*
Firewood	*hutb*

Emergencies

Help!	*tis-ai-adnee!*
I'm lost	*ana taiyeh*
There's an accident!	*fee hadtha!*
I have a problem	*andee mishkilla*
I'm ill	*ana mureed*

I have diarrhoea	*andee iss-hal*
I'm diabetic	*ana mureed bil sukkar*
I'm asthmatic	*ana mureed bil rabwa*
It's broken	*maksoor*
Heart attack	*azma galbeya*
Coma	*gayboba*
Snake / Scorpion	*thiabairn / akrab*
I need a doctor	*aiyeez duk-tor*
Is there a helicopter?	*fee helicobter?*
Do you have medicine?	*andak dawwa?*
I have insurance	*andee ta-meen*
Hospital	*mostashfa*
Embassy	*safaara*
Landmine	*laghm*

Getting around

Where is the...?	*fayn il...?*
How many kilos?	*kairm keelo?*
minutes?	*dageega?*
Here / There	*hinna / hineck*
Left / Right	*shemel / yimeen*
Straight	*alatool*
Before / After	*gubbl / baa-ad*
Behind / Near	*warra / guraiyib*
Far	*bai-eed*
Up / Down	*foag / taht*
North / South	*shamairl / janoob*
East / West	*shark / garb*
Is there a bus to..?	*fee utubees li...?*
Bus / microbus	*utubees / microbas*
Car / Jeep	*arabeeya / seeyaara*
Taxi	*taxi, tax*
Aeroplane / Ferry	*teeyaara / markib*
Petrol	*banzeen*

Some places

Bank	*bank*
Shop	*dukairn*
Chemist	*sai-dillay-ya*
Post office	*bosta*
Police Station	*gissm el bolees*
Toilet	*hamam, toowaleet*
Bus station	*mahattat utubees*
Port / Airport	*meena / mataar*
Egypt / Sinai	*Maasr / Seena*
St Katherine	*Katreen*
Cairo	*Al Qaheera*
Alexandria	*Iskanderaya*

Time and dates

| Minute / Hour | *dageega / say-ah* |
| Day / Week | *yoom / isboowah* |

Now	*delwagtee, el an*
Later	*badayn*
Today / Tomorrow	*innaharda* / *bokra*
After tomorrow	*baa-ad bokra*
Morning	*sobh*
Evening / Night	*layla* / *lil*
What's the time?	*say-ah kairm?*
How long?	add *ay?*

NB: To answer the question *say-ah kairm?* – what's the time? – learn the numbers.

Two 'o clock is *say-ah itneen*, Three o' clock *say-ah teleta* etc.

For half past add *w-nus*: ie *say-ah itneen w-nus*.

For quarter past add *w-roba*: ie *say-ah itneen w-roba*.

For quarter to it's the hour being approached *illa roba*: ie quarter to three would be *say-ah teleta illa roba* etc.

Accommodation and eating

Hotel	*fundoog*
Room	*awda, gurfa*
Do you have a room?	*andak awda* / *gurfa?*
Can I see?	*mumkin ashoof?*
Is there a menu?	*fee menyu?*
Can I have the bill?	*mumkin el hisairb?*
Bread	*ai-ish*
Meat / Fish	*lahma* / *samak*
Milk / Tea	*laban* / *shay*
Turkish coffee	*gahwa*
Instant coffee	*Nescafe*
Sugar	*sukkar*
I'm vegetarian	*ana nabairtee*
Delicious!	*lazeez!*

Money, haggling, hassle

Money	*filoos*
Small change	*fakka*
Tip / Backhander	*baksheesh*
One pound	*gnay*
Half a pound	*nus gnay*
How much?	*bi-kairm?*
Too much!	*kiteer!*
I don't want it	*mish aiyeez*
That's enough! / All sorted	*kifaya! Halas*
I'm married	*ana mitjaweza*
Are you mad?	*enta majnoon?*
Go away / Jog on	*imshee*/ *goor!*

Quantities

All / Everything	*kulu*
Nothing	*mafeesh*
Quarter / Half	*roba* / *nus*
Big / Small	*kibeer* / *sugaiyar*
More! / Less	*aktar!* / *agal*
Enough / Not enough	*kifaya* / *mish kifaya*
Kilo	*keelo*

Numbers

0	*sifr*	·
1	*wahid*	١
2	*itneen*	٢
3	*teleta*	٣
4	*arbaa*	٤
5	*hamsa*	٥
6	*seta*	٦
7	*saba*	٧
8	*tamaneeya*	٨
9	*tesa*	٩
10	*aashara*	١·
11	*hedaashar*	١١
12	*itnaashar*	١٢
13	*tele-taashar*	١٣
14	*arbaa-taashar*	١٤
15	*hamas-taashar*	١٥
16	*si-taashar*	١٦
17	*saba-taashar*	١٧
18	*taman-taashar*	١٨
19	*tesa-taashar*	١٩
20	*ishreen*	٢·
21	*wahid w ishreen*	٢١
22	*itneen w ishreen* etc	٢٢
30	*teleteen*	٣·
40	*arbaayeen*	٤·
50	*hamseen*	٥·
60	*siteen*	٦·
70	*sabaayeen*	٧·
80	*tamaneen*	٨·
90	*tesayeen*	٩·
100	*meeya*	١··
110	*meeya w aashara*	١١·
120	*meeya w ishreen*	١٢·
121	*meeya w wahid w ishreen*	١٢١
122	*meeya w itneen w ishreen* etc	١٢٢
200	*mitayn*	٢··
300	*toltomaya*	٣··
400	*robamaya*	٤··
500	*homsomaya*	٥··
1000	*elf*	١···

APPENDIX C: GPS WAYPOINTS

The GPS waypoints below (downloadable from 🖳 www.trailblazer-guides.com) are arranged by route; each has its own special numbered set. Each waypoint also has a map reference and a written description to make it easier to identify. GPS co-ordinates can be written in different formats; the format here is Lat/Long. There are different map datums too – complicated grids used to plot co-ordinates; the datum here is WGS 84. Both the co-ordinate and the map datum formats are amongst the most commonly used in the world and they're usually the default settings on a Garmin GPS.

Remember: GPS isn't always completely accurate, especially where satellite reception is limited. Never let it take your eye off traditional route finding.

THE HIGH MOUNTAIN REGION
Northern Peaks Circuit

Map No	GPS waypoint/description
1	1 N28 34.131 E33 57.950 Kharazeen
1	2 N28 34.667 E33 57.869 High pass
1	3 N28 34.609 E33 57.774 Jebel Suna
1	4 N28 35.247 E33 57.631 Jebel el Ojar
1	5 N28 35.972 E33 57.508 Wadi junction
1	6 N28 36.266 E33 57.373 High pass 2
2	7 N28 36.766 E33 56.876 Farsh Faria
2	8 N28 37.938 E33 57.157 Wadi Abu Zeituna
3	9 N28 38.808 E33 56.220 Jebel Banat path
3	10 N28 38.843 E33 55.851 Jebel Banat
3	11 N28 39.168 E33 55.765 Sed el Nugra diversion
3	12 N28 39.260 E33 54.556 Small dam
4	13 N28 38.993 E33 53.838 Al Karm Ecolodge
4	14 N28 38.198 E33 53.841 Small rocky gorge
4	15 N28 37.762 E33 53.949 Naqb el Hawa, bottom
5	16 N28 35.909 E33 55.432 Naqb el Hawa, top
5	17 N28 35.296 E33 55.850 Abu Seila, mosque/school
5	18 N28 35.668 E33 55.480 Naqb Abu Seila, top
5	19 N28 35.372 E33 55.170 Naqb Abu Seila, bottom

Northern Peaks Circuit (cont'd)

Map No	GPS waypoint/description
5	20 N28 35.078 E33 55.320 Dr Ahmed's garden
6	21 N28 34.028 E33 56.059 Path after Wadi Talla
6	22 N28 33.855 E33 56.222 Last pass to town

Galt el Azraq

Map No	GPS waypoint/description
7	1 N28 35.296 E33 55.850 Abu Seila, mosque/school
7	2 N28 35.668 E33 55.480 Naqb Abu Seila, top
7	3 N28 35.372 E33 55.170 Naqb Abu Seila, bottom
7	4 N28 35.653 E33 54.995 Wadi Shagg
7	5 N28 35.445 E33 54.839 Wadi Shagg path
7	6 N28 35.054 E33 54.132 Kharazat Shagg
7	7 N28 34.735 E33 54.076 Wadi Sagr, turn-off
8	8 N28 34.333 E33 53.736 Wadi Abu Tuweita
8	9 N28 34.527 E33 53.480 Wadi Abu Tuweita, exit path
8	10 N28 34.274 E33 52.933 Rock patterns
8	11 N28 34.148 E33 52.723 Wadi Talla (Kibeera)
8	12 N28 33.982 E33 52.474 Galt el Azraq water pool
8	13 N28 33.743 E33 52.445 Wadi Talla Kibeera (bottom)
8	14 N28 33.615 E33 52.513 Hidden spring, Abu Habak
9	15 N28 32.465 E33 52.885 Farsh Rummana
9	16 N28 32.345 E33 52.721 Naqb Bahriya, diversion

Galt el Azraq *(cont'd)*

Map	No	GPS waypoint/description
9	17	N28 32.039 E33 52.472
		Naqb Bahariya, turn-off
9	18	N28 31.993 E33 52.198
		Wadi Zatar
10	19	N28 32.238 E33 51.909
		Wadi Zuweitar
10	20	N28 32.103 E33 51.725
		Ein Najila
10	21	N28 32.044 E33 51.264
		Jebel Bab el Dunya
10	22	N28 31.360 E33 51.966
		Farsh Arnab
10	23	N28 31.212 E33 52.137
		Cliff trail start
10	24	N28 31.216 E33 52.336
		Jebel Masba Abu Garun
11	25	N28 31.135 E33 52.846
		Wadi Umm Siha
11	26	N28 31.380 E33 53.428
		Wadi Jibal, crossroads
11	27	N28 31.807 E33 54.051
		Wadi Jibal, garden
12	28	N28 32.434 E33 55.467
		Wadi Zawatin, arisha
12	29	N28 32.276 E33 55.755
		El Kheded junction
12	30	N28 32.795 E33 56.147
		Abu Jeefa pass
12	31	N28 33.450 E33 56.677
		El Milga

Jebel Katherina & Jebel Abbas Basha

Map	No	GPS waypoint/description
13	1	N28 33.684 E33 56.394
		Wadi Quweiz
13	2	N28 34.028 E33 56.059
		Wadi Talla fork
13	3	N28 33.198 E33 56.105
		Sed Daoud gully
13	4	N28 32.712 E33 56.035
		Isilibet junction
13	5	N28 32.276 E33 55.755
		El Kheded junction
13	6	N28 32.434 E33 55.467
		Wadi Zawatin, arisha
14	7	N28 32.710 E33 55.260
		Turn-off, Farsh Abu Mahshur
14	8	N28 33.343 E33 55.486
		Ascent gully, bottom
14	9	N28 33.011 E33 55.277
		Farsh Abu Mahshur basin

Map	No	GPS waypoint/description
14	10	N28 33.363 E33 55.239
		Jebel Abbas Basha
14	11	N28 33.603 E33 55.046
		Jebel Abbas Basha (palace)
14	12	N28 33.234 E33 54.847
		Sharafat Sakikriyeh
15	13	N28 31.749 E33 56.283
		Wadi Ahmar
15	14	N28 31.777 E33 56.883
		Turn-off to Jebel Katherina
15	15	N28 31.510 E33 56.972
		Wire enclosure
15	16	N28 31.366 E33 57.146
		Left turn to Farsh Umm Sila
15	17	N28 31.283 E33 57.356
		Farsh Umm Sila
15	18	N28 30.755 E33 57.238
		Jebel Katherina
15	19	N28 30.561 E33 57.331
		Jebel Zebir
16	20	N28 31.367 E33 57.617
		Ein Shanir
16	21	N28 32.048 E33 57.916
		Ramadan's garden
16	22	N28 33.282 E33 56.921 El Rasees

Mount Sinai/Jebel Musa

Map	No	GPS waypoint/description
17	1	N28 33.282 E33 56.921
		El Rasees trailhead
17	2	N28 32.125 E33 58.110
		Fork in path
17	3	N28 32.340 E33 58.083
		Trail up Jebel Safsafa
17	4	N28 32.858 E33 58.061
		Chapel of St Panteleimon
17	5	N28 33.155 E33 57.881
		Safsafa chapel
17	6	N28 33.116 E33 57.704
		Jebel Safsafa
17	7	N28 32.916 E33 58.190
		El Loza
18	8	N28 32.664 E33 58.490
		Farsh Elias
18	9	N28 32.318 E33 58.519
		Mount Sinai
18	10	N28 33.364 E33 58.598
		Monastery of St Katherine

Jebel el Deir

Map	No	GPS waypoint/description
19	1	N28 33.364 E33 58.598
		Monastery of St Katherine

Map	No	GPS waypoint/description

Jebel el Deir *(cont'd)*

Map No	GPS waypoint/description
19	2	N28 33.530 E33 58.636 — Bottom of ravine
19	3	N28 33.753 E33 58.593 — Trail after top of ravine
19	4	N28 33.936 E33 58.589 — High flat basin
19	5	N28 33.866 E33 58.685 — Hermit cell
19	6	N28 33.955 E33 58.752 — Ruined church
19	7	N28 33.614 E33 58.867 — Farsh Jamaam
19	8	N28 33.730 E33 58.936 — Jebel el Deir
19	9	N28 33.861 E33 58.883 — Descent gully
19	10	N28 33.783 E33 59.005 — Flatter wadi
19	11	N28 33.334 E33 59.008 — Small monastery

Jebel Umm Shomer

Map No	GPS waypoint/description
20	1	N28 23.563 E33 57.179 — Zeituna trailhead
20	2	N28 23.529 E33 56.889 — Turn-off on right
20	3	N28 23.286 E33 56.564 — Saddle between wadis
20	4	N28 22.966 E33 56.222 — Jebel Abu Shajara path
20	5	N28 22.611 E33 55.933 — Jebel Abu Shajara high point
21	6	N28 22.142 E33 55.491 — Low saddle, leopard trap
21	7	N28 21.708 E33 55.029 — Jebel Umm Shomer
21	8	N28 21.834 E33 56.334 — Deir Rimhan
21	9	N28 21.697 E33 56.499 — Camel path, boulder shelters
22	10	N28 21.332 E33 57.796 — Path enters wadi bottom
23	11	N28 20.287 E33 59.273 — Moiyet Zilega
23	12	N28 19.498 E33 59.651 — Wadi Thebt junction
24	13	N28 17.908 E33 57.499 — Wadi Isleh, narrow section
24	14	N28 17.162 E33 56.253 — Gigantic boulders
25	15	N28 16.321 E33 54.306 — Wadi Muwajid
25	16	N28 16.003 E33 53.839 — Greenery before gorge
25	17	N28 15.304 E33 53.268 — Hairpin bend
26	18	N28 14.542 E33 51.904 — Seil Isleh village

WADI FEIRAN
Jebel Serbal Circuit

Map No	GPS waypoint/description
27	1	N28 42.312 E33 38.275 — Seil Aleyat trailhead
27	2	N28 40.535 E33 39.293 — Wadi Aleyat, fork
28	3	N28 39.784 E33 38.832 — Naqb Shahrani
28	4	N28 39.197 E33 38.396 — Farsh Loza
28	5	N28 39.258 E33 38.624 — Jebel Serbal, ascent gully
28	6	N28 39.043 E33 38.673 — Jebel Serbal, crack passage
28	7	N28 39.096 E33 38.713 — Jebel Serbal
29	8	N28 38.638 E33 38.462 — Small pass
29	9	N28 38.294 E33 38.757 — Small pass 2
29	10	N28 38.064 E33 39.088 — Hajar Imbardia
29	11	N28 37.810 E33 39.538 — Wadi Rimm, head
30	12	N28 37.531 E33 39.628 — Darb Abu Selim
30	13	N28 37.219 E33 39.457 — Darb Abu Selim, exit path
30	14	N28 37.042 E33 39.075 — Wadi Sigillia, stone hut
30	15	N28 36.748 E33 38.065 — Wadi Sigillia, U-bend diversion
31	16	N28 36.720 E33 36.027 — Sed Sigillia/Wadi Mileihim
31	17	N28 37.261 E33 36.253 — Wadi Mileihim, path up left
32	18	N28 38.977 E33 36.618 — High pass 1
32	19	N28 39.609 E33 36.686 — High pass 2
33	20	N28 41.529 E33 37.231 — Turn-off, Jebel Salla

Jebel Serbal Circuit *(cont'd)*

Map	No	GPS waypoint/description
33	21	N28 42.223 E33 37.528
		Wadi Ajela, mouth

Jebel Salla

34	1	N28 42.223 E33 37.528
		Wadi Ajela, mouth
34	2	N28 41.529 E33 37.231
		Turn-off, Jebel Salla
34	3	N28 41.464 E33 36.916
		Wadi divides
34	4	N28 41.271 E33 36.505
		Rocky rake
34	5	N28 41.242 E33 36.448
		Jebel Salla

Wadi Feiran to Serabit el Khadem

35	1	N28 48.094 E33 27.644
		Wadi Mukattab, mouth
36	2	N28 49.684 E33 26.307
		Wadi Mukattab, open plain
36	3	N28 50.907 E33 25.564
		Wadi Mukattab, graffiti
37	4	N28 51.965 E33 24.439
		Wadi Sidreh, narrowing
38	5	N28 53.393 E33 22.313
		Sheikh Suleiman tomb
38	6	N28 53.762 E33 22.293
		Wadi Maghara, fork
38	7	N28 53.877 E33 22.112
		Wadi Maghara, bas relief
39	8	N28 54.497 E33 23.623
		Wadi Iqne, enters mountains
39	9	N28 54.949 E33 24.294
		Wadi Iqne, junction
39	10	N28 55.103 E33 24.232
		Wadi Amran, mouth
39	11	N28 55.249 E33 24.299
		Small notch pass
39	12	N28 55.418 E33 24.395
		Wadi Amran, stone hut
39	13	N28 55.650 E33 24.540
		Wadi Abu Dees, fork/dam
39	14	N28 56.190 E33 24.619
		Turn-off for Wadi Umm Retem
40	15	N28 56.553 E33 24.531
		Naqb Shaieer
40	16	N28 57.433 E33 24.948
		Wadi Umm Retem
40	17	N28 58.180 E33 24.941
		Sheikh Saadan (Wadi Sahu)

Wadi Feiran to Serabit el Khadem
(cont'd)

Map	No	GPS waypoint/description
41	18	N28 59.169 E33 25.085
		High pass, jeep track
41	19	N28 59.518 E33 25.079
		Jeep track, turn-off
41	20	N29 00.077 E33 24.949
		Re-join jeep track
41	21	N29 00.624 E33 25.005
		Wadi Lahian, jeep track fork
42	22	N29 01.395 E33 25.182
		Small watercourse mouth
42	23	N29 01.820 E33 25.623
		Jebel Hasaani, ridge
42	24	N29 02.336 E33 26.005
		Wadi Bala
42	25	N29 02.616 E33 26.268
		Serabit el Khadem, path
43	26	N29 02.345 E33 27.066
		Magharat el Teleha
43	27	N29 01.834 E33 27.359
		Magharat el Khaseef
43	28	N29 02.198 E33 27.544
		Temple of Hathor
43	29	N29 02.158 E33 27.849
		Descent trail
43	30	N29 02.327 E33 28.358
		Hut (Wadi Khaseef)
44	31	N29 03.461 E33 26.156
		Serabit village

THE DESERT

Ras Shaitan to Ein Hudera

45	1	N29 08.747 E34 40.716
		Wadi Melha, mouth
45	2	N29 09.361 E34 39.240
		Wadi Melha, narrows
45	3	N29 09.567 E34 38.833
		Wadi Wishwashi
46	4	N28 09.439 E34 37.955
		Wadi Melha, crossroads
46	5	N29 09.519 E34 37.878
		Moiyet Melha, palms
46	6	N29 09.367 E34 37.842
		Farsh Fureh, palms
46	7	N29 09.108 E34 37.654
		Naqb Fureh
46	8	N29 08.987 E34 37.553
		Small wadi
46	9	N29 08.822 E34 37.699
		Wadi Melha Atshana

Ras Shaitan to Ein Hudera (*cont'd*)

Map	No	GPS waypoint/description
47	10	N29 07.542 E34 36.214
		Turn-off to Coloured Canyon
47	11	N29 08.552 E34 35.893
		Wooden shack
47	12	N29 08.839 E34 35.642
		Coloured Canyon
47	13	N29 07.429 E34 36.074
		Camel trail to Coloured Canyon
47	14	N29 08.306 E34 35.947
		Sandy basin, left turn
47	15	N29 08.283 E34 35.673
		High shacks
48	16	N29 07.143 E34 35.061
		Wadi el Abraq
48	17	N29 05.316 E34 35.036
		Big bend/junction
49	18	N29 02.902 E34 33.214
		Ein Furtaga
51	19	N28 59.937 E34 30.144
		Wadi Mileihis
52	20	N28 58.154 E34 27.862
		Wadi Ghazala fork
53	21	N28 56.208 E34 26.862
		Wadi Hudera, divides up
54	22	N28 54.721 E34 26.136
		Closed Canyon turn-off
54	23	N28 53.984 E34 26.225
		Closed Canyon
54	24	N28 53.821 E34 25.346
		Ein Hudera
55	25	N28 52.999 E34 24.860
		Ein Hudera, pass
55	26	N28 52.431 E34 24.476
		Cafeteria Jomaa
55	27	N28 53.420 E34 25.527
		White Canyon, trail up right
55	28	N28 52.765 E34 25.815
		White Canyon, top

The Haduda Dune

56	1	N28 52.309 E34 22.512
		Nawamis, turn-off
56	2	N28 51.581 E34 22.936
		Nawamis village
56	3	N28 51.328 E34 22.414
		Nawamis tombs
56	4	N28 50.289 E34 21.770
		Jebel Mutamir, bottom
56	5	N28 50.293 E34 21.675
		Jebel Mutamir, summit

The Haduda Dune (*cont'd*)

Map	No	GPS waypoint/description
57	6	N28 49.632 E34 21.979
		Small wadi, mouth
57	7	N28 49.052 E34 21.613
		Small wadi, fork
57	8	N28 48.216 E34 22.460
		Wadi after crossroads
58	9	N28 47.347 E34 22.367
		Acacia tree, turn-off
58	10	N28 47.054 E34 22.617
		Jebel Barqa view
59	11	N28 46.154 E34 23.740
		Jebel Barqa, gully
59	12	N28 46.340 E34 23.836
		Jebel Barqa, summit
59	13	N28 46.282 E34 24.657
		Jebel Mahroom
60	14	N28 46.284 E34 26.037
		Haduda Dune
60	15	N28 46.414 E34 26.319
		Wadi Haduda
60	16	N28 45.841 E34 28.315
		Wadi Haduda, end

Desert Traverse

61	1	N28 48.303 E34 17.924
		Wadi Arada, hamlet
61	2	N28 48.613 E34 17.605
		Wadi Arada, crossroads
61	3	N28 49.290 E34 17.165
		Ancient graffiti
62	4	N28 50.238 E34 16.284
		Arada Canyon, turn-off
62	5	N28 50.812 E34 16.765
		Jebel Gunna, camel trail
62	6	N28 51.468 E34 17.113
		Farsh Abbeya, view
63	7	N28 52.197 E34 17.887
		Watercourse, turn-off
63	8	N28 52.298 E34 17.857
		Minor pass 1
63	9	N28 52.571 E34 17.973
		Minor pass 2
63	10	N28 52.977 E34 18.336
		Minor wadi fork
63	11	N28 53.183 E34 18.516
		Minor pass 3 (last)
64	12	N28 53.883 E34 18.548
		Wadi Umm Hamata
64	13	N28 53.984 E34 18.622
		Bir Umm Hamata

Desert Traverse *(cont'd from p283)*

Map	No	GPS waypoint/description
64	14	N28 54.432 E34 19.281
		Waterfall cliff
65	15	N28 54.766 E34 20.527
		Wadi Ghlim
65	16	N28 55.973 E34 20.648
		Bir Ghlim
66	17	N28 58.692 E34 20.440
		Dam, Wadi Ghlim
67	18	N28 59.766 E34 22.102
		Pass over low hills
68	19	N28 59.670 E34 23.764
		Sandy wadi, start
68	20	N28 59.546 E34 24.935
		Jebel Berqa, ascent canyon
68	21	N28 59.134 E34 24.683
		Halfway up Jebel Berqa
68	22	N28 59.065 E34.24.957
		Jebel Berqa, summit
68	23	N28 59.717 E34 24.719
		Hidden water pool
68	24	N28 58.919 E34 23.264 Big plain
69	25	N28 58.154 E34 23.299
		Naqb Moehis, start
69	26	N28 58.070 E34 23.775
		Naqb Moehis 1
69	27	N28 57.912 E34 24.069
		Naqb Moehis 2
69	28	N28 57.397 E34 24.330
		Naqb Moehis 3
70	29	N28 56.706 E34 24.490
		Naqb Moehis 4
70	30	N28 56.423 E34 24.738
		Naqb Moehis 5
70	31	N28 55.940 E34 24.623
		Wadi Medaila

Map	No	GPS waypoint/description
70	32	N28 55.984 E34 25.518
		Wadi Medaila, crossroads
71	33	N28 54.706 E34 25.173
		Wadi Rum
71	34	N28 54.661 E34 25.765
		Wadi Rum, black ridge
71	35	N28 54.721 E34 26.136
		Closed Canyon wadi
71	36	N28 53.984 E34 26.225
		Closed Canyon
71	37	N28 53.821 E34 25.346
		Ein Hudera
72	38	N28 53.420 E34 25.527
		White Canyon, trail up right
72	39	N28 52.765 E34 25.815
		White Canyon, top
72	40	N28 52.689 E34 26.115
		Sandy descent gully
72	41	N28 52.946 E34 27.132
		Majaaza/Wadi Ghazala
72	42	N28 53.716 E34 27.958
		Wadi Disco, mouth
73	43	N28 54.274 E34 28.584
		Wadi Disco, shacks
73	44	N28 54.742 E34 28.779
		Jebel Mileihis, path
73	45	N28 55.237 E34 28.386
		Jebel Mileihis
73	46	N28 53.462 E34 28.177
		Canyon Salema
73	47	N28 53.220 E34 28.489
		Canyon Salema, end
74	48	N28 52.078 E34 27.775
		Ras Wadi Ghazala

INDEX

Page references in **bold** type refer to maps

TRAILBLAZER TITLE LIST

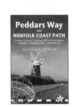

Adventure Cycle-Touring Handbook
Adventure Motorcycling Handbook
Australia by Rail
Australia's Great Ocean Road
Azerbaijan
Coast to Coast (British Walking Guide)
Cornwall Coast Path (British Walking Guide)
Corsica Trekking – GR20
Cotswold Way (British Walking Guide)
Dolomites Trekking – AV1 & AV2
Dorset & Sth Devon Coast Path (British Walking Gde)
Exmoor & Nth Devon Coast Path (British Walking Gde)
Hadrian's Wall Path (British Walking Guide)
Himalaya by Bike – a route and planning guide
Inca Trail, Cusco & Machu Picchu
Japan by Rail
Kilimanjaro – the trekking guide (includes Mt Meru)
Morocco Overland (4WD/motorcycle/mountainbike)
Moroccan Atlas – The Trekking Guide
Nepal Trekking & The Great Himalaya Trail
New Zealand – The Great Walks
North Downs Way (British Walking Guide)
Norway's Arctic Highway
Offa's Dyke Path (British Walking Guide)
Overlanders' Handbook – worldwide driving guide
Peddars Way & Norfolk Coast Path (British Walking Gde)
Pembrokeshire Coast Path (British Walking Guide)
Pennine Way (British Walking Guide)
The Ridgeway (British Walking Guide)
Siberian BAM Guide – rail, rivers & road
The Silk Roads – a route and planning guide
Sahara Overland – a route and planning guide
Scottish Highlands – The Hillwalking Guide
Sinai – the trekking guide
South Downs Way (British Walking Guide)
Tour du Mont Blanc
Trans-Canada Rail Guide
Trans-Siberian Handbook
Trekking in the Everest Region
The Walker's Anthology
The Walker's Haute Route – Mont Blanc to Matterhorn
West Highland Way (British Walking Guide)

www.trailblazer-guides.com

(Opposite) After your trek, spend some time relaxing by the Red Sea. You can snorkel or scuba dive over coral reefs teeming with marine life (**top photos**; © Tim Simond, *Original Diving*), laze on the cushions in waterfront cafés or shop in bustling markets. Sharm el Sheikh's Old Market is a good place to try traditional Egyptian drinks like *asir asab* (**middle, left**), made from crushed sugar cane. As well as the popular resorts of Sharm el Sheikh (see pp95-108), Nuweiba (pp222-8) and Dahab (pp109-15) there are numerous deserted beaches such as this one (**bottom**) at Ras Abu Galum (see pp115-6).